Pan-Slavism and Slavophilia in Contemporary Central and Eastern Europe

"This collection is an important contribution in both the historical and contemporary analysis of Pan-Slavism. It places this concept in context of Yugoslavism, as well as Russian appeals to Slavic and Orthodox solidarity and competing European identity. This book will become a standard study on the topic through its comprehensive and systematic approach, covering most Slavic countries and not treating Pan-Slavism as just a type of failed meta nationalism, but as an important idea informing the Slavic world today."
—Florian Bieber, *Professor of Southeast European History and Politics, University of Graz, Austria*

"The heyday of Pan-Slavism may be long gone, but the idea of the brotherhood of Slavs continues to inspire a range of cultural, civilisational and geopolitical imaginations in Europe. This book is a veritable treasure trove for anyone interested in the curious evolution of this understudied phenomenon and its contemporary ramifications."
—Filip Ejdus, *Associate Professor at Faculty of Political Science, University of Belgrade, Serbia*

Mikhail Suslov · Marek Čejka ·
Vladimir Đorđević
Editors

Pan-Slavism and Slavophilia in Contemporary Central and Eastern Europe

Origins, Manifestations and Functions

palgrave
macmillan

Editors
Mikhail Suslov
Department of Cross-Cultural
and Regional Studies
University of Copenhagen
Copenhagen, Denmark

Marek Čejka
Department of Territorial Studies
Mendel University Brno
Brno, Czech Republic

Vladimir Đorđević
Department of Territorial Studies
Mendel University Brno
Brno, Czech Republic

ISBN 978-3-031-17874-0   ISBN 978-3-031-17875-7 (eBook)
https://doi.org/10.1007/978-3-031-17875-7

© The Editor(s) (if applicable) and The Author(s), under exclusive license to Springer Nature Switzerland AG 2023
This work is subject to copyright. All rights are solely and exclusively licensed by the Publisher, whether the whole or part of the material is concerned, specifically the rights of translation, reprinting, reuse of illustrations, recitation, broadcasting, reproduction on microfilms or in any other physical way, and transmission or information storage and retrieval, electronic adaptation, computer software, or by similar or dissimilar methodology now known or hereafter developed.
The use of general descriptive names, registered names, trademarks, service marks, etc. in this publication does not imply, even in the absence of a specific statement, that such names are exempt from the relevant protective laws and regulations and therefore free for general use.
The publisher, the authors, and the editors are safe to assume that the advice and information in this book are believed to be true and accurate at the date of publication. Neither the publisher nor the authors or the editors give a warranty, expressed or implied, with respect to the material contained herein or for any errors or omissions that may have been made. The publisher remains neutral with regard to jurisdictional claims in published maps and institutional affiliations.

Cover credit: © Alex Linch/shutterstock.com

This Palgrave Macmillan imprint is published by the registered company Springer Nature Switzerland AG
The registered company address is: Gewerbestrasse 11, 6330 Cham, Switzerland

Preface

The term 'Pan-Slavism' may sound quite archaic in the context of today's world as if being some sort of a utopian pan-ideology that belongs only in the pages of history textbooks. Perhaps this impression is also helped by the current political situation, in which two of the largest Slavic nations—the Russians and the Ukrainians—are immersed in a brutal conflict caused by the Russian invasion. And although the Slavic nations of the Balkans are no longer, as they were in the 1990s, at war with each other, their mutual relations are certainly no model of fraternal coexistence. The concept of Pan-Slavism, which has so strongly resonated among the Slavic nations since the nineteenth century, thus seems to be, at face value, dead.

The situation, however, is much more complicated, with Pan-Slavism still having a strong potential for political and societal mobilisation. Even a pan-nationalist—in our case Pan-Slavic—emphasis on 'equality' among fraternal nations can be but one of the driving forces of future disputes and, possibly, conflicts in the Slavic world. Where is the line that separates the attitude: *They are like us, let's be friends*—as between today's Russians and Serbs—from the attitude: *They are like us, but in the meantime they have become traitors and fascists*—as between today's Russians and Ukrainians? Can it not also be a Pan-Slavic line that, apart from its emphasis on geopolitical friendship, also produces enormous internal tensions between 'fraternal' nations, even mutual hatred? In other words, are there also certain elements of Pan-Slavism that cause not only 'fraternal love' to flourish between 'Slavic brothers' but also cruel fratricidal struggles and conflicts as well? This publication, consisting of contributions by numerous experts on the subject, provides answers to the above questions, taking into consideration both historical and contemporary perspectives.

Conceptually, Pan-Slavism belongs to the so-called pan-nationalisms or macro-nationalisms, the origins of which are associated with the rise of the era of national awakenings and nationalism and their parallel 'pan-variants' of the nineteenth century. The main underlying idea can be identified as an attempt to transcend more isolated national identities and create a higher, 'pan-national' identity, which could have involved—in the spirit of the geopolitics of the time—a significantly larger, more readily defensible, and economically more independent territory than the area of just one nation state.[1] In this context, Pan-Slavism, which was constituted approximately in the period 1830–1840, was the first modern politically conceptualised pan-nationalism.[2] But pan-nationalisms could also serve as a veil for the pragmatic interests of imperial states, which in the case of Pan-Slavism was Tsarist Russia; in the case of Pan-Germanism, Germany; and in the case of Pan-Turkism, the Ottoman Empire (or as still perceivable when speaking about the ambitions of the current Turkish president, Recep Tayyip Erdoğan).

Pan-Germanism, having originated slightly before Pan-Slavism and being partly defined in cultural terms,[3] preceded other pan-nationalisms, such as Pan-Arabism and Pan-Scandinavism. Although pan-nationalisms resonated with many of their supporters until the end of the nineteenth century, they could not ultimately compete with other nationalisms in terms of political mobilisation and ideological convincingness, insofar as

---

[1] See Suslov, M. (2012). 'Geographical Metanarratives in Russia and the European East: Contemporary Pan-Slavism', *Eurasian Geography and Economics*, 53(5): 575–595. Also, Đorđević, Vladimir, Marek Čejka, Ondřej Mocek, and Martin Hrabálek. (2021). 'Beyond Contemporary Scholarship and toward Exploring Current Manifestations of Pan-Slavism', *Canadian-American Slavic Studies*, 55(2): 147–159.

[2] Adams, I. (2001). *Political Ideology Today*. Manchester: Manchester University Press. p. 73.

[3] See Kohn, H. (1949). 'Arndt and the Character of German Nationalism.' *The American Historical Review* 54(4): 787–803. Also, Kohn, Hans. (1952). 'Pan-Slavism and World War II', In *American Political Science Review*, 46(3), 1952: 699–722. Also, Đorđević, Vladimir, Marek Čejka, Ondřej Mocek, and Martin Hrabálek. 2021. "Beyond Contemporary Scholarship and toward Exploring Current Manifestations of Pan-Slavism", *Canadian-American Slavic Studies*, 55(2): 147–159.

one of the main problems of pan-nationalisms was their vagueness and low practical feasibility, as they could not compete with more clearly defined particularist nationalist programmes.[4] In addition, the vague definition of 'Slavic unity', which relativised the differences between the individual Slavic nations, proved to be one of the greatest weaknesses of Pan-Slavism. Although Russia later became the most well-known 'protector' of Pan-Slavist ideas, at least the first significant variant of Pan-Slavism did not count on Russian political influence: 'Austro-Slavism' (circa 1846–1918) and later also 'Neo-Slavism' (circa 1908–1918) embodied the efforts of the many Slavic nations living in the Habsburg Empire towards a comprehensive emancipation, which, however, was to take place within the liberalising atmosphere of the Habsburg empire rather than under the whip of Russian Tsarist autocracy.[5] Gradually, however, Russia started increasingly using Pan-Slavism in its imperialist policies.

This 'classical' era of Pan-Slavism was subsequently ended definitively by the disintegration of Austria-Hungary after the First World War, when the more particular emancipatory ambitions of many Central and South Slavic nations were fulfilled. The Pan-Slavism born in Habsburg Austria thus lost its relevance, and the most significant state in the Slavic world, Russia, was transformed into Soviet Russia (and then the USSR), which started using other concepts besides Pan-Slavism in its foreign policy, for instance Eurasianism. Pan-Slavism[6] is often seen today as an historical and extinct form of pan-nationalism.[7] As indicated above, this perception ignores the fact that today we can witness the revitalisation of

---

[4] Đorđević, V., Čejka, M., Mocek, O. and Hrabálek, M. (2021). 'Beyond Contemporary Scholarship and toward Exploring Current Manifestations of Pan-Slavism', Canadian-American Slavic Studies, 55(2): 147–159.

[5] Ненашева, Зоя Сергеевна. (1984). Идейно-политическая борьба в Чехии и Словакии в начале XX в: чехи, словаки и неославизм, 1898–1914. Москва: Nauka. Also, Đorđević, Vladimir, Marek Čejka, Ondřej Mocek, and Martin Hrabálek. (2021). 'Beyond Contemporary Scholarship and toward Exploring Current Manifestations of Pan-Slavism', *Canadian-American Slavic Studies*, 55(2): 147–159.

[6] Laruelle, M. (2008). Russian Eurasianism – An ideology of Empire, Baltimore: The John Hopkins University Press. Also, Laruelle, Marlene. 2008. 'Alternative Identity, alternative religion? Neo-paganism and the Aryan Myth in contemporary Russia', In *Nations and Nationalism*, 14 (2): 283–3.

[7] Đorđević, V., Čejka, M., Mocek, O. and Hrabálek, M. (2021). 'Beyond Contemporary Scholarship and toward Exploring Current Manifestations of Pan-Slavism', *Canadian-American Slavic Studies*, 55(2): 147–159.

this concept in updated and reinterpreted forms, hence the usage 'historical' Pan-Slavism, either in a more comprehensive way or only with respect to certain aspects of it. Even these new forms of Pan-Slavism are very vague, and—like the traditional ones—are perhaps even more difficult to define and grasp. For some aspects of this Pan-Slavic revival, it would be more appropriate to use the term Slavophilia, as they may also contain political aspects of Slavic unity and often oscillate on the border of largely romantic-cultural perception of today's Slavic identity. Very often, contemporary references to Pan-Slavism may highlight Russian influence in various political (largely nationalist) and cultural contexts and discourses, at times being about directly pro-Russian politics, only shrouded in a certain Pan-Slavic garb.[8]

New forms of Pan-Slavism/Slavophilia have in the last decade been visibly (ab)used for illiberal political agendas in the Slavic societies where the Christian Orthodox milieu often plays a major role in identity politics—primarily in contemporary Russia under the rule of Vladimir Putin, with that country's foreign policy ambitions having grown significantly and some aspects of Pan-Slavism having re-emerged (or been introduced).[9] However, similar tendencies can be found in other Slavic countries without a predominantly Orthodox milieu, as the case of the very secular Czech Republic indicates.[10] These new forms of Pan-Slavism/Slavophilia may manifest themselves in both domestic and foreign policy, where they can disproportionately favour Russian attitudes and ambitions; deepen anti-democratic, anti-civic, and populist tendencies; and at the same time threaten EU integration.[11]

---

[8] Đorđević, V., Čejka, M., Mocek, O. and Hrabálek, M. (2021). 'Beyond Contemporary Scholarship and toward Exploring Current Manifestations of Pan-Slavism', *Canadian-American Slavic Studies*, 55(2): 147–159.

[9] Suslov, M. (2012). 'Geographical Metanarratives in Russia and the European East: Contemporary Pan-Slavism', *Eurasian Geography and Economics*, 53(5): 575–595. Also, Đorđević, Vladimir, Marek Čejka, Ondřej Mocek, and Martin Hrabálek. (2021). 'Beyond Contemporary Scholarship and toward Exploring Current Manifestations of Pan-Slavism', *Canadian-American Slavic Studies*, 55(2): 147–159.

[10] Đorđević, V., Čejka, M., Mocek, O. and Hrabálek, M. (2021). 'Beyond Contemporary Scholarship and toward Exploring Current Manifestations of Pan-Slavism', *Canadian-American Slavic Studies*, 55(2): 147–159.

[11] Đorđević, Vladimir, Marek Čejka, Ondřej Mocek, and Martin Hrabálek. (2021). 'Beyond Contemporary Scholarship and toward Exploring Current Manifestations of Pan-Slavism', *Canadian-American Slavic Studies*, 55(2): 147–159.

Last of all, what also needs to be mentioned, and what this volume also addresses, are the more current and rather specific forms of Pan-Slavism, whereby a certain number of cultural (and, in most cases, quite apolitical) conceptions of Slavic unity have also begun to emerge, inspired by the more contemporary trend of the rise of various neo-pagan movements.[12] Therefore, this multifaceted nature and the differences in understandings of contemporary manifestations of Pan-Slavism are important, though (unjustly) neglected, and pose a challenge for the research of nationalisms and related issues in the context of the Slavic world. This volume, therefore, is intended to bring a deeper and more systematic insight to these complex issues, providing an update to the field that is both well-deserved and an invitation to further research on the topic at hand.

Brno and Copenhagen
May 2022

Marek Čejka
Mikhail Suslov
Vladimir Đorđević

---

[12] See Golovneva, E. (2018). *The Native Faith: Religious Nationalism in Slavic Neo-Paganism* September 5, 2018, Online: https://brewminate.com/the-native-faith-religious-nationalism-in-slavic-neo-paganism/. Also, Laruelle, Marlene. 2008. 'Alternative Identity, alternative religion? Neo-paganism and the Aryan Myth in contemporary Russia', In *Nations and Nationalism*, 14 (2): 283–3.

Contents

Introduction

Examining Pan-Slavism: Conceptual Approach, Methodological Framework, and the State of the Art   3
Mikhail Suslov, Marek Čejka, and Vladimir Đorđević

Structure of the Volume   27
Mikhail Suslov, Marek Čejka, and Vladimir Đorđević

Pan-Slavism as History

Russian Pan-Slavism: A Historical Perspective   35
Mikhail Suslov

A Short History of Pan-Slavism and Its Impact on Central Europe in the Nineteenth and Twentieth Centuries   47
Jakub Woroncow

Pan-Slavism in the Balkans: A Historical View   59
Susan Baker

Pan-Slavism as a (Political) Tool

New Wine in an Old Wineskin: Slavophilia and Geopolitical Populism in Putin's Russia   77
Mikhail Suslov

Ideational Travels of Slavophilia in Belarus: From Tsars
to Lukashenka 101
Veera Laine, Aliaksei Lastouski, and Ryhor Nizhnikau

On Pan-Slavism, Brotherhood, and Mythology: The
Imagery of Contemporary Geopolitical Discourse in Serbia 123
Dejana Vukasović and Miša Stojadinović

Intermarium or *Hyperborea?* Pan-Slavism in Poland After
1989 155
Przemysław Witkowski

On Pan-Slavism, Identity, and Other Issues

A Distant Acquaintance: Reflecting on Croatia's
Relationship with Pan-Slavism 185
Tin Puljić and Senada Šelo Šabić

On Pan-Slavism(s) and Macedonian National Identity 207
Cvete Koneska

Invented 'Europeanness' Versus Residual Slavophilism:
Ukraine as an Ideological Battlefield 231
Mykola Riabchuk

On Pan-Slavism, East vs. West Divide, and Orthodoxy

Bulgaria's Backlash Against the Istanbul Convention:
Slavophilia as the Historical Frame of Pseudo-Religious
Illiberalism 261
Nevena Nancheva

Montenegrin Squaring of the Circle: Between Russophilia,
Pan-Orthodoxia, and Competing Nationalism 283
Vladimir Vučković and Miloš Petrović

Pan-Slavism and Slavophilia in the Czech Republic Within
the Context of Hybrid Threats 309
Miroslav Mareš and Petra Mlejnková

Slovakia: Emergence of an Old-New Pseudo-Pan-Slavism
in the Context of the Conflict Between Russia and Ukraine
After 2014   329
Juraj Marušiak

An Ethnographic Look on Pan-Slavism

Manifestations of Pan-Slavic Sentiments Among South
Slavic Diaspora Communities in the United States
of America   359
Jasmin Hasić and Maja Savić-Bojanić

Interethnic Ritual Kinship as Pan-Slavism in Bosnia
and Herzegovina   379
Keith Doubt

Afterword   399

Appendix   403

Index of Persons   417

Index of Subjects   421

NOTES ON CONTRIBUTORS

Susan Baker took her Ph.D. in American Studies from Case Western Reserve University in Cleveland. She taught American history and Western Civilisation for eighteen years in Ohio, Missouri, and Utah. In 1997 she began participating in election monitoring and training missions with the Organization for Security and Cooperation in Europe. Between 1997 and 1998, she worked in Bosnia, preparing for elections and being a trainer for incoming monitors. Since then, she has monitored elections in Ukraine, Belorussia, Macedonia, and Albania. In 2001, she received a second M.A. degree from the School of International and Public Affairs at Columbia University, having done research on Southwestern Europe. In 2002, she received the Harriman Institute East Central Europe Certificate.

Marek Čejka is an associate professor at the Department of Territorial Studies of Mendel University in Brno, Czech Republic, a former assistant at the Constitutional Court of the Czech Republic, and a former researcher at the Institute of International Relations in Prague, Czech Republic. He specialises in the Israeli-Palestinian conflict, the Middle East and Maghreb regions, exploring the relationship between religion, politics, and ideology in the Middle East while researching Arab nationalism, (radical) Islamism, and Christian fundamentalism. He was the coordinator of a project entitled **'Hey Slavs'**,[1] sponsored by the Grant Agency[2] of the Czech Republic, a Czech Science Foundation body providing funding for scientific research. He has published in academic outlets such as the *Czech Journal of Political Science* and *Central European Journal of International and Security Studies* and co-edited a volume entitled 'Rabbis of our Time: Authorities of Judaism in the Religious and Political Ferment of Modern Times' (Routledge, 2016). He has also produced the volumes in the Czech language, the latest ones being a co-edited 'Muslimské bratrstvo v současnosti' [Contemporary Muslim Brotherhood] (Academia, 2017) and a single-authorship volume of 'Korán, meč a volební urna' [Quran, Sword, and Ballot Box] (Academia, 2020).

Vladimir Đorđević is an assistant professor at the Department of Territorial Studies of Mendel University in Brno, the Czech Republic, and a Visiting Lecturer at the Faculty of Social Studies, Masaryk University, Brno. He specialises in the Western Balkans, Europeanisation, democratisation, nationalism, and security-related agendas of the said region. He has published in journals such as *Communist and Post-Communist Studies*, *European Security*, *Balkan and Near Eastern Studies*, *Nationalities Papers*, and *Journal of Slavic Military Studies*.

Keith Doubt is a professor emeritus at Wittenberg University. He has published articles on various social theorists: Harold Garfinkel, Georg Simmel, Hans-Georg Gadamer, George Herbert Mead, Jürgen Habermas, Talcott Parsons, Erving Goffman, and Kenneth Burke. His recent books are *Through the Kinship: Kinship and Elopement in Bosnia-Herzegovina* (CEU Press, 2014), *Ethnic and National Identity in Bosnia-Herzegovina: Kinship and Solidarity in a Polyethnic Society* with Adnan Tufekčić (Lexington Books, 2019), and *Sociocide: Reflections on Today's Wars* (Lexington Books, 2020).

---

[1] This volume was supported by and included in the **Czech Science Foundation (GAČR)** grant number **GA20-07592S**. See more information at: https://starfos.tacr.cz/en/project/GA20-07592S.

[2] The editors of this volume would like to express their gratitude to **Evan McElravy**, B.A., alumni of McGill University, Canada, mail: evan.mcelravy@gmail.com, a writer, editor, translator, and teacher in Brno, Czech Republic, for his excellent copy-editing skills. In addition, the editors would like to thank **Amar Khairi**, Ph.D. Candidate at Mendel University, Czech Republic, mail: amar.khairi@mendelu.cz, for his help in managing the formal aspects of this volume.

Jasmin Hasić is an associate professor of International Relations and International Law at Sarajevo School of Science and Technology. He holds a Ph.D. in political and social sciences from the Universite libre de Bruxelles (ULB) and LUISS Guido Carli of Rome. His recent publications include *Bosnia and Herzegovina's Foreign Policy since Independence* (Palgrave Macmillan, 2019). His research interests include peacebuilding, diaspora studies, and demographic changes associated with post-conflict migration. He has done consulting work with several international organisations, including International Organization for Migration (IOM), United Nations Development Programme (UNDP), United Nations Population Fund (UNFPA), and the World Bank. He is an alumnus of the United Nations Alliance of Civilizations (UNAOC) Fellowship in New York, the British-Bosnian Fellowship in London, and the Humanity in Action Diplomacy and Diversity Fellowship in Washington and Paris.

Cvete Koneska's primary research interest is in post-conflict politics in the Balkans, focusing on ethnopolitics, power-sharing, and the identity transformations related to European integration. She completed her doctoral research at the University of Oxford on post-conflict power-sharing in Bosnia-Herzegovina, and Macedonia and has since then continued to write on foreign policy, ethnic communities, and institutional reforms in the region. Beyond academic research, Cvete advises businesses, governments, and investors on political, security, and cyber risks in challenging environments. She heads AN advisory practice of a leading intelligence and risk consultancy in London.

Veera Laine is a postdoctoral research fellow at the Finnish Institute of International Affairs, focusing on Russian politics and society. Her Ph.D. in political history at the University of Helsinki received in 2021 deals with nationalism(s) in contemporary Russia.

Marlene Laruelle is a research professor and director of the Institute for European, Russian, and Eurasian Studies (IERES) at the Elliott School of International Affairs, the George Washington University, Washington, USA. At IERES, she is also directing the Illiberalism Studies Program, the Central Asia Program, and co-directing PONARS-Eurasia. She has widely published on Russia's ideologies, nationalism, Russia's foreign policy, and soft power strategies. Her latest monograph is *Is Russia Fascist? Unraveling Propaganda East and West* (Cornell University Press, 2021). She is now researching the notion of illiberalism and is the editor of the Oxford Handbook of Illiberalism (Oxford University Press, 2023).

Aliaksei Lastouski is an affiliated researcher at IRES, Uppsala University. He is also a senior research fellow at the Institute for Political Studies ("Political Sphere"), Lithuania, and a researcher at the Centre of Belarus and Regional Studies at European Humanities University. He completed his Ph.D. in Sociology in 2007 at the Institute of Sociology, National Academy of Sciences of Belarus. He is one of the organisers of the International Congresses of Belarusian Studies, held annually since 2011. In March 2022, he was dismissed from Polotsk State University for political reasons. He has published articles on cultural and collective memory, national identity, and cultural geography.

Miroslav Mareš is a professor at the Department of Political Science, Faculty of Social Studies of the Masaryk University in Brno (Czech Republic). He is the head of the Security and Strategic Studies study programme and a researcher at the International Institute of Political Science. He focuses on extremism, terrorism, and security policy issues in the Central European context. He is a member of the European Expert Network on Terrorism Issues, an expert in the expert pool of the Radicalization Awareness Network, and an expert in the European Centre of Excellence for Countering Hybrid Threats. He is the co-author, with Astrid Bötticher, of the volume *Extremismus—Theorien—Konzepte—Formen* (Oldenburg Verlag, 2012), co-editor, with Tore Bjørgo, of *Vigilantism against Migrants and Minorities* (Routledge, 2019), and author and co-author of more than 300 scientific publications.

Juraj Marušiak is a political scientist and historian. Since 1996, he has worked as a senior research fellow at the Institute of Political Science, Slovak Academy of Sciences, Bratislava. His research is on the history of Slovakia in the twentieth century, the political development of Slovakia after World War II, and comparative politics and international relations in Central and Eastern Europe since 1989, primarily in the V4 countries, Russia, Ukraine, Belarus, and Moldova. In 2002–2003, Marušiak was the recipient of the Lane Kirkland scholarship at Warsaw University, specialising in East European Studies. He authored *Slovenská literatúra a moc v druhej polovici päťdesiatych rokov* [*Slovak Literature and Power in the Second Half of the 50's*] (Prius, 2001), *(Dez)integračná sila stredoeurópskeho nacionalizmu* [*The (Dis)integration Power of Central*

European Nationalism. A Study of the Visegrad Group Countries] (UKB, 2015; in co-authorship with Mateusz Gniazdowski and Ivan Halász), and *Príliš skoré predjarie… Slovenskí študenti v roku 1956 [An Early Spring That Came Prematurely… Slovak Students in 1956]* (Veda, 2020).

Petra Mlejnková is an assistant professor in the Department of Political Science, Faculty of Social Studies, Masaryk University (FSS MU), and a researcher at the International Institute of Political Science at the same faculty. She focuses on extremism and radicalism in Europe, propaganda, and information warfare. She is a member of an expert network called Radicalisation Awareness Network, the European Expert Network on Terrorism Issues, and the Czech RAN CZ expert network coordinated by the Ministry of the Interior of the Czech Republic. She has published on disinformation and propaganda and the European Far-Right. Recently, she co-edited a volume entitled *Challenging Online Propaganda and Disinformation in the 21st Century* (Palgrave Macmillan, 2021).

Nevena Nancheva is a senior lecturer in Politics, International Relations, and Human Rights at Kingston University London. She is also a researcher at the Centre for Communities, Identities, and Difference. Her research expertise covers Bulgaria and the Bulgarians abroad and relations of identity and belonging in the post-communist Balkans, including social networks, digital diasporas, and Europeanisation. She is currently leading a research project on ethnic food entrepreneurship and migrant inclusion in Europe.

Ryhor Nizhnikau is a senior research fellow at the EU's Eastern Neighbourhood and Russia programme at the Finnish Institute of International Affairs. He received his Ph.D. from Johan Skytte Institute of Political Studies, University of Tartu, Finland. He focuses on Russia's and EU's policies in the post-Soviet space and domestic developments in this region.

Miloš Petrović is a research fellow at the Institute of International Politics and Economics and a visiting professor at the Faculty of Political Sciences, University of Belgrade, Serbia. He graduated from a US-based high school, earning his M.A. degree from the Europa-Institut, the University of Saarland in Saarbruecken, Germany, and his Ph.D. from Belgrade's Faculty of Political Sciences. His research stays abroad include the one at the Faculty of Social Studies of Masaryk University in Brno,

Czech Republic, as well as those with several NGOs. His research interests include EU enlargement, neighbourhood policies, and contemporary political developments in SEE and CEE.

Tin Puljić earned his B.A. and M.A. degrees in Political Science *summa cum laude* at the Faculty of Political Science in Zagreb, Croatia. In his MA, he focused on the influence of religion on foreign policy discourse in the Middle East. He is pursuing a Ph.D. in International Relations at the same institution. He has written several analytical texts for Croatian NGOs Faktograf and GONG, including the ones on the Israeli-Palestine conflict, American presidential elections, and the regulation of big tech.

Mykola Riabchuk is a senior research fellow at the Institute of Political Studies of the Academy of Sciences of Ukraine and a lecturer at the University of Warsaw and Ukrainian Catholic University in Lviv. He penned several books and articles on civil society, state/nation-building, nationalism, national identity, and post-communist transition in Eastern Europe. Five of them have been translated into Polish, one into French (De la petit Russie á l'Ukraine, 2003), German (Die reale und die imaginierte Ukraine, 2005), and Hungarian (A ket Ukraina, 2015). He received numerous national and international awards and fellowships, including Fulbright (1994, 2016), Reagan-Fascell (2011), EURIAS (2013), and l'Institut d'études avancées de Paris (2021). His most recent books published in English are Eastern Europe since 1989: *Between the Loosened Authoritarianism and Unconsolidated Democracy* (Warsaw University, 2020) and *At the Fence of Metternich's Garden. Essays on Europe, Ukraine, and Europeanisation* (*ibidem*-Verlag, 2021). From 2014 to 2018, he headed the Ukrainian PEN Centre and was awarded the title of Honorary President at the end of his term.

Senada Šelo Šabić is a senior research associate at the Institute for Development and International Relations in Zagreb, Croatia. Her research focuses on issues related to the Balkans, primarily foreign policy, security, democratisation, and migration. She holds Ph.D. in political and social science from the European University Institute in Florence, Italy, and has two M.A. degrees: one in international relations from the University of Zagreb, Croatia, and one in peace studies from the University of Notre Dame, USA.

Maja Savić-Bojanić is an associate professor of Political Science at Sarajevo School of Science and Technology. She holds a Ph.D. in political science from the University of Buckingham, UK. Her recent publications include several articles published in *European Societies* (Taylor and Francis), *Southeastern Europe* (Brill), and the *Journal of Balkan and Near Eastern Studies* (Taylor and Francis). Her research interests include migration studies and transnationalism, national minorities, political participation, and post-conflict spaces.

Miša Stojadinović is a senior research fellow at the Institute for Political Studies, Belgrade, Serbia, and Faculty for International Politics and Security at the Union Nikola Tesla University, Belgrade. He is an executive editor of a leading academic journal *Serbian Political Thought* that is published by the Institute for Political Studies in Belgrade, and he was the secretary of the project "Democratic and National Capacities of Political Institutions of Serbia in the Process of International Integrations", financed by the Ministry of Education, Science, and Technological Development of the Republic of Serbia. He did his postdoctoral specialisation at the Institute for Postgraduate Studies of the University of National and World Economy of Sofia, Bulgaria. During his academic career, he has published numerous scientific papers in domestic and international journals and four monographs in Serbian, English, and Russian.

Mikhail Suslov is an associate professor at the Department of Cross-Cultural and Regional Studies of the University of Copenhagen, Denmark, and a former researcher at the Uppsala Centre for Russian and Eurasian Studies, Sweden. He specialises in and teaches Russian (intellectual) history, political ideology, geopolitics, Russian Orthodox Church, contemporary Russian politics and society, and the history of Eastern and Southern Europe. He has published in journals, such as Eurasian Geography and Economics, Russian Politics and Law, Geopolitics, and Europe-Asia Studies. Besides this, he is the author of the monographs Putinism—The Regime Ideology in Post-Soviet Russia (Routledge, forthcoming in 2023) and *Geopolitical Imagination: Ideology and Utopia in Post-Soviet Russia* (Stuttgart: Ibidem, 2020).

Vladimir Vučković is a visiting lecturer at the Department of International Relations and European Studies of Masaryk University, Brno, Czech Republic, and he does research on European Union, populism in Europe, and Western Balkans politics. He has held visiting fellowships at the Department of Political Science at the University of Stockholm (2017) and the Centre for Southeast European Studies at the University of Graz (2021). He is the author of *Europeanizing Montenegro: The European Union, the Rule of Law, and Regional Cooperation* (2021) and editor of the volume *Balkanising Europeanization: Fight against Corruption and Regional Relations in the Western Balkans* (2019). His publications have appeared in the *Journal of Slavic Military Studies*, *Romanian Journal of European Affairs*, *Europe-Asia Studies*, and *Political Studies Review*, among others.

Dejana Vukasović is a principal research fellow at the Institute for Political Studies, Belgrade, Serbia, and a visiting professor at the Faculty of Political Sciences of the University of Belgrade. She graduated from the Faculty of Political Sciences of the University of Belgrade (Department of International Relations). She holds LLM in European Union Law and a postgraduate degree in European Civilization from the University of Lorraine, France, where she also did her Ph.D. in European Union Law (Faculty of Law, Economics and Management of the University of Lorraine). During her academic career, she has published numerous scientific papers in domestic and international journals and four monographs in Serbian, English, and French.

Przemysław Witkowski holds his Ph.D. in political science, is an assistant professor at Collegium Civitas in Warsaw, Poland, and works as a senior research director at the Institute of Social Safety in Warsaw. He was a two-time holder of a scholarship awarded by the Polish Ministry of National Education and Sport (2005, 2006), recently authoring the following publications: *Glory to superman. Ideology and pop culture* (Instytut Wydawniczy Książka i Prasa, 2017), and *Laboratory of Violence. The political history of the Roma* (Instytut Wydawniczy Książka i Prasa, 2020). His academic specialisation includes radical political movements and groups, extreme-right political movements (neo-Nazism, neo-fascism, nationalism, monarchism, neo-pagan, integral traditionalism, Eurasianism, national Bolshevism), and their international contacts, with the specialisation in neo-pagan and nouvelle droite groups. He lectured at Gen. Tadeusz Kościuszko Academy of Land Forces, University of Lower Silesia in Wrocław, Adam Mickiewicz University in Poznań, Jagiellonian University in Kraków, and University of Wroclaw.

Jakub Woroncow earned his M.A. degree at the University of Warsaw, Poland, while attaining his Ph.D. from SWPS University of Social Sciences and Humanities, Warsaw. He works as a researcher and expert at the Institute of Social Safety in Warsaw. He specialises in World War II affairs, historical and modern totalitarian doctrines and movements, and issues related to terrorism and political extremism.

List of Figures

Examining Pan-Slavism: Conceptual Approach, Methodological Framework, and the State of the Art

Fig. 1   Pan-nationalism in the 'family' of related ideational phenomena   18

Bulgaria's Backlash Against the Istanbul Convention: Slavophilia as the Historical Frame of Pseudo-Religious Illiberalism

Fig. 1   Visual for the 'Petition against the EU's accession to the Istanbul Convention', run by the organisation Rod International (*Source* https://rod-bg.com/articles/petition-against-joining-of-eu-in-ic.html)   273

Fig. 2   Protest against the Istanbul Convention depicting a slogan which reads 'Save Children from Debauchery (*Source* BGNES for Bulgarian National Radio on 11th Jan 2018. Available at: https://bnr.bg/vidin/post/100918948/vredna-za-balgarskoto-obshtestvo-li-e-istanbulskata-konvencia)   274

Montenegrin Squaring of the Circle: Between Russophilia, Pan-Orthodoxia, and Competing Nationalism

Fig. 1   Russophilic and Pan-Orthodox patterns in Montenegro   286

Appendix

Fig. 1	All-Slavic Congress in Prague 1848—Ceremonial Mass (Photo: Archive of authors)	403
Fig. 2	All-Slavic Congress in Prague 1997—information brochure about the progress of the convention (Photo: Miroslav Mareš)	404
Fig. 3	All-Slavic Congress in Moscow 2015—promotional graphics (Photo: Archive of authors)	405
Fig. 4	Sticker of football fans of the Sparta Prague football club with the depiction of the Pan-Slavic symbol "kolovrat" (spinning wheel) and pro-Serbian inscriptions (Photo: Miroslav Mareš)	406
Fig. 5	The 'Night Wolves' motorcycle gang on one of their 'Freedom Journeys' on the occasion of the end of the Second World War, Brno, Czech Republic 2021 (Photo: Marek Čejka)	407
Fig. 6	Various pro-Russian and pan-Slavic symbols are often found at the events of the 'Night Wolves' motorcycle gang, Brno, Czech Republic 2021 (Photo: Marek Čejka)	408
Fig. 7	Various pro-Russian and pan-Slavic symbols are often found at the events of the 'Night Wolves' motorcycle gang, Brno, Czech Republic 2021 (Photo: Marek Čejka)	409
Fig. 8	The ribbon of St. George is a frequent symbol of pro-Russian and pan-Slavic attitudes. The photo shows one of the members of the 'Night Wolves' biker gang (Photo: Marek Čejka)	410
Fig. 9	Pan-Slavic inscription 'Brother for brother' (written in Russian alphabet) stuck on a Slovak car (Photo: Marek Čejka)	411
Fig. 10	Ultra-nationalist demonstration in Brno (Czech Republic, 2015) at which a number of pro-Russian and Pan-Slavic symbols appeared (Photo: Marek Čejka)	412
Fig. 11	From Pan-Slavism to Pan-Orthodoxy? T-shirt on a stand in Belgrade, 2021 (Photo: Marek Čejka)	413
Fig. 12	Slavic symbols on the flags of the paramilitary organization 'Slovak Conscripts' (Photo: Miroslav Mareš)	414
Fig. 13	Slavic symbols on the flags of the paramilitary organization 'Slovak Conscripts' (Photo: Márty Surma)	415

List of Tables

Invented 'Europeanness' Versus Residual Slavophilism: Ukraine as an Ideological Battlefield

Table 1	Ukrainians' changing attitudes toward Russia, Russian leadership, and the project of the Russian-led East Slavonic Union, with the 2014 as the turning point	243
Table 2	People variously define themselves in different categories. To what degree you feel that you are: Source: Quantitative Surveys on Ukrainian Regionalism (2013–2015). University of St. Gallen, Center for Governance and Culture, 2017, https://www.uaregio.org/en/surveys/methodology/	245
Table 3	Support for the two competing systems of values among the major social and demographic groups (%) (*Source* Українське суспільство: моніторинг соціальних змін. 2014 Випуск 1(15). Том 1, pp. 125–132. http://nbuv.gov.ua/UJRN/ukrsoc_2014_1%281%29__14)	254

Interethnic Ritual Kinship as Pan-Slavism in Bosnia and Herzegovina

Table 1	Interethnic Ritual Kinship by Age Mareco Index Bosnia, Sarajevo, September 2017 (X^2 [4, $N = 1766$] = 3.96, $p > 0.05$)	394
Table 2	Interethnic Ritual Kinship by Ethnicity Mareco Index Bosnia, Sarajevo, September 2017 (X^2 [4, $N = 1766$] = 3.96, $p > 0.05$)	395

Introduction

Examining Pan-Slavism: Conceptual Approach, Methodological Framework, and the State of the Art

Mikhail Suslov, Marek Čejka, and Vladimir Đorđević

Introduction

Pan-nationalisms—notably Pan-Slavism, Pan-Arabism, Pan-Germanism, Pan-Turkism, Pan-Scandinavianism, and others—have rightfully acquired a reputation for being 'losers' in politics and ideology, as their prime cause—nationalism—was simultaneously their own gravedigger. They were fated to failure and oblivion precisely because they could not compete with nationalisms in terms of political mobilisation, collective

---

M. Suslov (✉)
Department of Cross-Cultural and Regional Studies, University of Copenhagen, Copenhagen, Denmark
e-mail: mikhail.suslov@hum.ku.dk

M. Čejka · V. Đorđević
Department of Territorial Studies, Mendel University Brno, Brno, Czech Republic
e-mail: marek.cejka@mendelu.cz

V. Đorđević
e-mail: vladimir.dordevic@mendelu.cz

© The Author(s), under exclusive license to Springer Nature Switzerland AG 2023
M. Suslov et al. (eds.), *Pan-Slavism and Slavophilia in Contemporary Central and Eastern Europe*,
https://doi.org/10.1007/978-3-031-17875-7_1

solidarity, and ideological convincingness.[1] However, this volume maintains that pan-national affinities and sentiments do continue to play an important role in international relations, trade, tourism, and business, while usually being maintained in political discourse by increasingly authoritarian leaders, as the examples of Russia under Putin and Turkey under Erdoğan suggest.

Born in the era of national awakening, pan-nationalisms aimed to create supra-national identities on top of already-existing political formations, such as the Pan-Slavic union that was imagined as a new geopolitical entity embracing several already-existing Slavic nations. We propose to differentiate pan-nationalisms from macro-nationalisms, the latter being an expression of an imperial nation's desire to embrace kindred peoples, which accordingly is a matter of imagining a nation-state writ large, on a greater scale, incorporating irredentist and diasporic imaginings or, for instance, the project of a larger Russian nation to include the Ukrainians and Belarusians.[2] In today's world, the project of the 'Russian World' is another manifestation of macro-nationalistic imagery, whose ultimate goal is to stretch the qualities of 'Russianness' to include territories and peoples outside of the Russian Federation, rather than to create a qualitatively new pan-national state.[3]

There is a tendency in the literature to group these two national imaginations together. For example, Louis L. Snyder defined these movements in a largely synonymous way, claiming they both 'paint nationalism on a much broader canvas to include all (pan) those who by reason of geography, race, religion, or language, or by a combination of any or all of them, are included in the same group category'.[4] Both pan-nationalism and macro-nationalism have remained easily available ideological 'software', supplying political actors with convenient memories, emotions,

---

[1] Giladi, A. (2020). 'Origins and Characteristics of Macro-Nationalism: A Reflection on Pan-Latinism's Emergence at the Turn of the Nineteenth Century', *History*, 105, pp. 252–267.

[2] E.g. Miller, A. (2015). 'The Romanov Empire and the Russian Nation', In: Berger, S. and Miller, A. (eds) *Nationalizing Empires*. Budapest: CEU Press, pp. 309–368.

[3] E.g. Suslov, M. (2018). '"Russian World" Concept: Post-Soviet Geopolitical Ideology and the Logic of "Spheres of Influence"', *Geopolitics*, 23(2), pp. 330–353.

[4] Snyder, L. L. (1984). *Macro-Nationalisms: A History of the Pan-Movements*. Westport, CT and London: Praeger, p. 4.

metaphors, and ideas required for the legitimation of a particular course of action or line of thinking.

It should be noted that the dividing line between pan-nationalism and macro-nationalism is not straightforward, and both types of geopolitical and nationalist imagination can intertwine. For example, the idea that Russia, Ukraine, and Belarus are naturally destined to become a single state could be inspired both by a macro-nationalist vision of a large Russian nation—'Holy Russia', 'Mother Russia', or the 'Russian World'— and by a pan-nationalist project of a union of East Slavic peoples. Having established that pan-nationalism implies a supra-national and ethnically coloured identity, we need to enunciate the difference between pan-nationalisms and continentalisms. The latter advance visions of a 'large space' whose parameters are defined by spatial proximity and by belonging to the highest geographical taxonomy, a continent.[5] In reality, however, ethnic pan-nationalism could be inseparably connected with geographical continentalism, when it comes to Pan-Africanism,[6] for example, or to some versions of Eurasianism that not only foreground the existence of the Eurasian continent but also the primordial ethnic unity of the Slavic-Turkic peoples inhabiting it. European integration is arguably the most obvious example of the amalgamation of a pan-national European identity and continentalist visions.

Political motives for pan-national imagery are many, but here we would like to spotlight one central—arguably indispensable—idea, that of enlarging scale for the purpose of fighting for international recognition. Pan-nationalism in this sense is always a by-product of securitisation, when a political leadership perceives an existential threat to the existence of their political body, or even just damage to the country's honour and respect shown to it by the 'meaningful others'. One can claim

---

[5] On continentalist geopolitical imagination see Calder, K. E. (2012). *The New Continentalism: Energy and Twenty-First-Century Eurasian Geopolitics*. New Haven, CT: Yale University Press. Also, Lewis, M. W. and Wigen, K. E. (1997). *The Myth of Continents: A Critique of Metageography*. Berkeley: University of California Press.

[6] E.g. Aydin, C. (2013). 'Pan-nationalism of Pan-Islamic, Pan-Asian, and Pan-African Thought', In: Breuilly, J. (ed.) *The Oxford Handbook of the History of Nationalism*. Oxford: Oxford University Press, pp. 672–693; Shepperson, G. (1962). 'Pan-Africanism and "Pan-Africanism": Some Historical Notes', *Phylon*, 23(4), pp. 346–358.

that pan-nationalism is a weapon of the weak.[7] This explains why pan-nationalisms' constitutive element is antagonism to a powerful external enemy, such as Germany for Pan-Slavism and Pan-Scandinavianism,[8] Russia for Pan-Germanism and Pan-Turkism, and the Anglo-Saxon world and 'Germanism' for the project of a single *'race latine'*.[9]

This argument becomes especially pertinent to the outsiders of the Western world—and especially to the non-Western empires, whose proud history and sense of global mission clashes violently with their lowered status in the modern world.[10] Thus, three empires—the Russian, the Ottoman, and the Japanese—whose status and honour were badly damaged in modern history developed three powerful pan-nationalisms in the second half of the nineteenth century: Pan-Slavism, Pan-Turkism, and Japanese Pan-Asianism.[11] By extension, it is common that pan-nationalisms are harboured by imperial states and have one pronounced centre of gravity, such as Russia for Pan-Slavism, or Germany for Pan-Germanism. On the other hand, more dispersed and egalitarian forms of pan-nationalism are possible as well, as is demonstrated by Pan-Scandinavianism, Pan-Latinism, or Pan-Arabism.[12] Inside the family of Pan-Slavisms, there exists also a multitude of ideas that exclude Russia

---

[7] Puntigliano, A. R. (2011). "Geopolitics of Integration" and the Imagination of South America', *Geopolitics*, 16(4), pp. 846–864; Puntigliano, A. R. (2017). '"21st Century Geopolitics: Integration and Development in the Age of "Continental States"', *Territory, Politics, Governance*, 5(4), pp. 1–17.

[8] E.g. Glenthøj, R. (2019). 'When Size Mattered: The Threshold Principle and the Existential Fear of Being too Small: Pan-Scandinavism in a European Context', In: Broers, M. and Caiani, A. A. (eds) *A History of the European Restorations: Governments, States and Monarchy*. London: Bloomsbury, pp. 245–256.

[9] The term comes from Vibert, P. (1903) *L'Avenir de la Race Latine*. See also: Al-Matary, S. (2010). *La communauté au secours de la nation: politiser l'identité latine', un gage de compétitivité dans les sociétés mondialisées de la fin du XIXe siècle?*, paper presented at the conference 'Les littératures francophones, hispanophones, lusophones et la notion de latinité', University of Paris Ouest, 20–21 May; Hyman, A. (1997). 'Turkestan and Pan-Turkism Revisited', *Central Asian Survey*, 16(3), pp. 339–351; Wertheimer, M. S. (1971). *The Pan-German League, 1890–1914*. Hemel Hempstead: Octagon Press.

[10] Zarakol, A. (2011). *After Defeat, How the East Learned to Live with the West*. Cambridge: Cambridge University Press.

[11] Landau, J. M. (1995). *Pan-Turkism: From Irredentism to Cooperation*. Bloomington: Indiana University Press.

[12] Dawn, C. E. (1988). 'The Formation of Pan-Arab Ideology in the Interwar Years', *International Journal of Middle East Studies*, 20(1), pp. 67–91.

and promote a more horizontal geopolitical project without a single uncontested leader. (Austro-Slavism is a case in point here.)

By extending the argument about the 'selective affinity' between empires and pan-nationalisms, it should be mentioned that some metropolitan states, originating from pre-modern (especially contiguous) empires, now experience difficulties with national self-identification. Turkey and especially Russia are the most glaring examples of an uncertainty and fragility in national identity. In Russia, *russkii* (ethnically Russian) and *rossiiskii* (civic Russian) identities compete, and this indeterminacy makes supra-national projects thinkable, such as the 'Russian World', Eurasianism, or 'Slavic civilization' for that matter.[13] Moreover, the failure to establish a civic Russian (*rossiiskii*) nation has pushed the political mainstream towards a more ethnically oriented conceptualisation of what Russia is. To be sure, this has given an additional impetus for the reinvigoration of pan-nationalistic ideas. Looked at from the other way around, states with strong national identities provide fewer possibilities for supra-nation-building.

It is claimed that pan-nationalisms are amorphous and 'thin-centred' ideologies[14] aiming at (political) frameworks and bodies superseding the nation-state framework in international relations,[15] which at the same time makes them both flexible and attractive. On the other hand, the confessional, linguistic, ethnic, cultural, territorial, and socio-political heterogeneity of the world today makes pan-nationalisms a conceptual Lego, combining many configurations of identities for the purpose of promoting a particular international or domestic policy. Scandinavian solidarity, partially institutionalised and partially informal, is a good example of this. Moreover, examples of ads in Russia about opportunities for spending holidays or founding a business in, or even relocating to, Serbia, Montenegro, or Bulgaria are also not uncommon. These opportunities are embellished by references to a similar language, common '*mentalité*',

---

[13] On the Russian nationalism see, among others: Laruelle, M. (2019). *Russian Nationalism: Imaginaries, Doctrines, and Political Battlefields*. London: Routledge; Kolstø, P. and Blakkisrud, H. (eds) (2016). *The New Russian Nationalism: Imperialism, Ethnicity and Authoritarianism*. Edinburgh: Edinburgh University Press.

[14] Freeden, M. (1998). 'Is Nationalism a Distinct Ideology?', *Political studies*, 46(4), pp. 748–765.

[15] Cederman, L. (2000). 'Nationalism and Bounded Integration: What It Would Take to Construct a European Demos', *EUI Working Papers*, 34, pp. 1–40.

and their supposed friendliness towards Russians. Likewise, in different (more official) discourses, Russia's friendly relations with (some) Slavic countries are often framed in terms of Pan-Slavic rhetoric. It is, of course, notoriously difficult to establish causal links or calculate the impact of pan-nationalisms on our everyday life and policymaking, but the starting point for our volume is that this impact remains, at least in our opinion, significant.

By way of anatomising the phenomenon of pan-nationalism, it should be noted that one of its most striking features is its ability to re-emerge after long periods of dormancy. It could be argued that pan-nationalisms are all 'potential nationalisms'[16] because the residual historical aura of experiences of solidarity, strong national emotions, and mutual sacrifice tends to persist and form a fertile soil for subsequence political instrumentalisation. Take, for example, the uprising in Bosnia and Herzegovina in the period 1875–1877, led by a largely Christian population against the decaying Ottoman Empire. This event triggered a stormy reaction in the then-tsarist Russia, with sympathies towards the Balkan Slavs—somewhat dormant in the previous three decades of the nineteenth century—quickly growing to a significant, empire-wide proportion. This caused thousands of Russian volunteers to rush to the rescue of the Serbs, prodding the Russian government to declare war on the Ottoman Empire in 1877. This latent Russian 'Slavophilia' resurfaced again with the outbreak of the First Balkan War in 1912, unleashing a series of 'Slav banquets' and demonstrations. In this atmosphere, the country glided into the First World War as an ally of the Kingdom of Serbia, responding aggressively to the 'July crisis'[17] that was the introduction to this conflict. The resurgence of Slavic solidarity during the NATO air raids on the Federal Republic of Yugoslavia (Serbia and Montenegro) in 1999 had yet another fatal

---

[16] The term is borrowed from Gellner, E. (1983). *Nations and Nationalism*. Ithaca, NY: Cornell University Press, p. 43.

[17] Kohn, H. (1960). *Pan-Slavism: Its History and Ideology*. New York: Vintage Books; Boeckh, K. (2016). 'The Rebirth of Pan-Slavism in the Russian Empire, 1912–13', In: Boeckh, K. and Sabine, R. (eds) *The Balkan Wars from Contemporary Perception to Historic Memory*. Cham: Springer International Publishing, pp. 105–137. Also, MacKenzie, D. (1967). *The Serbs and Russian Pan-Slavism, 1875–1878*. Ithaca, NY: Cornell University Press.

consequence for Russia, whereby Pan-Slavism served as a catalyst for the crystallisation of the regime ideology of Putinism.[18]

Manifestations of Pan-Slavism in Today's World

Speaking of Putinism, it appears that this had reached a new level ideologically by 2021, when the Russian president penned a piece highlighting the supposed 'historical unity of Russians and Ukrainians',[19] setting the stage for Moscow's incursion into Ukraine starting in February 2022 and still ongoing in the time of finalising this volume. Emphasising common culture, tradition, history, and even mentality, while claiming that the Russian and Ukrainian languages are similar, Putin referred to, among other things, history in justifying the need for his subsequent invasion.[20] Mixing references to historical events while grounding his approach on the ideology of the 'Russian'—read: Anti-Western—'World' to which Ukraine was to belong was ideationally associated with various Pan-Slavic solidarity discourses that remain an important part of Russian foreign policy.[21] Additionally, Putinism is a sort of authoritarian political system characterised by an increasingly repressive (police) regime, ideologically backed by and relying on elements of Russian spirituality and exceptionality by virtue of being Slavs (and therefore culturally different to the West) and heavily centred on an ideology of Russian patriotism that is

---

[18] DeDominicis, B. E. (2017). 'Pan-Slavism and Soft Power in Post-Cold War Southeast European International Relations: Competitive Interference and Smart Power in the European Theatre of the Clash of Civilizations', *The International Journal of Interdisciplinary Civic and Political Studies*, 12(3), pp. 1–17. Also, Suslov, M. (2012). 'Geographical Metanarratives in Russia and the European East: Contemporary Pan-Slavism', *Eurasian Geography and Economics*, 53(5), pp. 575–595.

[19] Putin, V. (2021). 'On the Historical Unity of Russians and Ukrainians', Presidential Executive Office, available at: http://en.kremlin.ru/events/president/news/66181 [Accessed on 21st April 2022].

[20] Ibid. Also, Marples, D. R. (2022). 'Vladimir Putin Points to History to Justify His Ukraine Invasion, Regardless of Reality', available at: https://theconversation.com/vladimir-putin-points-to-history-to-justify-his-ukraine-invasion-regardless-of-reality-177882 [Accessed on 21st April 2022].

[21] Lewis, C. (2020). 'Contemporary Russian Messianism Under Putin and Russian Foreign Policy in Ukraine and Syria', *The Slavonic and East European Review*, 98(3), pp. 531–559. Also, Suslov, M. (2012). 'Geographical Metanarratives in Russia and the European East: Contemporary Pan-Slavism', *Eurasian Geography and Economics*, 53(5), pp. 575–595.

abundant with the right-wing political ideas that have become dominant in Russian domestic politics in the last two decades.[22]

The anti-Western discourse that has characterised Putinism was increasingly elevated in Russian foreign policy and domestic politics until it reached the point of identifying the West, and later on the Ukrainian government and especially Ukrainian President Zelenskyy, as Nazis and/or Nazi collaborators and supporters, making Russian intervention in Ukraine both necessary and justified, with the West vilified as the ultimate opponent of the Russian state.[23] Hence, the term 'denazification'—warranting the 'special operations of the Russian Army'[24] in Ukraine—de facto became 'a reminder that the term "Nazi" has become a generic term for "absolute evil" that is completely disconnected from its original historical meaning and context',[25] remaining ready for use in political purposes when needed. As Pisanty stated in her volume on the recent return of xenophobic right-wing ideas, 'new political formations are pushing alternative counter-histories, many based on latent memories, suppressed rancour, and national myths once thought to be dead and buried, but which now reveal an unexpected vitality'.[26] Therefore, this

---

[22] *Le Monde Diplomatique.* (2022). 'The Rightwing Ideologues Who Fueled Putin's Dream of an Expansionist Russia', available at: https://mondediplo.com/2022/04/03ideology-podcast [Accessed on 21st April 2022]. Also, NPR. (2022). 'Putin's Claim of Fighting Against Ukraine 'Neo-Nazis' Distorts History, Scholars Say', available at: https://www.npr.org/2022/03/01/1083677765/putin-denazify-ukraine-russia-history?t=1650619455966 [Accessed on 21st April 2022]. Also, UChicago News. (2022). 'How Putin's Invasion of Ukraine Connects to 19th-Century Russian Imperialism', available at: https://news.uchicago.edu/story/putin-invasion-ukraine-russian-empire-19th-century-imperialism-history [Accessed on 19th April 2022].

[23] NPR. (2022). 'Putin's Claim of Fighting Against Ukraine 'Neo-Nazis' Distorts History, Scholars Say', available at: https://www.npr.org/2022/03/01/1083677765/putin-denazify-ukraine-russia-history?t=1650619455966 [Accessed on 17th April 2022]. Also, Lewis, C. (2020). 'Contemporary Russian Messianism Under Putin and Russian Foreign Policy in Ukraine and Syria', *The Slavonic and East European Review*, 98(3), pp. 531–559.

[24] Putin, V. (2021). 'On the Historical Unity of Russians and Ukrainians', Presidential Executive Office, available at: http://en.kremlin.ru/events/president/news/66181 [Accessed on 17th April 2022].

[25] NPR. (2022). 'Putin's Claim of Fighting Against Ukraine 'Neo-Nazis' Distorts History, Scholars Say', available at: https://www.npr.org/2022/03/01/1083677765/putin-denazify-ukraine-russia-history?t=1650619455966 [Accessed on 22nd April 2022].

[26] Pisanty, V. (2021). *The Guardians of Memory and the Return of the Xenophobic Right.* New York: CPL Editions, p. 18.

decontextualisation and disconnection not only serves to provide legitimacy to Russian actions[27] but additionally furnishes an ideological basis for the rule of the Russian regime by creating an ideological counter-narrative that will likely continue to exist as long as Putin's regime is alive and well.

Ironically, the war in Ukraine also activated Pan-Slavic imagery in Russia. On the surface, the proposition of a Pan-Slavic revival against the background of a fraternal war between closely related East Slavic nations sounds outlandish and evokes René Girard's reflection on the dangers of sameness and similarities in geopolitics.[28] Indeed, one can surmise that it is the intensity of reflection on the closeness of Russia and Ukraine to each other that has laid the ground in Russia for thinking about Ukraine as a 'monstrous double'—a traitor or a brother turned fratricidal Cain—which appeared to be a self-fulfilling prophesy when Russian bombs began to fall on Ukrainian cities.

Under close scrutiny, however, we can find a raft of Pan-Slavic ideas, proposals, and visions triggered by the war. For example, the leader of the left-patriotic party Just Russia—For Truth, Sergei Mironov came up with a proposal to establish a League of Slavic States inspired by the Arab League. In his understanding, the war in Ukraine is a proxy war of the West against the Rest, most significantly against the Slavic nations, represented today by Russia, Belarus, and Serbia. In his vision, the Slavic League would help the Slavic nations to rid themselves of Western sway, to stop being 'Western marionettes', and finally to serve as a core for a union of all states 'which are ready to withstand the dictatorship of the American and West European leaders'.[29] In other words, the Russian official representation of its war in Ukraine shifts focus towards Russia's

---

[27] NPR. (2022). 'Putin's Claim of Fighting Against Ukraine 'Neo-Nazis' Distorts History, Scholars Say', available at: https://www.npr.org/2022/03/01/1083677765/putin-denazify-ukraine-russia-history?t=1650619455966 [Accessed on 21st April 2022].

[28] In the context of Girard's mimetic theory, 'mimetic doubles' are locked in a conflict, which escalates 'to the point that every difference has been erased and the rivals stand in from of each other as matching images' (Farneti, R. (2015). *Mimetic Politics: Dyadic Patterns in Global Politics. East Lansing: Michigan State University Press*, p. 10).

[29] Mironov, S. (2022). 'My dolzhny sozdat' "Ligu slavianskikh gosudarstv"', *Tsargrad.tv*, 25 June (Сергей Миронов: Мы должны создать "Лигу славянских государств"), available at: https://tsargrad.tv/articles/sergej-mironov-my-dolzhny-soz dat-ligu-slavjanskih-gosudarstv_571079?ysclid=l50uo5x2vq933313523.

confrontation with the West and Westernised domestic elites and resuscitates the metaphor of Russia as liberator of the Slavs. It is also thinkable that, in the event of Russia's military success, the issue of ideological support for annexationist policies would bring to the fore Pan-Russian or even Pan-Slavic geopolitical visions such as 'Novorossiya'.[30] Another example is the celebration of the Day of Slavic Unity on 25 June 2022 in Briansk (Russia), which featured representatives from the non-recognised Donetsk and Luhansk People's Republics, as well as from Belarus, which looked like a rehearsal of one possible geopolitical configuration for the post-war period.[31]

It goes without saying that the Russian incursion has brought into question the stability of the European continent while also creating a rift in the domestic politics of many Slavic states. While those Slavic countries that are members of the EU continued to largely condemn the invasion, some, such as Serbia or Belarus, found themselves in a peculiar position. While Belarus, whose authoritarian leader largely stood by the Russian president—though being awfully quiet about it—while allowing the Kremlin's troops to attack Ukraine from where they were stationed in Belarus, Serbia officially condemned the Russian invasion in the UN but otherwise refused to sign up to EU sanctions against Moscow, supposedly trying to remain neutral between East and West.[32]

As already shown, residual pan-nationalistic ideologies provide ample possibilities for politicians to build from these traditions their own legitimising strategies, policies, and concepts, however whether or not these possibilities will be used is an open-ended question. With the rise of illiberal and identitarian politics in recent years, nationalist and populist platforms have become increasingly influential, impacting the quality of democracy and at the same time eroding it in (not only) Europe. It is specifically in Europe that this sort of illiberal narrative has come to oppose the ideas of the democratic political order, pitting itself against

---

[30] On 'Novorossiya' see: Suslov, M. (2017). 'The Production of "Novorossiya": A Territorial Brand in Public Debates', *Europe-Asia Studies*, 69(2), pp. 202–221.

[31] 'V Brianske proshel Mezhdunarodnyi festival'...' (2022). *TV Soyuz*, 28 June (В Брянске прошел Международный фестиваль славянских народов «Славянское единство-2022»), available at: https://www.youtube.com/watch?v=AeDqu2PCJSw.

[32] Radio Slobodna Evropa. (2022). 'Rusija i Kina kao prepreka usklađivanju Srbije sa EU', available at: https://www.slobodnaevropa.org/a/srbija-uskladjenost-eu-sankcije-rusija/31814285.html [Accessed on 22nd April 2022].

the related narrative of the supra-national union that the EU stands for.[33] Having mixed anti-immigrationist and anti-elitist approaches with a peculiar civilisational and national exclusion,[34] political parties and leaders hostile to the common European project have thus become more vocal. At the same time, a geopolitical split between the East and the West has started to grow,[35] coming to somewhat resemble the Cold War division.[36] This division has been partly influenced by ideas stemming from Pan-Slavism, ideologically propagated by Russia and playing an increasing role in both non-EU states, such as Serbia, Ukraine, and Russia, and EU ones, such as the Czech Republic and Slovakia.[37]

In this context, Pan-Slavic discourses in today's world imbricate the conservative-identitarian search for hidden roots and forgotten legacies with the leftist criticism of the global hegemony of 'the West'. At the same time, Russia, in its assertive foreign policy and increasingly anti-Western ideology, seems to be reclaiming the role of leader of the 'Slavic world'. The ideology of the 'Russian World', which motivated and legitimised the war in Ukraine, largely taps into discourses of Pan-Slavic solidarity. As a symbolic reciprocation of the Russian volunteers' movement in Serbia in 1876–1877, the Serbian squad 'Jovan Šević' fought on the side of pro-Russian forces in Donbas in 2014 (followed by similar activities that volunteers from other Slavic states engaged in).

Another example in this regard is the pronounced Pan-Slavic rhetoric among Russian skinheads (i.e. Dmitry Demushkin's Slavic Union) and proponents of Slavic paganism. A third area where Pan-Slavic ideas and

---

[33] Enyedi, Z. (2016). 'Paternalist Populism and Illiberal Elitism in Central Europe', *Journal of Political Ideologies*, 21(1), pp. 9–25.

[34] Brubaker, R. (2017). 'Between Nationalism and Civilizationism: The European Populist Moment in Comparative Perspective', *Ethnic and Racial Studies*, 40(8), pp. 1191–1226.

[35] Foreign Policy. (2019). 'A New Cold War Has Begun', available at: https://foreignpolicy.com/2019/01/07/a-new-cold-war-has-begun/ [Accessed on 9th September 2020].

[36] Tsygankov, A. P. (2008). 'Russia's International Assertiveness: What Does It Mean for the West?', *Problems of Post-Communism*, 55(1), pp. 38–55. Also, Giles, K. (2016). 'Russia's "New" Tools for Confronting the West. Continuity and Innovation in Moscow's Exercise of Power', *Research Paper*, Chatham House. Also, Jaitner, M. (2015). 'Russian Information Warfare: Lessons from Ukraine', In: Geers, K. (ed) *Cyber War in Perspective: Russian Aggression Against Ukraine*. Tallinn: NATO CCD CEO Publications, pp. 87–94.

[37] Ibid.

visions can be found in abundance is the religious Orthodox-Christian milieu. Church-inspired intellectuals draw on the 'civilisational' rhetoric of the Orthodox Church to substantiate the existence of a separate and unique Slavic-Orthodox civilisation, often under the wings of Russia. A fourth intellectual niche for Pan-Slavic sentiments, associated with the previous one, is Messianism, which has in historical terms powered much of Russia's foreign policy in the Balkans, and whose elements have been regenerated in nationalist circles following the collapse of the Soviet Union. (See, for instance, Lewis's article discussing, among other things, Dugin's work in Russia.[38]) Fifth, contemporary Pan-Slavism is considerably inspired by continentalist discourses and policies.[39] Sometimes there may be a clash between the discovered identity of Russia as a Eurasian power and Slavophilia, but often Eurasianism and Pan-Slavism are superimposed on each other, creating a vision of a large geopolitical entity (*Grossraum* or 'large space' according to Carl Schmitt) stretching from the Adriatic to the Pacific. In these and other cases, the history of Pan-Slavism and its intellectual legacy facilitates the coalescence of illiberal, identitarian, civilisational, and anti-Western ideas in Slavic countries today, which makes Slavophilia a relevant ideological, political, and geopolitical phenomenon.

With respect to the points made, the key issues treated in the case studies are as follows:

1. The sources of contemporary Pan-Slavism as well as the relationship between contemporary and historical Pan-Slavism (the continuity vs. discontinuity debate);
2. Ideological aspects related to Pan-Slavism in terms of ethnonationalist politics, nationalist-populist standpoints, and the political and social actors therein, as well as the multi-faceted relationship of Orthodox Christianity to Pan-Slavism;
3. Displays/representations/manifestations of Pan-Slavism having political, social, and/or cultural implications in specific settings, such as among a relatively large Slavic diaspora;

---

[38] Lewis, C. (2020). 'Contemporary Russian Messianism Under Putin and Russian Foreign Policy in Ukraine and Syria', *The Slavonic and East European Review*, 98(3), pp. 531–559.

[39] See, for example, Calder, K. E. (2012). *The New Continentalism: Energy and Twenty-First-Century Eurasian Geopolitics*. New Haven, CT: Yale University Press.

4. Ethnographic approaches to examining Pan-Slavism, whereby interethnic ritual kinship is analysed; and
5. The various (social) functions Pan-Slavic ideas and discourses serve in the societies discussed, for example, both political goals and projects countering the Union and also the more-on-the-ground purposes these discourses serve for the 'ordinary' people. It is, in this regard, necessary to mention the role of EU conditionality, with various local oppositions[40] to it having arisen in recent years in several Slavic states that are either EU candidates or potential candidates (e.g. fears that the EU is trying to 'export' its 'superior' norms to more 'inferior' (Slavic) countries). This has in recent years been followed by a partial backlash against Brussels, as seen across the political spectrum of Slavic states, some of which are Union members.

Theoretical and Methodological Notes

The conceptual problem of studying residual Pan-Slavism lies in its elusive, dormant nature, which often flies under the radar of scholarship interested in socio-political movements, policies, and articulated ideological doctrines. To grasp its essence, we propose the term 'Slavophilia', which usefully points to the need to substitute the *-ism* in Pan-Slavism with *-philia*, that is to conceptualise Slavic pan-nationalism not as a coherent ideological platform but rather as a coalescence of ideas, emotions, visions, and metaphors, which—due to the shallowness of its political philosophy—is combinable with any ideological tradition. This helps clarify why, among other apparent contradictions, Slavophilia does not exclude the ideology of Eurasianism: for instance, a political figure can—despite taking seemingly opposed positions—preach Russia's Eurasian identity and simultaneously stand for Pan-Slavic solidarity. Similarly, 'Slavophilia' may inspire both liberal iterations of pan-nationalism (such as neo-Slavism in the beginning of the twentieth century) and conservative ones (as manifested in the imperialist Russian Pan-Slavism of the late nineteenth century). By way of making a methodological caveat, it is important to underline that 'Slavophilia' in our understanding has no

---

[40] See, for instance, Đureinović, J. (2020). *The Politics of Memory of the Second World War in Contemporary Serbia: Collaboration, Resistance and Retribution*. London: Routledge.

direct connection to Slavophilism, the mid-nineteenth-century Russian doctrinal mixture of cultural nationalism, conservatism, and populism. Importantly, this Slavophilism may or may not harbour Pan-Slavic sentiments, and hence, the term 'Slavophilism' is somewhat misleading and is also emphatically resisted by Slavophiles themselves.

To reiterate, despite the extinction of Pan-Slavism as an articulated Romantic-era geopolitical ideology, several related discourses have spilled over into mainstream debates and the popular imagination. To address this array of representations, the term Slavophilia seems to be useful. Our approach to it is mostly couched in terms of critical geopolitics.[41] This means that our primary concern is how geopolitical discourses shape the identity and policies of a community. To understand this, we need to delve into the host of geopolitical concepts that structure an otherwise amorphous discursive field. Slavophilia is here taken as one of those geopolitical concepts that span 'formal geopolitics' (i.e. expert theorisation and ideology), 'practical geopolitics' (the discourses of the political leadership), and 'popular geopolitics' (grassroots ideas, media, opinions, and emotions).[42] In this context (see the table below), geopolitical concepts provide the language in which elites and ideologists articulate political sentiments, metaphors, and visions about a community's identity, security concerns, role, mission in the world, and its desirable course in international relations.[43] In addition to this, geopolitical concepts define the country's 'strategic culture', meaning the complex of operational political representations among policy-makers.[44]

---

[41] Ó Tuathail, G. and Dalby, S. (1998). 'Introduction: Rethinking Geopolitics: Towards a Critical Geopolitics', In: Ó Tuathail, G. and Dalby, S. (eds) *Rethinking Geopolitics*. London: Routledge. Also, Mamadouh, V. and Dijkink, G. (2006). 'Geopolitics, International Relations and Political Geography: The Politics of Geopolitical Discourse', *Geopolitics*, 3(11), pp. 349–366. Also, Dodds, K. (2001). 'Political Geography III: Critical Geopolitics After Ten Years', *Progress in Human Geography*, 3(25), pp. 469–484.

[42] Ó Tuathail, G. (1999). 'Understanding Critical Geopolitics: Geopolitics and Risk Society', *Journal of Strategic Studies*, 2–3(23), pp. 107–124.

[43] On the notion of 'geopolitical vision' see Dijkink, G. (1996). *National Identity and Geopolitical Visions: Maps of Pride and Pain*. London: Routledge.

[44] On Russian strategic culture see, for instance, Staun, J. (2018). *Russisk strategisk kultur under Putin*. Copenhagen: Forsvarsakademiet. Also, Skak, M. (2018). 'Om russisk strategisk kultur før og nu', In: Bisgaard, L., et al. (eds) *Utopi og Realiteter: Festskrift til Erik Kulavig*. Ødense: Syddansk Universitetsforlag, pp. 121–132. Also, Skak, M.

In that regard, Slavophilia and other geopolitical concepts are constitutive parts of geopolitical culture in general.[45] To a researcher, these concepts provide frames for understanding popular geopolitical representations in social media and cultural production (such as in media, films, books, music, video clips). Therefore, the above-mentioned theoretical framework is to serve as the basis for the authors of this volume. We believe that our multi-dimensional and coherent approach to the study of Slavophilia is at the same time an important methodological 'selling point' of this volume. Hence, our team of authors takes a methodological approach that makes our study specific, above all when considering the number of case studies included in this volume as well as the breadth of our analysis relying chiefly on the application of qualitative methods. This is exactly where we see the added value of our volume, as it discusses a topic that has been only partially discussed in English language academic scholarship so far. This point will be argued in the concluding section of this chapter, in which we present considerations on the state of the art and our contribution to the field.

Types of geopolitical discourses	Theoretical approaches	Examples of sources for Slavophilia
Political (elites, policymakers) Intellectual/academic (intellectuals, academics)	Geopolitical ideology	Nationalist, conservative, and identitarian party programmes
Policymakers	Strategic culture	Statements of officials, official discourses
General public	Popular geopolitics	Cultural products (media, films, literature, music video clips, theatre, etc.)

The meaning of pan-nationalism emerges at the intersection of nationalistic and geopolitical iterations of identity (see Fig. 1). At a high level of

---

(2016). 'Russian Strategic Culture: The Role of Today's Chekisty', *Contemporary Politics*, 3(22), p. 324–341. Also, Adamsky, D. (2020). 'Russian Campaign in Syria: Change and Continuity in Strategic Culture', *Journal of Strategic Studies*, 1(43), pp. 104–125.

[45] On the concept of 'geopolitical culture' see, among others, O'Loughlin, J., Ó Tuathail, G. (Toal, G.) and Kolossov, V. (2005). 'Russian Geopolitical Culture and Public Opinion: The Masks of Proteus Revisited', *Transactions of the Institute of British Geographers*, New Series 30(3), pp. 322–325.

abstraction, pan-nationalism is about the contours of the 'us' community—who 'we' are, where 'we' are, where 'we' end and 'the others' begin, and to what extent 'they' are still part of 'us'. There are two kinds of tightly intertwined discourses that map out the contours of 'us': the domestic and the international, which correspond respectively to the nationalistic and the geopolitical visions.

First and foremost, by its very definition, a pan-nationalism is a nationalist idea, stating that there is a unity of kindred nations, as defined in terms of culture, language, and history (or common 'destiny'), with an emphasis on the need for this unity to be enhanced politically and economically, eventually within the geographical borders of a single state. As with any nationalist idea, pan-nationalism acquires blood and flesh in its horizontal juxtaposition to other pan-national bodies, such as a Pan-German union or, more commonly today, (regional) integrationist projects, such as the European Union, NATO, or similar.

Pan-nationalism 'feels at home' within yet another ideological family, this being that of populism. At this point, it is important to stress that pan-nationalisms, to a greater extent than nationalisms proper, tend to introduce a vertical dimension to their ideological worldview by comparing a 'self-community' with 'others' who are not just 'others' but

Fig. 1 Pan-nationalism in the 'family' of related ideational phenomena

also 'masters'.[46] Similarly to how canonical populism revolves around the juxtaposition of the authentic people and the corrupt elite, Pan-Slavic ideologists relate this logic to geopolitics by assigning the role of the 'simple people' and 'colonial underdogs' to the Slavs, while the others—be they Germans, Westerners in general, or Brussels bureaucrats specifically—are seen as 'corrupted masters'. This logic of course presupposes the nationalist idea about a relatively homogeneous 'us'—the wretched but nevertheless authentic people.[47]

As an ideology of geopolitical populism, pan-nationalism differs significantly from the ideology of multiculturalism in how it interprets the 'corruptness' of the imagined masters. Unlike the liberal-multiculturalist claim about justice (i.e. that a subordinate culture should be treated on an equal footing with the hegemonic culture, because this is only fair), pan-nationalism is instead aligned with the identitarian claim that the subordinate culture should have rights to self-realisation—or in other words, that the imagined community of all Slavs should be recognised not because it is fair to recognise them as part of the global community but because they are fundamentally different and should have the right to develop their differences to their logical limits.[48] This fixation on identity and community entrenches pan-nationalism in the camp of fascist-like ideologies, defined by their desire to rediscover the supposed purity of the community in the past. Indeed, racist, skinhead, and radical nationalist circles often adopt elements of Pan-Slavism to substantiate their idea of white supremacy. This is, for instance, the case in both Russia and Eastern

---

[46] Belous, V. (2019). 'The Opposition of Own/Alien as a Source of the External Threat: Reflections on Supra-State Sovereignization Politics and 19th-Century Pan-Slavism', In: Crailsheim, E. and Pérez-Grueso, M. D. E. (eds) *The Representation of External Threats. From the Middle Ages to the Modern World.* Leiden: Brill, pp. 56–66.

[47] Kallis, A. (2018). 'Populism, Sovereigntism, and the Unlikely Re-emergence of the Territorial Nation-State', *Fudan Journal of the Humanities and Social Sciences*, 11(3), pp. 285–302; Mudde, C. (2004). 'The Populist Zeitgeist', *Government and Opposition* (London), 39(4), pp. 541–563; Rydgren, J. (ed.) (2018). *The Oxford Handbook of the Radical Right*. New York: Oxford University Press; Kaltwasser, R. C. et al. (eds) (2017). *The Oxford Handbook of Populism*. 1st Edition. Oxford: Oxford University Press.

[48] Olivera, L. H. (2021). 'Difference and Recognition: A Critical Lecture on Axel Honneth, Jacques Rancière and Nancy Fraser', In: *Rethinking Vulnerability and Exclusion*. Cham: Palgrave Macmillan, pp. 137–159; Spencer, V. A. (2020). 'Introduction to Dialogue: Revisiting the Politics of Recognition', *Politics, Groups, and Identities*, 8(5), pp. 1043–1046.

Europe, where skinhead groups are much more nationalistic than in the West where the movement was born.

Pan-nationalism can also be contextualised as part of conservative communitarianism, with its emphasis on cultural affinities and communal solidarity, which according to this ideology precedes any rational constructions such as laws or institutions. Reflecting on Edmund Burke's thoughts, Roger Scruton avers that 'there cannot be a society without this experience of membership' or without a shared identity, otherwise disagreements and individual egoisms would make community impossible.[49] This is precisely what Pan-Slavist imagery proposes: the shared experience of a similar culture, language, and episodes of solidary actions form the basis for an all-Slavic union because these primordial ties are more important than the rules of the game in international relations. Communitarian connections to pan-nationalist imagery make it especially receptive to fascist-like movements emphasising ideas of holistic national unity.[50]

Unlike other national projects, pan-nationalisms necessarily implicate a sort of geopolitical thinking about the rightsizing of a state's territory, and how it exerts influence abroad or competes with others in the international arena. Hence, the methodological contention of this volume is to look at Pan-Slavic imagery from a broader perspective that is not limited to perceiving just a 'poor relation' in the family of nationalisms but aims at simultaneously tackling a relatively influential geopolitical concept. The geopolitical dimension of pan-nationalisms tallies with the communitarian belief that the experience of solidarity is more solid and primordial than existing political institutions, and—as a corollary of this—that some manifestations of a state's sovereignty are thinkable outside of its borders. In order to conceptualise this, scholars speak about 'phantom territories', 'spheres of influence', 'backyards', and 'auras'.[51] In Russian academia,

---

[49] Scruton, R. (2015). *How to Be a Conservative*. Reprint Edition. London: Bloomsbury, p. 33.

[50] For instance, Fraixe, C., Piccioni, L. and Poupault, Ch. (eds) (2014). *Vers une Europe latine: acteurs et enjeux des échanges culturels entre la France et l'Italie fasciste*. Bruxelles: Peter Lang.

[51] Billé, F. (2014). 'Territorial Phantom Pains (and Other Cartographic Anxieties)', *Environment and Planning D: Society and Space*, 32(1), pp. 163–178; Hast, S. (2014). *Spheres of Influence in International Relations: History, Theory and Politics*. Burlington, VT: Ashgate Pub. Company.

Mikhail Il'in introduced the term *khoritika*, which means roughly a cultural halo around a large geopolitical body.[52] Adrian Pabst and John Milbank theorised the possibilities of such 'auratic bodies'[53] as the British Commonwealth, La Francophonie, or the Russian World by arguing that there could be a 'society of nations and peoples who are bound together by social ties and cultural bonds that are more primary than state guaranteed rights and market contracts'.[54] In this light, religious solidarity plays the central role in imagining and promoting such movements as Pan-Islamism or the unity of Orthodox Christian nations.

'Auratic geopolitics' identifies pan-nationalisms as objectively existing but 'weak interactions' in the field of international politics, which demonstrate sovereignty's spill-over effects. In contrast, the concept of a *Grossraum* contextualises pan-nationalisms as normative and futuristic projects of a state's rightsizing and securitising. *Grossraum*-like pan-nationalisms inspired political thinking and practice in the nineteenth century, whereas today projects of a single pan-national state are relatively rare. Snyder's definition of pan-nationalism (in his understanding, a synonym of macro-nationalism) mentioned earlier incorporates precisely the process when a 'we-group enlarges its unity to include all those who "should belong" to a fatherland or motherland'.[55] Historical sources of inspiration for pan-nationalisms as a *Grossraum* are three: the Monroe Doctrine, which echoed in the projects of 'Asia for the Asians'[56] and the 'Slavic Monroe Doctrine'[57]; German unification; and Italian irredentism. In Carl Schmitt's interpretation, the concept of *Grossraum* became a synonym for sovereignty and anti-globalist criticism,[58] which was eagerly

---

[52] Il'in, M. 'Global'noe pogranich'e', available at: http://www.archipelag.ru/geocul ture/new_ident/geocultruss/verge [Accessed on 26th May 2021].

[53] Billé, F. (2021). 'Auratic Geographies: Buffers, Backyards, Entanglements', *Geopolitics*, ahead-of-the-print, https://doi.org/10.1080/14650045.2021.1881490.

[54] Milbank, J. and Pabst, A. (2016). *The Politics of Virtue: Post-liberalism and the Human Future*. London and New York: Rowman & Littlefield, p. 334.

[55] Snyder, 1984, p. 189.

[56] For example, Weber, T. (2018). 'Asianism During World War One: Macronationalism or Micro-worldism?', In: *Embracing 'Asia' in China and Japan*. Cham: Palgrave Macmillan, pp. 107–166.

[57] Sharapov, S. (1886). *Russkoe delo*, no. 20, p. 2.

[58] Schmitt, C. (1941). *Volkerrechtliche Großraumordnung: mit Interventionsverbot für raumfremde Mächte: ein Beitrag zum Reichsbegriff im Völkerrecht*. Berlin: Duncker &

picked up by contemporary critics of 'Western hegemony' as well as proponents of the civilisational approach to international relations. In today's Russia, Pan-Slavism has been revived in association with terms such as 'Slavic civilisation', 'Orthodox civilisation', and 'Russian civilisation', the bottom-line of which is precisely that *Grossraum*-related idea of ultimate sovereignty.

In that respect, pan-nationalism as a spatial metaphor in political debates could be used in four possible ways. The first and most important one latches onto the idea of security by offering a vision of a stronger and more respected country *vis à vis* its geopolitical adversaries. The second promotes the idea of development by arguing that a pan-national project would provide an impetus for economic development.[59] The third metaphor advocates the idea that pan-national rightsizing simultaneously means a return 'home' or achieving a greater authenticity by means of, for example, restoring ancient Slavic unity. Pan-Latinism likewise capitalised on the shared legacy of classical antiquity to advance projects of unity of the Romance-language countries.[60]

Finally, pan-nationalism massively borrows from the political metaphors of brotherhood and common family. With regard to these theoretical considerations, our volume develops the given framework via the examination of several case studies including all the Slavic states apart from Slovenia, as explained in the chapter outlining the structure of this volume. We consider the given approach an additional contribution to developing the field at hand, as no such volume has to this day (to the best knowledge of the authors) been published, as the state-of-the-art discussion to conclude this chapter shows.

Humblot; Haushofer, K. (1931). *Geopolitik der Pan-Ideen*. Berlin: Zentral-Verlag; Hooker, W. (2009). *Carl Schmitt's International Thought: Order and Orientation*. Cambridge: Cambridge University Press.

[59] Metaphors of security and development ('shelter of security', 'springboard of opportunity') are discussed in: Williams, C. and Smith, A. (1983). 'The National Construction of Social Space', *Progress in Human Geography*, 7(4), pp. 502–518.

[60] Amotz, G. (2020). 'Origins and Characteristics of Macro-nationalism: A Reflection on Pan-Latinism's Emergence at the Turn of the Nineteenth Century', *History* (London), 105(365), pp. 252–267; Amotz, G. (2013). 'L'idéologie panlatine et les méandres des rapports franco-italiens: Le cas de La revue des nations latines (1916–1919)', *La revue des revues* (1), pp. 44–56.

State of the Art and Contribution to the Field

Scholarship in the English language has so far been somewhat disjointed,[61] and our volume serves the purpose of filling this research gap. The logic of this volume is, as already mentioned, to address contemporary Pan-Slavism in the Slavic states, most of which has never been done before, at least not to our knowledge and anyway not in an orderly manner. Therefore, we hope that our volume will not only serve academics and professionals in the field, but also students of international relations and political science, who will be able to get an insight into the political, social, and cultural backgrounds and realities of the selected states.

There has been a fairly low number of academic studies written in the English language on the topic at hand, at least in the last two decades or so, showing that the field is populated by contributions not necessarily having links with each other.[62] Existing contributions address contemporary Pan-Slavism via case studies examining its political and social manifestations. For instance, work by Laruelle,[63] Suslov,[64] Grigorova,[65]

---

[61] Đorđević, V., Čejka, M., Mocek, O. and Hrabálek, M. (2021). 'Beyond Contemporary Scholarship and Toward Exploring Current Manifestations of Pan-Slavism', *Canadian-American Slavic Studies*, 55(2), 147–159. https://doi.org/10.30965/22102396-05502005.

[62] Ibid.

[63] Laruelle, M. (2012). 'Larger, Higher, Farther North ... Geographical Metanarratives of the Nation in Russia', *Eurasian Geography and Economics*, 53(5), pp. 557–574.

[64] Suslov, M. (2012). 'Geographical Metanarratives in Russia and the European East: Contemporary Pan-Slavism', *Eurasian Geography and Economics*, 53(5), pp. 575–595.

[65] Grigorova, D. (2019). 'The Post-Yugoslav Balkans in the Ideological War Between Russia and NATO', In: Vuković, N. (ed) *David vs. Goliath: NATO War Against Yugoslavia and Its Implications*. Belgrade: Institute of International Politics and Economics, pp. 292–303.

Mitrofanova,[66] DeDominicis,[67] and Kolossov and O'Loughlin,[68] respectively, discuss Pan-Slavism from different perspectives, addressing more contemporary Russian ideological settings, examining the power of Pan-Slavic ideas and Russian geographical metanarratives emanating from Pan-Slavism, Russian foreign policy in the Balkans (with particular attention paid to the 1990s and its NATO air raids during the Kosovo conflict), and the issues around the political implications of the Orthodox religion and the issue of 'soft power'.[69]

One major and quite recent study in the field has been produced in the German language,[70] with the literature produced in this language, as well as in some Slavic languages, being somewhat richer than the one in the English language.[71] This study of ours is an attempt to level the field, with this volume attempting to build bridges to the above-mentioned contemporary scholarship by offering pathways towards exploring related topics that we believe should be investigated in the future.[72] We believe in the significance of the topic at hand and therefore consider this volume as an important step towards treating the topics related to the contemporary political, social, and cultural backgrounds of the selected Slavic

---

[66] Mitrofanova, A. V. (2016). 'The Prospect for Politicization of Orthodox Christianity', In: Chumakov, A. N. and Gay, W. C. (eds) *Between Past Orthodoxies and the Future of Globalization*. Leiden: Brill, pp. 157–170.

[67] DeDominicis, B. E. (2017). 'Pan-Slavism and Soft Power in Post-Cold War Southeast European International Relations: Competitive Interference and Smart Power in the European Theatre of the Clash of Civilizations', *The International Journal of Interdisciplinary Civic and Political Studies*, 12(3), pp. 1–17.

[68] Kolossov, V. and O'Loughlin, J. (2002). 'Still Not Worth the Bones of a Single Pomeranian Grenadier: The Geopolitics of the Kosovo War 1999', *Political Geography*, 21(5), pp. 573–599.

[69] Đorđević, V., Čejka, M., Mocek, O. and Hrabálek, M. (2021). 'Beyond Contemporary Scholarship and Toward Exploring Current Manifestations of Pan-Slavism', *Canadian-American Slavic Studies*, 55(2), 147–159. https://doi.org/10.30965/22102396-05502005.

[70] Gasior, A., Karl, L. and Troebst, S. (eds) (2014). *Post-Panslavismus: Slavizität, slavische Idee und Antislavismus im 20. Und 21. Jahrhundert*. Moderne Europäische Geschichte Bd. 9. Göttingen: Wallstein-Verl.

[71] Đorđević, V., Čejka, M., Mocek, O. and Hrabálek, M. (2021). 'Beyond Contemporary Scholarship and Toward Exploring Current Manifestations of Pan-Slavism', *Canadian-American Slavic Studies*, 55(2), 147–159. https://doi.org/10.30965/22102396-05502005.

[72] Ibid.

states. Unfortunately, many undemocratic and largely uncivic ideas and agendas have in recent years become very influential in (not only) the Slavic states, some of which have, at least partly, found an ideological basis in Pan-Slavism, with one particularly strong current of these illiberal political platforms being largely anti-EU-oriented and questioning the very nature of European integration.[73] Therefore, our volume will also shed some light on these political, social, and cultural realities (some bearing international prominence) inside the Slavic states.

This volume is, therefore, the first examination of its kind to systematically deal with all the Slavic countries (except, in our case, Slovenia). In that respect, by approaching the given concept across many Slavic countries that we will be able to fully understand how it works on the ground and how it resonates across geographic, political, social, and cultural contexts, among other things.

Moreover, the volume is the first-ever to discuss Pan-Slavism and Slavophilia in a systematic manner by encompassing different Slavic countries and taking into consideration not only their politics but also other spheres of public life, as will be discussed in more detail in the following chapter.

Finally, the volume includes treatment of the political use and abuse of Pan-Slavic and Slavophilic ideas in questioning and undermining (Western) democracy and supra-national institutions and ideas, such as the EU. Therefore, it helps us understand how this and related identitarian projects challenge the ideas of democracy and the EU in general, allowing us to address a wider European political context, offering a way towards gaining a better understanding of the apolitical/cultural currents of contemporary Pan-Slavism (or pan-ideologies in general) that are both quite widespread and influential in the Slavic states today.

---

[73] Ibid.

Structure of the Volume

Mikhail Suslov, Marek Čejka, and Vladimir Đorđević

As already noted, the chapters in this volume offer political, social, and cultural perspectives on Pan-Slavism, delving into aspects of both the domestic and foreign policy of the case studies at hand; touching on elements of Pan-Slavic and Slavophilic ideas in terms of the formation of national identity, as well as their role in politics and culture; tackling the issue of identitarian politics and its ideological roots in Pan-Slavism and Slavophilia; analysing the nationalist-populist political perspective and the actors espousing Pan-Slavic ideas; and investigating the multi-faceted relationship between Pan-Slavism and Orthodox Christianity. The very plasticity and flexibility of Pan-Slavic ideas, as they can fit with almost

---

M. Suslov (✉)
Department of Cross-Cultural and Regional Studies, University of Copenhagen, Copenhagen, Denmark
e-mail: mikhail.suslov@hum.ku.dk

M. Čejka · V. Đorđević
Department of Territorial Studies, Mendel University Brno, Brno, Czech Republic
e-mail: marek.cejka@mendelu.cz

© The Author(s), under exclusive license to Springer Nature Switzerland AG 2023
M. Suslov et al. (eds.), *Pan-Slavism and Slavophilia in Contemporary Central and Eastern Europe*,
https://doi.org/10.1007/978-3-031-17875-7_2

any ideological agenda, are well-exemplified in our case studies, where it is shown that Pan-Slavism may be instrumentalised for political purposes and often having no independent agenda of its own. Although there are no mainstream forces in the politics of the Slavic states standing for the creation of a Slavic union today, the concept of Slavic brotherhood is eagerly used on an everyday basis to express many other related ideas. In addition, the rising popularity of identity politics leads national elites to reconsider their Slavic origins, whereby Pan-Slavic agendas have been experiencing a certain renaissance.

With respect to the above-mentioned points, our volume is structured in the following manner. After presenting introductory methodological-theoretical points in the previous chapter and the structure of the volume in this one, we follow up with a *second part* introducing the chapters that discuss historical aspects and the background of Pan-Slavism in chronological terms, treating the topic by tackling three different geographical areas: Eastern, Central, and Southeast Europe. The chapters here provide insight into the background of the issue at hand, highlighting primary historical developments and containing valuable information on nationalist, national liberation, and even left-wing ideas 'communicating' with Pan-Slavism in the given regions of Europe, without which understanding our case studies would not be possible. The authors herein show how varying degrees of Pan-Slavic agendas and ideas fed into national liberation agendas, as seen particularly in the Balkans and somewhat also in Central Europe; how they 'spoke' to nationalist and anti-imperialist/hegemonic movements and groups all the way from Imperial Russia to Central and Southeast Europe; and how they manifested oddities in being flexible enough to acquire both democratic and anti-hegemonic and at the same time imperialist, nationalist, and illiberal forms and traits in a given geographic space. The case studies, encompassing all the Slavic states apart from Slovenia, follow in the third through sixth parts, and they are at the very heart of this volume. The case of Slovenia was intentionally dropped from consideration after a careful inspection of the country indicated that contemporary Slovenian politics and society do not reflect any noteworthy Pan-Slavic or related ideas or notions, making this case unlike any of the other ones examined here.

The *third part* is comprised of chapters on Russia, Belarus, Serbia, and Poland, countries where Pan-Slavism formerly played—or to varying extents continues to play to this very day—an important role in, above all, politics, and to a certain degree also in social and cultural life. In addition, these countries have been grouped together to show the very intricacies and complexity of the idea of Pan-Slavism, showing considerable discrepancies and paradoxes—particularly in today's Poland; while Pan-Slavism still matters—chiefly in terms of its (occasional) political instrumentalisation—in Russia, Belarus, and (to a much lesser degree) Serbia, Poland remains an interesting example of how this ideology largely lost its ground after 1989, becoming much less significant politically and in most cases being equivalent to nationalist ideas or to political platforms based on Eurasianism. Poland, for that matter, displays the intriguing contradictions of Pan-Slavism. On the one hand, it has had to 'fight' with Russia for leadership in the Slavic world—in a way partly like Serbia, which also, speaking from the political point of view, historically advanced the idea of its being well-deserving of holding the leading position among the Slavic nations the former Yugoslav state was comprised of. On the other hand, Pan-Slavism in Poland in political terms has paradoxically also meant close cooperation with Russia (and the former USSR), essentially becoming synonymous with anti-Westernism. Russia and Belarus have been given the leading spots in this part because Pan-Slavism has been most often instrumentalised for political gains and purposes by the Kremlin and the Minsk regime in their development of very strong mutual ties, indicating that contemporary Pan-Slavism in these countries is ideologically situated in the vicinity of illiberal ideologies, being based on identitarian politics, moral conservatism, political religion, and even right-wing populism, and is abused in domestic political life in maintaining the political status quo.

The *fourth part* includes chapters on Croatia, North Macedonia, and Ukraine. The authors of these chapters rightfully point out that Pan-Slavic ideas do not contemporarily boast any significant political or social force in the respective countries but do show how the set of ideas and platforms based on or associated with Pan-Slavism have influenced national identities. Hence, the issue of national identity has, speaking from a historical point of view, remained appealing to address in the case of both North Macedonia—as in the Macedonian nationalist agenda versus Bulgarian and Serbian nationalist platforms—and Croatia, with its opposition to Serbian identity and fears of Serbian expansion. The authors of the chapters on these two states additionally speak of a 'Yugoslavism', partly drawing on Pan-Slavic ideas and views and partly on social nostalgia for the Yugoslav past and socialist (Tito's) times, which at the same time exist alongside domestic political agendas somewhat based on Pan-Slavism that geopolitically highlight largely pro-Russian (and therefore anti-EU) agendas. This part concludes with a chapter on Ukraine, discussing how Pan-Slavism became instrumentalised by various political actors in attempting to mobilise the nation to accept anti-Western ideas, often by invoking social nostalgia for Soviet times in Ukraine having been part of the USSR. As concluded in this chapter, there is no permanent, institutionalised political force in today's Ukraine, nor a domestic mainstream discourse, based on the Pan-Slavic agenda, with Ukraine exemplifying, as in the case of the two previously mentioned states, a debate over the development of a national identity born in opposition to the Russian one.

The *fifth part* hosts chapters on Bulgaria, Montenegro, the Czech Republic, and Slovakia, with these countries having been chosen based on Pan-Slavism's formation of situational or—in the case of Montenegro recently—quite nuanced 'alliances' with various political agendas and towards numerous political goals. For that matter, while in Bulgaria Pan-Slavic ideas have largely and recently revolved around the identitarian agenda, coupled with societal debates on rediscovering Bulgaria's Slavic roots and on traditional and family values as opposed to what is considered the Western value agenda, Montenegrin politics and society have been characterised by quite a number of durable Russophilic attitudes, coupled with a 'Pan-Orthodoxia' (the idea of all Slavs of Orthodox faith being close to each other) that is chiefly motivated by the country's Orthodox religion and altogether replaces Slavophilia. As for the Czech Republic and Slovakia, the situation with Pan-Slavism is a bit different, taking a more non-religious and less identitarian turn. Both states boast quite a rich ideological landscape of Pan-Slavic ideas that have influenced various political and cultural platforms over the decades. At the same time, both display a variegated landscape of largely political platforms that have to some degree been influenced by Pan-Slavism and largely champion anti-Western (mostly but not exclusively anti-EU) attitudes, while portraying Russia as the supposed protector of all Slavs and a significant force in an alleged fight against globalisation—part of the ongoing identitarian and conservative reaction to contemporary global challenges and trends in international politics. The same motifs may in a similar degree be found in the domestic politics of Bulgaria and to a somewhat lesser extent of Montenegro as well.

The *sixth part* is the shortest one, having only two chapters: one on Bosnia-Herzegovina and one on the ex-Yugoslav diaspora in the United States. Both chapters are largely ethnographic examinations of the concept of Pan-Slavism, thus broadening the research scope and methods of the volume. While the chapter on BiH examines the principle of the interethnic ritual kinship common in this part of the Balkans, the so-called *kumstvo*, building on data from a representative survey conducted back in 2017, the chapter on the ex-Yugoslav diaspora in the United States presents a study on the resurgence of (Pan-)Slavic identity in the form of Yugoslavism within that community. Interestingly, both chapters highlight that this identity is still very much alive and well despite the Yugoslav conflicts that took place in the 1990s and that brought an end to the multi-ethnic Yugoslav state, deeply influencing both the Yugoslav expatriate community abroad as well as those who stayed in the country and experienced the conflict first-hand.

What follows is an afterword that draws on and shortly reiterates the main points made throughout the volume, while at the same time asking several important questions related to this research and indicating venues for future exploration of the topic that will certainly be useful. The volume is concluded by two indices, one listing the most important persons mentioned in each chapter and the other outlining the most significant subjects treated therein.

Pan-Slavism as History

Russian Pan-Slavism: A Historical Perspective

Mikhail Suslov

Introduction

Pan-Slavism as an ideology has its own history, which is also an important factor for its recurrent resurgence. In the nineteenth century, it became an important, even constitutive part of the ideologies of Slavophilism and neo-Slavophilism.[1] It entered the political and ideological arena in Russia in step with the national awakening in Eastern Europe in the first half of the nineteenth century as primarily a revolutionary movement, merging the democratization thrust in *anciens régimes* with the national liberation movement against empires. The outstanding Russian herald of anarchism Mikhail Bakunin entertained a romantic vision of the Slavic

---

[1] Fadner, F. (1962). *Seventy Years of Pan-Slavism in Russia: Karazin to Danilevskii, 1800–1870*. Washington, DC: Georgetown University Press; Kohn, H. (1953). *Pan-Slavism: Its History and Ideology*. Notre Dame, IN: University of Notre Dame Press; Petrovich, M. B. (1956). *The Emergence of Russian Pan-Slavism 1856–1870*. New York: Columbia University Press.

M. Suslov (✉)
Department of Cross-Cultural and Regional Studies, University of Copenhagen, Copenhagen, Denmark
e-mail: mikhail.suslov@hum.ku.dk

confederation in Europe, which would presuppose for him the destruction of the Russian absolutism.[2] Little wonder that the tsarist government observed the development of Pan-Slavism with scepticism and apprehension. The classic Slavophilism of the 1830–1840s, despite the delusive name of this movement, was primarily not about the Pan-Slavic solidarity; its major concern was Russia's own identity in the context of the massive Westernization of the eighteenth century. However, the identitarian and utopian-conservative standpoint of the Slavophiles injected new meanings into Pan-Slavism, which acquired anti-Western and Russo-centric overtones. Aleksei Khomiakov, the leading Slavophile of the nineteenth century, famously juxtaposed peaceful and creative nature of the Slavs to the aggressive-destructive nature of the Germanic tribes. In his reading of world history, the Slavs, who in antiquity inhabited the whole Europe from the Black Sea to the British islands, were conquered, destroyed, and assimilated by the Germans. Russia, according to this vision, remains the only independent island of truly Slavic civilization, but even it is now under the pressure of the second wave of the Germanic cultural conquest due to Peter the Great's reforms.

The Slavophiles themselves were in the troubled, oftentimes antagonistic relations with the Russian government, but their interpretation of Pan-Slavism has prepared soil for the limited acceptance of the Pan-Slavic agenda by the official St Petersburg, but the degree of involvement of the Russian government in Pan-Slavic region-making should not be exaggerated. The case in point here is the rebellion in Bosnia and Herzegovina against the Ottoman Empire in 1875. This event sparked a wave of Pan-Slavic sympathies among the Russians, several thousands of whom went to the Balkans as volunteers, while many more participated in Slavonic benevolent committees, gathering help for the insurgents and promoting the Pan-Slavic cause in the media and among the political elite. This Pan-Slavic momentum has created a painful dilemma for the Russian government: 'To forbid unofficial assistance and suppress the committees would alienate the public; to encourage the insurgents would antagonize the Powers'.[3] However, both the public pressure and the fears of a too

---

[2] Hepner, B. P. (1954). *Bakounine et le Pan-Slavisme révolutionnaire. Cinq essais sur l'histoire des idées en Russie et en Europe*. Bruxelles: Société pour le progrès des études philologiques et historiques.

[3] MacKenzie, D. (1967). *The Serbs and Russian Pan-Slavism. 1875–1878*. Ithaca: Cornell University Press, p. 74.

decisive victory of the Turks made the Russian Empire to step in April 1877. The difficult Russian victory in the war with the Ottoman Empire and the half-hearted conditions of the Berlin Peace Treaty (1878) left the Pan-Slavic intellectuals deeply dissatisfied, but the state was even more reluctant to take cues from the ideologists of Pan-Slavism. In 1878, after a heated speech by Ivan Aksakov, the leader of the Slavophiles and the head of the Moscow Slavonic Benevolent Committee,[4] this committee was closed by order of the government, while its St Petersburg branch was harshly suppressed. The new reign of Aleksander III did not bring about changes in this policy. The emperor emphatically claimed that the St Petersburg Slavonic Benevolent Society (SPSBS) should not interfere in state policy, and he did not heed the request of such influential figures as Konstantin Pobedonostsev and Mikhail Katkov to restore the Moscow Committee.[5]

Another important development of Russian Pan-Slavism in the second half of the nineteenth century is the growing dissociation from the original national liberal agenda. Instead, the Russian official and right-wing ideologists filled Pan-Slavism with a completely new ideological content, which stood in sharp antagonism with the aspirations of other Slavic peoples of Eastern Europe for formation of their own democratic nation-states. The example of Vissarion Komarov, the editor-in-chief of the Panslav newspaper *Svet*, illustrates this point. Komarov imbricated the Panslav ideas with the ideas of Nikolai Danilevsky, who is credited to be the inventor of the concept of multiple civilizations. From this viewpoint, the Slavs are seen as a separate civilization, tortured, and suppressed by another civilization—Western Europe.[6] This standpoint, which would echo in many Pan-Slavic writings in the decades to come, also means that the desire of the Eastern Slavs for independence and democracy only tears them away from the core of the Slavic civilization—Russia, and makes them part of the 'Western civilization'.[7]

In the final two decades of Russia's imperial period, Pan-Slavism gradually gave way to other geopolitical ideas, which backed up Russia's

---

[4] Aksakov, I. (1886). *Sochineniia*. Vol. 1. Moscow: Tip. M. Volchaninova, p. 305.

[5] Khevrolina, V. (1997). 'Ideia slavianskogo edinstva vo vneshnepoliticheskikh predstavleniiakh pozdnikh slavianofilov', In: Aksenova, E. P., et al. (eds) *Slavianskii vopros: vekhi istorii*. Moscow: Institut Slavianovedeniia i balkanistiki RAN.

[6] Komarov, V. (1882). 'Lead Article', in *Svet*, 5 May, p. 1.

[7] Komarov, V. (1882). 'Lead Article', in *Svet*, 6 April, p. 1.

assertive policy in the Far East—ideology of the so-called Orientalists. In this context, Pan-Slavism came to be associated with something parochial and unambitious, which was totally out of line with Russia's promising global mission in Eurasia and on the Pacific. Discontent with the alleged 'ingratitude' of the Balkan Slavs became another important and long-lasting reason for Pan-Slavism to keep a low profile. One of the conservative intellectuals, Sergei Syromiatnikov, expressed this discontent as a need to abandon romantic attitudes to the Slavs. He argued that it was completely improper to tearing a piece of bread from Russia's own impoverished population in order to give it to the relatively well-off Slavs, who would never appreciate it anyway. The metaphor he was using implied that nobody would feed brothers at the expense of one's own children.[8]

This survey shows that already in the late imperial period, Pan-Slavism in Russia developed the main components of its ideological repertoire. There were cautious attempts of the state to instrumentalize it for its geopolitical ends without at the same time committing too much to it. Some intellectuals conceptualized the Pan-Slavic unity as a civilizational body, antagonistic to Western Europe, whereas others emphasized the pressing need to relate to the 'ungrateful' Slavs pragmatically, from the viewpoint of Russia's national interests, or, even more radically, they proposed to reorient the foreign policy towards Eurasia, away from the 'Slavic backwater'. On the other hand, forces of nationalism, which had brought Pan-Slavism to life in Eastern and Central Europe, soon rendered it irrelevant, when the Slavs in the Ottoman, Habsburg and Hohenzollern Empires developed strong national consciousness and identity, incommensurable with the idea of becoming part of the union under the Russian protection. After a short period of revival due to the Stalin's postwar policies of securitization in Central and Eastern Europe, Pan-Slavism seemingly hibernated for the forthcoming several decades.[9]

---

[8] Syromiatnikov, S. (1895). 'Deti i brat'ia: Moi mysli o slavianstve', In *Institute of Russian Literature at the Russian Academy of Science (IRLI RAN)*, fond 655, delo 1 [Archival material].

[9] Behrends, J. C. (2014). 'Stalins slavischer Volkskrieg. Mobilisierung und Propaganda zwischen Weltkrieg und Kaltem Krieg (1941–1949)', In: Gąsior, Agnieszka, Karl, Lars, und Troebst, Stefan (Hsg) *Post-Pan-Slavismus. Slavizität, Slavische Idee und Antislavismus im 20. und 21. Jahrhundert*. Göttingen: Wallstein Verlag, pp. 79–108; Kohn, H. (1953). *Pan-Slavism: Its History and Ideology*. Notre Dame, IN: University of Notre Dame Press, pp. 699–722.

Today, Pan-Slavism amalgamates with such geopolitical trends as civilizational ideology, 'large-space' thinking and isolationism, as well as with globalization.[10] The vision of the world, divided among a few giants, autarchic 'civilizations', which motivates Putin's leadership and among other things, fuels the war against Ukraine in 2022, goes very well together with the imagining of the all-Slavic space.

Sergei Sharapov's Pan-Slavic Programme
Major Arguments and Inspirations

This part of the chapter will focus on one representative Pan-Slavic thinker of the late Imperial period, Sergei Sharapov (1855–1911). His views absorbed the gist of the Pan-Slavic debates and new ideological developments in Russian society on the eve of the First World War. In the 1880s, in the aftermath of the Russo-Turkish War of 1876–1877, public intellectuals contemplated the reasons for the modest performance of Russia as the self-proclaimed liberator of the Balkan Slavs. In particular, they were appalled at what they called the 'base ingratitude' of Bulgaria, whose territory was liberated, soaked in Russian blood in the process, and which had nevertheless broken off diplomatic relations with Russia and taken an aggressively anti-Russian stance in international relations. Sharapov's understanding was that the problem resided in Russia's own imitative and servile attitudes to 'the West'. He posed the question: *what can the Slavs learn from Russia?* Russia's borrowed Western forms could just as well be borrowed directly from the West, without Russia's mediation. Russia's own Slavic ways had been forgotten, with the non-Russian Slavs preserving them in greater purity than the Russians. The bottom line of Sharapov's musings on this topic was a clarion call for the development of an alternative Slavic high culture, Slavic philosophy of religion, Slavic concepts of political liberty, Slavic principles of civil rights, Slavic private and public laws, and Slavic ideals of art.[11] The Pan-Slavic agenda in its most articulated form was, thus, used to present a Slavophile claim for authenticity and liberation from Western influences. Interestingly, Pan-Slavism was not only a critical argument; it was also seen as a remedy

---

[10] Hettne, B. and Söderbaum, F. (2000). 'Theorising the Rise of Regionness', *New Political Economy*, 5(3), pp. 457–472.

[11] Sharapov, S. (1886). 'Lead Article', *Russkoe delo*, no. 2, p. 3.

against imitative Westernization in Russia. Sharapov hoped that the democratic spirit of Slavdom would help Russia to get rid of its German-style bureaucratic traditions.[12]

Another interesting direction Sharapov pushed the Slavic question was the role and destiny of Poland, with its track record of anti-Russian revolts and anti-Orthodox attitudes, in the would-be Slavic union. His recipe for solving the problem verged on what we would today call populism. He argued that simple Polish peasants by their very nature adhered to Russia, whereas the Polish gentry, intelligentsia, and clergy incited the people to confront Russia and the whole of Orthodox Slavdom. The way out would be to align the 'organically Slavic' aspirations of the Polish people with Russia, and thereby to disconnect them from their own Westernized (and thus anti-Slavic) intelligentsia.[13] Striking anti-Semitic and Germanophobic notes, Sharapov proposed to protect Poland from German and Jewish influences. On top of that, he argued, all efforts should be made in order to separate the Polish Church from Rome and create an independent Polish Church in alliance with Orthodoxy.[14] This latter proposal became clear in the context of the so-called 'Old Catholic movement' which inspired many right-wing Russian intellectuals, who saw it as a harbinger of the future reunification of the Christian Churches on the basis of the shared dogma established by the first four Universal Church councils of the fourth through ninth centuries. The 'back-to-the-roots' thrust in religious life would create the possibility of communion between the Russian Orthodox Church and the (imaginary) Polish Old Catholic Church, ultimately eliminating political hostility between these two fraternal nations.[15]

Perhaps the central motive for his Pan-Slavic proposals lay in his extreme Germanophobia. In 1886, he wrote in an article, 'What is the German tribe? This is a wedge, historically driven between the Roman and Slavic worlds....'.[16] In his view, in order to contain and disarm

---

[12] Sharapov, S. (1898). 'Pis'mo k mitropolitu tyrnovskomu Klimentu', *Russkii trud*, special issue for no. 1, p. 20.

[13] Sharapov, S. (1886). 'Lead Article', *Russkoe delo*, no. 14, p. 1.

[14] Sharapov, S. (1889). 'Opyt Slavianskoi programmy', Gosudarstvennyi Arkhiv Smolenskoi oblasti, fond 121, delo 557, list 1 [Archival material].

[15] Suslov, M. (2020). 'Saving the Selves or Saving the Others? Responses to Old Catholicism in Late Imperial Russia', *Acta Slavica Iaponica*, no. 41: 91–109.

[16] Sharapov, S. (1886). 'Lead Article', *Russkoe delo*, no. 34 and 35, p. 3.

Germany, some territories should be restored to the Slavs, namely the Poznań region, while the Western Slavs should be consolidated and organized as a barrier to the German *Drang nach Osten*.[17] He admitted elsewhere that 'the Slavic question is first and foremost the question of how to secure Russia from the impending German peril'.[18] However, in the context of the diplomatic struggle to conclude an agreement with the German Empire (which resulted in the Reinsurance Treaty of 1887), Pan-Slavic propaganda sounded out of place. And so Sharapov's newspaper received a clear 'you are not welcome' message from the government, which suspended it several times by order of the Minister of the Interior—putting it on the brink of financial insolvency, only to be rescued only by a group of industrialists from Moscow who saw economic danger to their position in a Russo-German rapprochement.[19]

Contours of the Pan-Slavic Union

During his public career, Sharapov came up with several specific projects for uniting the Slavs. One of them was worked out in 1889, and it decisively broke with Russo-centric macro-nationalism, proposing broad rights to autonomy for all members of this union, which would consist of: (1) the Russian Empire, incorporating Galicia; (2) the Polish Kingdom, to be ruled by a king, who would be the Russian Tsar, and administered by his governor-general; (3) Finland, to be ruled by a Grand Prince (also the Russian Tsar) and his general-governor; (4) the Associated Land of Bulgaria, to be run by a governor elected by all the Slavic rulers and approved by the Russian Emperor; (5) the Associated Land of the Lusatian Sorbs (Lužički Srbi), to be governed like Bulgaria; (6) the free city of Constantinople; (7) the Kingdom of Serbs and Croats, to be ruled by the Serbian dynasty of Njegoš; (8) the Czech Lands, to be ruled as its people would decide; (9) the Land of Hungary, which in the case of its freely joining the Slavic Union would have the right to choose its own government; in the case of military opposition, it would be governed like Bulgaria; (10) the Kingdom of Greece, to be governed by

---

[17] Ibid., pp. 3–4.
[18] Sharapov, S. (1901). *Sochineniia*. Vol. 15. Moscow: tip. A. Vasil'eva, pp. 79–80.
[19] Sharapov, S. (1890). 'Lead Article', *Russkoe delo*, no. 7, p. 1.

the present dynasty; and (11) the Kingdom of Rumania, to be governed like Greece.[20]

As we can see from this outline, non-Slavic peoples were equally welcome in this imaginary union. Sharapov specifically discussed the autonomous status of Finland, as the relationship of Russia and Finland was 'a prototype of the future Slavic Union. The Slavic peoples of the Habsburg Empire would accept Russian supremacy on the same basis as today's Finland.... Violating Finnish home-rule would impede for a long time the natural resolving of the Slavic question, because the Slavs, who are ready to recognize the power of the Russian tsar, are not charmed by Russian bureaucracy'.[21]

In 1902, he penned another political fantasy, 'Fifty Years from Now', which featured an equally bombastic plan for a continental-sized Russian Empire, yet with a strong emphasis on federalization along national lines. This geopolitical utopia supposed the future disintegration of the Habsburg Empire, whose Slavic majority would enter the Russian Empire as autonomous regions. At this point, the protagonist of the utopia exclaimed, 'But we dreamt of the Slavic Union, where the Russian Empire would dissolve'. His guide answered,

> Look how immense Russia is and how small her Western appendage is. Would it have been just if the winner and the first people of Slavdom had squatted down for the sake of some equality with the Slavs? But they do not demand it at all. They have their national traditions, their lands, languages, and administration, and they are very content to be parts of the great Russian power.[22]

Flirting with Neo-Slavism

The Russo-Japanese War of 1904–1905 and the first Russian revolution of 1905–1907 undermined the imperial hubris of the Pan-Slavic intellectuals, making them more susceptible to the liberal demands of the neo-Slavists. In these years, Sharapov came back to the idea of the Slavs as the engine for Russia's own domestic transformation. In a private letter,

---

[20] Sharapov, S. (1889). 'Opyt Slavianskoi programmy', Gosudarstvennyi Arkhiv Smolenskoi oblasti, fond 121, delo 557, list 4 [Archival material].

[21] Sharapov, S. (1905). 'Lead Article', *Russkoe delo*, no. 6, pp. 17–18.

[22] Sharapov, S. (1902). *Cherez polveka*. Moscow: tip. A. Vasil'eva, p. 59.

Sharapov despondently observed, 'I think that here is the end of Russia as such. We have to offer our hands to the Poles and yell at the top of our voice "Long live the Slavs!" Everything is rotten in Russia.... Russia has fizzled out and became corrupt as a state and as a nation. We cannot be revived by our own strength. Our rebirth lies in Slavdom'[23] From the perspective of Slavophile eschatology, the revolution of 1905–1907 and the advent of parliamentarism marked the end of "Russian Russia", which had to become 'Slavic Russia' lest the Empire perish as Poland had in the eighteenth century.[24] Sharapov admitted that the decrepit Russian Empire needed the fresh forces of the Slavs, battle-hardened in their faith and liberty.[25] Contrary to his previous jingoistic discourses, in 1908 he perfectly recognized that Russia was solely a *part* of Slavdom, not Slavdom per se.[26] The Russian worldview was somewhat one-sided and required the 'persistence of the Czechs, the elegance and discipline of the Poles, the industriousness of the Bulgarians, the spontaneity and poetry of the Serbs.... We are too mild and negligent'.[27]

According to Sharapov, the Russians should follow the example of the South Slavs in order to learn an independent and self-respecting way of life, to acquire the skills of resistance to alien intrusions, etc. Referring to the example of the British Empire, he also implied that economic centralization of the Slavic world was more important, feasible, and desirable than political unification.[28] Already in 1901, he had suggested extending the Russian banking and monetary system to the Slavic lands so that departments of the Russian (or Slavic) State Bank could establish a common monetary union in these countries, whereby an isolated and

---

[23] Sharapov, S. (1906). 'A Letter to K. Paskhalov', Gosudarstvennyi Arkhiv Smolenskoi oblasti, fond 121, delo 545, list 16, 17 [Archival material].

[24] Sharapov, S. (1906). 'A Letter to the Editor of the Unknown Polish Newspaper', Gosudarstvennyi Arkhiv Smolenskoi oblasti, fond 121, delo 545, list 21ob. [Archival material].

[25] *Svidetel'*, 1908, no. 16–17, pp. 13, 17.

[26] Ibid., p. 12.

[27] Ibid., p. 13.

[28] Sharapov, S. F. (1908). *Samoderzhavie ili konstitutsiia?*. Moscow: Svidetel', pp. 62–63.

self-sufficient Slavic economy would appear and render any political unification redundant inasmuch as the Russian ruble 'would weld together the Slavic world stronger than an iron chain'.[29]

These thoughts indicate a considerable modernization of the intellectual outlook of Russian Pan-Slavs. In fact, Sharapov adopted the project of the neo-Slavists, who also advocated the economic unity of the Slavic world and particularly the organization of a Slavic Bank. Another new development was a more straightforward condemnation of the policy of Russification. In 1909, he insisted that Russia's failure to secure the support of the Slavs in the Habsburg Empire was due to Russification, which naturally drove the other Slavic peoples away.[30] Sharapov's criticism, couched in neo-Slavist terms, caused dissatisfaction among other Russian Pan-Slavists (such as the St. Petersburg Slavonic Benevolent Committee, Aleksandr Bashmakov, Platon Kulakovskii, Dmitry Vergun) and put him closer to Russian liberals like Pavel Miliukov.[31]

However, Sharapov's willingness to go ahead with neo-Slavist proposals was limited. Two things repulsed him from this movement: their principle of religious toleration was incompatible with the Orthodox fundamentalism espoused by Sharapov, and their allegiance to Western constitutionalism contradicted the Slavophile plea for a more patriarchal, pastoral, and archaic political order. On top of this, Sharapov's thought was not 'nationalistic' enough to coincide with the liberal and bourgeois nationalism of the neo-Slavists. His nationalism was much too contaminated with Messianism and imperialism to produce convincing nationalist arguments that would bring him closer to the neo-Slavists. Another deviation from the canon of neo-Slavism was an attempt to play with racial themes. Namely, Sharapov believed that the Slavs and the Anglo-Saxons (Germany was intentionally excluded) were, he prophesied, the two Aryan races destined to rule the universe and to check the 'yellows' and the Muslims for the further glory of the 'White race'.[32]

---

[29] Sharapov, S. F. (1901). *Sochineniia*. Vol. 12. Moscow: tip. A. Vasil'eva, pp. 57–58.

[30] Aksakov, N. and Sharapov, S. (1909). *Germaniia i Slavianstvo*. Moscow: Svidetel', p. 6.

[31] *Svidetel'*, no. 22 (April 1909), pp. 30–40.

[32] *Svidetel'*, no. 13 (July 1908), pp. 53–55.

Conclusion

An examination of Sergei Sharapov's Pan-Slavic views shows the considerable complexity and flexibility of late Imperial Pan-Slavism, which easily entered into situational ideological alliances and reinforced various political ideas. Among others, we can observe imbrications of Pan-Slavism and anti-Germanism, Pan-Slavism and Slavophile identitarian conservatism, Pan-Slavism and populist sentiments about the 'simple people', Pan-Slavism and religious Messianism, Pan-Slavism and racism, and many others. Sharapov's playing with a more liberal version of Pan-Slavism was a sign that he had spotted the most important dilemma of Pan-Slavism, which is pertinent even for today's Russia: it is all too seductive for the state to use Pan-Slavism for its own practical geopolitical purposes, but this is exactly the greatest liability of Pan-Slavism, because it is tainted by its strategic alliance with a non-democratic state and illiberal ideologies.

A Short History of Pan-Slavism and Its Impact on Central Europe in the Nineteenth and Twentieth Centuries

Jakub Woroncow

Introduction

In 1826 the Slovak lawyer Ján Herlek, inspired by the Czech and Slovak revival movements, published his work *Elementa universalis linquae Slavicae*, in which he took steps to create a universal Slavic language.[1] That was probably the first time the word 'Pan-Slavism' had ever been written down, but the roots of the idea are older, and scholars have identified it in the ideas of Adam Kollár and Pavol Šafárik. They are called, respectively, the first poet and the first politician of Pan-Slavism,[2] but besides these we can also name as early Pan-Slavists the Czechs, Josef Dobrovský and Josef Jungmann; the Slovaks, Jan Kollár and Ľudovít Štúr; and the Poles,

---

[1] Herlek, J. (1826). *Elementa universalis linguae Slavicae e vivis dialectis eruta et sanis logicae principiis suffulta*. Typis Regiae Universitatis Hungaricae.

[2] Kohn, H. (1960). *Pan-Slavism. Its History and Ideology*, p. 4.

J. Woroncow (✉)
SWPS University of Social Sciences and Humanities, Warsaw, Poland
e-mail: jakub.woroncow@gmail.com

© The Author(s), under exclusive license to Springer Nature Switzerland AG 2023
M. Suslov et al. (eds.), *Pan-Slavism and Slavophilia in Contemporary Central and Eastern Europe*,
https://doi.org/10.1007/978-3-031-17875-7_4

Joachim Lelewel, Jerzy Lubomirski, August Cieszkowski, Agenor Gołuchowski, and Wicenty Pol.[3] Jan Kollár's Czechoslovak orientation had its roots in Slovak Protestantism.[4] He is the author of the poem 'Slávy dcera' ('Slava's Daughter'), in which he idealized the past of the Slavs. He claimed that Slavs were one single race and argued they should stop calling themselves only by their national designation and instead append to these the word 'Slav.'[5] Why did such an idea appear among Czechs and Slovaks? Friedrich Engels, a critic of Pan-Slavism, claimed:

> Austrian Poles have their natural centre of gravity in Russian Poland [....] In either case, the Austrian Slavs are only seeking their reunion either among each other, or with the main body of their separate nationalities. This is the reason why Pan-Slavism is not a Russian but an Austrian discovery. In order to secure the restoration of each Slavic nationality, the different Slavic tribes in Austria are beginning to work for a union of all the Slavic tribes in Europe.[6]

But Andrzej Walicki states that pro-Russian Pan-Slavism was born in Poland, with Stanisław Staszic's opus 'Myśli o równowadze politycznej w Europie' ('Thoughts about the political balance in Europe')—not just a brief concept but a political vision and program of uniting the nations that could be completed only with Russian hegemony. Staszic claimed that Poles should support this action as elder brothers of the Russians, and that Russians should understand that Poles could not be their slaves.[7] Such a position was possible under Alexander I, a quite liberal Tsar and probably the only Russian emperor who could support the idea of a Slavic federation.[8] Pan-Slavists of that period were also influenced by the ideas of the French Revolution and German Romanticism. Among friends of the

---

[3] Wisłocki, T. (1927). *Kongres słowiański w r. 1848 i sprawa polska*, p. 6.

[4] Auty, R. (1952). 'Jan Kollár, 1793–1852', *The Slavonic and East European Review*, 31(76), p. 81.

[5] Pražák, A. (1928). 'The Slovak Sources of Kollár's Pan-Slavism', *The Slavonic and East European Review*, 6(18), p. 590.

[6] Engels, F. (1855). *Pan-Slavism and the Crimean War*, Originally published in *Neue Oder-Zeitung*, 21 April, available at: https://www.marxists.org/archive/marx/works/1855/04/21.htm.

[7] Walicki, A. (2000). *Idea narodu w polskiej myśli oświeceniowej*, p. 72.

[8] Guins, G. (1949). 'The Politics of "Panslavism"', *The American Journal of Economics and Sociology*, 8(2), p. 125.

Slavs we can name writers like Jakob Grimm, Johann Gottfried Herder, and Johann Wolfgang Goethe.[9]

While Czechs, Slovaks, and Moravians lived in the Habsburg Empire, Poles were divided among three empires, Russia among them. Between 1807 and 1815, they briefly had an independent state, the Duchy of Warsaw, but after the Congress of Vienna, the Western part was incorporated into Prussia, while the rest was transformed into the Kingdom of Poland with the Tsar as king. Krakow became an 'independent' republic under the control of three empires and was finally incorporated into Austria in 1846 after a democratic rising led by Jan Tyssowski.

The Polish state disappeared from the map in 1794, but Czechs had not had their own since the fifteenth century. In the eighteenth and nineteenth centuries, the Czech language was reborn through the publication of a Czech grammar book by Dobrovský in 1809 and a Czech-German dictionary by Jungmann in 1834–1839. The Slovak national revival was influenced by other intellectuals following Štúr.[10] Dobrovský, Jungman, and Karel Havlíček Borovský stood for the transformation of the Austrian monarchy into a democratic federation of free nations, an idea called Austro-Slavism.[11]

The Polish position on Austria was motivated by its incorporation of Krakow, while Russia as an oppressor was not seen as any kind of ally after the Polish national rising of 1830–1831. Czechs and Slovaks were not oppressed by the Russians, while Slovaks were in conflict with the Hungarians, who were not seen as enemies by the Poles.[12] Bronisław Trentowski, Lelevel, and Adam Mickiewicz believed in a Pan-Slavic alliance but with a democratic and liberal Russia.[13] Ludwik Mierosławski and Michał Czajkowski were critical of the Russian 'peoples' movement, while Franciszek Duchiński even claimed that Russians were not Slavs.[14]

In the spring of 1848, the idea of a Slavic Congress was announced in the Croatian paper *Narodne novine*. At the same time, the German

---

[9] Auty, R. (1952), p. 85.
[10] Majerek, R. (2011). *Pamięć, mit, tożsamość. Słowackie procesy autoidentyfikacyjne w okresie odrodzenia narodowego*, pp. 81–82.
[11] Kohn, H. (1960), pp. 17–26.
[12] Wisłocki, T. (1927), p. 80.
[13] Kohn, H. (1960), pp. 34–35.
[14] Ibid.

Confederation incorporated some parts of the Grand Duchy of Posen that had been the German part of the former Duchy of Warsaw. This motivated Poles of the Duchy to support the initiative of the committee led by František Palacký, Pavol Jozef Šafárik, and Karel Vladislav Zap.

The congress that started in Prague on 2 June was divided into three sections[15]: the first consisting of Czechs, Slovaks, Moravians, and Silesians; the second of Poles, Ruthenians, and the part of Polish-speaking Silesians residing in Austrian territory. Two Russians, the revolutionary Mikhail Bakunin and the Old Believer priest Olimpi Miloradov joined this section but spoke only during the parts of the discussions that referred to all Slavs themselves and not to the affairs of individual nations.[16] The third section consisted of Croatians, Slovenians, Dalmatians, Illyrians, and Serbians.[17] The temporary committee was composed of twenty Czechs and four Poles. Palacký became president of the congress alongside two vice-presidents, Lubomirski and Stanko Vraz.

The congress was described in the German press as a Russian initiative. But it did not stand against Germans and Hungarians per se but rather against oppression and the rule of one over another[18]; in fact, it also took the side of the Poles under Russian rule. The case for creating an independent South Slavic Kingdom under the emperor but with independence from Hungary was a problematic one for Polish delegates, who continued to see Hungarians as their allies.[19] Delegates worked on two manifestos: one to the people of Europe and one to the emperor. The next step was to create the goals of an alliance among Slavic nations standing for freedom.[20] They also chose a flag for the Slavic movement—blue, white, and red, similar to the flag of France that was a symbol of revolution—and an anthem, 'Hey Slavs' based on the poem 'Hey Slovaks' written by Samuel Tomášik and a melody composed for 'Mazurek Dąbrowskiego.'[21]

---

[15] Moraczewski, J. (1848). *Opis pierwszego zjazdu słowiańskiego*, p. 8.

[16] Ibid.

[17] Moraczewski, J. (1848), p. 10.

[18] Moraczewski, J. (1848), p. 14.

[19] Moraczewski, J. (1848), p. 18.

[20] Moraczewski, J. (1848), p. 20.

[21] 'Hey Słowianie' with the melody was a national anthem of Yugoslavia and it is Serbian anthem till today. 'Mazurek Dąbrowskiego' by Józef Wybicki is Polish national anthem.

The 12 June Prague Uprising erupted due to the Austrian garrison opening fire on a peaceful demonstration of residents that took place after a mass celebrated by the priest Jan Arnold, the brother of a radical Czech democrat, Emanuel. The revolt was spontaneous. Barricades in the streets were built mostly by students. The uprising ended after 5 days with 43 Czechs (and 14 Austrian soldiers) dead.[22] Because of those events, the delegates of the congress left Prague and the event was never completed. Thus, the first Pan-Slavists did not stand for Russian hegemony in Europe nor did they seek to destroy Austria. Mickiewicz in 1848 proclaimed a program of West Slavic unity against Russia, while Czechs like Borovský and Palacký wanted to transform Austria into a bulwark against Russian and German imperialism without destroying those states.[23] The goal of the Poles was independence of the Czechs, autonomy, and a stronger role in the monarchy. But the revolt in Prague changed this.

Pan-Slavism came to Russia quite late, after the Crimean War (1853–1856).[24] At first, it was just a cultural and philosophical idea, but later it did become an imperialist geopolitical concept supported by the Tsar and the Russian Orthodox church.[25] After the bloody pacification of the Polish National Uprising of 1863, it was impossible to find any followers of Slavic concepts in Poland because the idea of state Pan-Slavism was also becoming popular in Russia.[26] At the same time, Slavs from the Habsburg monarchy became more oriented toward Russia after the agreement between the Austrian government and the Hungarians that created the Austro-Hungarian dual monarchy in 1867. Such a situation doomed the Austro-Slavs because their conception of a federalist organization of the state was now obsolete and rendered impossible, but the Slavic movement still had followers. In 1867, *The Slavs and the World of the Future*, written in German by Štúr before his death, was published in Russia. Italian independence activist Giuseppe Mazzini believed that Italians and

---

[22] Staif, J. (1990). *Revoluční léta 1948–1949 a české země*, pp. 72–75.

[23] Kohn, H. (1960), p. 47.

[24] Petrovich, M. B. (1956). *The Emergence of Russian Pan-Slavism (1856–1870)*, p. 3.

[25] Eberhardt, P. (2010). *Rosyjski panslawizm jako idea geopolityczna*. Vol. 2. Przegląd Geopolityczny, p. 62.

[26] Walicki, A. (2002). *W kręgu konserwatywnej utopii. Struktura i przemiany rosyjskiego słowianofilstwa*, p. 400.

Slavs could together preserve European peace.[27] Tensions between Poles and Czechs grew. Edward Grégr wrote in his diary that Czechs could not achieve anything with the Poles and that the Russians were the only hope.[28] Russian Pan-Slavists like Vladimir Lamansky believed that their mission and the goal of Russian foreign policy was to unify Slavs just as the Kingdom of Piemonte had unified Italy.[29]

The first steps toward organizing another congress in Moscow, nineteen years after the Slavic Congress in Prague, were taken by the Slavic Committee in organizing an ethnographic exhibition. Palacký and Rieger sent there Czech exhibits, as did the Kashubian Florian Caynowa, and the Sorb-Lusatian Jan Smoler.[30] The idea of organizing a congress in Moscow later appeared as a spontaneous initiative.[31] The goal of the Russians organizing the Congress was to invite conservative and Russophile leaders of Pan-Slavic tendencies from all nations. The Polish press claimed that instead of pushing Slavs under Russian hegemony, the goal should be to nurture solidarity among the nations and to convince the Czechs that the goal of the Pan-Slavic movement was to stand for Polish rights under the Russian monarchy. Karol Sladovský, Antoni Zeithammer, Bedřich Schwarzenberg, and Václav Stule all refused to take part in the Moscow Congress.[32] The last named was in contact with Lubomirski and worked on rapprochement with the Poles.

Palacký and Rieger met in Paris with Hotel Lambert, a conservative political camp in exile that held its meetings in the hotel with a same name in Paris. Later, they went to Warsaw to visit the houses of major Polish aristocrats, none of which were at the time open to the idea of supporting the Russian initiative. Both Polish societies stood against the Russian initiative. Among prominent Czech independence activists, František Brauner, Karel Mattuš, Josef Hemerník, Jan Skrejšovský, Adolf

---

[27] Kohn, H. (1961). 'The Impact of Pan-Slavism on Central Europe', *The Review of Politics*, 23(3), p. 325.

[28] Grégr, E. (1908). *Dennik, Vydal a úvody opatril dr Zdenek V. Tobołka*, p. 133.

[29] Łamanskij, W. I. (1867). 'Izuczenije Sławianstwa i russkoje narodnoje obozrienije', Żurnał Ministierswa Narodnogo Proswieszczenija, Vol. 1, p. 150.

[30] Tanty, M. (1965). 'Geneza Zjazdu Słowiańskiego w 1867 r.', Studia z dziejów ZSRR i Europy Środkowej, Vols. 1–2, p. 11.

[31] Popov, N. A. (1868). 'Sławianskij sjezd w Pragie i godowszczina sjezda w Moskwie', Moskowskije Uniwersitietskije Izwiestija, p. 426.

[32] Tanty, M. (1965), p. 26.

Patera, and Karel Jaromír Erben planned to attend. The Poles boycotted the Moscow congress as a Pan-Slavist event. Despite the situation, the Young Czech Party did not break with the Pan-Slavist path, and even Polish political circles in Austria and Prussia continued to back the pro-unity tendency. In 1901, the Slavic Circle in Krakow was founded, transformed later into the Slavic Association.[33]

Pan-Slavic currents were criticized by Marxists from the very beginning. Even as early as 1849, Friedrich Engels was claiming that

> Pan-Slavism immediately gave proof of this reactionary tendency by a double betrayal: it sacrificed to its petty national narrow-mindedness the only Slav nation which up to then had acted in a revolutionary manner, the Poles. It sold both itself and Poland to the Russian Tsar.[34]

Meanwhile Ignacy Daszyński, leader of Polish Social-Democratic Party (PPSD), claimed in 1899,

> The only idea that in Poland for the whole century they fought was this ridiculous Pan-Slavism that I would call the philosophy and ethic of Russian Tsarism. But even if those compromisers were right that Russia would be as gentle as Austria for us, I do not see any reason to stand for Slavia. This is not any kind of national politics, this is the insanity of a race war....[35]

FROM THE TWENTIETH CENTURY ON

The early twentieth century was a period of a limited revival of the Slavic idea. Neo-Slavism was a short-lived part of the Pan-Slavist movement. A tendency that appeared in the early twentieth century was against the Germanisation of the Slavs but without any Russian domination over them.[36] This current was influenced by positivism rather than

---

[33] Jaroszewicz-Kleindienst, B. (1974). 'Towarzystwo Słowiańskie w Krakowie. Zarys działalności', *Pamiętnik Słowiański*, 24, pp. 151–170.

[34] Engels, F. (1849). 'The Magyar Struggle', First published: in *Neue Rheinische Zeitung* No. 194, 13 January.

[35] Daszyński, I. (1899). *Szlachetczyzna a odrodzenie Galicyi*, p. 28–29.

[36] Tuminez, A. S. (2000). *Russian Nationalism Since 1856: Ideology and the Making of Foreign Policy*. Lanham: Rowman & Littlefield, p. 125; Reddaway, W. F. (1971). *The Cambridge History of Poland*. CUP Archive, p. 405.

romanticism, more moderate and non-violent than revolutionary, and was popular among the Young Czechs.[37] As an essentially Czech creation,[38] Neo-Slavism was described by Edvard Beneš as the last historical manifestation of Austro-Slavism,[39] although Karel Kramář claimed to oppose the principles of the older concept.[40] As Paul Vyšný claims, the goals of Neo-Slavism were similar: united Slav political action, an elimination of inter-Slavic conflicts, and opposition to the Austro-Hungarian dual monarchy in order to transform the Empire into a federal state with a pro-Russian foreign policy rather than pro-German.[41] The Polish journal *Slavic World* (*Słowiański Świat*) claimed that inter-Slavic conflicts were the basis of all defeats.[42]

Austrian Poles did not join the movement. The concept of the movement led by Karel Kramář attracted another nationalist, pro-Russian political force in the Russian part of Poland, the National Democrats led by Roman Dmowski. The founding congress that took place in Prague on 12 July 1908, hosted a group of Polish delegates led by Dmowski. Both groups had been seeking contacts among the other.[43] Both Kramář and Dmowski were right-wing nationalists and Russophiles. Kramář even went to meet the then-Russian prime minister Peter Stolypin on his trip to Petersburg, where he had first met the Russian Slavists in May.

The place of the founding congress was not incidental: organizers intentionally chose Prague and the anniversary of the Pan-Slavic Congress of 1848. 'We must come to the great all-Slavic congress with a new great program. Let's call it the Neo-Slavic program. Let Neo-Slavism be based on the dogma: equality, freedom, and brotherhood of all Slavic nations,' claimed Kramář.[44]

Organizers also believed that this time Slavic politics was entering a new era, with the goal of preventing a '*Drang nach Osten*' as Mykola

---

[37] Judson, P. M. and Rozenblit, Marsha L. (1 January 2005). *Constructing Nationalities in East Central Europe*. Berghahn Books, p. 128.

[38] Vyšný, P. (1977). *Neo-Slavism and the Czechs 1898–1914*, p. 248.

[39] Beneš, E. (1947). *Úvahy o slovanstvi*, p. 68.

[40] Kramář, K. (1926). *Na obranu slovanské politiky*, p. 14.

[41] Vyšný, P. (1977), p. 248.

[42] Giza, A. (1984). *Neoslawizm i Polacy 1906–1910*, p. 59.

[43] Giza, A. (1984), pp. 83–95.

[44] Hribar, I. (1928). *Moji spomini*, 1. del: Od 1853. do 1910. leta, p. 232.

Hlibowyćkyj claimed, and a focus on improving 'difficult' Polish-Russian affairs.[45] Kramář, Hlibowyćkyj, and Ivan Hribar publicly expressed their optimism concerning the Russian-Polish situation. Dmowski and his movement stood against the Socialists who had fought for Polish independence in 1905, and he also claimed that the German threat was stronger than the Russian. Poles from German and Austrian lands did not take part in the congress and neither did the Galician Ruthenians and Sorb-Lusatians.

After the conference in Prague, two less important meetings took place in Petersburg before the second congress in Sofia opened on July 7, 1910, with no delegates from Poland.[46]

The congress in Bulgaria was the breaking point of the Neo-Slavic movement because after that the idea disappeared. Its initiators resigned from continuing any actions. Politics in all the Slavic nations were so different that any political debate or agreement were hardly possible. That is why Neo-Slavists had avoided the key topics of their vision of a future Europe.

During World War I, Czech and Slovak politicians including Tomáš G. Masaryk tried to organize a Czechoslovak Legion in Russia. The goal of this initiative was to take part in the war against Germany and Austria. After the Russian Revolution, three divisions of Czechs and Slovaks took part in the Russian Civil War rather than the war in Europe. But the political initiative was still in progress. In April 1918, Masaryk came to the USA via Canada and started his campaign for the independence of the Czechs and Slovaks, supported by the Ruthenians. In his book *The New Europe*, published in English in 1918, he stated that the Austro-Hungarian Empire was a house of nine nations ruled by dynasty, aristocrats, the army, and the Church in which a minority ruled over the majority, and quoted Adam Mickiewicz to compare the Empire to the East-Indian Campaign: 'The real federation of nations will come only when nations are free and united. This is the development of Europe.'[47]

The Pittsburgh Agreement of 31 May 1918, stated that both Czechs and

---

[45] Agičić, D. (2020). 'Chorwaci a zjazd neoslawistów w Pradze w 1908 roku (na podstawie ówczesnej prasy chorwackiej)', *Zeszyty Naukowe Uniwersytetu Jagiellońskiego – Prace Historyczne*, 147/2, p. 365.

[46] Vyšný, P. op. cit., pp. 191–192.

[47] Masaryk, T. (1920). *Nová Evropa: stanovisko slovanské*, citation by: G. Kovtun (1988), *Masaryk & America: Testimony of a Relationship*, p. 77.

Slovaks would create a common republican state. Masaryk also convinced the American president to destroy Austria-Hungary as the most important ally of Germany in order to win the war and organized the evacuation of the Czechoslovak Legion from Russia. As an expert in Russian affairs, he advised not intervening in the Russian Civil War.

After the war, the empires—German, Russian, and Austro-Hungarian—that had oppressed Slavic nations all fell. On the territory of the former Habsburg monarchy, there appeared new states including Czechoslovakia; the Kingdom of Serbs, Croats, and Slovenes; and Poland, built out of the former territories of all three empires. Pan-Slavic conceptions seemed not to be any longer current and afterward appeared only accidentally, for example, as an initiative of the Polish, Bulgarian, and Czech peasant movements. In 1924, a Slavic Union of Village Youth was founded and agitated for similar societies in other countries in order to establish cooperation based on economic and agrarian strategy ideas.[48] Slavic thought was also present in the Polish Fascist, modern pagan, and New Age movements of the 1930s. The National Radical Movement 'Falanga' believed that the only way to preserve the future of the world was the creation of a Slavic empire ruling over Warsaw, Prague, and Kiev.[49] Poland never joined the Little Entente created by Czechoslovakia, Yugoslavia, and Romania in the early 1920s.

Fascist movements in Europe were further steps in the destruction of the Slavic unity concept as two anti-Slavic regimes used inter-Slavic conflicts to destroy Slavic nations by supporting the separatist tendencies of Slovaks, Carpathian Ruthenians, Ukrainians, and Croatians. Before World War II, when Nazi Germany annexed the Czech part of Czechoslovakia and the Tizso regime emerged, Poland used the opportunity to annex the Czech part of Zaolzie (Těšínsko), land that had been divided between the two countries after 1918.

During World War II, the most serious initiative was the project of a Polish-Czechoslovak federation to be created after the war. The proposal—supported by Great Britain—came from Poland. Both governments in exile met and started negotiations. The National Democrats were opposed and supported the idea of a Polish national state with the

---

[48] Dec, J. and Załęski, Z. (1925). 'Słowiański Związek Młodzieży Wiejskiej', available at: http://lewicowo.pl/slowianski-zwiazek-mlodziezy-wiejskiej/.

[49] Piasecki, B. (1937), *Zasady programu narodowo-radykalnego*, p. 18.

borders of the Commonwealth.[50] Various organizations from the Christian Democrats to the radical left supported the initiative.[51] Nationalist and radical right resistance organizations created conceptions to build Slavic empires and subject other nations to Poland.[52] Milan Hodža and Jan Masaryk firstly supported that idea, while Edvard Beneš remained passive. But the Soviet Union seemed to be the more important ally in the war against Nazi Germany: the Polish government understood that.

The communists weaponized elements of Pan-Slavism after the Nazi invasion of the Soviet Union. On 10 and 11 August 1941, a Slavic Congress was organized in Moscow.[53] The delegates' aim was to stand against Russia's enemy number one, which was Germany.[54] On 5 September 1941, the Pan-Slavic Committee was founded. Milovan Đilas was shocked:

> The Pan-Slavic Committee, which had been created in the course of the war, was the first to arrange banquets and receptions for us. But one did not have to be a Communist to perceive not only the artificiality but also the hopelessness of this institution. Its activity was centred on public relations and propaganda, and even in this it was obviously limited. The Committee was composed almost entirely of Communists from the Slavic countries – the émigrés in Moscow who were in fact alien to the idea of Pan-Slavic reciprocity.[55]

As Hans Kohn wrote, 'Traditional national values were restored without any reference either to class war or the revolutionary struggle.'[56] The Pan-Slavic Committee was led by the Soviet general Aleksandr Siemionowicz Gundorow and Alexiey Tolstoy, Dymitr Szostakowicz, and

---

[50] Łojek, J. 'Federalizm, antysocjalizm i doktryna narodowa', w: Kalendarium Historyczne pt. 227, p. 443.

[51] Kisielewski, T. (1991). *Federacja Środkowo-Europejska*, pp. 233–245.

[52] Read more: Fertacz, S. (2000). *Polska myśl słowiańska w okresie II wojny światowej*.

[53] Polniak, Ł. (2011). *Patriotyzm wojskowy w PRL: w latach 1956–1970*, p. 26.

[54] Ibid., p. 26.

[55] Dilas, M. (2014). *Conversations with Stalin*, p. 27.

[56] Kohn, H. (1952). 'Pan-Slavism and World War II', *The American Political Science Review*, 46(3), p. 700. It is interesting that before aggression against the USRR Hitler claimed about Stalin: „he identifies himself with the Russia of the Czars, and he has merely resurrected the tradition of Pan-Slavism", J. Toland, 673 (1992 Anchor edition) Adolf Hitler. The definitive biography.

the Polish communist Wanda Wasilewska. As Đilas claimed, Stalin not only weaponized the Pan-Slavic concept but really believed in such an order under his hegemony.[57]

The end of the war did not break the Nationalist and Slavic trend in either the Soviet Union or in Poland or Czechoslovakia, which both became parts of the Eastern Bloc. Władysław Gomułka, leader of the Polish Workers' Party, claimed in 1947 at the international meeting in Szklarska Poręba that 'Slavic solidarity' was priority number two after the alliance with the Soviet Union.[58] In 1948, a plenum of national Slavic Committees was organized in Prague. Zdeněk Nejedlý was among those who understood that ideologies connected with militarism were more useful tools to legitimize the regime, its order, and its international relationship with Moscow.

Conclusion

The history of the Pan-Slavic idea shows that the concept could deeply evolve over the course of a hundred years, and an idea to liberate the oppressed that was praised by democrats could transform into a propaganda tool of oppression in the hands of totalitarian movements and regimes in a quite different political and geopolitical context.

---

[57] Dilas, M. (2014), p. 81.

[58] Borodziej, W. (1990). *Od Poczdamu do Szklarskiej Poręby: Polska w stosunkach międzynarodowych 1945–1947*. London, p. 37.

Pan-Slavism in the Balkans: A Historical View

Susan Baker

INTRODUCTION

In reviewing Balkan Pan-Slavism, one might consider Peter Christoff's observation, labelled the 'descent of an idea'. Beginning in an abstract sphere, he contended, with religion or philosophy, an idea moves to the level of ideology and ultimately takes concrete form as 'tactics, organization, and action'. In its most extensive, ideological phase, the idea powerfully influences social and political problems and indicates solutions. In its concrete form, however, it encounters reality and human imperfections and sometimes becomes unrecognizable.[1] In the Balkans, this general progression occurred, albeit there were ebbs and flows in the force of the movement. The flows occurred in five waves: the Illyrianists, the adherents of Greater Serbia, the followers of Bishop Strossmajer, the pre-World War I flowering of creativity, and the Titoists. Between these flows of Pan-Slavic expression, there were ebbs.

[1] Christoff, P. K. (1991). *An Introduction to Nineteenth-Century Russian Slavophilism: Iu. F. Samarin.* New York: Westview Press, pp. 4–5.

S. Baker (✉)
Nehalem, OR, USA

© The Author(s), under exclusive license to Springer Nature Switzerland AG 2023
M. Suslov et al. (eds.), *Pan-Slavism and Slavophilia in Contemporary Central and Eastern Europe*,
https://doi.org/10.1007/978-3-031-17875-7_5

Pan-Slavism—the search for and discovery of Slavic identity and unity—flowered under the influence of nineteenth-century Romantic philosophers. In middle European universities, students studied the evolutionary civilizational theories of German philosophers like Hegel and Herder. Johann Gottfried von Herder, an East Prussian clergyman, developed a philosophy of civilizations based on the *nation* as the 'unit of evolution'. A people (or *Volk*), he said, progressed through an evolution of consciousness into nations. In this process, nations became 'suprapersonal' units, striving to realize themselves by linguistic and cultural works.[2] Although Herder as a German urged German pride in their achievements, he saw the Slavs as the harbinger of the future. They lived 'quiet, freedom-loving, agricultural' lives and 'scorned to take up the sword in self-defence', 'content to cultivate the peaceful arts', he wrote They would lead mankind to 'freedom, cooperation, equality and universal benevolence', the goals of the historic process.[3] Central to Herder's system were the factors of *consciousness* and *language*. Growth in a people's consciousness developed from their use of language.

Balkan Pan-Slavism was also inextricably intertwined with political developments. In the reactionary period after the Napoleonic wars, the eastern empires reimposed 'legitimacy' and dominated diplomacy. Within Austria, German culture dominated. The Ottoman Empire, with its nearly impenetrable borders between Christian and Muslim cultures, loomed on the southern and eastern borders of Russia and Austria. Balkan Slavs within both empires were vastly underrepresented. In Austria, what is now Croatia was divided between counties directly administered by Vienna and those that came under Hungarian rule. Croatia had enjoyed no unity or independent existence since medieval times.[4] In the early nineteenth century, its parliament, the *Sabor*, was made up of landed nobility, many of

---

[2] Fadner, F. (1962). *Seventy Years of Pan-Slavism in Russia: Karazin to Danilevskii, 1800–1870*. Washington, DC: Georgetown University Press, pp. 1–2; Kohn, H. (1960). *Pan-Slavism: Its History and Ideology*. 2nd Edition. New York: Random House, pp. ix–x.

[3] Fadner, pp. 4–5. One must note that Herder's characterization of the Slavs—at least as it applied to Russian Slavs—ignored the obvious histories of Peter the Great and Catherine II, whose military conquests marked their legacies.

[4] And it would not unify until 1918.

whom were foreign, representatives of the clergy, or delegates from independent cities—a tiny fraction of the population.[5] It is not astounding that Slavs followed the ideas of teachers like Herder.

Herderian ideas spread from Czech and Slovak universities southward. Leading scholars like Jan Kollar in Budapest, Ljudovit Štur in Bratislava, and Paul Joseph Šafarić in Novi Sad attracted and taught many leading South Slav intellectuals, including Ljudovit Gaj, Vuk Karadžić, and Jovan Skerlić.[6]

One community in particular was instrumental in transmitting northern Pan-Slavism to the south. The Serbs in southern Hungary had become educated and active in commerce; they now formed the nucleus of an intelligentsia. Teodor Pavlović, a Hungarian Serb, serves as an example. As editor of *Serbskii narodni list* in Pest, he originally published Kollar's book, *Reciprocity Between the Various Tribes and Dialects of the Slavic Nation*.[7] Kollar's concept of literary 'reciprocity' (by which he meant two-way exchanges of literary pieces, translations, publications, collections of old manuscripts, and folk ballads) became a core concept of early Pan-Slavism, and his book of poems, *Daughter of Slava*, stood as the 'national bible of early Pan-Slavism'.[8]

Although the pursuit of reciprocity and the interest in Slav history and collections of Slav texts similarly characterized both northern and southern Western Pan-Slavism, the movements starkly contrasted in the obstacles they faced. The Czech and Slovak movements aimed at greater recognition *within* the Austrian Empire. From the beginning, South Slavs confronted larger obstacles. Not only did they resist German and Hungarian dominance in the Austrian Empire, but they inhabited two deeply different cultures. The border between the Austrian and Ottoman

---

[5] Despalatović, E. M. (1975). *Ljudevit Gaj and the Illyrian Movement*. New York: East European Monographs, No. XII, p. 12; Tanner, M.C. (1997). *A Nation Forged in War*. New Haven & London: Yale University Press, p. 59.

[6] Milojkovic-Djurić, J. (1994). *Panslavism and national Identity in Russia and in the Balkans 1830–1880: Images of the Self and Others*. Boulder, CO: East European Monographs, pp. 14–17. As this author sees it, the geographical triangle between Budapest, Bratislava, and Novi Sad provided a fertile ground for Pan-Slav thinking in this early period. The inclusion of Novi Sad belies Hans Kohn's contention that the South Slavs were irreparably behind because of a 'belt of German, Magyar, and Rumanian settlement'. Kohn, p. 55.

[7] Milojkovic-Djurić, p. 14.

[8] Ibid., pp. 8–9; Kohn, p. 9.

Empires was nearly impenetrable. In addition, even if that barrier were to be overcome, the differences between Catholic and Orthodox Christian cultures remained, religion being the traditional marker of cultural identification. Even so, however, enormous steps were taken towards the goal of unification between Croats and Serbs.

In the early years of the 1820s and 1830s, two individuals from either side of the Austrian-Ottoman divide took up the challenges of literary unity. In Zagreb, Ljudovit Gaj led what became known as the Illyrian School. In Belgrade, Vuk Karadzić reformed and unified the Serbian language. Unexpectedly, they ended up with a common linguistic solution.

Gaj, a German-Croat, had studied in Budapest, met Kollar, and was strongly influenced by the theory of reciprocity. The term Illyrian for the Balkan Pan-Slavs developed from the French occupation of Dalmatia in the Napoleonic era. The French governor had revived the Roman term Illyrica to designate the French-controlled areas of Istria, Dalmatia, and northern Croatia. He left behind an impulse towards unity, tolerance, and liberalism. When Austria resumed control, that impulse remained.[9]

Simultaneously, Hungarians were initiating their own national revival. Intent on gaining parity with Germans, they substituted Hungarian for Latin in official documents and imposed the Hungarian language in schools, without allotting local choices to the minorities under their rule.[10] Thus, the Illyrian movement had both a positive (Dalmatian) and a negative (Hungarian) impetus.

In these years, diverse dialects were used in the Croatian provinces: three major and several minor ones. The first step to unity, Gaj thought, was agreement on the form for a written language. To this end, he published *A Short Outline of Croat-Slovene Orthography*.[11]

From this beginning, Gaj—with a circle of colleagues in Zagreb—devoted himself to Illyrian/South Slav literary expression. The group founded the first Croatian newspaper, *The Croatian, Slovenian, and Dalmatian Newspaper*, in 1835, using his new orthography. The next year, he began using the Štokavian dialect, the most widely used form and

---

[9] Kohn, pp. 59–60.

[10] Banac, I. (1984). *The National Question in Yugoslavia: Origin, History, Politics.* Ithaca, NY & London: Cornell University Press, pp. 75–76.

[11] Kohn, pp. 60–61.

the ancient literary dialect of Ragusa. It would be the basis for the unified identity of all parts of Croatia and answer the threat of Hungarian cultural dominance.[12] The newspaper's literary supplement, *Danica*, offered an outlet for young Croatian writers. Gaj also promoted the establishment of reading rooms in large cities to encourage literacy. With Count Janko Drasković, a wealthy northern Croatian landowner, he formed the Croatian *Matica*, the lasting Croatian cultural centre in Zagreb. The Slovenian poet, Stanko Vraz—despite tensions with other Slovenes—wholeheartedly supported the movement.[13]

In contrast to Gaj, Vuk Stefanovic Karadžić began his career during the Ottoman control of Serbia. From a peasant background, Karadžić matured during the first Serb revolution 'in the thrall of Ottoman misrule'.[14] A talented linguist, he argued that the basis for written language should be 'write as you speak'.[15] In 1818, he published a new Serbian dictionary, using the Štokavian dialect, challenging the Orthodox hierarchy's chosen dialect.[16] For this, the Church heavily criticized him. Karadžić contended that all people who used the dialect were Serb, whether they called themselves so or not; the terms Bosnian, Montenegrin, and Slavonic merely alluded to geographic areas.[17]

Karadžić lived much of his life in Vienna, collaborating with the Slovene Catholic scholar Jernej Kopitar. He was in touch with Gaj, travelling with him from Dubrovnik, the old centre of Štokavian literature, to Montenegro at the height of their popularity.[18] It seemed literary agreements might in reality set the basis for further unity.

---

[12] Despalatović, p. 65; Banac, pp. 75–78.
[13] Despalatović, pp. 134–135; Kohn, p. 63.
[14] Banac, p. 80.
[15] Tanner, p. 74.
[16] Banac, p. 80; Tanner, p. 74.
[17] Ibid., p. 80; Tanner, p. 103. For a critique of Karadžić's methods and accuracy, see Pavlović, A. and Atanasovski, S. (2016). 'From Myth to Territory: Vuk Karadžić, Kosovo Epics and the Role of Nineteenh-Century Intellectuals in Establishing National Narratives', *The Hungaian Historical Review*, 5(2), pp. 357–376.
[18] Tanner, p. 78.

From Cultural and Literary to the Political and Ideological Realm

So far, the movement had existed in the cultural and literary sphere. Its leaders represented Balkan Pan-Slavism's abstract phase. But by the 1840s, Gaj's movement had become political and entered the ideological realm. Gaj and his followers formed the Illyrian Party. By 1843 they were openly espousing unification of all South Slavic lands within the Austrian Empire, thereby challenging Hungarian dominance.[19] Gaj actively participated in the Austrian government's attempts to derail Hungarian nationalism, as the empire played one faction off against another, often overtly favouring the Illyrians. In 1848, Gaj led the Croatian support for Austria against the Hungarian rebellion.[20]

In Serbia, after partial autonomy in 1830, the ideology of Greater Serbia was born. Interior minister Ilija Garašanin, influenced by the Polish refugee Franjo Zah, devised a plan for the foreign relations of the new nation, called *Nacertanje* (Outline). Garašanin contended that Serbia had not yet completed its nation-building mission; it should serve as the centre of a widening Serb kingdom, incorporating all South Slavs, creating a bulwark against either Austrian or Russian hegemony in the area.[21]

Garašanin became Foreign Minister under Prince Michael Obrenovic, and together they began to implement *Nacertanije* in the 1860s. Michael created alliances with Bulgarians, Greeks, and Romania in preparation for a general Christian uprising throughout the Ottoman Empire. However, when he was assassinated in the Spring of 1867, that plan fell apart.[22]

But Russian intellectuals had also experienced the 'identity crisis' implied by Herder's attribution of future leadership to the Slavs. Beginning in the 1820s, a small group of Russian writers had advocated a more

---

[19] Gazi, S. (1973). *A History of Croatia*. Philosophical Library, Inc., pp. 139–146.

[20] Tanner, p. 78. In 1839, for instance, the emperor awarded Gaj a diamond ring for his service. In 1840, he ordered the Illyrian language to be taught in Croatian schools.

[21] MacKenzie, D. (1985). *Ilija Garasanin: Balkan Bismarck*. Boulder, CO: East European Monographs, esply pp. 55–56.

[22] Judah, T. (1997). *The Serbs: History, Myth & The Destruction of Yugoslavia*. New Haven: Yale University Press, pp. 56–61.

robust foreign policy for the dynasty.[23] After the Crimean War, the tone shifted and became a strident call for Russian power and leadership in the Balkans. Writers like the scientist Nikolai Danilevsky and the militarist General Rostislav Fadeev revived Catherine the Great's dream of recapturing Constantinople and establishing a Balkan Slav Confederation as a bulwark against Western hostility. Austria had to be defeated first; the path to Constantinople lay through Vienna, Fadeev claimed.[24]

Count Nikolai Ignat'ev, avid Russian Pan-Slavist and ambassador to Constantinople between 1864 and 1877, undertook to actualize the dreams of Fadeev and Danilevsky. He created a 'fantastic medley of agents and informers' in the Balkan states (Serbia, Bulgaria, Bosnia and Herzegovina, and Montenegro), coordinating work towards an eventual uprising against the Ottomans.[25]

Although Serbian Prince Michael's plans had evaporated in 1868, a villager revolt that broke out in Herzegovina in July 1875 and quickly spread to Bosnia provided the opportunity Russian and Serbian Pan-Slavs had been looking for. Ignat'ev manipulated the diplomats in Constantinople as the uprising began to alarm Europeans. The insurgents held out for a year until Serbia and Montenegro declared war on the weakened Ottoman forces in July 1876. Having considered calling on Fadeev as their commanding general, the Serbs ultimately chose General Mikhail Cherniaev, founder of the Pan-Slavic journal *Russkii Mir* in Moscow and known for successes in the Caucasus.[26] Russian volunteers

---

[23] Petrovic, M. B. (1956). *The Emergence of Russian Panslavism 1856–1870*. New York: Columbia University Press, pp. 28–39; for Russian efforts to attract and hire three leading Czech Pan-Slavs, see Fadner, pp. 20–22.

[24] Fadeyev, R. (2018). *Opinion on the Eastern Question*, trans. T. Michell. London: Edward Stanford, 1871, reprinted by Forgotten Books, pp. 34–40; Fadner, pp. 314–338; Kohn, pp. 184–186, and 190–208; MacMaster, R. E. (1967). *Danilevsky: A Russian Totalitarian Philosopher*. Cambridge, MA: Harvard University Press.

[25] Sumner, B. H. (1962). *Russia and the Balkans, 1870–1880*. London: Archon Books, p. 32. Among the Pan-Slav consuls actively pursuing these goals were Naiden Gerov and Prince Aleksei Tseretelev in Bulgaria, Alexander and Vladimir Jonin in Ragusa and Mostar respectively, and Alexander Hilferding, Consul in Sarajevo, author of *The Western Slavs* and later Desk Chief of the Asiatic Department.

[26] Pejić, J. B. (2016). 'Rostislav Fadeev and the Eastern Question', *Historical Review*, 65, p. 215.

streamed into Serbia and Bosnia on Chernyaev's coattails, numbering 5,000 by September 1876.[27]

But Ottoman troops crushed Chernyaev, and at the end of October, Alexander II delivered an ultimatum for a cease-fire to the Ottomans on behalf of the Serbs. But Ultimately, Alexander acquiesced to Pan-Slavic pressure at home and declared war himself on the Ottomans in April 1877.

Russian and Serbian Pan-Slavists had believed the new war meant the end of the Ottoman Empire, Russian occupation of Constantinople, and the creation of their Balkan Confederation. But Cherniaev's losses and Russian troops' actual behaviour appalled the Serbs.[28] Furthermore, the Russians had ignored the trepidation that the strident tone of late Pan-Slavism evoked in English, French, and Austro-Hungarian minds.[29] When the English ordered the activation of the British Navy in the Bosporus, after Russian troops arrived there at the end of 1877, Alexander and Foreign Minister Gorchakov prohibited troops from entering Constantinople. At the Berlin Congress of June 1878, Russia was forced to accept the decisions of the Great Powers, which cut the newly created 'Big Bulgaria' in half and handed Bosnia and Herzegovina over to the Austro-Hungarian Empire. The belligerent Russian Pan-Slavic dream of hegemony in the Balkans, as a nineteenth-century ideology, was dead.[30]

The more modest dream of Balkan South Slavic unity survived, however. After 1848, Bishop Josip Juraj Strossmajer replaced Gaj as head of the Illyrian movement and brought the Pan-Slavic movement back to its spiritual, abstract sphere. The Illyrian Party was re-named the National Party. Strossmajer, a Catholic German-Croat like Gaj, educated by Franciscans in Djakovo, Budapest, and Vienna, became Bishop of Djakovo

---

[27] Geyer, D. (1987). *Russian Imperialism*. New Haven: Yale University Press, p. 72n.17; Judah, p. 66. The Montenegrins rejected offers of Russian military leadership and, much to their advantage, succeeded in fighting side by side with the insurgents and stymying Ottoman troops in the south.

[28] MacKenzie, D. (1996). *Serbs and Russians*. Boulder, CO: Eastern European Monographs, 1996, pp. 11–12.

[29] Kohn, pp. 125–136. In these pages, Kohn explores the various shades of feelings towards Europe among Russian intellectuals and the influences of those feelings on their identity.

[30] The parallels with the current confrontation over Ukraine are too striking not to mention.

in 1850 and remained there for the rest of his life.[31] He built on what Gaj had begun by founding the Yugoslav Academy and the Croatian University to foster South Slavic education, arts, and scientific research. He and his colleague Canon Franjo Rački—a leading historian and the first president of the Yugoslav Academy—brought scholars from Russia, Bulgaria, Slovenia, Dalmatia, Serbia, and Bosnia to promote the unification of Austrian and Ottoman Slavs.[32] Strossmajer's treasured dream was to end the schism between the Eastern and Western Christian churches. As a Catholic in good standing, he courageously opposed papal infallibility. He and Rački worked for full Slavic representation within the Hapsburg Monarchy. In the short term, their *Jugoslavenski* programme, the core of the National Party agenda, meant unification of all disparate Slav parts within the Austrian empire. In the longer term, however, they wanted to see a federal South Slav state, built on the ashes of the Empire and allied with the Serbs. At the same time as Prince Michael was trying to establish a Balkan alliance, Strossmajer agreed to a step-by-step creation of an 'allied state', envisioning an independent, federal South Slav nation, including Serbia and Montenegro.[33] Strossmajer was a true spiritual leader, but he represented both the abstract and the ideological spheres of the Pan-Slavic idea, supporting as he did both cultural and political projects. His example of harmony and tolerance guided the Croatian Pan-Slavic movement throughout the entire second half of the nineteenth century.

Simultaneously, however, narrower political voices were heard. In 1852, the National party split; exclusionary Croatian nationalists formed the Party of Rights under Ante Starčević, who wanted a unified Croatia, directly responsive to Austrian authorities in Vienna and free of Hungarian jurisdiction, while rejecting Serb legitimacy.[34] This party later divided into the Party of Pure Rights under Josip Frank, which

---

[31] Tanner, pp. 96–97.

[32] Banac, p. 89.

[33] Ibid., p. 90; Tanner, p. 98.

[34] Tanner, pp. 104–106. Starčević's position amounted to the theory of trialism in the Empire, whereby the third nationality, the unified Slavs, would be represented in Vienna on an equal political basis with Germans and Hungarians. Even so, Strossmajer hated Starčević.

became hostile to the *Jugoslavenski* idea and developed into the Croatian *Ustaše* under Ante Pavelić in the 1930s. The other half of Starčević's party eventually rejoined Strossmajer's National Party.[35]

Two developments hindered progress for the *Jugoslovenski* programme. First, in 1867 the *Ausgleich* established parity between Hungarians and Austrians, creating the new Austro-Hungarian Empire and thereby hindering Slavic equality. The *Nagodba*, accompanying the *Ausgleich*, regulated Hungarian-Croat relations, re-establishing Hungarian dominance. Appointed as Ban in 1883 under this regime, the Hungarian landowner, Count Karoly Khuen-Herdervary imposed an oppressive Magyarization policy, playing off Serbs against Croats and substantially increasing distrust and animosity between the two.[36]

Second, independent Serbian policies were effectively eclipsed after 1878. In secret agreements prior to the Russo-Turkish War of 1877, Russia and Austria-Hungary had carved out spheres of influence in the Balkans. Russia abandoned support for Bosnia-Herzegovina in return for control over Bulgaria and required Serbia to regard Austria as its primary patron. Serbia became an Austrian puppet until 1903. These developments drove many militant anti-Austrian and pro-unification movements into the underground.

The year 1903 was a turning point in the fate of *Jugoslovenski* ideas for four reasons. Khuen-Hedervary left office as Ban of Croatia; Alexander Obrenović was assassinated in Belgrade and Peter Karadjordjević replaced him, determined to resume Serbian independence; the United Croatian Opposition was created, a majority coalition in Croat lands; and the Hungarians demanded their own separate military, threatening anew Austrian control.

From these factors and others, two Dalmatian politicians, Frano Supilo and Ante Trumbić, believing that Croatian survival was impossible within the Austro-Hungarian Empire, revived the spirit of Pan-Slavism and reached out to Serbs. In Dalmatia, they negotiated a new agreement, publicly pronouncing in 1905 that 'the Croats and Serbs of Dalmatia will work shoulder to shoulder as blood brothers in national and political questions....'[37] The paradoxical effect of oppression under

---

[35] Ibid., p. 106.
[36] Ibid., pp. 108–110; Banac, pp. 91–95.
[37] Banac, pp. 96–97; Tanner, pp. 110–111.

Khuen-Hedervary had been to increase, not decrease, feelings of solidarity between Croats and Serbs.

As a result of the changes in 1903, a plethora of cultural activities reminiscent of the 1830s occurred. The First Yugoslav Artistic Exhibit was held in 1904, in conjunction with the First Congress of South Slav Youth, demonstrating anew enthusiasm for collaboration. The Third Conference of Yugoslav Writers, held in 1905, established a literary journal and renamed itself the Association of Yugoslav Writers and Journalists, *Slovenski Jug*.[38] In addition, the Pan-Slavic Congress of 1908 repudiated the idea of Russian dominance, and revived the principle of reciprocity.[39]

A new age of rebellion and social ferment occurred among students. They encountered exciting teachers like Tomáš Masaryk and Jovan Skerlić, who urged solid social improvements and renewed linguistic unity respectively. The expanded franchise also encouraged political expression among new voting populations, increasingly conscious of the sources of their oppression. Students—the sons of village leaders, the first to leave the village and travel—struggled with trade union jobs and encountered left-wing thought. They faced poverty and oppressive work conditions; they read widely, conversed in coffee houses, and dreamed of a better future. They championed the possibility of liberation.[40]

Personifying this burst of Pan-Slavic enthusiasm was Ljuba Jovanović-Čupa, a student activist in the Law Faculty at the University of Belgrade, who formed the first pro-Yugoslav Serbian journal, *Slovenski Jug*. He saw the Yugoslavs as one people whose future depended on the renunciation of narrow nationalism, combining the ideological and concrete spheres of Pan-Slavism.[41]

When Austria-Hungary annexed Bosnia-Herzegovina in 1908, Serbian anti-Austrian resentments flared. Members of the radical Young Bosnians,

---

[38] Milojković/Djurić, J. (1988). 'The Roles of Jovan Skerlić, Steven Mokranjac, and Paja Jovanović in Serbian Cultural History, 1900–1914', *Slavic Review*, 47(4), pp. 687–701.

[39] Levine, L. (1914). 'Pan/Slavism and European Politics', *Political Science Quarterly*, 29(4), pp. 664–686, pp. 675–677. Levine was intent on showing that Russian Pan-Slavism was defunct.

[40] Ibid., p. 214. For a detailed treatment of many of members of the conspiracy that led to the death of Franz Ferdinand in 1914, see Dedijer's 'Primitive Rebels of Bosnia', pp. 175–234.

[41] MacKenzie, D. (1996). 'Ljuba Jovanović-Čupa and the Search for Yugoslav Unity', In *Serbs and Russians*. Boulder & New York: East European Monographs, pp. 11–127.

frustrated at the Serbian government's passivity, took matters into their own hands, killing Archduke Franz Ferdinand. Thus, anger at oppression, with South Slavic unity as the focal point of a tangle of problems, plunged Europe into the worldwide conflict that the Great Powers had avoided since 1815.

During the war, leading Yugoslav politicians persevered in their search for unification. The Dalmatian Croats, Supilo and Trumbić, along with the sculptor Ivan Mestrovic, formed the Yugoslav Committee (JO). They travelled to gain support and were especially successful in France and England.[42] The Serbian government in exile in Corfu under Prime Minister Nikola Pašić declared that, with military victory, it would create a 'powerful southwestern Slavic state: all the Serbs, all the Croats, and all the Slovenes would enter its composition'.[43] In July 1917, the JO and the Serb exiles cooperated in the Corfu Declaration, proclaiming that Serbia, Croatia, and Slovenia would form an independent state under a 'constitutional, democratic and parliamentary monarchy headed by the Karađorđević dynasty'.[44] A third group, headed by the Slovene Anton Korošec, had continued to work for unity and equal representation within the Austrian Empire as the Zagreb National Council but ultimately joined the others in 1918.[45]

With Austrian defeat, these groups, internationally supported, took the final steps towards unity. On October 29, 1918, the Croatian Sabor declared Dalmatia, Croatia, Slavonia, and Rijeka to be one independent, unified state. The next day, the Zagreb Sabor dissolved itself and transferred its authority to the National Council. And on October 31, 1918, the National Council declared its readiness 'to enter into a common state with Serbia and Montenegro'.[46]

In Serbia, Pašić—formerly an exclusive Greater Serbia proponent—recognized the National Council as 'the legitimate government of the Serbs, Slovenes, and Croats' of the former Austro-Hungarian Empire.

---

[42] Banac, pp. 118–119. Intellectuals like R. W. Seton Watch and Henry Wickham Steed were among the leading British sympathizers. For the ongoing French support for Yugoslavia, see Kolaković, A. (2020). 'La France, Protectrice des Slaves', *Revue des études slaves*, 91(1/2) (Paris, 1921), pp. 115–129.

[43] Banac, pp. 116–117.

[44] Ibid., p. 123.

[45] Ibid., p. 127.

[46] Ibid., p. 128.

After intense negotiations in Geneva, he declared Serbia, ready to join in a greater Yugoslav state.[47] All sides agreed on a transitional common ministry, which would operate until a Constituent Assembly was elected. On November 9, the United Kingdom of Serbs, Croats, and Slovenes was publicly announced. King Alexander formally proclaimed the new state in Belgrade on December 1, 1918.[48]

Towards a Conclusion: Pan-Slavism and the Yugoslav State

For the first time, Balkan Pan-Slavism had achieved its goal. Two political entities from opposite sides of the formerly impenetrable Austro-Hungarian-Ottoman border, with contrasting cultural and political backgrounds, had united. The crumbling of the Austrian and Ottoman Empires, which had hindered Slavic self-expression, enabled the realization of the original South Slavic dream. Slavs benefited also from the support of Western states, and above all from the continuous work of those who believed in the dream of unification. Its creators could justifiably celebrate the achievement.

However, once unification had been achieved and imperial oppression was removed, leaders had to face concrete governmental problems and the voices of competitive, narrow nationalism. Portents of future problems appeared. The Zenith Group of Ljubomire Micić pushed anew Fadeev's image of a war of civilizations with the South Slavs as the vanguard of offensive action.[49] In late 1928, a Montenegrin radical killed the Croatian Peasant Party leader, Stjepan Radić on the floor of the Yugoslav Parliament. King Alexander, frustrated by democratic disorder, formed a monarchical dictatorship. In 1934, he was assassinated. Ante Pavelić, leader of the old exclusivist Croatian Party of Rights and implicated in

---

[47] Ibid., p. 134.

[48] Tanner, p. 120.

[49] Banac, p. 208; Glisic, I. and Vujoseic, T. (2016). 'I Am Barbarogenius: Yugoslav Zenitism of the 1920s and the Limits of Performativity', *The Slavic and East European Journal*, 60(4). This artistic movement transferred the old Russian resentment and fear of European leadership onto the new Yugoslav *Barbarogenius*, picturing the effect of the new, young, energetic but fractious Yugoslavia on an old, decrepit, effete Europe. Too radical, Micić was forced to flee to Paris—an ironic end to his career, so loudly critical of Europe.

the assassination, formed the *Ustaše* Croatian Liberation Movement to 'liberate Croatia from alien rule', where 'only the Croatian nation would rule'.[50] Pavelić collaborated with Mussolini to form the Independent State of Croatia during World War II.

Meanwhile, Josip Broz Tito, having matured in much the same milieu as the Progressive Youth of pre-World War I days, joined the Communist Party in the early 1920s, worked his way up through the ranks, and became Yugoslav Party Chair in 1937.[51] During the war, Tito fought doggedly against both Pavelić's *Ustaše* forces and Serbian monarchist Chetniks. As the war dragged on and he gained backing, Tito and his coterie proclaimed the new communist Yugoslav government at the end of November 1943.[52] The second Yugoslavia, like the first, was thus created from the ashes of world war. It lasted until 1989, when Tito's legacy unravelled in the face of other nationalist intransigencies.

In 1948, Tito defied Stalin's power in the newly formed COMINFORM. Yugoslavia was expelled from that body. Although they expected it, the Yugoslavs were not invaded and survived. Yugoslavia then became 'Titoist', developing its own form of socialism and a non-aligned international position. As in 1876, South Slavs confronted Russian hegemony and spurned it.

In many ways, Tito—a hard-boiled, ambitious, pragmatic politician, saturated with communist ideology—may be considered an example of Christoff's concrete form of the Pan-Slavist idea, where the idea encounters reality and sometimes becomes unrecognizable. Strossmajer's spiritual goal of uniting Eastern and Western Christianity had become Tito's Communist Yugoslavia. Tito persisted in defending his concept of Yugoslavia throughout anarchic wartime; he adhered to its concepts of unity and brotherly love; he forced non-nationalist behaviour on his people. He attempted to develop the federalist conception of the state, a major theme in earlier Pan-Slavist thinking. To a large degree, the cross-cultural dreams of Gaj, Strossmajer, and the pre-war Progressive Youth were realized in Titoist Yugoslavia. But, as Milovan Djilaš has pointed out,

---

[50] Banac, p. 125.

[51] Pavlowitch, S. K. (1992). *Tito: Yugoslavia's Great Dictator—A Reassessment.* Columbus, OH: Ohio State University Press, pp. 15–25.

[52] West, R. (1994). *Tito and the Rise and Fall of Yugoslavia.* New York: Carroll & Graf, Inc., p. 172. For a treatment of the discussions about the new state, see pp. 162–174.

Tito conflated Yugoslavia and himself.[53] Because he did so, he developed no process for succession. This was a major reason why, in the 1990s, radical nationalist voices, like those raised in the 1920s, divided Titoist Yugoslavia. Time will tell whether another Balkan Pan-Slavic Yugoslavia can be created.

---

[53] Đjilaš, M. (1980). *Tito: The Story from Inside*. New York: Harcourt Brace, Chapter 13, pp. 169–179. This is the most searching assessment of Tito and his legacy that has been made.

Pan-Slavism as a (Political) Tool

New Wine in an Old Wineskin: Slavophilia and Geopolitical Populism in Putin's Russia

Mikhail Suslov

Introduction

This chapter discusses the relevance of Slavic affinities and the importance of Pan-Slavic ideas in Putin's Russia. It argues that shifts in the geopolitical culture and regime ideology of Russia have infused Pan-Slavism with new meanings suitable for expressing new political concerns and ideas. This chapter does not consider Pan-Slavism to be a coherent ideology, rather a loose collection of political ideas, policies, geopolitical visions, and sentiments, whose common denominator is the belief that all peoples of Slavic origin, culture, and language have or should attain a considerable degree of cultural and political unity among themselves. The term 'Slavophilia' is used in this chapter in order to grasp the hybrid and fluid nature of Pan-Slavic attitudes today and to juxtapose it to historical forms of Pan-Slavic ideological articulation. Slavophilia is a child of its age, not a holdover of the nineteenth-century national awakening in Eastern

M. Suslov (✉)
Department of Cross-Cultural and Regional Studies, University of Copenhagen, Copenhagen, Denmark
e-mail: mikhail.suslov@hum.ku.dk

© The Author(s), under exclusive license to Springer Nature Switzerland AG 2023
M. Suslov et al. (eds.), *Pan-Slavism and Slavophilia in Contemporary Central and Eastern Europe*,
https://doi.org/10.1007/978-3-031-17875-7_6

Europe. It is, by contrast, one among many other forms of contemporary identity politics,[1] whose political thrust stems from the question 'Who are we?' rather than from the canonical ideological question 'What should be done?'. Hence, unlike classic forms of pan-nationalism, which explicitly contained projects for future policies aimed at forging a supranational union, contemporary identitarian Pan-Slavism shifts its focus from actions to the static condition of remaining faithful to an imagined 'Slavicness'. This claim to preserving Slavic identity may or may not entail some political actions, such as 'saving' brother Slavs from external enemies or promoting integrationist projects. What is invariable in such an interpretation is the securitisation of the identity, which can acquire internal and external forms: the former is about the condemnation of those who have 'betrayed' their Slavicness; the latter deals with the geopolitical dimension and contains a vision of powerful and threatening enemies versus the suffering Slavs.

The chapter shows that in post-Soviet Russia, Slavophilia has emerged as an identity-related language, used to convey concerns about belonging and distinctiveness as well as to express emotional and moral attitudes to a situation in which 'we' are represented as an underprivileged, threatened, and victimised group of the 'wretched of the earth'. In this capacity, Slavophilia has become part of the Kremlin's newly crystallised ideology of multiple civilisations and resistance to the Western hegemonic project. This vision of Slavic solidarity does not exclude the possibility of using the trademark trick of the Russian political elite since the mid-nineteenth century: to instrumentalise Pan-Slavic rhetoric as a smokescreen for hegemonic discourses and politics.

These two faces of contemporary Slavophilia, the political and the ideological, display different dynamics. While Russia's economic and political presence in the Slavic countries and specifically in the Balkans has been weakening in the past two decades,[2] the ideological relevance of the Slavs remains significant, demonstrating a potential for growth. The regime

---

[1] See among others: Bernstein, M. (2005). 'Identity Politics', *Annual Review of Sociology*, 31(1), pp. 47–74; Fraser, N. (1999). 'Social Justice in the Age of Identity Politics: Redistribution, Recognition, and Participation', In: Ray, L. and Sayer, R. A. (eds) *Culture and Economy After the Cultural Turn*. London: Sage, pp. 25–52.

[2] Hake, M. and A. Radzyner (2019). 'Western Balkans: Growing Economic Ties with Turkey, Russia and China', *BOFIT Policy Brief*, 1; Beliaev, S. (2018). 'Ekonomicheskie vzaimootnosheniia Rossii i stran Balkanskogo poluostrova', *Regional'nyi vestnik*, 6, pp. 33–34. Beliaev's calculation of the trade turnover between Russia and the Balkan countries is

ideology of Russia insists on the increasing irrelevance of the 'West', which is meant to be waking up to the fact that it is only one of several great global civilisations, and in this light, the ideological struggle for the Slavs is intensified. They are challenged by various ideologists to choose their side: either they lose their identity inside the 'collective West', or they celebrate their Slavic distinctiveness in a union with Russia. For example, in an interview with Serbian president Aleksandar Vučić in 2019, the Russian TV anchor Vladimir Solov'ev implied that Serbia had been moving towards the 'West' but that, in the changing global situation, it might well happen that there would be 'nowhere to come to (*nekuda budet prikhodit*)'.[3]

A few words should be said by way of setting the ideological context and clarifying the term 'political mainstream'. This term is used to denote the ideology of the Russian political elite, the 'regime ideology'.[4] It reflects the fact that the regime of Putinism has gradually consolidated its authoritarianism over the past 23 years, while niches of the opposition and free speech have correspondingly shrunk.[5] This process ended in Spring 2022 when, against the backdrop of the war in Ukraine, the last disloyal media outlets were banished. This means that the regime has acquired a certain degree of ideological unanimity, despite the obvious fact that there are notable discrepancies and variations inside the regime. Uniformity in political thinking means that an ideological core has been formed, and within this consensus on the most fundamental principles, there may be endless variations.[6] The methodological corollary of this observation implies that all public discourse about Slavophilia is now in some kind of conformity with the ideological consensus, and this fact eases the task of establishing the representativity of the sources for this study.

---

grounded on the information from the web-portal 'Vneshniaia Torgovlia Rossii', available at: Внешняя Торговля России (https://russian-trade.com/).

[3] Solov'ev, V. (2019). 'Bol' Iugoslavii', *Youtube*, 25 March, available at: https://www.youtube.com/watch?v=XbLIJqWBthc.

[4] Chen, C. (2016). *The Return of Ideology: The Search for Regime Identities in Postcommunist Russia and China*. Ann Arbor: University of Michigan Press.

[5] E.g. Taylor, B. (2018). *The Code of Putinism*. New York: Oxford University Press; Langdon, K. and Tismaneanu, V. (2019). *Putin's Totalitarian Democracy: Ideology, Myth, and Violence in the Twenty-First Century*. Cham: Springer International Publishing AG.

[6] Laruelle, M. (2021). *Is Russia Fascist? Unraveling Propaganda East and West*. Ithaca: Cornell University Press; Lewis, D. (2020). *Russia's New Authoritarianism: Putin and the Politics of Order*. Edinburgh: Edinburgh University Press.

Another preliminary advisory should pertain to the content of the regime ideology of Putinism. We can use a raft of terms to describe the ideological core of Putinism indirectly: populism, identitarian conservatism, right-wing communitarianism, fascism, fundamentalism, cultural nationalism, 'civilisationalism', anti-Westernism, Messianism, and so on. The problem with these descriptions is that none of them grasps Putinism in its entirety. This is because Putinism is indeed a new and unique ideological phenomenon, whose essence cannot be boiled down to any of the aforementioned concepts. In brief, Putinism is a consistent repudiation of canonical liberalism with its fundamental assumption 'that all men are created equal, that they are endowed by their Creator with certain unalienable Rights, that among these are Life, Liberty, and the pursuit of Happiness'. By contrast, Russia's mainstream ideology maintains that humanity consists of several civilisations with different basic matrices of values, so though the Americans may value life, liberty, and the pursuit of happiness, this does not entail that the Chinese or the Russians hold the same values dear: they stick to their own values. However, due to its hegemonic and hubristic nature, the 'West' is trying to impose its regionally specific set of values on the rest of the world, thereby only wreaking havoc. Russia, in this view, is vested with the lofty mission of protecting the 'rest' from the 'West' and ushering in a more fair system of autonomous civilisations, which would supplant the failed projects of Western-driven globalisation and multiculturalism.[7] In this context, Russian Slavophilia is one among other practical extensions of this global vision, in which the 'Slavs' are imagined as a separate civilisation, fundamentally different from the 'West' but, by virtue of their geographical proximity to it, historically the first and the most wretched victims of Western imperial aggression.

People and organisations using the term 'Pan-Slavism' in their ideological speeches are part of this political mainstream, or, as recently, have been tending to move from the margins towards the political centre. Roughly speaking, there are three ideological 'points of growth' for Slavophilia: (1) nationalism in all its hues, from inclusive civilisationism to radical Russian supremacism and racism; (2) anti-globalism and socialism; and (3) the Orthodox church and political religiosity. Quite often, all three of these dimensions of Slavophilia come together. For example, the

---

[7] Suslov, M. (2020). *Geopolitical Imagination: Ideology and Utopia in Post-Soviet Russia.* Stuttgart: Ibidem Verlag.

All-Slavic Union, presided over by the nationalist and Holocaust-denier Oleg Platonov and arguably the best connected Pan-Slavic organisation in Russia, stands at the centre of the nationalistic camp but also propagates religious fundamentalism and a vision of the Slavic mission for liberating humanity from Western global capitalism.[8] The same could be said about Sergei Baburin, editor of the journal *Slaviane* and rector of the International Slavic Academy.[9] Baburin is part of the national-socialist niche of Russian politics, with an emphasis on the latter, leftist aspects.[10] Among these intellectuals, especially close to Baburin, the idea of the 'Slavic alternative' is gaining currency. This concept means that, due to their special natural characteristics, the Slavs provide the most fertile soil for a 'third way' between capitalism and Soviet-style socialism.[11] The Slavic 'third way' implies that a collectivistic consciousness, with egoism and greed suppressed while searching for religious meanings and holiness, and emphasis on traditions and the values of child-rearing and family life would give the Slavs the historic chance towards creating a new model of a moral and eco-friendly civilisation. This civilisation would become the real alternative to the consumerist capitalism of the global West.[12]

Two remarks delimiting the scope of the present study are due. First, Slavophilic rhetoric is occasionally used to legitimise Russia's aspirations for the creation of an East Slavic union with Belarus and Ukraine.[13] However, the logic of these revanchist ideas about the restoration of a bygone unity is different from Pan-Slavism, which is essentially about

---

[8] Platonov, O. (2015). 'Vsemirnaia missiia slavianstva', *Izborskii Klub*, 26 May, available at: Олег Платонов. ВСЕМИРНАЯ МИССИЯ СЛАВЯНСТВА | Изборский клуб (https://izborsk-club.ru/5652); Platonov (2017). 'Vsemirnaia zadacha slavianstva – sozdanie sodruzhestva nezavisimykh slavianskikh gosudarstv', *ruskline.ru*, 19 June, available at: Всемирная задача славянства - создание содружества независимых славянских государств (https://ruskline.ru/monitoring_smi/2017/iyun/2017-06-19/vsemirnaya_zadacha_slavyanstva_sozdanie_sodruzhestva_nezavisimyh_slavyanskih_gosudarstv/).

[9] 'Slavianskaia Akademiia', available at: Славянская Академия (slav-academ.ru).

[10] 'Mezhdunarodnyi Slavianskii Sovet', available at: (2) Международный Славянский Совет | Facebook (https://www.facebook.com/mslavsovet/).

[11] Baburin, S. (2018/2019). 'Slavianskaia al'ternativa', *Slaviane*, 13 (4/1), p. 1.

[12] Zagorov, O. (2018). 'Slavianskaia dukhovnost' – kul'turnyi kod bolgarskoi natsional'noi identichnosti', *Slaviane*, 12(3), p. 17; N.A. (2018). 'Za Slavianskoe edinstvo, druzhbu i mir s drugimi narodami: Manifest', *Slaviane*, 11(2), p. 30.

[13] Luzan, A. (2018). 'Panslavizm – ideologiia budushchego', *Slaviane*, 11(2), p. 28.

imagining a supranational unity among already independent states. Thus, this paper will consider only political thinking about the need for solidarity between Russia and those Slavic countries *outside* of the former Soviet Union. These discourses usually revolve around Serbia and—less often—Bulgaria and Slovenia. Second, it is also necessary to exclude from this analysis various soft-power attractions and intrastate 'philias' that are not directly related to the argument of national affinity. For example, we can imagine that political elites in Kazakhstan, Hungary, and elsewhere may well be Russophilic, but that obviously does not imply that they are motivated by Pan-Slavic visions and ideas, and thus these will not be taken into consideration in this examination. This distinction poses a certain conceptual challenge when it comes to the pro-Russian discourses and policies of the Slavic countries. To what extent, for example, does Pan-Slavism account for the Serbophilia of the Russian political mainstream, and to what extent is it the result of strategic and economic calculations? In other words, is Pan-Slavism a means or an end of Russian political leadership? The chapter will address these questions by assessing the role and place of Slavophilia in the Russian political mainstream.

Essentialisation of Slavicness

In the framework of Kremlin's dominant ideology, Slavophilia is based on the assumption that the Slavic world is a natural, 'organic' phenomenon, uniting nations believed to have something more in common than just linguistic kinship. In extreme cases, this assumption implies geographical and biological determinisms. The conservative prose writer Valentin Rasputin picked up on this idea in the following way: 'We [Slavs] were born from direct contact with rocks of the mountains and waters of rivers, grasses of the steppes, and birds' cries.... So we learned to love, suffer, cry, and laugh in our own way—in accordance with the spirit of the mountains and valleys which surrounded us'.[14] Both Rasputin and Nikita Moiseev, another late-Soviet guru of the conservative camp, emphasised the scientific 'naturalness' of cultural-territorial entities. Moiseev, for example,

[14] Rasputin, V. (1992). 'Chto dal'she, brat'ia slaviane? Moi manifest', available at: Что дальше, Братья-Славяне? Мой манифест — Журнал Клаузура (https://klauzura.ru/2020/01/chto-dalshe-bratya-slavyane-moj-manifest/).

insisted that qualities of a landscape and climate shape a civilisation's cultural traits.[15]

The book *Slavic Union: Its Necessity and Possibility* (2015), written by a collective of authors affiliated with the Stavropol Agricultural University, is couched in this peculiar terminology, characteristic of the regime ideology, which presents a mixture of anti-globalist discourses, primordial nationalism, racism, and moral conservatism. The authors insist that a Slavic union would become a fortress against global capitalism, as headed by the United States, and later on—by way of explicating why the Slavs are different from others—they identify specific qualities of the Slavs: peacefulness, introspection, tolerance, calmness, morality, and so on.[16] These qualities, according to the book, developed thanks to the specificity of the geographical, climatic, and historical conditions of the Slavic experience. For example, the endless spaces of the East European plain instilled a love for freedom and independence among the Slavs, while the abundance of food and natural resources contributed to the formation of such qualities as kindness, forgiveness, and tranquillity. As a concession, the authors point to the partial corruption of the Slavic character from admixtures of 'Finnish blood' in the 'Great Russians' and of the blood of 'Asiatic predators' in the 'Little Russians'.[17]

Oft-quoted neo-Slavophile Nikolai Danilevsky has struck the same note, emphasising the difference between the Slavic and the German national characters and pointing to a Slavic contemplative nature, lack of aggression, Christian kindness, and resignation. In today's discourses, Danilevsky is credited for expressing the idea of a 'genetically based peacefulness (*geneticheski obuslovlennoe miroliubie*)' of the Slavs.[18] In the context of the war in Ukraine, this idea about a biological substratum of 'Slavicness' received unexpected support in the Russian media when

---

[15] Moiseev, N. (2000). *Sud'ba tsivilizatsii: Put' razuma*. Moscow: Iazyki slavianskoi kul'tury, pp. 50–78.

[16] Aseev, Iu., Kants, N. and Kravchenko, I. (2015). *Slavianskii soiuz: Neobkhodimost' i vozmozhnost'*. Stavropol': SGAU, 4, pp. 15–16.

[17] Ibid., pp. 19–22.

[18] Danilevsky, N. (1995). *Rossiia i Evropa* (1868). St Petersburg: Izd. St. Peterburgskogo un-ta. On his contemporary relevance for Pan-Slavism, see: Karachev, G. (2021). 'Sushchestvuet li slavianskoe edinstvo, ili V chem slaviane pokhozhi mezh soboi', *The Russian Times*, 25 June, available at: Существует ли «славянское единство», или В чем славяне похожи между собой (https://therussiantimes.com/narody-mira/414 338.html).

some political figures started to talk about secret 'Western' laboratories in Ukraine preparing an 'ethnic weapon' that would selectively target people of Slavic origin.[19]

Typically, however, the idea of the 'naturalness' of Slavic unity is couched in cultural and religious terms, but this is still far from the liberal understanding of a community as *'un plébiscite de tous les jours'*.[20] The firm belief that the Slavs possess some unchangeable qualities and moral characteristics, such as solidarism, collectivism, altruism, non-violence, and so on, is quite widespread in Russian political discourse. This idea is certainly not the invention of present-day Pan-Slavists but rather stems from mid-nineteenth-century Slavophiles like Aleksei Khomiakov, who argued (among other things) that the Slavs belonged to the 'Iranian' peoples and thus were characterised by creativity and a peace-loving nature.[21] On top of this, the peacefulness and natural tolerance of the Slavs make these nations the most suitable role model for a non-liberal multiculturalism, preserving the national identity of various communities and, at the same time, creating the foundations of their peaceful coexistence.[22]

The vision of some primordial but half-forgotten shared Slavic legacy inspired the sculptor and patriotic activist Viacheslav Klykov, who argued that the 'Serbs are like Russians a long time ago…. Discovering Serbia is like discovering the self and reconnecting with our own nature'.[23] Today, when civilisational discourses are coming to the fore in Russia, a vision of Slavic 'civilisation' is also interpreted as a 'regathering' of Slavic unity, which should help the Slavs restore their forgotten cultural roots.[24] These two discourses about Slavic civilisation and the common historical past intersect in the argument that Russia and Serbia were the most faithful

---

[19] Rogozin, D. (2022). 'Biooruzhie na Ukraine', *RT.com*, 21 March, available at: Рогозин: биооружие на Украине действует на репродуктивную систему россиянок — РТ на русском (https://therussiantimes.com/narody-mira/414338.html).

[20] Renan, E. (1882). 'Qu'est-ce qu'une nation?', available at: Renan - Qu'est-ce qu'une nation? (http://www.iheal.univ-paris3.fr/sites/www.iheal.univ-paris3.fr/files/Renan_-_Qu_est-ce_qu_une_Nation.pdf).

[21] Khomiakov, A. (1900). 'Semiramida', In: Khomiakov, *Polnoe sobranie sochinenii*, vols. 5–7. Moscow: Universitetskaia tip.

[22] Lazarov, K. (2018). 'Ne pogasit' togo, chto ne gasnet', *Slaviane*, 11(2), p. 23.

[23] Ushakova, I. (2021). 'Za chest' Rossii i Serbii', *Nash sovremennik*, 31 March.

[24] E.g. Lazarov, K. (2019). 'Slaviane i global'nye vyzovy', *Slaviane*, 14(2), pp. 7–8.

heirs of the East Roman Empire, thus representing Orthodox civilisation in its purest form.[25]

As a case in point, Patriarch Kirill time and again touches upon the concept of Slavic unity in the context of the need to preserve the spiritual-cultural identity of the people in a world of aggressive globalism. In this sense, faithfulness to the Orthodox religion and to the legacy of Saints Cyril and Methodius, who brought literacy and Christianity to the Slavic lands in the ninth century, is a cultural bedrock of the Slavic world and the guarantee of its unity.[26] Religious ideologists connect 'Slavicness' with Orthodox Christianity, thereby excluding non-Orthodox Slavs from their vision of a 'Slavic civilisation'.[27] This emphasis on the Orthodox Church harks back to the nineteenth-century Russian exceptionalist policy and Messianic ideology, and so bears its principal 'birth defect': the alienation of the non-Orthodox constituency of Russia itself, as well as of all the non-Orthodox Slavs outside of Russia.

However, the broadest channel for supplying the Russian population with Slavic themes and discourses is Slavic fantasy, which had acquired substantial popularity already in the 1990s in the vein of Western Celtic, Arthurian, and other sub-genres of epic fantasy. Despite its name, this genre's interest in Slavic unity is minimal, whereas its primary preoccupation is forging a historical genealogy of the Russian nation through references to its pre-Christian past and depiction of fights with non-Slavic peoples. Pulp literature, films, and video games in the genre of Slavic fantasy establish a tight association between 'Slavicness' and the primordial and Messianic visions of antiquity and the past glories of the Russian nation, while it should be noted that 'Slavicness' as such is typically not

---

[25] Krshlianin, V. (2021). 'Rossiia, Serbiia i Balkany: Perspektivy', *Valdai Club*, 22 June, available at: Россия, Сербия и Балканы: перспективы — Клуб «Валдай» (https://ru.valdaiclub.com/a/highlights/rossiya-serbiya-i-balkany-perspektivy/?sphrase_id=512195).

[26] 'V Smolenske proshli torzhestva', *mospat.ru*, n.d., available at: В Смоленске прошли торжества, посвященные Дню славянской письменности и культуры: новость ОВЦС (http://mospat.ru/ru/news/64888/); 'Nasledie Kirilla i Mefodiia i edinstvo pravoslavnogo, russkogo i slavianskogo mira', *Vsemirnyi Russkii Narodnyi Sobor*, n.d., available at: Наследие Кирилла и Мефодия и единство православного, русского и славянского мира (https://vrns.ru/news/nasledie-kirilla-i-mefodiya-i-edinstvo-pravoslavnogo-russkogo-i-slavyanskogo-mira/?sphrase_id=990).

[27] E.g. Vedeneeva, N. (2018). 'Professor Sokolov predskazal ob"edinenie Rossii, Belorussii i Ukrainy', *MK*, 20 August; Andrei Savinykh's statement, quoted from: Zabrodin, A. and Baikova, T. (2020). 'Eks-traditsii', *Izvestiia*, 7 August 2020.

problematised, serving as a synonym for the loosely defined pagan past of Russia.[28]

The essentialisation of Slavicness means that belonging to this community cannot be a question of free individual deliberation. Valentin Rasputin, the foremost representative of 'village prose' and a conservative ideologist, expressed this idea with the utmost power, arguing that to be a Slav 'is not our will, it is our destiny (*ne volia nasha, a nasha dolia*)'.[29] This conservative-communitarian interpretation of a supranational community implies that all political forms and interactions can only be based on the fundamental 'natural' kinship among the nations. Roger Scruton famously declared that a society's 'binding principle is not a contract, but something more akin to love',[30] because without this unmediated and emotional relation to strangers, people are unlikely to agree upon any contract, which entails the limitation of their free will and diminishes their available resources. John Milbank and Adrian Pabst in their book extended this consideration to interstate relations by arguing that 'the international system is not so much a society of sovereign states but rather…a society of nations and peoples who are bound together by social ties and cultural bonds that are more primary than state-guaranteed rights and market contracts'.[31]

Geopolitical Populism

An important dimension of communitarian geopolitics is what could be called geopolitical populism. The canonical understanding of populism claims that it is grounded on a juxtaposition between the 'people' and the 'elite'. This juxtaposition emerges from concerns about the failure of democracy to represent the 'people' properly, as well as from a communitarian vision of the 'people' as an entity with a stable, unchangeable

---

[28] Breeva, T. and Khabibullina, L. (2015). '*Russkii mif' v slavianskom fentezi*. Kazan': KFU; Safron, E. (2012). '*Slavianskaia' fentezi: Fol'klorno-mifologicheskie aspekty semantiki*. Diss. Petrozavodsk: PSU.

[29] Rasputin, V. (1992). 'Chto dal'she, brat'ia slaviane? Moi manifest', available at: Что дальше, Братья-Славяне? Мой манифест — Журнал Клаузура (https://klauzura.ru/2020/01/chto-dalshe-bratya-slavyane-moj-manifest/).

[30] Scruton, R. (2014). *How to Be A Conservative*. London: Bloomsbury, p. 29.

[31] Milbank, J. and Pabst, A. (2016). *The Politics of Virtue: Post-Liberalism and the Human Future*. Lanham: Rowman & Littlefield, p. 334.

identity. The question of representation, in this case, comes down to striving to discover a mechanism to express this identity in a better way than through representative democracy, such as by means of a 'true' people's leader or by studying history (hence, the emphasis on securitising history in populist regimes). Geopolitical populism also envisages a nation as a community with a stable core of identity, but the elites are represented as a geographically external force, such as 'Brussels bureaucrats' or 'globalists'. In Russian regime ideology, populism is expressed through two discourses: the antagonistic juxtaposition of the Slavs and the 'West' on the one hand, and the belief that the 'West' is the master and 'we' are the underdogs, fighting for liberation, on the other.

The rhetoric of Slavs as 'common people' in juxtaposition to arrogant Westerners has been developed by the journal *Slaviane,* edited by Sergei Baburin. The journal, for example, maintains that, unlike other people, the Slavs 'are close to nature', and that their lifestyle is the lifestyle of a 'common person (*prostoi chelovek*)'. This argument is used to conclude that the Slavs have developed the highest and the most consistent type of 'humane civilization (*gumanisticheskaia tsivilizatsiia*)'.[32] The Russian press eagerly quoted renowned film director Emir Kusturica saying that moral and spiritual values 'naturally belong (*iskonno prisushchie*)' to the Slavs.[33] Populism reconfigures Pan-Slavism as criticism of the domestic, liberal, and Westernised elites. Once again, Pan-Slavic ideologists voice the assumption that the Slavic peoples are instinctively attracted to each other and naturally strive for a kind of political unity with Russia, while their elites push them apart, into the embrace of the 'West'.[34] Il'ia Chislov, for example, argues that 'Slavic and Orthodox countries remain our [Russian] trustworthy and faithful allies, if we are talking about countries and peoples, in spite of the resilience of the elites, journalists, and spin-doctors'.[35] Aleksandr Dugin has expressed geopolitical

---

[32] Lazarov, K. (2019). 'Slaviane i global'nye vyzovy', *Slaviane,* 15(5), pp. 8–9; Cf. Zakhariev, Z. (2018). 'Russkaia kul'tura i slavianskii mir: Pered vyzovami tsivilizatsionnykh peremen', In: *Rossiia i mir: Razvitie tsivizatsii,* Vol. 1. Moscow: Institut mirovykh tsivilizatsii, pp. 52–57.

[33] Pavliutkina, I. (2018). 'Serby smotriat v storonu Moskvy', *Krasnaia Zvezda,* 2 February.

[34] Platonov, O. (2017). 'My ob"iavliaem pokhod za edinstvo slavianskogo mira!' *Slovo,* 16 June. Cf also: Aseev, Kants, Kravchenko (2015). *Slavianskii soiuz,* 180.

[35] Chislov, I. (2018). 'Bog udachu daet otvazhnomu', *Slovo,* 25 May.

populism in crystal-clear form, maintaining that not a single Serb wanted to join NATO; the Serbian elite had 'considerably alienated itself from the people. Our *Russian* elite is not like this'.[36] In an article penned for the patriotic think tank Izborsky Club, journalist Slobodan Stojićević argues that the people in Serbia 'want one thing'—union with Russia—whereas the country's elite wants another—integration with the European Union.[37]

As an identitarian ideology, Slavophilia in our understanding belongs to the family of other ethnonationalisms. Its central metaphor is that of kinship or ethnic 'brotherhood' among the Slavs, which highlights the idea of masculine solidarity with a hint of resistance to a hostile environment.[38] Slavophilia massively capitalises on the metaphor of a 'brotherhood in arms'—a powerful device for the pan-nationalistic imagination. This metaphor is chosen even by central media outlets such as newspaper *Izvestia*.[39] The importance of the brotherhood metaphor becomes obvious when we consider the choice of the name for the joint Russian-Belarusian-Serbian military exercises in 2019–2021: Slavic Brotherhood.[40]

This populist approach to geopolitics accentuates attention on the stability of the community's identity over time and space, as well as its clear-cut differentiation from other identities. In this context, increasing animosity between the Russian political elite and the 'West' is reflected in anti-Western themes, which tend to dominate in Pan-Slavic discourses. This is certainly not a recent invention. Slavophile argumentation is exhumed and reinforced in the discourses of religious-nationalistic media

---

[36] Dugin, A. (2020). 'Serby – nashi samye vernye soiuzniki', In: *Izborskii Klub*, 6 January, available at: Александр Дугин: Сербы — наши самые верные союзники | Изборский клуб (https://izborsk-club.ru/18531).

[37] Stojićević, S. (2016). 'Gde granitsy Russkogo mira?', *Izborskii Klub*, 13 April, available at: Слободан Стойичевич. Где границы Русского Мира? | Изборский клуб (https://izborsk-club.ru/9378).

[38] Kaplan, D. (2021). 'Imagining National Solidarity: Strangers-Turned-Friends-Turned-Brothers', *European Journal of Cultural and Political Sociology*, Ahead-of-Print: 1–26.

[39] Filimonov, G. (2017). 'Na iazyke bratskikh narodov', *Izvestiia*, 3 April.

[40] 'Serbia vyrazila nadezhdu na uchastie v ucheniiakh "Slavianskoe bratstvo"', *Izvestiia*, 14 October 2020, available at: Сербия выразила надежду на участие в учениях «Славянское братство» | Новости | Известия | 14.10.2020 (https://iz.ru/1073652/2020-10-14/serbiia-vyrazila-nadezhdu-na-uchastie-v-ucheniiakh-slavianskoe-bratstvo).

outlets, such as ruskline.ru, which repeats the idea about the dichotomy between the material-rationalistic spirit of the 'West' and the spiritual-emotional worldviews of the Slavs.[41] Pan-Slavic activists today still recycle the Messianism of the Slavophiles and Dostoevsky, which allocates to the Slavs a very special place in world history as those who would reconcile and combine the best qualities of the East and West, such as a sharp analytical mind with a striving for harmony and goodwill.[42]

Oleg Platonov, for example, refers to a fake document, the so-called Dulles Plan, as proof that the 'West' has always tried to set the Slavs against each other.[43] Valentin Rasputin emphasised that the Slavs have always stood in the way of the 'West's' global dominance, which explains why they are so hated there.[44] The image of a powerful enemy is surely conducive to the consolidation of pan-nationalisms. Historically, Pan-Slavism was fuelled mostly by anti-German and anti-Ottoman ideas and visions. Today, the 'West', as an undifferentiated whole, is seen as an enemy.[45] Sergei Baburin, for example, maintains that it is 'globalism and neo-liberalism' that is the actual foe of the Slavs.[46] The documentary *The Russian Cross above the Balkans*, produced in 2009 by Aleksei Denisov, editor-in-chief of the state-owned TV channel History, defined the Slavic enemy as the 'Euro-Atlantic civilization', always trying to set the Slavs

---

[41] Plamenats, I. (2017). 'Vliianie dukha Zapada kak glavnaia prichina slavianskogo needinstva,' *ruskline.ru*, 13 June, available at: Влияние духа Запада как главная причина славянского неединства (https://ruskline.ru/news_rl/2017/06/13/vliyanie_duha_zapada_kak_glavnaya_prichina_slavyanskogo_needinstva/).

[42] Platonov, O. (2017). 'My ob"iavliaem pokhod za edinstvo slavianskogo mira!' *Slovo*, 16 June.

[43] Ibid.

[44] Rasputin, V. (1992). 'Chto dal'she, brat'ia slaviane? Moi manifest', available at: Что дальше, Братья-Славяне? Мой манифест — Журнал Клаузура (https://klauzura.ru/2020/01/chto-dalshe-bratya-slavyane-moj-manifest/).

[45] Belous, V. (2019). 'The Opposition of Own/Alien as a Source of the External Threat: Reflections on Supra-State Sovereignization Politics and 19th-Century Pan-Slavism', In: Crailsheim, E. and Dolores Elizalde, M. (eds) *The Representation of External Threats: From the Middle Ages to the Modern World*. Leiden: Brill.

[46] Baburin, S. (2014). *Strazh natsii: Ot rasstrela parlamenta do nevooruzhennogo vosstaniia RGTEU*. Moscow: Knizhnyi mir, p. 483.

against each other and rejoicing when they suffered.[47] Patriotic journalist Il'ia Polonsky strikes the same note when he argues that the 'West tries to set all Slavs against each other for the purpose of their ultimate de-Slavisation'.[48] Mikhail Iudin, director of the Institute of Slavic Culture at the Russian State University of Design and Technology, points at a specific enemy, the United States—which, as he argues, exerts enormous influence on the non-Russian Slavs and cultivates Russophobia among them.[49]

In this context, the trope of the perpetual and unfathomable sufferings of the Slavs occupies an important place in the Pan-Slavic imagination. The aforementioned documentary *The Russian Cross above the Balkans* indulges in lengthy descriptions of how the Turks tortured the subjugated Slavs. In historical discourses about World War II, the war is presented as an attack by the West in general against the whole Slavic world.[50] In Pan-Slavic discourses, NATO, the European Union, the United States, and other Western organisations are likely to be compared to fascism in order to strengthen the parallel between the current geopolitical context and World War II—and thereby highlight the West's aggressiveness.[51] Even in respected academic circles, Slavophobia is believed to be part of the Western identity, defined by its 'craving for dominance in Eastern

---

[47] 'Russkii krest nad Balkanami', documentary by Aleksandr Denisov, *Telekanal Rossiia*, 2009, available at: Русский крест над Балканами - YouTube (https://www.youtube.com/watch?v=Xu9fzXk-pAA).

[48] Polonsky, I. (2019). 'Den' edineniia i druzhby slavian i pechal'noe nastoiashchee slavianskogo mira', *Voennoe obozrenie*, 25 June, available at: День единения и дружбы славян и печальное настоящее славянского мира (https://topwar.ru/159371-den-edinenija-i-druzhby-slavjan-i-pechalnoe-nastojaschee-slavjanskogo-mira.html).

[49] Iudin, M. (2021). 'Glavnoe, chto mozhet vernut' edinstvo slavianam, - kul'tura', *Ukraina.ru*, 25 Мая, Юдин: Культура может вернуть единство славянам (https://ukraina.ru/interview/20210524/1031447744.html).

[50] N.a. (2018). 'O bor'be protiv fal'sifikatsii istorii', *Slaviane*, 12(3), p. 64; Tejkowski, B. (1998). 'Geopoliticheskoe i natsional'noe polozhenie slavianstva i perspektivy slavianskogo sodruzhestva', In: Troitskii, E. (ed) *Russko-slavianskaya tsivilizatsiia: Istoricheskie itogi, sovremennye geopoliticheskie problemy, perspektivy slavianskoi vzaimnosti*. Moscow, p. 254; Mialo, K. (2004). 'Mify i real'nost' slavianskogo edinstva na grani vekov', *Nash sovremennik*, 9, pp. 219–220; Troitskii, E. (2009). *Ukreplenie russkogo mira i konkurentsiia. Vozvrashchenie sootechestvennikov*. Moscow: Granitsa, p. 208.

[51] Milošević, B. (2011). *Nepobezhdennyi. K 70-letiiu so dnia rozhdeniia Slobodana Miloshevicha*. Moscow.

Europe, [by] insurmountable striving to baptise the baptised, to enlighten the enlightened, to teach the learned'.[52] This motif of a powerful external enemy tormenting the Slavs is a handy rhetorical device to explain the lack of political unity among them. Sergei Baburin and his co-authors, for example, claim that the 'Slavic world' has been 'violently dismembered' but remains 'mentally united'.[53] The official *Izvestiia* capitalised on the same argument in an article claiming that 'the European Union, NATO, and the U.S.A. are at pains to drive a wedge between Russia and Serbia'.[54] Platonov elsewhere argued that 'the whole politics of the West after the Second World War has consisted of the destruction of friendly ties and partnership among the Slavic countries'. The Cold War, in this interpretation, was primarily a war of NATO against the Slavs.[55]

One of the editorial articles of the journal *Slaviane* describes the Slavic world as a 'spring, compressed by its enemies to its limit'.[56] Likewise a scholar of the Russian Academy of Sciences, Elena Gus'kova argues that the bombing of the former Yugoslavia in 1999 was part of a coherent programme implemented by NATO for the purpose of suppressing, splitting, and marginalising the Slavic peoples.[57] The narrative of perpetual Slavic suffering amalgamates with the term 'de-Slavization (*deslavianizatsiia*)' as a systematic process and Western policy of eradicating the Slavic identity.[58] The Russian poet Vlas Veresen' penned the following

---

[52] Nikiforov, K. (2000). 'Vozmozhnost' sblizheniia pravoslavnykh stran', In: Nosov, B. V. (ed) *Slavianskie narody: Obshchnost' istorii i kul'tury*. Moscow: Indrik, p. 472.

[53] Baburin, S., Simchera, V. and Simchera, Ia. (2016). 'Slavianskii mir: Edinstvo i bor'ba proivopolozhnostei', *Slaviane*, 3, p. 9.

[54] Laru, D. and Zabrodin, A. (2017). 'Krym i Sevastopol' – chast' Rossii', *Izvestiia*, 21 April.

[55] Platonov, O. (2013). 'O evraziitsakh i Slavianskom Soiuze', *livejournal.com*, 10 July, available at: Олег Платонов о евразийцах и Славянском Союзе (https://alexsrb.livejournal.com/176694.html).

[56] Baburin, S. (2018). 'Tiazhkoe ispytanie Tret'ego Rima', *Slaviane*, 12(3), p. 1.

[57] Gus'kova, E. (2013). *Agressiia NATO protiv Iugoslavii v 1999 godu i protsess mirnogo uregulirovaniia*. Moscow: Indrik, p. 260.

[58] Polonskii, I. (2019). 'Den' edineniia i druzhby slavian i pechal'noe nastoiashchee slavianskogo mira', *Topwar.ru*, 25 June, available at: День единения и дружбы славян и печальное настоящее славянского мира (https://topwar.ru/159371-den-edinenija-i-druzhby-slavjan-i-pechalnoe-nastojaschee-slavjanskogo-mira.html).

verses, entitled 'The March of Slavic Unity', in which he expressed his premonition of times of dramatic troubles for the Slavic world:

> The smoke of conflagrations wafts again,
> Crows circle as a sign of trouble,
> Time has come, get ready, comrade,
> Let our ranks become stronger!
> Black clouds have covered the sky,
> There will be tears and calamities enough for everyone.
> Brother, stand up, whoever you are:
> A Russian, a Bulgarian, a Serb, or a Czech.[59]

It has been mentioned that the securitisation of history is an important populistic device for imagining a community's identity throughout centuries. Russian regime ideology today is to a large extent a commentary on Russian history, predominantly the history of the Great Patriotic War.[60] Pan-Slavic discourses have absorbed this idea, too, as, for example, when the head of External Intelligence, Sergei Naryshkin called for Russian-Serbian solidarity for the purpose of protecting 'our version of World War II' and fighting back against 'attempts to falsify history'. As a symbolic gesture of brotherhood between the Russians and the Serbs, a particle of the eternal flame from the memorial of the Unknown Soldier in Moscow was transferred to Belgrade under Naryshkin's auspices.[61] In exchange, the president of Serbia, Aleksandar Vučić took part in the Immortal Battalion manifestation on Red Square in 2018[62] and used other media occasions to discuss the 'Slavic victory' in World War II for a Russian audience.[63] In this context, Pan-Slavism could be interpreted as a

---

[59] Veresen', V. 'Marsh slavianskogo edinstva', *chitalnya.ru*, n.d., available at: Марш славянского единства ~ Песни (Авторская песня) (https://www.chitalnya.ru/work/2037948/).

[60] Platonov, O. (2017). 'My ob"iavliaem pokhod za edinstvo slavianskogo mira!' *Slovo*, 16 June.

[61] 'V Moskve proshla tseremoniia perenosa vechnogo ognia...' *Vzgliad*, 14 December 2020.

[62] Smirnov, D. (2018). 'Putin vyvel Vuchicha i Netan'iakhu na "Bessmertnyi polk"', *Komsomol'skaia Pravda*, 9 May, available at: Путин вывел Вучича и Нетаньяху на «Бессмертный полк» - https://www.kp.ru/daily/26827.4/3866641/.

[63] Vučić, A. (2020). 'K 75-letiiu Velikoi Pobedy', *Rossiia 24 / Youtube*, available at: Президент Сербии Александр Вучич. К 75-летию Великой Победы - Россия 24 - YouTube.

process of recollecting bygone unity: the pre-historical unity of Slavs, the first stages of the Pan-Slavic movement in the nineteenth century, military comradeship during World War I,[64] and Slavic brotherhood in the war against Nazi Germany. According to this interpretation, neglecting Slavic affinity is akin to an obliteration of shared memory. In February 2020, the speaker of the State Duma, Viacheslav Volodin came up with a proposal to establish a joint Russo-Serbian Institute for the Defence of Historical Memory.[65] As an extension of this initiative, in November 2021 Belgrade hosted a forum called Memory of the Victors, which included State Duma MPs and other members of the Russian political leadership (for example, the coordinator of the Immortal Battalion movement).[66]

Russia's Mission

The vision of the 'cosmic struggle' between the Slavs and the 'West' gives a Messianic flavour to Slavophilia. Through this prism, the Slavs are seen as a very special community with a special 'third way' and a global mission. This mode of thinking is especially visible within the socialist-nationalist ('red-brown') milieu. Among these intellectuals, especially those close to Baburin, the idea of the 'Slavic alternative' is gaining currency. This concept means that due to the special natural characteristics of the Slavs, they provide the most fertile soil for a 'third way' between capitalism and Soviet-style socialism.[67] The Slavic 'third way', as already said, is largely associated with collectivistic consciousness, with the importance of religiosity, holiness, and the values of family life where egoism and greed are suppressed, allowing the Slavs to try and invent a different, moral and eco-friendly, civilisation that, for Zagorov, would challenge the global

---

[64] 'Naryshkin: Serbiia s Rosiei solidarna', *Parlamentskaia gazeta*, 8 May 2014.

[65] N.A., 'Viacheslav Volodin predlozhil sozdat' mezhdunarodnyi institut zashchity istoricheskoi pamiati', *Duma.gov.ru*, 12 February 2020, available at: Вячеслав Володин предложил создать международный институт защиты исторической памяти (http://duma.gov.ru/news/47769/).

[66] Shapovalova, A. (2021). 'Mezhdunarodnyi forum 'Pamiat' pobeditelei' zavershilsia v Belgrade', *Lenta.ru*, 5 November, available at: Международный форум «Память победителей» завершился в Белграде: Общество: Россия: https://lenta.ru/news/2021/11/05/forum/.

[67] Baburin, S. (2018/2019). 'Slavianskaia al'ternativa', *Slaviane*, 13(4/1), p. 1.

West in being the real alternative to the consumerist capitalism.[68] For the left flank of the political spectrum, the Slavs stand for the colonial underdogs of the globalised world dominated by the Anglo-Saxons, and hence the issue of Slavic liberation and unification merges together with the anti-globalist and social-democratic agendas. Among those individuals and organisations are the largest left-wing party in Russia, the CPRF, the heir to the omnipotent CPSU. A number of spin-off parties, such as Just Russia and the International Slavic Movement entertain Pan-Slavic ideals, as well.

Another member of the ASU is Nikolai Burliaev, an actor, film-director, and chair of the international forum of Slavic cultures called the Golden Knight.[69] Burliaev stands on a more conservative-nationalistic-religious platform than socialist-oriented Baburin, yet his anti-globalist agenda connects him with other left-wingers. The honorary trustees of the Golden Knight are Patriarch Kirill; the former governor of St. Petersburg, Poltavchenko; and the renowned film director and an ideologist of conservatism, Nikita Mikhalkov. Burliaev is not particularly explicit about his vision of the Slavic unity; he usually limits himself to referencing Dostoevsky's words that Russia has two missions: the Slavic world and Orthodoxy.[70] Mikhalkov has vocally denied the independence of Kosovo on the grounds that the Kosovo conflict was only one episode in the global fight against Orthodoxy.[71]

Imagining the role and mission of Russia in the Slavic world has recently undergone the most fundamental changes in step with Russia's

---

[68] Zagorov, O. (2018). 'Slavianskaia dukhovnost' – kul'turnyi kod bolgarskoi national'noi identichnosti', *Slaviane* 12(3), p. 17; 'Za Slavianskoe edinstvo, druzhbu i mir s drugimi narodami: Manifest', *Slaviane*, 11(2) (2018), p. 30.

[69] 'Mezhdunarodnyi Forum "Zolotoi Vitiaz'," available at: Международный Форум «Золотый Витязь» — Международный Форум «Золотой Витязь» (http://zolotoyvityaz.ru/).

[70] Burliaev, N. (2010). 'O Slavianskom voprose', *ruskline.ru*, 19 June, available at: О славянском вопросе (https://ruskline.ru/analitika/2010/10/02/o_slavyanskom_voprose).

[71] Mikhalkov, N. (2006). 'Ia priekhal, chtoby podderzhat' sokhranenie Kosova v sostave Serbii', *ruskline.ru*, 5 October, available at: Никита Михалков: "Я приехал, чтобы поддержать сохранение Косова в составе Сербии" (https://ruskline.ru/news_rl/2006/10/05/nikita_mihalkov_ya_priehal_chtoby_podderzhat_sohranenie_kosova_v_sostave_serbii/).

growing confidence on the international stage, since especially the Russo-Georgian War and the annexation of Crimea. The dominant tendency of the 1990s and the 2000s was glorifying Serbia as the bastion of the Slavic world[72] and castigating Russia and Russia's policies for their indeterminacy and Western orientation. Right-wing politician Vladimir Zhirinovsky voiced these concerns in the State Duma when he called Serbia 'our Brest Fortress', evoking the powerful image of the unprecedented resilience of the fortress's defenders, who withstood the invading forces of the Nazi Wehrmacht from June 22 to 29, 1941.[73] For many a conservative Slavic intellectual, the battle for Serbia was a battle for independence from the West, from globalisation, and from the 'New World Order', a euphemism for the Judeo-Masonic conspiracy.[74]

The NATO bombardment of Serbia in 1999 has spotlighted the theme of Serbian 'martyrdom', 'crucifixion', and its 'Golgotha path'.[75] This rhetoric was also systematically used to describe Belarusian resistance to Westernisation.[76] For example, Zhirinovsky has argued that Belarus 'is sacrificing itself [in the name of] Slavic geopolitical interests'.[77] The theme of Russia's guilt before the Serbs, Belarusians, and even Trans-Carpathian Ruthenians reinforces the impression that Russia is surrendering her rights to spatial and historical centrality.[78]

This rhetoric changed in the 2010s, when the Russian leadership reimagined the country as one, and arguably the most important, pole

---

[72] Zhirinovsky, V. (2002). *Politicheskaia klassika*. Moscow, vol. 82, p. 5; Dzhuretic, V. (2003). *Razval Yugoslavii*. Moscow: Stroispetsmontazh, p. 555; Greshnevikov, A. (2006). 'Serbskaia Golgofa', In: A. Greshnevikov, *Khranitel' russkogo lada*. Rybinsk: Rybinskoe podvor'e, p. 35.

[73] 'Stenogramma zasedaniia 14 Maya 1999 g.', *Russian State Duma*, available at. http://transcript.duma.gov.ru/node/2369/.

[74] Skobelev, E. (2003). 'Esli slaviane vystupiat...', *Nash sovremennik*, 3, p. 244; Nazarov, M. (2005). *Vozhdiu Tret'ego Rima*. Moscow: Russkaia Ideia, p. 913; Kalajić, D. (2006). *Tret'ia Mirovaia Voina*. Moscow: IHTIOS, pp. 47, 111.

[75] Ryzhkov, N., & Teterkin, V. (2003). *Raspiataia Yugoslaviia*. Moscow: Rus. nov', p. 6; Burliaev, N. (2011). *Slavianskii venets: Letopis' 'Zolotogo Vitiazia'*. Moscow, Russia, vol. 3, p. 67.

[76] Ziuganov, G. (2006). *Zashchishchaia nash mir: O vneshnepoliticheskoi deiatel'nosti KPRF*. Moscow: ITRK, p. 46.

[77] Zhirinovsky, V. (2007). 'Rossiia i Belorussiia', *Nash sovremennik*, no. 7.

[78] E.g. Mialo, K. (2003). *Mezhdu Zapadom i Vostokom. Opyt geopoliticheskogo i istoriosofskogo analiza*. Moscow: Rus. Nats. Fond, p. 59.

of the multipolar world, the flag-bearer of the liberation of the 'rest' from the 'West'. In this new context, Slavophilia has acquired a role in telling the old story of how Russia has been called by Providence and history to save other Slavic nations. The new Messianic narrative of Russia as a 'provider of global stability' inspires the vision of Russia's pacifying mission in the Balkans.[79] In the film *Battalion*, a graphic scene depicting a Russian trooper saving a little Serbian girl and carrying her away from a minefield evokes other historical parallels. One of them is the iconic sculpture of the Liberator Soldier with a German girl in his arms in Berlin's Treptower Park, which has become a condensed expression of the Red Army's mission of liberating Europe from fascism.

In the same film series, a Russian officer tells the NATO troops stationed in Kosovo, 'Serbia is our business. Learn history'. Elsewhere, in an argument about Russia's role in the Balkans, one of them responds that his country is preventing the massacre of civilians, and when a group of exasperated Serbs, chased by the Kosovars, runs to the Russian garrison and is let in, in circumvention of the regulations, it is because they said, 'We have nowhere else to go. Let us in the Russian Federation'. Oleg Rozov, a member of the nationalistic-conservative Izborsky Club think tank, referred to the Messianic concept of Katechon (the Retainer), while arguing that Russia's 'sphere of responsibility' looks like concentric circles: the Russian world, the Slavic world, and the whole world.[80]

On a more humorous note, a recent romantic comedy film called *Hotel Belgrade* (directed by Konstantin Statsky, 2020) continues to exploit the same topic of Russia's benevolent help to the otherwise hopeless Serbs. In the film's cheesy, exoticising depiction of the Balkans, there is an episode in which the Russian female protagonist, well-versed in martial arts, protects her ne'er-do-well Serbian boyfriend from the local criminal boss. A dash of anti-Westernism (this mafioso is a fan of 'degenerate' Western contemporary art) and positive valorisation of family values add to the big picture.

Contrary to the nineteenth-century narrative, the struggle between the Orthodox Slavs and the Muslim world has been downplayed

---

[79] Korovin, K. (2021). 'Pravo serbskogo naroda,' *Izborskii klub*, 13 July, available at: Валерий Коровин: Право сербского народа | Изборский клуб (https://izborsk-club.ru/19618).

[80] Rozanov, O. (2015). 'Vpered, slaviane!' *Izborskii klub*, 8 August, available at: Олег Розанов. ВПЕРЁД, СЛАВЯНЕ! | Изборский клуб (https://izborsk-club.ru/6499).

or completely reinterpreted within the new ideological framework of Eurasianism. The film *The Balkan Frontier*, for example, features a Russian Special Forces squad, deliberately manned by people of different nationalities: a Russian, a Belarussian, a Tartar, an Uzbek, an Ingush, a Serb, and an Albanian. The film emphasises that some members of this group are practising Muslims. One of the Serbs repeats the Serbian idiom that 'We are 200 million, together with the Russians' only to receive a disgruntled remark from a Tartar: 'And how many are you with the Tartars?' In this way, the filmmakers correct the Pan-Slavic cliché in accordance with the new ideological reality: the point is not about Russian-Serbian brotherhood but about Serbs being a respected member of a much larger and more powerful Eurasian family. The emphasis on the multinational and multi-confessional nature of Russia gives a new interpretation to the old narrative about Russia's brotherly ties with the Serbs. Now it highlights Russia's unique ability to reconcile Christianity and Islam, bring peace to the Balkans, and serve as a pacifying force in religious conflicts. The theme of the special relations between the Serbs and Russia is not completely gone either: a Serbian soldier, wounded and mutilated by enemy fire, covers the retreat of the Russian squad, knowing that he has no chance to survive. This feat evokes an appreciative remark from one of the protagonists: that he was 'a real Serb'. In this way, the importance of the Serbs through the prism of this new Pan-Slavism lies in their ability to share the same values as Russia and their desire to fight the same enemy, rather than in their ethnic kinship with the Russians.

In the last twenty years, and especially after 2015–2016, the Russian political elite has decisively turned to the East. Sergei Karaganov, one of the most prominent pro-Kremlin analysts, argues that the West is now on the losing side of history, whereas the economic success of China has showed to everyone that a country can be powerful and successful without adopting alien, Western lifestyles and values. Against this background, Eurasian ideology has received a new impetus and is now the vanguard of Russian geopolitical thinking, whereas the Slavs remain in the shadows. In 2015, the Eurasian Economic Union (EAEU) became operational, and the next year Putin voiced an idea of setting up a 'Larger Eurasia' partnership, to include the EAEU, China, and possibly also other Asian countries. This new geopolitical thinking intertwines with Pan-Slavic themes, giving the non-Russian Slavs a new, less important, but still ample place in the Russian geopolitical imagination.

An attempt to reconcile Eurasianism with Pan-Slavism was recently made by the father-founder of neo-Eurasianism, Aleksandr Dugin. He insists on Serbia's Eurasian nature, as a country which combines elements of the East and West in itself. Moreover, he argues that the Balkans became a hospitable home for the Turanic peoples, who came there from Central Asia in time immemorial. In Dugin's understanding, 'Eurasian Serbia' has two missions: to become the centre of confessional dialogue and to serve as the avant-garde of non-Western, essentially Eurasian values in Europe.[81] Most of the proponents of Slavophilia, in actuality, see the Slavic integrationist project as commensurable with the Eurasian one.[82] Some ideologists such as Boris Iskhakov, president of the International Slavic Academy, and Kim Smirnov, rector of the International Slavic University, have put forward the term 'Slavo-Eurasian Union'.[83]

The film series *Battalion* offers a more decisive rupture from the Pan-Slavic canon. It contains two romantic plotlines, in both of which the Russian Spetsnaz officers develop relationships with, respectively, an Albanian and a Roma woman, whereas the Serbs play a rather insignificant role as walk-ons who are saved by Russians, and who occasionally even betray their own saviours. In one episode, a Serbian civilian, whom Russians let onto the airport grounds in order to save them from the rage of the Kosovar Muslims, films the facility on the orders of the British military command. When caught, he explains that the dire economic condition of his family pressed him to commit this act of treachery, and as we can assume he is benevolently pardoned.

This episode evokes parallels with the discourse about the treachery of the non-Russian Slavs liberated by Russia in the war with the Ottoman Empire of 1877, who immediately turned their back on Russia and participated in wars against their saviour. This has never been forgotten, and now—pointing to the aspirations of the Slavic nations to enter NATO and

[81] Dugin, A. (2017). 'Balkanskaia shkola geopolitiki', *Izborskii klub*, 19 December, available at: Александр Дугин: Балканская школа геополитики | Изборский клуб (https://izborsk-club.ru/14521); Dugin, A. (2012). *Geopolitika Rossii*. Moscow: Gaudeamus, p. 74.

[82] Baburin, S. (2012). *Vozvrashchenie russkogo konservatizma*. Moscow: Inst. Russkoi Tsivilizatsii, pp. 97, 483; Bondarenko, V. (2011). *Russkii vyzov*. Moscow: Inst. Russkoi Tsivilizatsii, p. 75.

[83] Smirnov, K. and Kataeva, O. (2000). Istoricheskii vyzov slavianskomu soobshchestvu (Moscow), 6; Troitskii, E. (2011). *Slavianskoe edinenie—faktor mogushchestva Rossii*. Moscow: Granitsa, p. 87.

the EU—Russian commentators never miss an opportunity to mention Fedor Dostoevsky and Konstantin Leont'ev's disparaging remarks about the Slavs.[84] Referring to Dostoevsky, Valentin Rasputin mourned that today 'former Turkish Slavs openly regret that they were liberated from the Turks, and the former German Slavs regret that they were liberated from the Germans, while sending curses to their liberators'.[85] The writer and political analyst of Chechen origin, German Sadulaev levelled the most devastating critique of the Slavs in the following manner:

> While some Slavs were fighting fascism, other Slavs were serving in the SS troops…. They say Cain was Abel's brother. But do we need such brotherhood? These brothers are different from non-brothers in their ability to covertly punch in the solar plexus, or stab a knife in the back, or pour gas and set fire when you do not expect it.[86]

Sadulaev expresses the crystallising consensus about Russia's historical destiny as by and large a Eurasian country, whose loose and deceptive ties with the European Slavs are significantly less important than ties with its own Turkic, Caucasian, Finno-Ugric, and other non-Slavic peoples. Even Nikita Mikhalkov, quite supportive of the Slavic cause, has recently developed a more critical stance with reference to the same passage in Dostoevsky.[87] Egor Kholmogorov reverentially quoted another pre-revolutionary conservative thinker, Konstantin Leont'ev, who prophesied: 'The establishment of a single Slavic state would usher into the world the end of Russia'.[88] To further distance Russia from the Slavs,

---

[84] N.A., 'Ne brat ty mne?', *AiF*, 6 January 2015.

[85] Rasputin, V. (1992). 'Chto dal'she, brat'ia slaviane? Moi manifest', available at: Что дальше, Братья-Славяне? Мой манифест — Журнал Клаузура (https://klauzura.ru/2020/01/chto-dalshe-bratya-slavyane-moj-manifest/).

[86] Sadulaev, G. (2015). 'Ne brat'ia, ne vragi. Prosto postoronnie', *Komsomol'skaia pravda*, 12 September. Cf. also Tsipko, A. (2021). 'Ottorzhenie ot Rossii: Pochemu ot nas otvorachivaiutsia brat'ia-slaviane', *Moskovskii Komsomolets*, 2 July.

[87] Mikhalkov, N. (2021). 'Vremia, otpushchennoe Dostoevskim, isteklo', *tsargrad.tv*, 22 March, available at: Время, отпущенное Достоевским, истекло: Михалков вынес приговор "братьям-славянам" (https://tsargrad.tv/news/vremja-otpushhennoe-dostoevskim-isteklo-mihalkov-vynes-prigovor-bratjam-slavjanam_335365).

[88] Leont'ev, K. (1996). *Vostok, Rossiia, i slavianstvo* [1873]. Moscow: Respublika, p. 39; Kholmogorov, E. (2005). *Russkii proekt. Restavratsiia budushchego*. Moscow: Eksmo, p. 298.

Kholmogorov argues that, though Slavic by language, Russians belong to 'Nordic civilization' by culture, race, and 'mentality'.[89]

Conclusion

We can assume that the growing popularity of the conservative-communitarian worldview among the Russian elite has inevitably increased the importance of Pan-Slavism. This study shows that despite the obvious anachronism of this kind of pan-nationalistic thinking, it serves as an underlying basis for new ideological constructions. Namely, Pan-Slavism has rediscovered itself as an identitarian ideology, whose purpose is primarily the securitisation of the imagined shared Slavic identity, rather than a direct call for action. In spite of its relatively static nature, contemporary Pan-Slavism (Slavophilia) can be used as a prop for advancing a whole spectrum of illiberal ideas, mostly of conservative-communitarian provenance. These ideas include nationalism, conservatism, religious fundamentalism, and nationally oriented socialism, as well as a vision of a just world order, which should consist of several autonomous civilisations. In this sense, the galvanisation of the half-forgotten Pan-Slavic topics is both a symptom of the formation of the regime ideology in Russia and its consequence.

---

[89] Kholmogorov, E. (2006). *Russkii natsionalist*. Moscow: Evropa.

Ideational Travels of Slavophilia in Belarus: From Tsars to Lukashenka

Veera Laine, Aliaksei Lastouski, and Ryhor Nizhnikau

Introduction

In July 2005, on the eve of the Belarusian Independence Day, Aliaksandr Lukashenka hosted in Minsk the participants of the Ninth All-Slavic Assembly, which was used to demonstrate the centrality of Slavic brotherhood to the Belarusian state. Lukashenka underlined the symbolism of gathering representatives of brotherly Slavic peoples in Minsk, while the then-Deputy Chief of Staff of the Presidential Administration and chief

---

V. Laine
Ministry of Foreign Affairs of Finland, Helsinki, Finland
e-mail: veera.laine@formin.fi

A. Lastouski
Uppsala University, Uppsala, Sweden
e-mail: aliaksei.lastouski@ires.uu.se

European Humanities University, Vilnius, Lithuania

R. Nizhnikau (✉)
Finnish Institute of International Affairs, Helsinki, Finland
e-mail: ryhor.nizhnikau@fiia.fi

© The Author(s), under exclusive license to Springer Nature Switzerland AG 2023
M. Suslov et al. (eds.), *Pan-Slavism and Slavophilia in Contemporary Central and Eastern Europe*,
https://doi.org/10.1007/978-3-031-17875-7_7

ideologist of the state, Oleg Proleskovsky, noted that 'Belarusians will always welcome and support any initiatives of Slavic unity'.[1] In 2021 in an address to the nation, Lukashenka put the narrative of the unity of the Slavic people at the core of his speech, stating, 'We are native Slavic peoples, people from the same baptismal font. Our roots are from time immemorial, and this must be preserved, no matter the cost. No matter what someone wants, we will return our Ukraine to the bosom of our Slavs. We will definitely do it.'[2]

This chapter looks at the evolution and trajectory of Slavophilia in Belarus and its instrumentalisation by the Belarusian state. Slavophilia has had a blurry status and role in the Belarusian state and Belarusian society. Since Lukashenka's election in 1994, Belarus has often been seen as 'a safe haven for Slavophile ideas', central to the survival and diffusion of Pan-Slavism.[3] The concept of the 'Slavic peoples' has always been of great importance in the political and intellectual culture of Belarus. The Belarusian president was considered the main champion of Slavophilia in the post-Soviet region, while some Pan-Slavic ideas were integrated in the early stages of the Belarusian nation-building project. They highlighted common beginnings and ethno-linguistic and ideational ties that surpassed state or ethnic boundaries. Yet, despite the regular featuring of Slavophile ideas in the narratives of state officials and state ideology in the 1990s and early 2000s, and the presence of active lobbyists, these were becoming alienated from mainstream public discourse and did not translate into state policies in a consistent and coherent manner. At the same time, the very comprehension of the Slavic community has been shifting with time, within which principles of inclusion and exclusion set new cultural boundaries.

---

[1] President.gov. (2005). 'Prezident strany Aleksandr Lukashenko prinyal uchastiye v torzhestvennom sobranii, posvyashchennom Dnyu Nezavisimosti Respubliki Belarus' (Dnyu Respubliki)', 1 July 2005, available at: https://president.gov.by/ru/events/prezident-strany-aleksandr-lukashenko-prinjal-uchastie-v-torzhestvennom-sobranii-posvjaschennom-dnju-2220.

[2] RBC. (2022). 'Lukashenko poobeshchal vernut' Ukrainu v "lono slavyanstva"', available at: https://www.rbc.ru/politics/28/01/2022/61f3c4249a79476a826448e6.

[3] Rudling, P. (2011) 'Lukashenka and the "Red-Browns": National Ideology, Commemoration of the Past and Political Belonging', In: *Forum für Osteuropäische Ideen- und Zeitgeschichte*, 15, pp. 95–126.

This chapter makes two main points. First, it argues that in a myriad of competing concepts and imageries, the dominant interpretation has gradually shifted towards and embraced a narrow understanding of Slavophilia as the unity of the three East Slavic peoples, the Russians, the Ukrainians, and the Belarusians. However, that very sequence already establishes a certain hierarchy, with Russians in the status of the 'big brother', which in some interpretations may furthermore lead to a merger of the 'Slavic' with the 'Great Russian'—terminology which also denotes quite specific political attitudes, including an orientation towards an alliance with Russia.

Second, attitudes towards and application of Slavophilia have been rather instrumental, largely following the political and geopolitical manoeuvring of the Lukashenka regime. In this regard, distancing from and rapprochement with Moscow have respectively had direct implications for the role of Slavophile ideas in official discourse and nation-building policies. The rapid rise of new ideologies, such as 'the Russian World (*russkii mir*)' and Eurasianism, have created new risks and challenges for Slavophilia in Belarus.

This chapter proceeds as follows. First, it discusses the historical roots and background of Slavophilia in Belarus and its place among the main intellectual and political debates, specifically juxtaposing it to the concept of 'West Russism (*zapodnorussizm*)'. Second, it looks at the role of Slavophilia in contemporary Belarus and its application by the Lukashenka regime. Finally, the chapter illustrates the instrumentalisation of Slavophilia by the Belarusian Orthodox Church.

BELARUSIAN NATIONALISM AND THE SLAVIC IDEA

Belarus is located on the fault line between two powerful cultures, Polish and Russian, who each sought to include the land in their dominions. Based on these very conflicts and contradictions between Polish and Russian ideas that took place throughout the nineteenth century, it became possible to form the concepts of cultural autonomy and political sovereignty for Belarusians.

Both Polish and Russian cultures have developed their own complex and contradictory relationships with the idea of Slavic community. Although in the second half of the nineteenth century, Russia gradually began to be identified as the leader of the Slavic world, Poles were the first to appeal to the idea of a community of Slavic peoples.

This appeal took place in the context of the general European romantic fascination with folk culture that overlapped with the Spring of Nations, and in such a situation, Slavs had the potential to be the ones to build a common front of young nations confronting the decrepit empires. A special explanation, however, had to be sought for the case of the Russians, as Adam Mickiewicz (who was highly honoured in the Belarusian-Lithuanian lands) and Franciszek Duchiński excluded them from the Slavic world as being alien not only to Slavs but to all of Europe in their racial origins. In this paradigm, blood correlates with culture: Slavic blood organically belongs to European civilisation, where the freedom and dignity of man are revered. Russian despotism, based on a lack of rights and slavish obedience to the authorities, was explained by the 'non-Slavic' nature of Russia, the result of an infusion of 'Mongolian blood'. Poland, on the other hand, had a special mission—to lead the Slavic peoples to freedom.[4]

For the Belarusian national project—which gradually grew out of ethnographic and historical studies and gained political expression—at the turn of the twentieth century, it was also extremely important to withdraw Belarus from the imperial project. Belarusians were assigned the role of representatives of the great Russian people, though according to the Russian anthropology of the nineteenth century, their racial origin was spoiled by the influences of Poles and Jews.[5] Without real power, the oppressed seeks to demonstrate superiority in the symbolic field. The politically and economically oppressed Belarus was presented as an organic part of Europe with a brilliant legal and cultural tradition, while Russia (and this is an obvious borrowing from Polish authors) was excluded from the European tradition. Yet again the reasoning of blood and origin was used: Belarusians were defined as 'anthropologically purer'[6] Slavs, 'nearly the purest type of the Slavic tribe'.[7] The purity of the Slavic blood of Belarusians was naturally contrasted with the mixed blood of

---

[4] Górny, M. (2011). 'Pięć wielkich armii naprzeciw wrogom naszym. Przyczynek do historii rasizmu', *Kwartalnik Historyczny*, 4, pp. 681–706.

[5] Marfina, O. (2015). *Istoriya antropologicheskikh issledovaniy v Belarusi*. Minsk: Belaruskaya navuka.

[6] Karski, Y. (1903). *Belorusy. T. 1*. Warsaw: Tipografiya Warshavskoho Uchebnoho Orkruha, p. 34.

[7] Dounar-Zapolski, M. (2011). *Istoriya Belorussii*. Minsk: Belarus, p. 24.

the Russians, with their Tatar and Finnish influences. The imperial domination of Russia, therefore, no longer had the legitimation of the rights of 'big brother', being instead perceived as the barbaric yoke of a people of lower origins over the 'pure Slavic tribe'.[8]

Pan-Slavism in its classical form (with an appeal to the supranational community of Slavic peoples—united in origin—from which common political tasks follow) has always been alien to Belarusian nationalism. Moreover, until 1918 one of its main political goals was the restoration of the Grand Duchy of Lithuania together with the Lithuanians,[9] and Pan-Slavism was completely irrelevant to such a goal.

Cautious statements by scientists of the early twentieth century acquired a completely different sound in the 1920s, at a time when an intensive Belarusianisation policy was unfolding in the BSSR within the framework of the 'empire of affirmative action'.[10] Theses about primordial Slavic (Aryan) purity filled the history textbooks by Usevalad Ihnatouski (1926, p. 10) and those by Arkadzi Smolich on geography:

> Among the peoples of Eastern Europe, the Belarusian is the purest representative of the Slavic type. Its eastern Moscovian neighbour, the Great Russian people, grew up on the Finnish base and arose from the mix of Slavic colonists with Mongols and Finns. Belarusians have stayed on their land since ancient times, and history does not recall any other significant natives of a non-Slavic type in the area.[11]

This fictitious genealogy, tied up in racial issues, had the very clear purpose of separating the 'more delicate', 'more subtle' Belarusians, real Europeans and true Slavs, from the Russians. This was acceptable as part of the post-colonial emancipation carried out by the Bolsheviks in the 1920s. But with the curtailment of this policy under Stalin, the cultural

---

[8] Rudling, P. A. (2014). *The Rise and Fall of Belarusian Nationalism, 1906–1931*. Pittsburgh: University of Pittsburgh Press, pp. 51–52.

[9] Michaluk, D. and Rudling, P. A. (2014). 'From the Grand Duchy of Lithuania to the Belarusian Democratic Republic: the Idea of Belarusian Statehood during the German Occupation of Belarusian Lands, 1915–1919', *Journal of Belarusian Studies*, 7(2), pp. 3–36.

[10] Markova, A. (2021). *The Path to a Soviet Nation. The Policy of Belarusization*. Leiden: Brill.

[11] Smolich, A. (1922). *Geagrafiya Belarusi*. Vilnius: Belaruskaye vydavectva B. Kleckina, p. 126.

and political elite of the BSSR was destroyed, textbooks were banned, and the old imperial myth of the Great Russian people in its Soviet connotation came back to stay for many years.

The return of the Belarusian national movement in the political space in the late 1980s was complemented, among other things, by an active reprinting of works from the beginning of the twentieth century, but the theme of the 'pure Slavic tribe' did not return. The 'Slavic' label was firmly stuck on representatives of the pro-Soviet and pro-Russian forces, from the camp of which Aliaksandr Lukashenka came to power.

In an intellectual attempt to get out of this trap of the Slavic world, the project of 'Kryvia' (a legendary pagan country whose name is devoid of the humiliating stem 'Rus'') arose, and local intellectuals (Todar Kashkurevich, Siarhey San'ko, and Aliaksei Dzermant) initiated a persistent search for the Baltic roots of Belarusians, revealing these in etymology, archaeological discoveries, and folk calendar songs.[12] The term 'Slavic' in this perspective was seen as an alien definition of Belarusians in contrast to their roots and values. Naturally, Baltic self-determination had very specific geopolitical consequences. There was a plan to create an alliance of the peoples from the Baltic to the Black Sea, which was supposed to become an obstacle to the Eurasian monster. Paradoxically, the movement died out around 2010, when one of the main ideologists of the movement, Aliaksei Dzermant, moved to the Eurasianist camp. The self-determination of Belarusians through 'non-Slavism' gradually faded away.

With the disappearance of the 'Slav' category, however, the essence of cultural borders remains the same, and it is still vital for Belarusian nationalism to draw a distinct border with the Russian world, replacing the 'Slavic' self-determination with a 'European' one. Accordingly, it is implied that—based on its history and cultural traditions—Belarus belongs to European civilisation, with its values of democracy and legal culture. The rule of Lukashenka (who denies these values) is thus perceived as an aberration from the correct trajectory of development, as a mistake that must be corrected. The European nation again confronts Asian despotism.

---

[12] Kazakevich, A. 'Karotkaya hieniealohiya kryuskaj idei', *Palitychnaya sfera*, 6, pp. 4–10.

West Russism: A Local Version of the Russian World?

In the nineteenth century, one more version of Belarus's self-determination (who are we? who are we with?) was formed, which experienced an unexpected renaissance at the beginning of the twenty-first century. This was West Russism, which began to take shape in the middle of the nineteenth century and was associated with the need for intellectuals (historians, journalists, writers, etc.) to form a local identity that would at the same time be loyal to the Russian imperial project.

The fundamental contradiction in this ideological project was the fact that advocating for the identity of the local history of Western Rus, and even its language and culture, was not in contradiction with also considering Belarusians to be an integral part of the Russian supernation. Accordingly, ethnographic differences were not regarded as a basis for separation from the Russians; moreover, their unity of origin was seen as an imperative for political unity under the auspices of the Russian Empire.

When referring to the history of the ancient Slavs, Mikhail Kayalovich, a key representative of this trend, saw civilisational characteristics in it that were directly opposite to the conclusions reached by Polish and Belarusian authors. Instead of despotism, he focused on the *veche* system and the development of a sense of citizenship.[13]

West Russists assigned a huge role to Orthodoxy, which was considered to be the basis for self-identification by the population of Western Rus', while the Poles who brought their political and spiritual yoke to these lands were regarded as enemies. The very name 'West Russism' had already been formulated in the 1920s by Belarusian national democrats, who saw this trend as a form of colonial subordination to the Russian imperial project. The return of West Russism to the intellectual orbit occurred in the 1990s, when the Belarusian Orthodox Church began to actively publish the works of Mikhail Kaialovich on the history of the Uniate Church liquidation. Gradually, by the early 2000s, a circle of authors had formed around the site Western Rus', quite unambiguously marking their continuity with the classical West Russism of the nineteenth century. Some of these authors were directly related to the Belarusian Orthodox Church as 'church historians' teaching at the Theological

---

[13] Kaialovich, M. (1893). *Istoriia russkago samosoznaniia po istoricheskim pamiatnikam i nauchnym sochineniiam*. Saint Petersburg: Sinodalnaia tipografiia.

Academy (Aliaksandr Bendin, Valiantsina Tsiaplova); some worked in the administration of the president of the Republic of Belarus, Aliaksandr Lukashenka (Vadzim Hihin, Leu Kryshtapovich).

The ideological core of this project is a consideration of Belarusians as an integral part of the Russian people, something Kayalovich could undoubtedly agree with. The Russian people are understood as a super-ethnos encompassing the Great Russians, Little Russians (Ukrainians), and Belarusians (White Russians). For this super-ethnos, the unity of language and culture as well as commonality of values and mentality is distinctive. Briefly, this main prescription of *zapadnorussism* can be formulated as follows: 'A Belarusian, like a Great Russian and a Ukrainian, is a Russian man by his theoretical and practical life; and Belarus, like Russia and Ukraine, are parts of a unified all-Russian civilisation.'[14] This results in prescriptions for alliance with Russia as a major geopolitical objective for Belarus. Slightly peripheral to this political project are references to Slavic brotherhood and 'Slavic civilisation'.

Thus, the world in the ideology of West Russism is perceived strictly dualistically, divided rigidly into two parts, between which there are no crossings or compromises: East vs. West, Good vs. Evil, God vs. Satan, etc. Naturally, the Russian people—or its semantic substitute, the Slavic world—constitute the positive pole. In fact, it can even be claimed that 'humanity' and 'humaneness' equate to the Russian/Slavic world. Only the Russian people possess spirituality, culture, and—consequently—civilisation. Everything else around is perceived as a space completely subordinate to the forces of evil striving to destroy the last bastion of civilisation and high spirit. The Russian people are carrying out a unique providential mission, which reaches the scale of salvation of the whole world. According to the views of the ideologists of West Russism, the world is already at the brink of a catastrophe, full extinction, and only the Russian people can prevent its destruction. The forthcoming (and perhaps inevitable?) disaster has two primary dimensions: a spiritual one and one of natural resources. Oddly enough, the struggle for vanishing resources is becoming the main explanatory motive for many processes occurring in the modern world. The collapse of the Soviet Union is exclusively described as a carefully planned and technologically implemented action by the Western world, caused by a desire to possess the vast raw material

---

[14] Kryshtapovich, L. (1999). *Belorussia i Russkaia tsivilizatsiia*. Minsk: ISPI, pp. 134–135.

reserves of this state. Another important dimension of the crisis of the modern world lies in the spiritual realm. Western civilisation is described as degenerate, spiritless, and materialistic. Furthermore, this degraded and decaying West is aggressively trying to subdue the last bastion of civilisation—Russian culture—primarily through mass culture and mass media. Thus, modern reality is described as a permanent spiritual and information war against the Slavic world.[15]

Direct access to elite political circles in Belarus allows the West Russists not to remain limited within a narrow circle of history admirers. It's no doubt they have direct influence on both public rhetoric and the practices of the Belarusian authorities. It should be noted that the topic of Pan-Slavism as a community of all Slavs is practically absent in Belarusian political discourse. 'Slavs' are almost always Eastern Slavs by default. At the same time, the civilisational separation from the alien Western world is not determined only by East Slavic origins (which form special collective values) but also by belonging to the Orthodox religion. Naturally, Poles fall into the enemy camp because of their Catholicism. It may sound strange, but the only Slavs to the west of the Bug who arouse sympathy are the Serbs; however due to the political and geographical distance, appeals to the community around this people are rare.

Thus, the Slavic idea in Belarus basically takes the form of a Slavic-Orthodox civilisation, so it is worth looking closely at how the idea of 'the Russian World' is reiterated in domestic politics by the Belarussian regime, and additionally how the understanding of the said idea as a spiritual community of East Slavic peoples is articulated by the Belarusian Orthodox Church.

Lukashenka and Slavophilia

Since the beginning of his presidency in 1994, Aliaksandr Lukashenka has actively relied upon and promoted the ideas of Slavic brotherhood. Pan-Slavic ideas about the unity of Eastern Slavs and their growing juxtaposition to the West fitted both his political and personal views. Lukashenka's official rhetoric streamlined the brotherhood of Slavic peoples and increasingly stressed the special role of Belarus in their union.

---

[15] Lastouski, A. (2011). 'Rusocentrism as Ideological Project of Belarusian Identity', *Belarusian Political Science Review*, 1, pp. 23–46.

He stated in 1995 that 'Belarus is regarded as the saviour of Slavic civilisation, and we must save this civilisation'.[16] The main Pan-Slavic movement, the International Slavic Committee, officially declared Lukashenka the 'only Slavic president who has not sold out to Washington'.[17]

Lukashenka's election in 1994 was supported by the Slavic Sobor 'Belaia Rus'', in its very name clearly referring to the ideas of the nineteenth-century Slavophiles. The traditional ideological mix of Russian national patriotism (Holy Rus' as the Slavic world's stronghold; the sacred struggle against the eternal enemy, the West; outright anti-Semitism; and a strong belief in the Judeo-Masonic conspiracy) was accompanied by a special stake in Lukashenka, who was supposed to restore the unity of the Great Russian people.

Slavophilia has become an integral part of state ideology and foreign policy discourse. The Belarusian state ideology has described Belarus as a 'cradle of Eastern-Slavic civilisation'.[18] It has also highlighted Belarus's central role in 'East Eurasianism' and its status as the 'spiritual leader' of Eastern-Slavic civilisation, a defender of values and promoter of Slavic unity. In his analysis of Lukashenka's presidential discourse, Lysyuk[19] writes, 'In the semantic space of the discursive model of state leadership in Belarus, the key words are the following: "my Belarusian people", "Slavic brotherhood", and "integration with Russia".'

Pan-Slavism has also transcended symbolic and institutional spaces in Belarus. The military exercise with Russia and Serbia called Slavic Brotherhood went along with the main cultural event of the country, the Slavjanskiy Bazar in Vitsiebsk, which showed the cultural unity of the Slavic peoples. Lukashenka's power vertical actively promoted Slavophilia.[20] Members of the Slavic Sobor 'Belaia Rus'' provided manpower for his

---

[16] Rudling, P. (2011). 'Lukashenka and the "Red-Browns": National Ideology, Commemoration of the Past and Political Belonging', In: *Forum für Osteuropäische Ideen- und Zeitgeschichte*, 15, pp. 95–126.

[17] Kommersant. (2001). 'Slaviane snova pytaiutsia ob"edinit'sia', 3 April, available at: https://www.kommersant.ru/doc/252452.

[18] Leshchenko, N. (2008). 'The National Ideology and the Basis of the Lukashenka Regime in Belarus', *Europe-Asia Studies*, 60(8), pp. 1419–1433.

[19] Lysuk, A. (2008). *Sotsiokul'turnaia determinatsiia politicheskogo liderstva: soderzhanie, sposoby, evoliutsiia*. Chernovtsi: Bukrek, p. 298.

[20] As Mitrofanova (2005) underlines, Belaruskaya Dumka, the journal of the Presidential Administration, was one of the main hubs of the Slavic ideas.

first presidential administration. And his history teacher at Mahiliou Pedagogical University, Yakau Trashchanok, received unprecedented access to the education system in Belarus. Trashchanok actively promoted the idea that it was West Russians who represented the Belarusian national idea, based on their belonging to the original East Slavic Orthodox civilisation. Belarusians are completely identified with the Orthodox culture:

> Today, a Belarusian may profess any religion or be an atheist, but what makes him a Belarusian is a real belonging to the genetically Eastern Christian subsystem of European civilisation and East Slavic (all-Russian) culture, of which Belarusian culture is an integral part.[21]

His textbooks on the history of Belarus were very much reminiscent in their content to the Russian national patriots' journalism (of Aleksandr Prokhanov's circle). Siarhei Kastsyan, the chair of the committee on foreign affairs of the Belarusian parliament, headed the Belarusian Slavic Committee, set up in 1998. Local officials formed local Slavic Committees. For instance, the Mazyr Slavic Committee was chaired by a city official and included some 50 members.[22] The Belarusian Slavic Committee officially included ten thousand members and was even a part of Lukashenka's All-People's Assembly, which has endorsed every five years the plans for his presidential term.

Furthermore, elements of Pan-Slavism such as its highlighting of distinct values and juxtaposition to the West fit Lukashenka and his elites' worldview. They saw sanction pressure on the regime as an expansion of the Western liberal world aimed not just at regime change in Belarus but at the destruction of Slavic unity. Slavic unity was intended to become an anti-Western voice that would also stop the expansion of 'globalism'.

---

[21] Trashchanok, Y. (2006). *Gosudarstvennaia ideologiia i natsional'naia ideia Respubliki Belarus'*. Mahiliou: MHU, p. 35.

[22] Mazyr by (2013). 'Belorusskii slavianskii komitet: my budem rady videt' novykh molodykh liudey v nashei organizatsii', 20 November, available at: https://www.mazyr. by/2013/11/belorusskij-slavyanskij-komitet-my-budem-rady-videt-novyx-molodyx-lyudej-v-nashej-organizacii/.

Siarhei Kastsyan actively lobbied for the creation of the Slavic Parliamentary Union, stating that 'due to the absence of such a body, we often cannot defend our Slavic interests at international forums'.[23]

For Slavophile organisations and movements, such an ideological leaning of the Belarusian state carved out a special status for Belarus, which was endowed with the soteriological status of 'saviour of the world', since all human civilisation was equated with Rus':

> So far, only Belarus retains the potential capability to arouse the rest of Rus' to great deeds.... Even now Lukashenka unconsciously acts in the spirit of the Slavic teachings. As an example, we can take the union of Belarus and Russia. Meanwhile it is only a formal union, but if it is filled with content, Rus' will not only save itself, but will also save other peoples from the approaching disaster.[24]

It endows the political confrontation with a visionary dimension, wherein the defenders of the values of Slavic civilisation regard themselves as the last defenders of the Good: 'We declare holy war on Universal Evil. In spite of everything, we grain by grain will lay the foundation of the future Greatness and Rebirth.'[25]

However, the regime's support for Slavophilia has been pragmatic, and the discourse is far from being entrenched in the power system and state ideology. Rather, it has been subordinated to Lukashenka's domestic and foreign policy interests, which make its position unsustainable. Slavophile ideas were instrumental to Lukashenka's Russia policy in the 1990s and early 2000s, winning him significant support in Russian society and among the Russian elite, who considered the dissolution of the USSR a mistake. For instance, the CPRF and its leader Gennady Ziuganov actively participated in the All-Slavic Movement. Gennady Seleznev, the speaker of the Russian Duma, initiated the Sobor of Slavic Peoples in 2001 and was the head of the organising committee of the Eighth International Slavic

---

[23] Cherepica, V. (2015). 'Grodnenskii istoricheskii kaleidoskop', available at: https://zapadrus.su/bibli/geobib/grodnok/1314-v-n-cherepitsa-grodnenskij-istoricheskij-kalejdoskop-glava-7-zaklyuchitelnaya.html.

[24] Niamchynau, Y. (2002). "Slavianskoe uchenie – prirodopostigaiushchaia Rus'", In: *Slavianskoie veche*. Minsk: BelSOES 'Chernobyl', p. 175.

[25] Hierashchanka, A. (1994). 'Pod cherno-zolotisto-belym flagom!'. *Rus' Belaia*, no. 1.

Congress in Moscow.[26] Belarus actively backed and promoted these integration initiatives and attempted to embed the Union State of Belarus and Russia into these projects.

In this regard, when Vladimir Putin in the 2000s challenged the premises of Belarusian-Russian relations and the ideological leadership of Lukashenka as a reintegrator in the post-Soviet space,[27] the regime's interest in Slavophilia dropped. Ideas of (neo-) Eurasianism and the political project of 'the Russian World (*russkii mir*)' adopted by the Russian political leadership directly threatened Lukashenka's political interests. As a response, Lukashenka launched a new policy of nation-building.[28] Nevertheless, the state ideology continued to host Slavophile ideas and actively use them in bargaining with Russia. Yet these ideas evolved and were increasingly blended with the necessity of enhancing Belarusian statehood and independence as Lukashenko redefined himself from being a post-Soviet integrator to the builder of his country's independence and defender of its sovereignty.

This led to a natural split within the West Russist movement: some remained with Lukashenka, while other former apologists for the Slavic world's saviour began to criticise him harshly for betraying his mission and for his venality towards the insidious West. But those who criticised Lukashenka from such positions were dealt with rather harshly, facing forced emigration and prison terms.

After the Ukrainian crisis of 2014, when Lukashenka attempted to play the role of mediator, rhetoric about the 'Slavic peoples' (predictably reduced to the Russians, Ukrainians, and Belarusians) was actively used to justify the role. Appeals to primordial unity and kinship were used to demonstrate the fundamental fallacy underlying the confrontation between Russia and Ukraine. On the other hand, geopolitical opportunity went hand in hand with the new security challenges and Minsk's growing sense of insecurity regarding its dependence on Moscow.[29] As a result, Belarus attempted to increase its ideological distance from Moscow. Minsk initiated a policy of soft Belarusianisation and *inter*

---

[26] Newsru.com. (2001). 'Otkrylsia S'ezd slavianskikh narodov', 1 June, available at: https://www.newsru.com/russia/01jun2001/slavyane.html.

[27] Rudling (2011); see also Nizhnikau, R. and Moshes, A. (2020). 'Belarus in Search of a New Foreign Policy: Why It Is So Difficult', *Danish Foreign Policy Review*.

[28] Leshchenko (2008).

[29] Nizhnikau and Moshes (2020).

alia repositioned itself from being a centre only of Eastern Orthodox civilisation to a being bridge between East and West, between Eastern European Orthodox and Western European Catholic civilisation. Belarus, partially due to its geographical position at the 'centre of Europe' and its '(religious) tolerance', was proclaimed as a bearer of European civilisation, which naturally combined three families of values: Catholic, Orthodox, and Protestant.[30] Such a turn went hand in hand with EU—Belarus normalisation and an active search in Belarusian foreign policy for new ties with the West.

However, the direct threat to the regime from the popular uprising of 2020—and Moscow's integral part in the regime's survival[31]—suspended the ideological manoeuvres of the Belarusian regime and brought ideas of Slavic brotherhood and unity back to the forefront of nation-building. Slavophilia, nevertheless, has been facing competition from Eurasianism. Paradoxically, Aliaksei Dzermant, who previously called for the creation of a Baltic-to-Black Sea geopolitical alliance that would protect European civilisation from a destructive and aggressive Eurasia, has turned into one of the main apologists for Eurasianism in Belarus. The challenge of harmonising the political subjectivity of Belarus (with the entrenched Lukashenka) with Russia's geopolitical projects is resolved by Belarus's special mission. In the opinion of the Belarusian Eurasianist circle, it is Belarus that should formulate the mission for a Greater Russia, which is a 'compulsion to integrate'.[32]

For apologists of the Eurasian idea in Belarus, Lukashenka has established a vector of movement towards the unification of space into a single civilisational field, with Belarus as the first initiator of this post-Soviet spatial reintegration. What role is assigned to Belarus in the geopolitical construction of the Eurasian space? The need to include Belarus in the Eurasian programme leads to the replacement of the uncomfortable term 'limitrophe' with the much nicer sounding 'frontier'. Firstly, without such a frontier, it is impossible to imagine a full-fledged Russian geopolitical subjectivity. (And the success of Belarus is a weighty argument in the

---

[30] Belarus segodnia (2014).

[31] Moshes, A. and Nizhnikau, R. (2021). 'The Belarusian Revolution: Sources, Interim Outcomes, and Lessons to Be Learned', *Demokratizatsiya: The Journal of Post-Soviet Democratization*, 29(2).

[32] Dziermant, A. (2020). *Belarus – Evraziia. Pogranich'e Rossii i Evropy.* Moscow: Rodina.

struggle for Ukraine.) And secondly, the Western frontier appears to be a source of various threats from the ontologically hostile Euro-Atlantic civilisation. Belarus acquires special significance as a stable state (being the Brest Fortress of West Eurasia), ensuring stability and security on the western frontier and preventing the anti-Russian alliance from uniting along the Baltic-to-Black Sea *Intermarium*.

After the Belarusian Revolution, Lukashenka only re-embraced Slavophile narratives. He continuously underlined the centrality of Slavic unity, its spiritual and moral values, and thus the necessity of reintegration for survival. On the day of the Russian invasion of Ukraine, in which Belarus played an integral part, he addressed the Ukrainian authorities: 'We are Slavs, three Slavic peoples. Let us sit down and decide our fate for the future, forever.'[33]

In 2022, Lukashenka also launched a complete overhaul of nation-building and memory policies in the country to further stress historical ties with Russia and common legacies:

> [W]e need to enter a new stage, as the experts say, to start defining and shaping meanings in the national-historical development of the Belarusian nation and the state. We have to prevent new challenges and threats in the sphere of national memory. Otherwise, we, our children will once again repeat the dark days of history when we were forced to live under the yoke of foreign masters on our land.[34]

He specifically characterised the Belarusian state, including Great Duchy of Lithuania, in the following way: 'The dominant faith is Orthodox Christianity. The territory is mostly Belarusian, Ukrainian, partially Russian lands. The people are 80% ours. Slavs. And these are the main attributes and signs of statehood.'[35] He also differentiated Eastern Slavs from the Poles and Lithuanians: '[W]hen the Principality of Polotsk and the Principality of Turov thundered across Europe as centres of spirituality and enlightenment, Lithuanians' ancestors were still living in the

---

[33] Belta. (2022). 'Lukashenko nazval usloviia peregovorov Rossii s Ukrainoi', 24 February 2022, available at: https://www.belta.by/president/view/lukashenko-nazval-uslovija-peregovorov-rossii-s-ukrainoj-486663-2022/.

[34] President.gov. (2022). 'Soveshchanie po voprosam realizatsii istoricheskoi politiki', 5 January 2022, available at: https://president.gov.by/ru/events/soveshchanie-po-voprosam-realizacii-istoricheskoy-politiki.

[35] Ibid.

darkness of paganism and maintaining a primitive economy.'[36] At the same time Lukashenka did not forget the Soviet legacy—'Let us not forget that we were finally formed as a nation during the Soviet times. This is when the history of the Belarusian state began.'[37]—but also caught a new wave in ideological orientation: 'Let's replace the inexorably ageing Europe with the rapidly growing Asia. Psychologically, our society is prepared to become part of the new Eurasia, its outpost.'[38]

Pan-Slavism and the Belarusian Orthodox Church

The Belarusian Orthodox Church (BOC), which often automatically defined Slavs as Orthodox and underlined the centrality of Orthodoxy, was seen as an integral part of these reintegration (including Slavophile) projects. Slavophilia is an important element of Russian Orthodoxy, of which the BOC, as the third largest constituency of the Russian Orthodox Church (ROC), is an integral part. For the ROC, Pan-Slavic connections form the very basis of its self-understanding because of history and the myth of Holy Russia (*Svyataya Rus'*) that intertwines present-day Ukraine, Belarus, and Russia. In this vision, the baptism of the Kievan Rus' and the baptism of Prince Vladimir in the year 988 confirmed the unity of the three political entities in the eyes of God.[39]

After the collapse of the Soviet Union, when the Russian Orthodox Church intensified the rebuilding of its structures within Russian society and abroad, it endorsed the key motto of the Pan-Slavic movement—'Three countries—one people' as a key element in advancing its goal of the union of the Eastern-Slavic states. Aleksii II (Ridiger) tended to underline that Russia, Ukraine, and Belarus were 'baptised in a single Kiev font', have one history, and 'cannot live without each other', as they

---

[36] Belta. (2022). 'Lukashenko vystupil za adekvatnuiu otsenku istoricheskikh periodov, vkliuchaia vremena VKL i Rechi Pospolitoi', 6 January 2022, available at: https://www.belta.by/president/view/lukashenko-vystupil-za-adekvatnuju-otsenku-istoricheskih-periodov-vkljuchaja-vremena-vkl-i-rechi-478283-2022/.

[37] Ibid.

[38] Belta. (2021). 'Lukashenko obratilsia k mirovomu soobshchestvu: net smysla shatat' Belarus'!', 26 May 2021, available at: https://www.belta.by/president/view/lukashenko-obratilsja-k-mirovomu-soobschestvu-net-smysla-shatat-belarus-443022-2021/.

[39] TASS. (2018). 'V RPTS zaiavili, chto Kreshchenie Rusi predopredelilo ves' put' slavianskoi tsivilizatsii', 28 July 2018, available at ttps://tass.ru/obschestvo/5410977.

constitute 'a single spiritual community'.[40] Moreover, the composition of the ROC is strictly hierarchical, and the Patriarch of Moscow *and All Rus'* is the spiritual leader of all the Churches on its canonical territory. Since the early 1990s, the ROC has actively supported the work of the Pan-Slavic movement, which in turn highlighted Orthodoxy as a key element. The World Russian Sobor and the Sobor of Slavic Peoples of Belarus, Russia, and Ukraine directly outlined in their programmes their 'support for a united canonical Orthodox Church.'[41]

These defining ideas of the ROC faced challenges in the erosion of the post-Soviet space and intensified state and nation-building processes on the ROC's canonical territory in the early 1990s. In theory, the canonical territory is the geographical entity to which the Church's jurisdiction is limited, and there should be only one Church operating on each canonical territory. But in practice, the boundaries of those territories are much disputed. The rhetoric of the ROC merges the idea of the Russian world with the concept of Holy Rus' and presents the latter as the absolute core or backbone of the former.[42] The Russian state leadership, in turn, uses the concept of the Russian World to refer to the 'mental' Russia, or the Russian-speaking diaspora, in a broad but mainly secular sense.[43]

The ROC's view on Slavic unity is not directly connected to the present-day states. Rather, it should be seen as an eschatological view of the lands constituting the Holy Rus' because of their spiritual legacy. Yet, the ROC's perception has conveniently backed the Russian state's power initiatives to support 'Russianness' outside the borders of the Russian Federation—and in the 'near abroad' in particular. In practice, state leadership has maintained rhetoric of 'compatriots' abroad, who together comprise the Russian World, creating and funding specific programmes and institutions to promote this idea since around the mid-2000s. In this

---

[40] Newsru.com. (2001). 'Otkrylsia S"yezd slavianskikh narodov', 1 June, available at: https://www.newsru.com/russia/01jun2001/slavyane.html.

[41] Radio svoboda. (2001). 'Slavianstvo - mif ili real'nost'?', 11 June, available at: https://www.svoboda.org/a/24226413.html.

[42] Suslov (2014), p. 70.

[43] See also Petro, N. N. (2015). Russia's Orthodox Soft Power. Carnegie Council, 23 March, available at: https://www.carnegiecouncil.org/publications/chapters_papers_reports/727.

Also Suslov, M. (2018). '"Russian World" Concept: Post-Soviet Geopolitical Ideology and the Logic of "Spheres of Influence"', *Geopolitics*, 23(2), pp. 330–353, available at: https://doi.org/10.1080/14650045.2017.1407921.

way, the ROC seems a natural anchorage of these ideas, especially since 2012, when Russian state leadership started increasingly to exploit the rhetoric of 'spiritual-moral values' as the basis of national identity.

Subsequently, Orthodoxy has become an important political and geopolitical instrument in both Belarus and Russia. The BOC is a key part of Belarusian domestic and foreign policies. Domestically, the BOC has been a key partner of the state, which slowly but steadily drew it into state projects during 2000s.[44] Belarusian law recognises the BOC's 'determining role' in the development of the spiritual, cultural, and state traditions of Belarus; moreover, the BOC is the only religious institution to receive state subsidies and maintain cooperation agreements with Belarusian state agencies. The choice was politically motivated and primarily stemmed from its ideological utility and the possibility of better control over Orthodox structures. The BOC was also traditionally, alongside the army, among the most trusted public institutions in the country, employing the regime's secular officials who facilitated the steering of the Church agenda.[45]

Patriarch Kirill underlined that the cooperation between church and state in Belarus is unique in the entire post-Soviet space in both its scale and in the level of cooperation.[46] In many areas, a collaboration between the church and the state—a *symphonia*—was established primarily to advance the state's goals. Since 2003, when the BOC and the state signed an agreement on cooperation, followed by a dozen of agreements on cooperation with the church by state ministries and departments, the Church has increasingly been employed in education, memory, and even public politics. The BOC also cooperated with the security structures.[47] According to Aleh Manaeu, the state power actively uses the Orthodox Church not as a factor in spiritual development but rather as an

---

[44] Interview with an activist.

[45] Interview with the priest.

[46] President. (2009). 'Gosudarstvennuiu ideologiiu neobkhodimo stroit' na fundamente khristianskikh tsennostei', 25 September, available at: https://president.gov.by/ru/events/gosudarstvennuju-ideologiju-neobxodimo-stroit-na-fundamente-xristianskix-tsennostej-4877.

[47] Church. (2019). 'Opyt patrioticheskoi deiatel'nosti tserkvi v gody Velikoi Otechestvennoi Voiny i sovremennost', 1 December, available at: http://church.by/pub/opyt-patriotichestkoj-dejatelnosti-cerkvi-v-gody-velikoj-otechestvennoj-vojny-i-sovremennost.

instrument of social control.[48] Lukashenka would regularly meet with the Synod of the BOC, during which he would de facto instruct and present his ideas on Church activities.

The episcopate of the BOC in the 1990s and 2000s consisted almost entirely of former inhabitants of Moscow monasteries and graduates of Russian seminaries. Within the BOC, the conservative movement had a strong following. The idea that Belarusian identity was synonymous with *zapodnorussizm* (Western Russism), and thus a part of the shared culture of all Eastern Slavs, was widely shared. Institutional ties and deepening of contacts only further solidified these ideational bonds.

In the 1990s, the BOC actively backed the regime's reintegration rhetoric and even participated in Pan-Slavic movements, such as the Sobor of Slavic Peoples. Orthodoxy was seen as a defining feature of Pan-Slavism, and the Church actively supported reunification ideas. Belarus was a part of a 'Slavic-Orthodox' civilisation, and any 'sovereignisation' of the country was rejected because a turn to 'provincial' nationalism would lead to a degradation.[49] Hence, the contemporary Belarusian national idea was Orthodox and derived from *zapadnorussizm*, as defined by the bishop Iosif Semashko.[50] Belarusian Pan-Slavic organisations such as the website Zapadrus.su regularly promoted Orthodox values and Orthodox traditions in Belarus, Russia, and Ukraine, and the underlying unity of this religion with the Russian national and imperial ideology.[51]

The BOC's ideological role, however, was not straightforward. During the 2000s, Lukashenko, a self-described 'Orthodox atheist', increasingly instrumentalised the Church as a key ideological partner. The clergy and the Church were increasingly tasked with promoting the regime's agenda, including the legitimisation of the official ideology. In this respect, the official state ideology proclaimed the BOC an ally and a pillar of the state

---

[48] Deutsche Welle. (2010). 'Oleg Manaev: Religioznyi renessans v Belarusi ne privel k smene tsennostei', 7 January, available at: https://www.dw.com/ru/олег-манаев-религиозный-ренессанс-в-беларуси-не-привел-к-смене-ценностей/a-5096412.

[49] Sobor.by. (undated). 'Dve belorusskie natsional'nye idei (katolicheskii natsional-separatizm i pravoslavnaia natsional'naia ideia)', available at: http://sobor.by/zametki.php [Accessed on 13th September 2021].

[50] Sobor.by (undated).

[51] Yeliseyeu, A. and Laputska, V. (2016). Anti-Belarus Disinformation in Russian Media: Trends, Features, Countermeasures. *EAST Media Review*, 1, available at: http://east-center.org/wp-content/uploads/2016/12/EAST-Media-Review.pdf.

ideology, which meant that the BOC should follow the regime's policies and adjust to its changes.

In practice, this put the BOC in a dubious position at times, especially during the deterioration of Belarus-Russia relations. Ideological and integration pressures between Russia and Belarus led to a swift ideological reconstitution in Belarus. For instance, after Russia's annexation of Crimea in 2014, when the Belarusian regime reconsidered its stance towards Moscow-championed ideologies and tried to distance itself from both the Russian World and Eurasianism in its official policies, it also directly affected the remnants of Slavophile ideas in the state ideology. The regime reconsidered the role of Slavic brotherhood and the Orthodox Church and proclaimed a new national idea—statehood.[52] Slavic roots were revised and became the foundation of Belarusian statehood, not the driver of Slavic reintegration. The Kievan Rus' became one of the stages of the country's history, not its defining moment.[53]

The BOC and other actors immediately limited the usage of Slavophile motifs in their official rhetoric. The BOC followed the state's policy of soft Belarusianisation by endorsing a wider usage of the Belarusian language in its documents and practices. The Church clergy changed their narratives and largely repeated the official line that stressed that the Belarusian people were equal to the Russians and had commonalities but also differences, including their own origin in the Polesie region. The Belarusian Orthodox Church was repurposed as a founder and a factor of the independent Belarusian state, rather than another uniting bond with Russia. In September 2016, at a meeting between the President and the Synod of the BOC, Lukashenko stressed, 'I am convinced that our further work will continue to be only constructive and will allow us to coordinate efforts to strengthen society and its spiritual enrichment…. The Church is conservative…[i]t stood and must stand guard over [Belarusian] values and statehood.'[54]

---

[52] Belta. (2019). 'Lukashenko: Belarus' nuzhdaetsia v natsional'noi ideye, kotoruiu podderzhit ves' narod', 1 March 2019, available at: https://www.belta.by/president/view/lukashenko-belarus-nuzhdaetsja-v-natsionalnoj-idee-kotoruju-podderzhit-ves-narod-338501-2019/.

[53] Belarus Segodnia. (2014). 'Chto takoe belorusskaia natsional'naia ideia?', 20 June, available at: https://www.sb.by/chapters/a-khto-tam-idze-165992.html.

[54] Sputnik (2016). 'Lukashenko prizval Sinod BPC', available at: sputnik.by/lukashenko-prizval-sinod-bpc-uvazhat-i-podderzhivat-drugie-konfessii-1025322001.html.

Any dissatisfaction on the part of the Russian Orthodox Church was countered with a veiled threat of autocephaly. For instance, on 16 December 2014, at a meeting of the clergy of the Minsk Metropolitanate, Metropolitan Pavel directly said that the current status looked 'offensive' for Belarusians and that he would 'raise the issue' of granting self-government for the Exarchate.[55] After the experience of Constantinople granting the newly organised Orthodox Church of Ukraine autocephalic status in 2019, resulting in the ROC losing a significant part of its influence abroad, these comments from within the BOC must have resonated strongly among the ROC leadership.

Yet the Belarusian Revolution and the following counterrevolution put a lid on these developments. The Belarusian regime's response reversed the national building process in the country and put an end to Lukashenka's ideational distancing from Moscow,[56] which led immediately to institutional and narrative changes in the Belarusian Orthodox Church. The BOC's discourse was recalibrated to reintroduce Pan-Slavism and combine it with pro-regime political narratives. Slavophile ideas returned to the repertoire of the BOC. Furthermore, as in other social groups and institutions, the BOC underwent a cleansing of 'disloyal' elements and ideological 'enemies'. The supporters of the protests were removed. Metropolitan Pavel, who supported the regime's distancing from Moscow in 2014–2020, was quickly replaced with the Bishop of the Barysau diocese, Veniamin (Tupeko), whose conservative stance made him a natural ally of a new ideological rapprochement with Moscow.

Conclusion

Slavophilia remains vividly present in contemporary Belarusian official discourse. The 'unity of Slavs' remains a powerful rhetorical tool for Lukashenka. The Belarusian Revolution and the Russian war against Ukraine only further increased the importance of 'Slavic' narratives in

---

[55] Perchin (2015).

[56] On the effects of the Belarusian revolution on Belarus-Russia relations, see Moshes, A. and Nizhnikau, R. (2021). 'Forever together? Relations between Moscow and Minsk after the Belarusian revolution of 2020', *PONARS Eurasia*, available at https://www.ponarseurasia.org/forever-together-relations-between-moscow-and-minsk-after-the-belarusian-revolution-of-2020/.

official discourse. The Belarusian regime largely relies on Slavophilia as a supranational project, which should unite three brotherly nations with the maintenance of a degree of political and cultural autonomy.

However, its appeal and relevance remain profoundly limited despite its use by state officials. There are several key factors that explain its limit. First, Slavophilia is an ambivalent concept that has been used both as a tool for excluding Russians from the community of civilised peoples (due to their Asian admixture) and as a justification for the cultural and political dominance of the Great Russians. Both motifs can be found in the intellectual landscape of Belarus, but the idea of the unity of the three East Slavic peoples dominates in the public discourse due to Aliaksandr Lukashenka's constant appeal to it.

Second, it is challenged by rival ideological concepts, which also underline the unity of the Slavic peoples and the role of common history, values, and culture—but under the dominance of the 'Great Russians'. In this regard, the ideological drift of the Belarusian authorities under the influence of a new wave of Eurasianists, for whom Slavophilia is hopelessly outdated, has only accelerated after the Belarusian Revolution and the growing dependence of the regime on Moscow's support. The need to resist the West and defend the Russian World is built into the new geopolitical contour of Eurasia, in which Belarus is the most important outpost on the border with Euro-Atlantic civilisation. The sentimental rhetoric of Slavic unity no longer works under exploding rockets; instead, the stakes are technocratic solutions and the struggle for resources.

Nevertheless, for the regime's domestic and foreign policy manoeuvring, Slavophile ideas have been instrumental, even if their utility has decreased during the integration and ideational conflicts with Russia. Pan-Slavism has remained in state policies, even if most of the Slavophile actors were marginalised in Belarus. The BOC was the only institutional exception. The central place of Orthodoxy in the Slavophile narratives, and the ROC's own perspective on the 'triune people', made the BOC a natural ideological ally to the Slavophiles, even if their ideas overlapped more than they coincided.

On Pan-Slavism, Brotherhood, and Mythology: The Imagery of Contemporary Geopolitical Discourse in Serbia

Dejana Vukasović and Miša Stojadinović

Introduction

Generally used to denote and promote a belief in Slavic unity,[1] the term 'Pan-Slavism' is characterized by a conceptual vagueness that has led to many different manifestations in the imagining of 'Slavic identities'. In this regard, the term Pan-Slavism can be viewed as an 'umbrella term'

---

[1] Cf. Maxwell, A. (2018). 'Effacing Pan Slavism: Linguistic Classification and Historiographic Misrepresentation', *Nationalities Papers*, 46(4), pp. 1–21.

D. Vukasović (✉) · M. Stojadinović
Institute for Political Studies, Belgrade, Serbia
e-mail: dvukcevic@yahoo.fr

M. Stojadinović
e-mail: misa.stojadinovic@ips.ac.rs

embracing myriad Pan-Slavic projects featuring ethnic, cultural, linguistic, confessional, and socio-political heterogeneity.[2]

In this chapter, we seek to analyse the impact of Pan-Slavic ideas on the framing of Serbia's contemporary collective identity. More specifically, we attempt to answer the question of whether, in what ways, and to what extent Serbian political leaders have framed Serbia's foreign policy, and thus also its identity, by mobilizing Pan-Slavic ideas starting from the period of the democratic changes in Serbia initiated in 2000. In so doing, we are focusing on discursive manifestations of Slavic solidarity through the 'special relations' between Serbia and Russia.

This task calls for some clarifications. Firstly, the term 'Pan-Slavism' used in this chapter is understood as a concept denoting the historical tendency of the Slavic peoples 'to manifest in any tangible way, whether cultural or political, their consciousness of ethnic kinship'.[3] In line with this conceptualization of Pan-Slavism, we argue that Pan-Slavic manifestations range from vague expressions of Slavic cultural solidarity to more or less specific programmes for the political unification or regional grouping of multiple Slavic nations. In this chapter, we also suggest that contemporary forms of Pan-Slavism generated by political elites after 1989 do not necessarily have the ambition of creating a greater, formally sovereign Pan-Slavic entity. They can also be viewed as a 'lower intensity sentiment' within Slavic polities today,[4] i.e., as various manifestations of solidarity and unity, based on Slavic ethnocultural kinship. It is this understanding of the term Pan-Slavism that this chapter is based upon.

Secondly, this chapter is oriented towards discursive manifestations of Pan-Slavic ideas through the relationship between Serbia and Russia. It is argued that post-1989 Pan-Slavism has lost its rationale as an instrument for the mass mobilization of Slavic nations and as a tool of legitimizing Soviet hegemony. In the case of Serbia, however, it has continued to exist

---

[2] Suslov, M. (2012). 'Geographical Metanarratives in Russia and the European East: Contemporary Pan-Slavism', *Eurasian Geography and Economics*, 53(5), pp. 575–595; Terzić, S. (2006). 'About Eastern and Western PanSlavism (in the XIX and the Beginning of the XX Century)', *Historical Review*, LIII, pp. 317–332.

[3] Petrovich, B. (1956). *The Emergence of Russian Panslavism 1856–1870*. New York: Columbia University Press.

[4] Cf. Dedominicis, B. (2017). 'Pan-Slavism and Soft Power in Post-Cold War Southeast European International Relations: Competitive Interference and Smart Power in the European Theatre of the Clash of Civilizations', *International Journal of Interdisciplinary Civic and Political Studies*, 12(3), pp. 1–17.

in some forms—not as an articulated ideology but more as a set of new and old myths.[5] This phenomenon is visible through the revival of the 'special relations' with Russia after 1989, which have assumed various discursive manifestations from the 1990s onwards. Hence, this concept is becoming something close to Russophilia, expressed in the discursive construction by political elites of a Serbian-Russian ethnocultural and religious closeness through the concepts of friendship and brotherhood, including solidarity, strong national emotions, mutual sacrifice, etc. It is argued that Pan-Slavic ideas in Serbia are manifested as a mythologized attachment to Russia with different degrees of 'sentiment intensity' depending on the specific context. The focus is on how and to what extent Serbian political elites produce geopolitical knowledge and thus legitimatize brotherly narratives between Serbia and Russia.

Thirdly, the period analysed in this chapter covers turbulent years in Serbian political history that highlight the importance of the impact of Slavic closeness on Serbian-Russian relations. Namely, all Serbian governments after 2000 have reaffirmed EU membership as their key foreign policy goal, showing their commitment to the European integration process and membership in the EU. However, unlike some other European post-communist states which, immediately after the Cold War and regime change, identified themselves with Europe/the EU, Serbia's process of collective identification with the EU is ambiguous, primarily due to its isolation from Europe and the negative 'reputation' built up during the 1990s—as well as being due, at the same time, to a strong emotional attachment to Russia. This isolation has also contributed to the prolongation of the use of Pan-Slavic ideas in Serbian-Russian relations. At the same time, there was also a need for 'a story' about the geopolitically imagined position of Serbia after 2000 as situated between the EU and Russia. Moreover, the contemporary geopolitical context marked by tensions between Russia and the EU amplifies the anxiety among Serbian political elites around their geopolitical imagination of Serbia. In the light of these trends, this chapter attempts to analyse how Serbian political leaders have discursively constructed a 'balance of anxiety' and, more specifically, how they have framed Serbian foreign policy in the contemporary context of East–West confrontation.

---

[5] Perica, V. (2009). 'Sumrak panslavenskih mitova', In: Čolović, I. (ed) *Zid je mrtav, živeli zidovi*, Biblioteka XX vek, Beograd, pp. 303–325.

The chapter draws upon official statements and speeches delivered by the Serbian political elite from 2000 onwards, including by prime ministers, presidents of the Republic, and party leaders. Political elites are understood as 'entrepreneurs of identity'.[6] In the process of promoting change or upholding the status quo, political elites 'are faced with the task of aligning their political goals with national identity in order to gain power and authority to shape collective action'.[7] Thus, as entrepreneurs of identity, political leaders discursively manage the relationship between continuity and change in identity over time, with a view to constructing the future of a nation.

The chapter relies on critical geopolitics and therefore considers geopolitical discourses as being associated with establishing practices of knowledge production.[8] Critical geopolitics highlights the importance of socially constructed geographies as ways of legitimizing foreign policy doctrines.[9] It understands geopolitics as a discourse that produces geopolitical knowledge. Knowledge is closely linked to power: all power requires knowledge, and all knowledge relies upon and reinforces existing power relations.[10] Thus, knowledge cannot be neutral but shapes power relations. Geopolitical discourses, therefore, are not the 'language of truth'

---

[6] Obradović, S. & Howarth, C. (2017). 'The Power of Politics: How Political Leaders in Serbia Discursive Lymanage Identity Continuity and Political Change to Shape the Future of the Nation', *European Journal of Social Psychology*, 48(1), pp. 25–35.

[7] Ibid.

[8] Dalby, S. (1991). 'Critical Geopolitics: Discourse, Difference, and Dissent', *Environment and Planning D: Society and Space*, 1(1), pp. 349–363; Ó Tuathail, G. (1996). *Critical Geopolitics*. London: Routlegde; Ó Tuathail, G. (1998). 'Thinking Critically About Geopolitics', in G Tuathail et al. (eds) *The Geopolitics Reader*. London: Routledge, pp. 1–12; Agnew, J. (2003). *Geopolitics. Revisioning World Politics*. 2nd Edition. London and New York: Routledge; Agnew, J. (2004). 'Is Geopolitics a Word that Should Be Endowed Only with the Meaning It Acquired in the Early Twentieth Century?', *Progress in Human Geography*, 28(5), pp. 634–637; Mamadouh, V. & Dijkink, G. (2006). 'Geopolitics, International Relations and Political Geography: The Politics of Geopolitical Discourse', *Geopolitics*, 11(3), pp. 349–366; Toal, G. (2003). 'Re-asserting the Regional: Political Geography and Geopolitics in World Thinly Known', *Political Geography*, 22(6), pp. 653–655.

[9] Agnew, J. (2003). *Geopolitics. Revisioning World Politics*.

[10] Jackson, R. & Sørensen. G. (2013). 'Post-Positivism in IR', In: Jackson, R. and Sørensen, G., *Introduction to International Relations. Theories and Approaches*. 5th Edition. Oxford: Oxford University Press, p. 235.

but 'seek to establish and assert their own truth'.[11] In other words, geopolitical discourses do not merely describe the world, or transmit statements and speeches, but rather give meaning or make sense of 'geographical reality'. They produce geopolitical knowledge 'to aid the practice of statecraft and further the power of the state'.[12] In this regard, critical geopolitics seeks to reveal the hidden politics of geopolitical knowledge, i.e., to deconstruct the ways in which geopolitical knowledge is created around international crises, actors, and events.[13] It highlights the need for the 'denaturalization' of geopolitical imageries through a critical approach towards the discourses that shape them, i.e., by challenging claims of objectivity and of the independent existence of truth. This chapter is focused on so-called practical geopolitics for the establishment of practices of knowledge production.[14] It examines the geopolitical discourses of the Serbian political elite in order to demonstrate how they socially construct and politically contest the geopolitical positioning of Serbia. In this regard, the chapter sheds light on how the Serbian political elites construct narratives about the Serbian-Russian 'special relationship' by using Pan-Slavic sentiments, how they represent this relationship to explain crisis situations, and how they develop strategies and solutions to these situations.

Academic literature exploring Pan-Slavism and Serbian-Russian relations is, with rare exceptions, almost exclusively focused on the nineteenth century. Some isolated events and periods are especially examined in this

---

[11] Ó Tuathail, G. (1998). 'Thinking Critically About Geopolitics', p. 3.

[12] Ó Tuathail, G. & Agnew, J. (1992). 'Geopolitics and Discourse. Practical Geopolitical Reasoning in American Foreign Policy', *Political Geography*, 11(2), p. 192.

[13] Ó Tuathail, G. (1998). 'Thinking Critically About Geopolitics', p. 3; Ó Tuathail G. (2002). 'Theorizing Practical Geopolitical Reasoning: The Case of the United States' Response to the War in Bosnia', *Political Geography*, 21, p. 603.

[14] Ó Tuathail G. and Dalby, S. (1998). 'Introduction: Rethinking Geopolitics. Towards a Critical Geopolitics', In: Ó Tuathail, G. and Dalby, S. (eds) *Rethinking Geopolitics*. London: Routledge, p. 5.

regard.[15] Despite a plethora of works from different angles on contemporary Serbian-Russian relations from 1990 onwards, those examining the role of Pan-Slavic sentiments in the Serbian-Russian relations of the period featured in this chapter are virtually non-existent, although there are some exceptions.[16] In Serbia, especially in the last 20 years, there has been a 'hyper-production' of books and articles related to Serbian-Russian relations and modern Russian politics and politicians. However, works linking Serbian-Russian relations since the 1990s with Pan-Slavic sentiments are virtually non-existent. Hence, the aim of this chapter is to fill this gap in the existing literature and to draw attention to the importance of this underexplored topic.

The chapter will be structured as follows. First, the mythologization of the Pan-Slavic geopolitical imagination in Serbian-Russian relations will be analysed. More specifically, this section focuses on deeply rooted perceptions of Russian-Serbian closeness, based on historical experience of war alliances, cultural kinship, and their shared Orthodox religion. The chapter then focuses on the period from the disintegration of Yugoslavia until the 2000 democratic changes in Serbia. It is argued that Serbia's 'exceptional' case in the 1990s created fertile ground for a revival of Pan-Slavic ideology through Serbian-Russian relations. The next section is devoted to the period from 2000 down to the present. It is argued that in this period, although it ceased to exist as an ideology, Pan-Slavic sentiments have persisted in the foreign policy discourse of the Serbian political elite through a resurgence of old myths of Slavic solidarity in order to construct the geopolitical 'specificity' of Serbia and to 'balance the anxiety' arising from East–West confrontation.

---

[15] E.g., Milojković Đurić J. (1994). *Pan-Slavism and National Identity in Russia and in the Balkans 1830–1880: Images of Self and Others*. New York: Columbia University Press; MacKenzie, D. (1967). *The Serbs and the Russian Pan-Slavism 1875–1878*. Ithaca: Cornell University Press; Petrovich, B. (1956). *The Emergence of Russian Panslavism*; Vovchenko, D. (2016). *Containing Balkan Nationalism: Imperial Russia and Ottoman Christians 1856–1914*. Oxford University Press; Kohn, H. (1960) *Pan-Slavism, Its History and Ideology*. New York: Vintage Books; Terzić, S. (2006). 'About Eastern and Western PanSlavism (in the XIX and the Beginning of the XX Century)'.

[16] Perica, V. (2009). 'Sumrak panslavenskih mitova'; Cohen, L. (1994). 'Russia and the Balkans: Panslavism, Partnership and Power', *International Journal*, 49(4), pp. 814–845; Vujačić, V. (2015). *Nationalism, Myth, and the State in Russia and Serbia*. New York: Cambridge University Press.

The Mythologization of the 'Brotherhood' Between Serbia and Russia

Historically, Pan-Slavic ideas in Serbia and Russia have not had a common focus; while Russian Pan-Slavism was primarily directed against Germany, Serbian Pan-Slavism was always more tied up with anti-Ottoman sentiments.[17] The Pan-Slavic 'traditional friendship' between Serbia and Russia can thus be regarded as the spreading of Russian Pan-Slavism, which emerged under the specific geopolitical context of the Balkan states striving to free themselves from Ottoman occupation. For Serbian political leaders under Ottoman rule, the Slavic idea was constructed in terms of support and help from Russia in their efforts to liberate themselves from foreign occupation. In their imagery, this was a 'special relationship' based on the cultural kinship and closeness between the two Slavic Orthodox nations. Throughout almost all the nineteenth century, Russia was perceived as Serbia's protector and patron in the Ottoman Empire. Moreover, this specific context enabled the construction of the relationship between Russia and Serbia around the concept of brotherhood, representing Russia as a 'powerful elder brother' who protected a smaller and weaker sibling. Thus, closeness between the two nations was constructed on an idea of a special relationship creating a meaningful, natural, almost-familial link between the two nations extending beyond formal diplomacy and realpolitik.[18]

On the other hand, the Russian Pan-Slavic ideology was constructed on the primacy of Russia among Slavic nations, and on their unity under its protection.[19] This was in line with the constructed picture of Russia as leader of an awakened Slavism in the geopolitical imagery of nineteenth-century Serbian political elites. Russia was constructed as a 'patron' (from the Latin *patronus*, 'protector'), enabling the construction of a metaphorical kinship between Serbia and Russia, i.e., a treatment of non-blood relations as kin, with all the duties, obligations, and expectations that

---

[17] Andersen, M. (2000). 'Russia and the Former Yugoslavia', In: Webber, M. (ed) *Russia and Europe. Conflict or Cooperation*. London: Macmillan, p. 183.

[18] Cf. Pierzynska, J. (2020). 'With a Little Help from New Friend? Ideas of International Brotherhood in Postcommunist Contexts', *Europe-Asia Studies*, 72(9), pp. 1554–1576.

[19] Petrovich, B. (1956). *The Emergence of Russian Panslavism 1856–1870*, p. 103.

entails.[20] Such imagined and fictional kinship is devoid of any claims to shared ancestry. At the same time, it also implies hierarchy, as reflected in the construction of Russia's historical development and its great power politics as being of great significance for the determination of the fate of small or otherwise disadvantaged states (e.g., Serbia). This patronage is well explained in the *Epistle from Moscow to the Serbs* written by Alexis Khomiakov in 1860:

> Let it be permitted to us, your brethren, who love you with profound and sincere love and who are spiritually pained at the very thought of any evil befalling you, to turn to you with some warnings and counsels (…) we are older than you in recorded history. We have passed through more varied if not more difficult trials than you.[21]

Closeness to Russia was also significant in cultural and religious terms: cultural closeness connected to a shared Byzantine heritage led to this patron relationship with and closeness to a Russia viewed as an empire linked to the Orthodox Christian peoples of the Balkans.[22] At the same time, Serbian society of that period was largely traditional, strongly influenced by patriarchal values, and 'burdened' by the past and deeply rooted myths.[23] Traditionally, Serbian people have perceived Russia as culturally civilizationally akin to Serbia. This is also due to the intense cooperation between the Serbian and Russian Orthodox Churches since the Middle Ages.

---

[20] Neumann, I. et al. (2018). 'Kinship in International Relations: Introduction and Framework', In: Haugevik K. and Neumann, I. B. (eds) *Kinship in International Relations*. London: Routledge.

[21] Petrovich, B. (1956). *The Emergence of Russian Panslavism 1856–1870*, p. 99.

[22] Petrović D. (2020). 'Russia and the Serbs (Serbia) from the Eastern Question to the Contemporary Relations', In: Stojanović, B. and Ponomareva, E. (eds) *Russia and Serbia in the Contemporary World: Bilateral Relations, Challenges and Opportunities*. Beograd: Institute of International Politics and Economics, p. 99.

[23] Varga, B. (2016). 'Beograd i Kijev izmedu Brisela i Moskve', In: *Politika srpskog identiteta: Antizapadnjatvo, rusofilstvo, tradicionalizam*. Beograd: Helsinški odbor za ljudska prava u Srbiji, pp. 163–203; Samardžić, N. (2018). 'Ruski mit u srpskoj istoriji', *Danas*, viewed 03. March 2018, https://www.danas.rs/nedelja/ruski-mit-u-srpskoj-istoriji/.

The domination of an emotional approach to politics based on stereotypes and myths is one of the constants of the Serbian political mentality.[24] The 'feeling' of political proximity between Serbia and Russia—personalized in the spreading of myths of a 'centuries-old friendship', 'Slavic and Orthodox brotherhood', and the 'traditional historical ties' of the Serbian and Russian people—led to the creation by nineteenth-century political elites of a notion of Russia as the 'protector' of the Serbs. This tendency towards the mythologization of historical experiences of solidarity, strong national emotions, and a common 'fate'(such as mutual sacrifice/struggle, similar injustice, etc.) has allowed for the persistence and (re)interpretation of Pan-Slavic ideas about Serbian-Russian relations in the discourse of the Serbian political elites over time. Mythical narrations of the past serve as discursive resources for the present. Mythology enables the construction of narratives that give meaning to concrete political actions.

The strength of a political myth is that it is rooted in 'common sense', as something that has always been because it is so normal.[25] As George Schöpflin notes, myths are based on 'perception rather than historically validated truth about the ways in which communities regard certain propositions as normal and natural and others as perverse and alien'.[26] A successful political myth is, as Vincent Della Sala rightly stresses, 'one that is rooted in a historical experience but is vague enough so that it can continue to serve the purposes for which it was devised'.[27] Hence, historical narratives are to be presented as 'found' in events rather than placed there by narrative techniques, and they cannot 'be closed' with the end of the events to be narrated. As Hayden White argues, 'the demand for

---

[24] Jovanović, M. (2010a). 'Two Russias: On the Two Dominant Discourses of Russia in the Serbian Public', In: Ž Petrović (ed) *Russia Serbia Relations at the Beginning of the XXI Century*, Belgrade: ISAC Fund, p. 13.

[25] Della Sala, V. (2010). 'Political Myth, Mythology and the European Union', *Journal of Common Market Studies*, 48(1), p. 9.

[26] Schöpflin, G. (1997). 'The Functions of Myth and a Taxonomy of Myths', in Geoffrey Hosking, Georg Schöpflin (eds.), *The Myths of Nationhood*, New York: Routledge, p. 19.

[27] Della Sala, V. (2010). 'Political Myth, Mythology and the European Union', p. 8.

closure (…) is a demand for moral meaning'.[28] In other words, a moral judgement of events is the principal force of narratives in political myths.

The myth of a heroic tradition of struggle is one of the most important elements of the traditional Serbian national identity. The idea of the heroism and conscious self-sacrifice of the Serbian people in the face of an invincible enemy is deeply rooted in the Serbian collective consciousness.[29] During the creation of the Serbian state in the nineteenth century, this myth represented a mixture of longstanding Serbian Orthodox Church mythology and nineteenth-century Serbian national history.[30] Thus, the mythical narrative of shared sacrifice, struggle, injustice, and heroism that was constructed between Serbia and Russia in the nineteenth century enabled the birth of Pan-Slavic sentiments and drove the political activity of the Serbian political elite towards Russia in their fight for independence from the Ottoman Empire.

Russian 'brotherly patronage' towards Serbia lasted until the major political turning point of 1878, when following the Treaty of San Stefano and the Berlin Congress, Serbia gained independence from the Ottoman Empire. At the same time, due to the 'Westernization' of the Serbian political elite, the importance of Russian Pan-Slavism began to fade. This was followed by the Russian reorientation of patronage towards Bulgaria, leaving Serbia to the Austrian sphere of influence.[31] Political proximity between Serbia and Russia was rebuilt during the twentieth century on very different and diffuse foundations, explained in a stereotypical manner as the political ties between the two states during World War I, or as political and ideological empathy between the regimes ruling during the Cold War.[32] Pan-Slavic sentiments were absent from the discourse of the

---

[28] White, H. (1980). 'The Value of Narrativity in the Representation of Reality', *Critical Inquiry*, 7(1), p. 24.

[29] Vujačić, V. (2015). *Nationalism, Myth, and the State in Russia and Serbia*, op.cit., p. 137.

[30] Savić, B. (2014). 'Where Is Serbia? Traditions of Spatial Identity and State Positioning in Serbian Geopolitical Culture', *Geopolitics*, 19(3), p. 691.

[31] Jovanović, M. (2010a). 'Two Russias: On the Two Dominant Discourses of Russia in the Serbian Public', p. 16.

[32] Jovanović, M. (2010b). 'In the Shadow of Gas and Politics: Cultural and Spiritual Contacts, Connections and Cooperation Between Serbia and Russia', In: Petrović, Ž. (ed) *Russia Serbia Relations at the Beginning of the XXI Century*, Belgrade: ISAC Fund, p. 184.

Serbian political elite until the end of World War II, only to be reawakened by Stalin's decision to establish the Pan-Slavic Congress as a centre of the new Pan-Slav movement,[33] along with the perception by Stalin of Yugoslavs as the 'second-ranking Slav nation' and, consequently, with the movement of the centre of the Congress from Moscow to Belgrade. The Pan-Slavic sentiment was well described in Marshal Tito's speech at the Sixth Congress in Belgrade:

> What would have happened if the glorious Red Army had not existed? What would have happened if this state of workers and peasants with Stalin, the man of genius, at its head, had not existed, which stood like a wall against fascist aggression and which with innumerable sacrifices and rivers of blood also liberated our Slav nations in other countries? For this great sacrifice which our brothers in the great Soviet Union made, we other Slavs thank them.[34]

This statement constructs the 'brothers from the Soviet Union' as protectors of other Slavs, up to their self-sacrifice and deaths in the liberation of Slavs from fascist aggression. However, this vision of Pan-Slavic ideology was also constructed around solidarity on an ethnic and cultural basis, without being tied to a particular imperial force. Thus, after Tito on 28 June 1948 openly rejected the Soviet Union's narrative that the Slav peoples could not preserve their independence without Russia's protection, and the resultant rift between him and Stalin marked the end of Yugoslav-Soviet Pan-Slavic solidarity, this was replaced by Pan-Russism, imposing Russian predominance and leadership not only on Slavic peoples but also on Hungarians, Romanians, Uzbeks, and Caucasians.[35] On the other hand, Titoist Yugoslavism was created, which can be regarded as having some Pan-Slavic characteristics, such as its concepts of brotherhood and unity (*'bratstvo i jedinstvo'*) and the adoption as the national anthem of a modified version of 'one of the hallmarks of nineteenth-century Pan-Slavism, the Slovak song *"Hej, Slované"* ("Hey, Slavs!")'.[36] At the same time, however, the Yugoslav political elites led by Tito

---

[33] Kohn, H. (1960). *Pan-Slavism, Its History and Ideology*, p. 305.

[34] Ibid., p. 306.

[35] Ibid., pp. 309–310.

[36] Perica, V. (2002). *Balkan Idols: Religion and Nationalism in Yugoslav States*. New York: Oxford University Press, p. 102.

promoted a new form of socialist identity, based on a 'third way' between the East and the West and focusing exclusively on the Yugoslav nations, while neglecting cultural connections with both the East and the West and developing a new collective identity that derived less from Pan-Slavic ideas.[37]

'Brotherhood' vs. 'Westernization' in the 1990s

The erosion of communist regimes after 1989 created a void in (South)Eastern Europe which was to be filled with alternative ideologies and revitalized religions.[38] Although Pan-Slavism had lost its rationale as an instrument for the mass mobilization of Slavic nations and as a tool for legitimizing Soviet hegemony after 1989, the 'exceptionalism' of Serbia proved fertile ground for a reawakening of Pan-Slavic ideology.

Unlike other East European countries, Serbia was an 'exceptional' example of a country in which the former communist elite managed to preserve essential elements of institutional and ideological continuity with the old system.[39] Also, and unlike in other cases of state disintegration (i.e., the Soviet Union, Czechoslovakia), the breakup of the Yugoslav Federation within and among Yugoslavia's successor states erupted in violence and led to civil war. In these specific circumstances, the regime of the 1990s led by Slobodan Milošević undertook the process of re-identifying with the myth of the heroic struggle of the Serbian people. The reactivation of national traditions and mythologies and the invocation of powerful external threats were at the heart of the Milošević regime's geopolitical discourse. The monopolization of discourse through the mass media went hand in hand with the creation of an impression of continuity between past conflicts and the current ones,[40] enabling the political

---

[37] Schwärzler, M. and Zimmermann, T. (2020). 'Construction of Brotherhood and Unity in Czechoslovakia and Yugoslavia After 1945: The Illustrated Magazines Československo and Jugoslavija', In: Zimmermann, T. and Jakir, A. (eds) *Remembering War and Peace in Southeast Europe in the 20th Century*. Split: Sveučilište u Splitu, Filozofski fakultet, pp. 101–108.

[38] Perica, V. (2009). 'Sumrak panslavenskih mitova', p. 304.

[39] Vujačić, V. (2004). 'Reexamining the 'Serbian Exceptionalism' Thesis', *Working Paper*, pp. 1–43, accessed 17 November 2020, https://escholarship.org/uc/item/1mg8f31q#author, pp. 1–2.

[40] Ibid., p. 15.

elite to become the defender of the 'national dignity' of the Serbs by re-mythologizing old legends and historical facts. At first, Slobodan Milošević's regime did not perceive the West as a threatening Other. It held a geopolitical perception of Serbia as a rampart and bastion of European civilization.[41] In his 1989 speech occasioned by the commemoration of the 600th anniversary of the battle in Kosovo, Milošević stated that in Kosovo, the Serbs had not only defended themselves but all of Europe as well. Therefore, anti-Europeanism was not at the heart of Milošević's policy; Serbia had always been in Europe, but it should remain so on its own terms.[42] However, after the 'disillusionment' with the policies of Serbia's old Western allies, which resulted in Serbia's international isolation, the old idea of Russia as the only great power protector of the Balkan Orthodox Slavs resurged.[43] In these circumstances, it was 'only natural' to turn towards Russia and mythologize the brotherhood between the two nations. Pan-Slavic ideas in this case performed the role of ideology: an ideological connection between the two 'brotherly socialist states' was constructed,[44] juxtaposing the Slavic world and its unity with the West. Thus, Serbia's identity was constructed around a discourse representing NATO, the United States, and other Western organizations in terms of negative identity formation, as opponents of Pan-Slavic solidarity and as ideologically anti-Yugoslav, i.e., anti-Serbian. In this geopolitical imagining, Serbia's role was conceived as the final defensive wall in the Western campaign against Russia,[45] which 'naturally' implied support and help from brotherly Russia for Serbian nationalist politics in order to re-establish a centralized Yugoslav federation.

[41] Savić, B. (2014). 'Where Is Serbia? Traditions of Spatial Identity and State Positioning in Serbian Geopolitical Culture', p. 699.

[42] Vujačić, V. (2004). 'Reexamining the 'Serbian Exceptionalism' Thesis', p. 31.

[43] Ibid., p. 10.

[44] Vukšić, D. (2008). 'Political-Military Relations Between the Republic of Serbia and the Russian Federation in the Process of Dismemberment of Yugoslavia', *Monitoring Russia Serbia Relations*. Belgrade: ISAC Fund, p. 62.

[45] As stated by Vojislav Šešelj, President of the Serbian Radical Party (SRS) and former Vice President of the government of the Republic of Serbia headed by Mirko Marjanović in 1998: 'The Serbs are persistently putting up resistance and defending their homeland. And Russia is sleeping. We are defending Russia as well, and trying to awake it at the same time' (Jovanović 2010, p. 17).

Anti-Westernism became a powerful tool in the geopolitical imagination of Serbia. On one hand, history was not simply equated with historical analogies that connected Serbia and Russia, but rather it was also interpreted as a fatalistic force with an inexplicable power to repeat itself, enabling different manifestations of the victimization of Serbia and the essentialization of Serbian-Russian relations. On the other hand, the concept of brotherhood generally made it possible to 'address' the marginalization of the brotherly nations. Thus, Serbian geopolitical 'exceptionalism' was constructed around the spatialized linkage between smallness, heroism, and victimhood. In this regard, the concept of smallness was linked to a self-image of strength and greatness in the Serbian geopolitical imagination.[46]

The power of Pan-Slavic ideas gained momentum during the NATO bombing campaign on the Federal Republic of Yugoslavia (FRY) in 1999. The Milošević regime appealed to Pan-Slavic sympathies in Moscow for support regarding Kosovo, emphasizing Slavic unity and solidarity.[47] NATO's military action against the FRY was perceived as an act of aggression by the powerful 'West', while NATO itself was constructed as immoral, brutal, and unjust, the threatening Other that jeopardized the country's pursuit of a peaceful solution to the conflict in Kosovo. The dichotomy between 'us' and 'them' was constructed through a narration of a foreign (Western) enemy endangering the FRY's greatest values of freedom and independence.

At the same time, the narrative of resistance against a foreign (NATO) enemy was interpreted as an act of solidarity and unity with Russia. Russia came as the natural stronger brother, ready to defend its weaker sibling. The essentialization of the concept of brotherhood between Serbia and Russia created the 'truth' about Serbia as a 'last line of defence' against 'Western' domination. This 'sentiment' was put forward by the Yugoslav Parliament, which voted on 12 April 1999 for Serbia to join the Union of Russia and Belarus, and the Russian Duma decided on it positively four

---

[46] Cf., Savić, B. (2014). 'Where Is Serbia? Traditions of Spatial Identity and State Positioning in Serbian Geopolitical Culture', p. 688.

[47] Dedominicis, B. (2017). 'Pan-Slavism and Soft Power in Post-Cold War Southeast European International Relations: Competitive Interference and smart power in the European theatre of the clash of civilizations', pp. 1–17.

days afterwards.[48] The Pan-Slavic impulse and the imagination of Serbia as important for the 'common Slavic cause' was further reinforced by the visit to Belgrade in April 1999 of the Belarusian President Aleksandr Lukashenko, who, as Mikhail Suslov points out, 'has always positioned himself as a standard-bearer of Pan-Slavism via the political project of the Union of Russia and Belarus'.[49] The current president of Serbia, Aleksandar Vučić declared during Lukashenko's visit to Belgrade in 2019 that his prior visit during the NATO bombing in 1999 was 'a visit to brothers and friends' and that his visit 'will never be forgotten'.[50]

Imagined as a 'brotherly space' among socialist countries, the Union of Serbia, Russia, and Belarus was a clear testimony of the 'highest degree of intensity' of Pan-Slavic sentiments, with the creation of some kind of mini-variant of the USSR. However, as Dušan Reljić points out, this initiative 'survived only on paper because none of the participants made any effort to achieve its great intentions'.[51] More importantly, the Russian political elite was suspicious of this Serbian initiative, and President Yeltsin eventually blocked the decision on Serbia's joining the Union of Russia and Belarus. Russia's anxieties over Kosovo were related to the use of force employed by NATO, which meant the scaling down of diplomatic efforts and concrete Russian participation.[52] Therefore, Russia asserted itself as an inevitable actor in the process of diplomatic mediation aiming to resolve the Kosovo issue (Chernomyrdin's shuttle missions). At the same time, Russia clearly stated that it would not be dragged into a conflict in the Balkans. As stated by Vladimir Putin, then-Secretary of the Russian Security Council, Russia could not 'engage in any military action [...] in its present state'.[53] In a similar vein, Viktor Chernomyrdin, when explaining his motives for involvement in the diplomatic effort, argued

---

[48] Suslov, M. (2012). 'Geographical Metanarratives in Russia and the European East: Contemporary Pan-Slavism', p. 580.

[49] Ibid., p. 576.

[50] BETA. (2019). 'Vučić sa Lukašenkom: Vaša poseta tokom bombardovanja nikada neće biti zaboravljena', accessed 3 December 2019, https://beta.rs/vesti/politika-vesti-srbija/120120-vucic-sa-lukasenkom-vasa-poseta-tokom-bombardovanja-nikada-nece-biti-zaboravljena.

[51] Reljić, D. (2009). *Rusija i zapadni Balkan*. Beograd: ISAC Foundation, p. 7.

[52] Andersen, M. (2000). 'Russia and the Former Yugoslavia', p. 199.

[53] Ibid., pp. 202–203.

that Russia 'stood by Serbia in 1914, but lost seven million people in WWI as a result'.[54]

After the end of NATO bombing and the signing of the Kumanovo Agreement on 9 June 1999, a battalion of Russian parachutists were the first to enter Priština and take over the airport, in spite of the impending NATO deployment. The arrival of the Russians gave the Serbian people hope that the fraternal help, expected during the NATO bombing, had finally arrived.[55] Welcoming ceremonies for the arrival of the Russian soldiers had been organized all over Serbia. As Vidosav Stojanović notes, 'The Serbs from Priština greeted the Russians like an army of liberation; they threw flowers at them, jumped on the tanks, and kissed their Eastern brothers'.[56] Finally, Russian troops agreed to withdraw without claiming an independent peacekeeping zone in Kosovo.[57]

'BROTHERHOOD' AND/OR 'EUROPEANIZATION' FROM THE 2000S

In September 2000, the Democratic Opposition of Serbia (DOS) won the election against Slobodan Milošević's regime. The political changes in Serbia after 5 October 2000 marked a break with the wars and isolation of the 1990s and the beginning of the country's democratic transition and integration. In this new context, continuity and change can be traced in the discursive construction, understanding, and interpretation of the special relationship with Russia as part of Serbia's geopolitical imagination.

The priority of the first pro-Western government, with Zoran Đinđić at its helm, was the country's democratization and Europeanization and the promotion of ties with the US and the EU, which opened the way,

---

[54] Ibid., p. 203.

[55] Politika. (2020). 'Rusi držali "Slatinu" pod kontrolom i pre dolaska padobranaca', viewed 12 June 2020, https://www.politika.rs/scc/clanak/456067/Drustvo/Rusi-drzali-Slatinu-pod-kontrolom-i-pre-dolaska-padobranaca.

[56] Stojanovic, V. (2004). *Milosevic: The People's Tyrant*. London and New York: I.B. Tauris, p. 167.

[57] Dević, A. (2019). 'The Eurasian Wings of Serbia: Serbian Affinities of the Russian Radical Right', In: Perry, V. (ed) *Extremism and Violent Extremism in Serbia: 21st Century Manifestations of an Historical Challenge*. Hannover: Columbia University Press, pp. 109–138; Reljić, D. (2009). *Rusija i zapadni Balkan*.

following the 2003 Thessaloniki European Council, towards its European integration, leading to the conclusion of the Stabilization and Association agreement (SAA) with the EU in 2008.[58] In parallel with this convergence with the EU, Serbia's political elite intensified its cooperation with NATO, which in December 2006 resulted in Serbia's membership in NATO's Partnership for Peace Program.

Đinđić's framing of Serbia was constructed around the West and Europe as an opposition to the pre-modern past of Serbia. As he put it, 'We want European structures and standards to become part of our society and for our state to become an equal member of the European community of values. Our task is to affirm European values everywhere we act, and to prepare the country for a true European integration'. Hence, notions of 'Europe-as-identity' and 'Europe-as-EU' were merged into one, a democratic polity where a democratic Serbia should secure its place.[59] Europe, as the desired end-goal of a democratic Serbia, was premised on the compatibility of Serbia's identity with Europe's.[60]

Soon, however, Serbia's 'return to Europe' found itself at stake. After Đinđić's assassination in 2003, the new government (2004–2008) headed by Vojislav Koštunica and the Democratic Party of Serbia (DSS) advanced national-conservative lines in its foreign policy discourse.[61] Although

---

[58] Vukčević, D. (2008). 'Srbija i pridruživanje Evropskoj uniji-značaj političkog dijaloga', in Subotić, M. and Đurić, Ž. (eds) *Srbija- politički i institucionalni izazovi*. Beograd: Institut za političke studije, pp. 235–246; Vukčević, D. (2013). *Evropska unija kao strateški akter. Teorija i praksa bezbednosne i odbrambene politike*. Beograd: Institut za političke studije.

[59] Kostovicova, D. (2004). 'Post-Socialist Identity, Territoriality and European Integration: Serbia's Return to Europe After Milošević', *GeoJournal*, 61, p. 24; Vukčević, D. (2013). 'Effects of the Socialization Process on Europeanization of EU Member States' National Identities', in Petrović, P. and Radaković, M. (eds) *National and European Identity in the Process of European Integration*. Beograd: Institut za međunarodnu politiku i privredu, pp. 41–54.

[60] Vukčević, D. and Stojadinović, M. (2011). 'Proces proširenja EU: koncept «prelivanja»', *Srpska politička misao*, 34(4), pp. 131–152; Vukasović, D. and Stojadinović, M. (2016). 'Srbija između evropskih i evroazijskih integracija', In: Milošević, Z. (ed) *Srbija i evroazijski savez, prijetnje*. Šabac: Centar akademske reči, pp. 252–264; Stojadinović, M. and Đurić Ž. (2017). *Politički mitovi neoliberalizma*. Beograd: Institut za političke studije; Stojadinović, M. (2014). *Noam Čomski i savremeno društvo*. Beograd: Institut za političke studije.

[61] Radeljić, B. (2004). 'The Politics of (No) Alternatives in Post-Milošević Serbia', *Journal of Balkan and Near Eastern Studies*, 16(2), pp. 243–259; Radeljić, B. (2019).

relations with Russia were only sporadic in the first years of the pro-democratic government, the 'Kosovo issue' led to the resurgence of the concept of brotherhood between the two countries in shaping a policy context that enabled Serbia to oppose the recognition of Kosovo's independence, despite external pressures from the West.[62]

Relations between Serbia and the EU were ambiguous (at least until 2008 and the arrival of the pro-European ruling coalition) for several reasons. First, after the fall of Slobodan Milošević's regime, key Serbian political parties were unable to agree about the issue of EU integration, either opposing it entirely, like the conservative politicians who presented Europe as 'anti-Serbian' (Serbian Radical Party-SRS), or refusing to give it the 'status of priority', which resulted in a lack of commitment to Europe as the foundational state identity.[63] On numerous occasions, Vojislav Koštunica himself as Prime Minister expressed anti-Western attitudes, especially regarding NATO bombing and cooperation with the ICTY, using nationalist rhetoric and boycotting progress towards EU integration. Second, the traumatic memory of NATO bombing in 1999, as narrated by the Milošević regime, was also endorsed by Koštunica's government, which incorporated it into the very identity of the Serbian state. Third, there was perception of a deeply rooted closeness between Serbia and Russia as expressed through ethnic kinship, cultural proximity, and a shared Orthodox religion. As a consequence, and unlike in other Central and South-eastern European countries, EU integration in Serbia has never been a 'straight line' but rather has had its ups and downs, ranging from direct confrontation and rejection to enthusiasm and cooperation.[64]

Serbian domestic and foreign policy after 2000 remained largely dominated by the Kosovo issue. A few months after internationally brokered

'Russia and Serbia: Between Brotherhood and Self-Serving Agendas', *ENC Analysis*, European Neighborhood Council, EU; Radeljić, B (2019). 'Tolerating Semi-Authoritarianism? Contextualising the EU's Relationship with Serbia and Kosovo', In: Džankić, J. et al. (eds) *The Europeanisation of the Western Balkans*. Springer Nature, pp.157–180.

[62] Marciacq, F. (2019). 'Serbia: Looking East, Going West?', In: Bieber, F. and Tzifakis, N. (eds) *The Western Balkans in the World*. London: Routledge, pp. 61–82.

[63] Stojić, M. (2018). *Party Responses to the EU in the Western Balkans*. Cham: Palgrave Macmillan; Subotić, J. (2010). 'Explaining Difficult States: The Problems of Europeanization in Serbia', *East European Politics and Societies*, 24(4), pp. 595–616.

[64] Ristić, I. (2009). 'Serbia's EU Integration Process: The Momentum of 2008', *Panoeconomicus*, 56(1), p. 115.

negotiations on the final status of Kosovo failed, leading to a unilateral declaration of independence by the Kosovo assembly on 17 February 2008, the Stabilization and Association Agreement (SAA) was concluded between Serbia and the EU. Soon, however, the signing of the SAA was discursively constructed by the Serbian government as a concession not only to strengthen reformist forces and the process of Europeanization, but also to pressure the Serbian government into recognizing Kosovo.[65] Nationalist, Eurosceptic notes were observable in the discourse of Prime Minister Koštunica, gradually strengthening towards the end of his term as prime minister, particularly after Kosovo's declaration of independence in 2008.[66] Addressing the protest rally in Belgrade occasioned by the unilateral declaration of Kosovo's independence, he stated,

> For as long as the State of Serbia exists, we will not recognize what was created by violating the principles on which the civilized world rests. We are not alone in that struggle. The Serbian people will not forget the friendship and unwavering support that President Putin, as head of the Russian state, has extended to Serbia.[67]

At the same time, Koštunica discursively linked the questions of Kosovo and EU membership, and thus enabled the construction of an incompatibility between Serbia's political and historical past (Kosovo status) and its potential future (EU membership). The Kosovo issue was constructed as the essence of the Serbian state, justifying rejection of the demands made by the EU.[68] At the same time, the collective identity narrative about the traumatic NATO bombing as an act of aggression translated into a policy of military neutrality.[69] On 26 December

---

[65] Subotić, J. (2010). 'Explaining Difficult States: The Problems of Europeanization in Serbia', p. 607.

[66] Savić, B. (2014). 'Where Is Serbia? Traditions of Spatial Identity and State Positioning in Serbian Geopolitical Culture', p. 710.

[67] *Serbian Orthodox Church* (2008). 'The Promise Is Given, Kosovo Is Serbia as Long as We Live', accessed 25 February 2008, http://www.spc.rs/eng/promise_given_kosovo_serbia_long_we_live.

[68] Obradović, S. and Howarth, C. (2017). 'The Power of Politics: How Political Leaders in Serbia Discursive Lymanage Identity Continuity and Political Change to Shape the Future of the Nation', pp. 25–35.

[69] Ejdus, F. (2014). 'Beyond National Interests: Identity Conflict and Serbia's Neutrality Towards the Crisis in Ukraine', *Südosteuropa*, 62(3), pp. 348–362.

2007, the National Assembly of Serbia adopted the Resolution on Protection of Sovereignty, Territorial Integrity and Constitutional Order, which was not, however, further elaborated in any of the strategic documents adopted later,[70] allowing for differing interpretations in different geopolitical contexts. In this very particular context, the adoption of the Resolution on Military Neutrality was primarily meant, as Filip Ejdus points out, 'to be a message of friendship to Moscow, from which Belgrade expected support in its legal and diplomatic battle to preserve its virtual sovereignty over Kosovo'.[71]

It is possible to trace some elements of continuity and change in the (Pan-)Slavic sentiments behind the Serbian-Russian relationship in the discourse of the Serbian political elite from the period 2004–2008. On the one hand, anti-Westernism represents a continuity with the discourse of the Serbian political elite under Slobodan Milošević. The question of Kosovo's independence was highlighted as an issue putting the country's territorial integrity at risk, inspiring ethnonational(ist) sentiments that created an environment conducive to the construction of an external, i.e., 'Western' threat. On the other hand, the 2004–2008 government revived old myths about the historical experiences of Slavic solidarity, strong national emotions, and mutual sacrifice and struggle, especially the historical debt to Russia for its centuries-long efforts to support Serbia's statehood, church, and people.[72] By stating that 'Serbia cannot exist

---

[70] Ejdus, F. (2014). 'Serbia's Military Neutrality: Origins, Effects and Challenges', *Croatian International Relations Review*, 20(71), pp. 43–69; Vukasović, D. and Mirović Janković A. (2016). 'Vojna neutralnost Srbije u kontekstu evro-atlantskih integracijać', In: Milošević, Z. (ed) *Srbija i evroazijski savez, prijetnje*. Šabac: Centar akademske reči, pp.173–188; Stojadinović, M. (2009). 'Srbija pred izazovima', *Srpska politička misao*, 25(3), pp. 213–230; Stojadinović, M. (2012). *Potraga za identitetom*. Beograd: IPS; Đurić, Ž. and Stojadinović, M. (2018). 'Država i neoliberalni modeli urušavanja nacionalnih političkih institucija', *Srpska politička misao*, 56(4), pp. 41–57; Stojadinović, M. (2019). 'Izazovi malih i srednjih država u multipolarnom svetu', *Srpska politička misao*, 64(2), pp. 125–138; Stojadinović, M. (2020). 'Urušavanje demokratije i rađanje neoimperijalnog tipa građanina', *Srpska politička misao*, 67(1), pp. 61–77; Stojadinović, M. (2012). 'Demokratija i,vrli novi svet', *Srpska politička misao*, 38(4), pp. 121–143.

[71] Ejdus, F. (2014). 'Serbia's Military Neutrality: Origins, Effects and Challenges', p. 51.

[72] Savić, B. (2014). 'Where Is Serbia? Traditions of Spatial Identity and State Positioning in Serbian Geopolitical Culture', p. 710.

without Russia',[73] Prime Minister Koštunica not only re-established the old myth of Russia as Serbia's patron but also constructed specific biopolitical bonds between the two countries.[74] Thus, the historical Russian Pan-Slavic mission was revived—reflected in a romanticized image of Russia as Serbia's older and stronger brother, ready to protect Serbia based on family ties—and liberated from formal diplomacy. Russia was equated with the romanticized picture of nineteenth-century Russia and its historical Pan-Slavic mission, making it in that way inherently pro-Serbian and thus the guardian of Serbia. Under this concept, Russia was Serbia's only 'way' for economic development and the preservation of Kosovo within its borders.

This discursive construction of Serbian-Russian relations went hand in hand with the internal economic and political consolidation of Russia under Yeltsin's successor, Vladimir Putin, who charted a conservative course of Russian historical traditionalism and interventionism. Russian opposition to the 'Western consensus' on Kosovo independence was an illustration of a new, more assertive Russia, ready to challenge Western initiatives, particularly when they touched upon sensitive issues such as military intervention or Russian domestic politics, including its new pan-Orthodox ambitions.[75] At the same time, Russian backing of Serbia was perceived by the Serbian government as 'natural' and 'self-evident', as a result of the imagined existence of special 'bonds' between the two states. Reacting to the signing of the Energy Treaty, Koštunica stated,

> With Serbia as a political and economic partner in the Balkans, Russia has a loyal ally in the heart of Europe, reaffirming its position as a key global player. The pipeline deal may also boost Russia's influence as energy supplier to the continent.[76]

---

[73] Vesti. (2011). 'Koštunica: Srbija ne može bez Rusije', accessed 23. September 2011, https://arhiva.vesti-online.com/Vesti/Srbija/166659/Kostunica-Srbija-ne-moze-bez-Rusije.

[74] Cf., Savić, B. (2014). 'Where Is Serbia? Traditions of Spatial Identity and State Positioning in Serbian Geopolitical Culture', pp. 684–718.

[75] Antonenko, O. (2007). 'Russia and the Deadlock over Kosovo', *Global Politics and Strategy*, 49(3), pp. 91–106.

[76] *Washington Post.* (2008). 'Putin's Likely Successor, Pledging Support for Serbia, Signs Pipeline Deal', accessed 26 February 2008, https://www.washingtonpost.com/wp-dyn/content/article/2008/02/25/AR2008022502484.html.

Thus, the concept of the Serbian-Russian partnership and alliance are used here to construct Russia as having an important role in counterbalancing the Western influence on Serbia's politics, and also as positioning Serbia closer to Russia and its sphere of influence. At the same time, it frames the image of Serbia as an 'exceptional' country because of its role in enabling Russia to reaffirm its position as a key player.

Between 2008 and 2012, after the rift between the Democratic Party (DS) and the Democratic Party of Serbia (DSS), the country was governed by a coalition consisting of the bloc 'For a European Serbia - Boris Tadić' (Democratic Party, SPO and G 17+) and the Socialist Party of Serbia (SPS). Within the coalition, a leading part was played by the Democratic Party, which made the European integration one of its key foreign policy priorities. This government headed by Mirko Cvetković made serious efforts in order to make progress in the European integration process. It forwarded the SAA to the National Assembly, took concrete steps in cooperation with the ICTY, and gained the UN General Assembly's endorsement for its initiative to have the International Court of Justice (ICJ) rule on the legality of Kosovo's independence.

At the same time, policies concerning Kosovo remained unchanged, with the government continuing to refuse to recognize its independence. However, the government was open to intense diplomatic efforts, including a proposal for the partition of Kosovo, in order to express its willingness to compromise.[77] In parallel with 'Serbia's return to Europe', the government maintained its 'special relations' with Russia. The political leadership used the concept of simultaneous friendship with the EU and Russia in order to represent the identification of Serbia with both the EU and Russia. As stated by former President Boris Tadić on the occasion of the 65th anniversary of the victory over fascism in Moscow,

> Today it was the opportunity to meet our (Russian) friends in an attempt to build a new peace on the planet, to meet our European friends and to remind them that the idea of a united Europe arose on the foundations of the struggle against fascism.[78]

---

[77] Ramet, S. (2010). 'Serbia Since July 2008: At the Doorstep of the EU', *Südosteuropa. Zeitschrift für Politik und Gesellschaft*, 58(1), p. 25.

[78] *BBC*. (2010). 'Dan pobede u Moskvi', accessed 9 May 2010, https://www.bbc.com/serbian/news/2010/05/100509_ve-day.

Referring to Serbia's path towards the EU, Tadić emphasized that this would not prejudice its relations with Russia. 'We will be Russia's best friend in the European Union. It will be helpful in all aspects of relations between the two countries'.[79] Hence, he constructed Serbia as a 'bridge' between the East and the West, projecting an image of Serbia as a liberal-democratic and economically, culturally, and technologically modernized country, which was ready to overcome its nationalist political culture.[80]

At the same time, it is possible to register a discursive shift from the previously strict pro-Western attitudes of the Democratic Party towards a more centrist position based on the 'in-betweenness' of Serbia in its geopolitical imagination. This framing of Serbia's identity added a vision of social and material benefits from its geopolitical exceptionality, as well as its progress and modernity in the future.[81] Hence, Cvetković's government marked a rupture with the previous government in its discursive manifestations of the concept of Serbian-Russian brotherhood: the brotherhood was not constructed on an EU-Russia binary (either/or) but rather on Serbia's role as a bridge between East and West, which would include the 'peaceful' coexistence of Serbia's identification with the EU and with Russia (both/and). In this geopolitical imagination, Serbian-Russian relations are constructed as deeply embedded in ethnocultural and spiritual terms throughout history. When visiting Moscow to meet with President Putin, then-President Tadić declared that

> the historical relations (between Serbia and Russia) are very profound – they run much deeper than those with other peoples and other nations. These relations have cultural and spiritual roots but are also based on economic cooperation between our countries.[82]

---

[79] *RTV.* (2009). 'Tadić: Srbija će biti najbolji prijatelj Rusije u EU', accessed 19 October 2009, http://www.rtv.rs/sr_lat/politika/tadic-srbija-ce-biti-najbolji-prijatelj-rusije-u-eu_153695.html.

[80] Savić, B. (2014). 'Where Is Serbia? Traditions of Spatial Identity and State Positioning in Serbian Geopolitical Culture', pp. 705–706.

[81] Ibid., p. 706.

[82] Putin, V. (2005). 'Kremlin Palace', Moscow, accessed 15 November 2005, http://en.kremlin.ru/events/president/transcripts/23272.

He added furthermore, 'And when I attentively studied Russian and Serbian history, I saw that these relations were never interrupted'.[83] This statement recalls the myth of a centuries-long friendship between Serbia and Russia and underlines the profoundness of the cultural and spiritual ties between the two countries. He evokes ethnocultural and spiritual links between Serbia and Russia as deeply embedded through history.

The vision of Serbia as a bridge was accompanied by the pursuit of a military neutrality policy by Serbia, while at the same maintaining military cooperation with NATO. As stated by Boris Tadić, 'Our country has been too immersed in wars throughout the twentieth century and everything we do in the future should be built in such a way that we are never involved in any war again, preserving above all human lives and our country'.[84] Hence, Serbia was discursively constructed as a country that broke away from its previous nationalist strategic culture. This vision included various arrangements in the framework of the PfP, but not membership (due to the low levels of public support for NATO membership in the late 2000s and fresh memories of the 1999 NATO bombing). In parallel with NATO, relations with Russia were also intensified by the 2009 signature of the agreement on establishing a Serbian-Russian humanitarian base (RSHC) in Niš, only 100 km from the borders of Kosovo and Bulgaria, with the aim of assisting Serbia and other Western Balkan countries in the event of natural disasters and emergency situations. Moreover, in 2008 Russia and Serbia signed in Moscow the Energy Treaty, which also addresses the issue of the South Stream gas pipeline that is supposed to transit through Serbia, as well as the sale of a 51% share in the Petroleum Industry of Serbia (NIS) to the Russian company Gazprom.[85]

The elections in May 2012 brought back to power political forces which had been part of the regime in the 1990s. The new government was led by the Serbian Progressive Party (SNS), created from a faction of the Serbian Radical Party (SRS) which had supported Milošević in the 1990s. On his first official trip abroad, when he met with the Russian

---

[83] Ibid.

[84] *B92*. (2012). 'Tadić: NATO bombardovanje je zločin', accessed 24 March 2012, https://www.b92.net/info/vesti/index.php?yyyy=2012&mm=03&dd=24&nav_cat egory=12&nav_id=593988.

[85] Jović- Lazić, A. and Lađevac, I. (2018). 'Odnosi Srbije I Rusije- uticaj na međunarodni položaj naše zemlje', In Proroković, D. and Trapara, V. (eds) *Srbija i svet u 2017. godini*, Beograd: IMPP, p. 175.

President Putin, the newly elected Serbian President Tomislav Nikolić declared, 'The only thing I love more than Russia is Serbia'.[86] In the same emotional manner, he declared in his farewell address to the outgoing Russian ambassador Aleksandr Konuzin that Serbia was 'his house' in which he was 'a good host, not just a welcomed guest'.[87] These statements raised several questions about the policies of 'alternatives' of the new government, including its low-key relations with the West and shift towards the East.

Although many expected a slowdown in European integration and a turn towards Russia, the new coalition government (with SPS) stepped up its efforts in the process of Serbia's European integration. It went further than the previous governments in resolving the issue of Kosovo by signing, in 2013, the so-called Brussels Agreement, accepting a move of negotiations with the Kosovo government towards the normalization of mutual relations. The Agreement opened the way for an intensification of relations with the EU, and starting in 2014, Serbia formally opened membership negotiations. While this policy shift on the issue of Kosovo was explained by an official narrative about the necessity of Serbia's 'making sacrifices' in order to 'survive', the old narrative of Kosovo's non-recognition was reaffirmed.[88] At the same time, official Belgrade maintained its 'balancing act' by attempting to keep both good relations with Brussels and Russia's diplomatic support in curbing Kosovo's attempts at becoming a full-fledged member of the international community of states.[89]

By signing the Brussels agreement and moving forward the EU integration process, the new government replaced the discourse of an 'outsider' with the discourse of a 'would-be insider' in terms of the EU.[90]

[86] *B92.* (2012). 'Tadić: NATO bombardovanje je zločin'.

[87] *Telegraf.* (2012). 'Srbija je vasa kuća: Nikolić pevao Oj Kosovo…naoproštaju Konuzina', accessed 13 September 2012, https://www.telegraf.rs/vesti/politika/337385-nikolic-konuzinu-srbija-je-vasa-kuca-ovde-ste-bili-dobar-domacin-video-foto.

[88] Subotić, M. and Igrutinović, M. (2019). 'Ambivalence of the Serbian Strategic Culture', In: Miklóssy, K. and Smith, H. (eds) *Strategic Culture in Russian's Neighbourhood. Change and Continuity in an In-Between Space.* London: Lexington Books, pp. 196–198.

[89] Kovačević, M. (2019). 'Understanding the Marginality Constellations of Small States: Serbia, Croatia and the Crisis of EU-Russia Relations', *Journal of Contemporary European Studies*, 27(4), pp. 409–423.

[90] Ibid.

Through the Brussels Dialogue and intense cooperation with the EU, the new government created an image of Serbia as an arduous 'defender' of the European integration process. Europe-as-identity was constructed as the most desired political goal. At the same time, Serbian leadership also advanced the country's cooperation with NATO. In January 2015, the procedure for the adoption of the Individual Partnership Action Plan (IPAP) with NATO was completed and was followed by the adoption of a law formalizing cooperation in the field of logistics and the regulation of the status of NATO forces on the territory of Serbia. These developments were attended by an official discourse that agreements with NATO, as well as IPAP, were not step towards NATO membership, and that Serbia would remain militarily neutral.[91] The ruling elite's discourse has rarely addressed topics related to cooperation with NATO, while at the same time often reiterating that Serbia remains military neutral and is not interested in joining NATO.

In parallel with the development of cooperation with NATO, Serbia's cooperation with Russia was also progressing. The brotherhood between the two countries assumed the form of a strategic partnership, concluded with Russia in 2013, as well as a bilateral agreement on military cooperation, materialized in the form of joint military exercises ongoing since 2014, when a drill called 'Srem 2014' took place in Serbia. Since 2015, annual military drills called 'Slavic Brotherhood' involving Serbian, Russian, and Belarusian troops have been carried out, while in the same period, Serbia and Russia have also jointly organized yearly flight and tactical exercises called the Brotherhood of Aviators of Russia and Serbia.

The new government thus framed Serbia around a long-term orientation towards the EU while simultaneously fostering a commitment to 'strategic relations' with Russia. As in the case of the previous government, Serbia is positioned as a bridge between two opposite geopolitical poles. At the same time, the government reinvented itself as the entrepreneur of Serbia's modern centre-right.[92] The uniqueness of Serbia

---

[91] Vukotić, D. (2015). 'Srbija nije ušla u NATO. A NATO u Srbiju?', *Politika*, viewed 25 March 2015, http://www.politika.rs/scc/clanak/322682/Srbija-nije-usla-u-NATO-A-NATO-u-Srbiju; Vukasović, D. & Mirović Janković, A. (2016). 'Vojna neutralnost Srbije u kontekstu evroatlantskih integracija'.

[92] Radeljić, B. (2019a). 'Russia and Serbia: Between Brotherhood and Self-Serving Agendas', op.cit.; Radeljić, B. (2019b). 'Tolerating Semi-Authoritarianism? Contextualising the EU's Relationship with Serbia and Kosovo'.

is constructed by its positioning 'at the crossroads'. This imagery posits a Serbia between Brussels (and Washington) and Moscow, connecting them mutually.[93]

Russia's annexation of the Crimea was the greatest challenge for the Serbian political elite in its imaginary positioning of Serbia as a bridge. Unlike the United States, the EU, and other European candidate and non-candidate countries that immediately condemned Russia's actions and urged Russia to withdraw its troops from Ukraine, while at the same time imposing sanctions on the leaders and businessmen involved, Serbia's leadership adopted a different stance, abstaining from the voting in the UN General Assembly and adopting, as stated by Tomislav Nikolić, 'a position of neutrality with regard to the situation in Ukraine'. Furthermore, then-Prime Minister Vučić reaffirmed, 'We support the territorial integrity of every country, including Ukraine. But, let's put it this way, I asked that Serbia, for the sake of traditional ties ... maintain its position and not introduce sanctions against Russia'.[94]

Furthermore, in the Serbian media—especially the tabloids—Kiev has for years been portrayed as an 'enemy' of Russia and Ukraine as an inferior state, while Ukrainians were represented as an 'artificial' nation that wanted to distance itself from its Russian roots.[95] This negative portrayal of Ukraine was not, however, present in the early 2000s and especially during the 'Orange Revolution', when the language used in the media space promoted a positive picture of Ukraine, similar to that of the 5 October Revolution in Serbia, as a symbol of non-violent resistance to dictators and rigged elections. At the time, numerous Serbian analysts considered the 'election-triggered colour revolutions' as a Serbian political 'export brand', while former Otpor movement activists who had participated in the protests in Serbia leading to the end of the Milošević regime travelled to Ukraine and other post-Soviet countries to advise their civil activists.[96]

---

[93] Savić, B. (2014). 'Where Is Serbia? Traditions of Spatial Identity and State Positioning in Serbian Geopolitical Culture', p. 704.

[94] Poznatov, M. (2014). 'Serbia's Careful Balancing Act on Ukraine', *Euractiv*, 9 May 2014, https://www.euractiv.com/section/enlargement/news/serbia-s-careful-balancing-act-on-ukraine/.

[95] Varga, B. (2016). 'Beograd i Kijev između Brisela i Moskve', p. 174.

[96] Varga, B. (2015). Evropa posle Majdana, *Srpski kulturni centar*, Novi Sad, p. 46.

The annexation of Crimea by Russia raised questions about the similarities between the cases of Kosovo and Crimea, including inconsistencies in Russia's approach towards the notion of territorial integrity. In his statement, President Putin made a parallel between Kosovo and Crimea by stating,

> (Russia's) western partners created the Kosovo precedent with their own hands. In a situation absolutely the same as the one in Crimea, they considered Kosovo's secession from Serbia legitimate while arguing that no permission from a country's central authority for a unilateral declaration of independence is necessary.[97]

This parallel has also been drawn in Serbian foreign policy discourse. While affirming respect for the territorial integrity of Ukraine, saying that 'Serbia was bombed and we know very well how it looks when someone is endangering your territorial integrity', the Prime Minister at the time, Aleksandar Vučić also stated, however, that 'it wouldn't be fair to introduce sanctions on the state that has never harmed us and has not introduced its own sanctions towards us'.[98]

Behind this policy of 'neutrality' on Crimea lies a hidden framing of events in Kiev through the prism of the 1990s wars in the Balkans. The Serbian political elite drew parallels between the 1990s thesis of the nationalist 'Serbian Yugoslavia' and the Ukrainian crisis. The conflict was constructed on anti-Westernism, i.e., the West was represented as seeking to harm Russia and its interests using Ukraine as its tool, while, on the other hand, Russia was trying to preserve the national interests of Orthodox Russian and the Serbs.[99] By discursively equating Kosovo and

---

[97] Radeljić, B. (2017). 'Russia's Involvement in the Kosovo Case: Defending Serbian interests or Securing Its Own Influence in Europe?', *Region: Regional Studies of Russia, Eastern Europe, and Central Asia*, 6(2), p. 293.

[98] Subotić, M. and Igrutinović M. (2019). 'Ambivalence of the Serbian Strategic Culture', p. 198.

[99] Subotić, M. and Igrutinović M. (2019). 'Ambivalence of the Serbian Strategic Culture', op.cit.; Varga, B. (2016) 'Beograd i Kijev između Brisela i Moskve'; Varga B. (2015). *Evropa posle Majdana*.

Crimea, Serbian official foreign policy discourse was marked by a representation of Russia as a victim of the West, just like Serbia was the victim in the Kosovo issue.[100] The anti-Western sentiments of the Serbian political elite were also visible later that year, when the commemoration of the centenary of World War I and the 70th anniversary of the liberation of Belgrade by the Red Army took place in Belgrade as an important symbol of solidarity between two countries. On that occasion, Russian President Putin was awarded the highest honour (Order of the Republic of Serbia) in an expression of the reaffirmation of close Russian-Serbian ties and historical solidarity. On that occasion, President Nikolić declared, 'Dear brother Vladimir, the Serbian people are proud that you carry the highest Serbian order. [...] Russia is a great supporter of Serbia on many issues, and Serbia is proof to Russia that it can have friends even among small countries'.[101] The concept of Serbia's smallness in this statement recalls the mythologization of the 'unbreakable bonds' with Russia, represented as a 'generous patron' towards a small and weak Serbia. Moreover, when asked if the organization of a military parade during a Russian military action in Ukraine and amid the criticism from the EU was controversial, Vučić responded,

> I do not think it is controversial because this was not just a pointless parade, it was a parade to mark the liberation of Belgrade. Sorry, but it was the Russians who took part in the liberation of Belgrade, not some other people. If others took part in it, we would invite them as well.[102]

The brotherly connections here are constructed primarily by the concept of 'brothers in arms' built on a myth of 'centuries-old friendship' and historical experiences of solidarity, thus highlighting the importance of history as the basis of the two nations' mutual trust, ever-closer rapport, and further deepening of cooperation.

[100] Subotić, M. and Igrutinović M. (2019). 'Ambivalence of the Serbian Strategic Culture'; Varga, B. (2016). 'Beograd i Kijev između Brisela i Moskve'.

[101] *RTV.* (2014). 'Predsedniku Rusije najviši orden Republike Srbije', accessed 16 October 2014, https://www.rtv.rs/sr_lat/politika/predsedniku-rusije-najvisi-orden-republike-srbije_527291.html.

[102] Prelec, T. (2017). 'Interview with Aleksandar Vučić', *LSE*, accessed 27 October 2017, https://blogs.lse.ac.uk/lsee/2014/10/29/interview-with-aleksandar-vucic-were-not-asking-for-mercy-but-reforming-serbia/.

After the 2016 parliamentary elections, followed by the 2017 presidential elections that consolidated the power of the Serbian Progressive Party (SNS), discussions around a more balanced policy between the EU and Russia are visible in the foreign policy discourse. The government repeatedly confirmed that Serbia's ultimate goal was membership in the EU, while at the same time highlighting the delay of the Kosovo issue. However, the ambiguity of EU policies in the enlargement process in the Western Balkans, together with the still distant possibility of EU membership, go hand in hand with the ambiguity of the geopolitical discourse of the Serbian political elite. Although avowedly supporting EU values, the slightest criticism coming from the EU results in an official narrative, as Branislav Radeljić points out, 'that the West wants to overthrow Vučić, that big powers are working against Serbia, and that Russia makes for a more honest and reliable friend'.[103]

Hence, a continuity with Koštunica's (but also with Milošević's) government is visible in the traditionalist and conservative rhetoric of the Vučić government's construction of Europe as a blackmailer of Serbia. However, it is also possible to detect a change in the 'nature' of the anti-Western sentiments of the current government as compared to Koštunica's (but also a similarity to the Milošević regime):behind the present brotherly relations with Russia lies a hidden political agenda of maintaining an alternative to the West, rather than a nurturing of common ethnocultural and spiritual ties, perceived as deeply rooted in history, between Serbia and Russia.

Conclusion

This chapter has focused on the question of whether, in what ways, and to what extent Serbian political leaders from the period of the 2000 democratic changes in Serbia onwards have shaped Serbia's foreign policy and thereby also its identity by mobilizing Pan-Slavic ideas. In so doing, the chapter has sought to elucidate discursive manifestations of Slavic solidarity through the 'special relationship' between Serbia and Russia. By arguing that Pan-Slavic ideas in Serbia are manifested as a mythologized attachment to Russia with different degrees of 'sentiment intensity' depending on specific contexts, the chapter aimed to demonstrate in what

---

[103] Radeljić, B. (2019). 'Russia and Serbia: Between Brotherhood and Self-Serving Agendas', p. 7.

manner and to what extent Serbian political elites produced geopolitical knowledge and thus legitimatized brotherly narratives about Serbia and Russia.

Building on the mythical perception of proximity between the two countries based on their historical experiences of solidarity, strong national emotions, and common 'fate' (e.g., mutual sacrifice/struggle, similar injustices), Serbian political elites framed Pan-Slavic sentiments in different ways. It has been shown that conservative, nationalist regimes put forward Pan-Slavic arguments mainly in terms of anti-Westernism, i.e., anti-Europeanism. Conversely, pro-democratic governments used Pan-Slavic sentiments in terms of a mythological perception of a deeply rooted closeness between Serbia and Russia based on ethnocultural kinship. At the same time, the chapter has shed some light on how Serbian political elites have used a constructed 'special relationship' narrative in order to spatially imagine the geopolitical positioning of Serbia. It has been shown that an idea of the 'spatial uniqueness' of Serbia was advanced, generating different imaginary 'realities' about Serbia's exceptionalism and thus framing its positioning within the scope of the present East–West confrontation.

Intermarium or *Hyperborea*? Pan-Slavism in Poland After 1989

Przemysław Witkowski

INTRODUCTION

It would seem that there is a fashion for Slavicness in Poland. 'Slavic cosmetics',[1] 'Slavic tattoos',[2] 'Slavic music',[3] 'Slavic fashion',[4] and 'Slavic

---

[1] Isham, Z. (2019). Słowiańskie kosmetyki - te marki czerpią z naszej wyjątkowej tradycji, *Elle*, https://www.elle.pl/artykul/slowianskie-kosmetyki-te-marki-czerpia-z-naszej-wyjatkowej-tradycji.

[2] Trzaska, M. (2021). 'Symbole słowiańskie - jak wyglądają i co oznaczają?' *Radio Zet*, https://stylzycia.radiozet.pl/Magia/Wrozby/Symbole-slowianskie-jak-wygladaja-i-co-oznaczaja-31408.

[3] Witkowski, P. (2021). 'Brunatny Dolny Śląsk. O czym jest ten serial (Odc. 2)', *Polityka*, https://www.polityka.pl/tygodnikpolityka/kraj/2119681,1,brunatny-dolny-slask-o-czym-jest-ten-serial-odc-2.read.

[4] Łacny, D. (2020). 'Moda na słowiańskość. Znów fascynują nas rusałki, wiły, utopce, szeptuchy', *Zwierciadło*, https://zwierciadlo.pl/lifestyle/420174,1,moda-na-slowianskosc-znow-fascynuja-nas-rusalki-wily-utopce-szeptuchy.read.

P. Witkowski (✉)
Collegium Civitas University, Warsaw, Poland
e-mail: przemek.witkowski@gmail.com

© The Author(s), under exclusive license to Springer Nature Switzerland AG 2023
M. Suslov et al. (eds.), *Pan-Slavism and Slavophilia in Contemporary Central and Eastern Europe*,
https://doi.org/10.1007/978-3-031-17875-7_9

gymnastics'[5] all appear on the market, while Janusz Bieszek's Turboslavic pseudoscience books sell tens of thousands of copies. But what is the political representation of a vision based on Slavic heritage? Are there any new attempts to revitalise the old Pan-Slavism? Or are completely new embodiments of this old concept emerging?

It is very difficult to preach Pan-Slavism in Poland today. One problem immediately arises: Russia. This is because Russia has been the main centre for spreading Pan-Slavism in the last two centuries. And yet competition with Russia has been one of the main geopolitical axes of Poland's activities for at least the last four hundred years. At the same time, Russia's significant demographic advantage and position as the centre of Orthodox Christianity has given it a much better position to play the role of global leader of the Slavs. Most often, this political concept was associated with a close alliance with Russia and an aversion to the West. In addition, while Russian Pan-Slavists in the nineteenth century talked about the liberation of the Slavs (Southern or Western) thanks to Russia, much of Poland had already been ruled by the Russian Empire ever since the Partitions of Poland. Also, during the ideological offensive of Pan-Slavism, Russia faced strong resistance in the form of the November Uprising (1830–31), the January Uprising (1863–64), and the events of the 1905 Revolution. At the same time, Pan-Slavic ideas were a weapon of Russia in the fight against Austria-Hungary for the lands and the 'soul' of the South Slavs, Poles in the Habsburg state enjoyed wide autonomy and presented a generally loyalist position.[6]

In terms of demographics, economy, and its military, Russian domination over other Slavic states was (and still is) indisputable, and thus any equality in partnership between Slavic nations outside Russia is highly questionable. Because of all that, Polish political elites were often very reluctant about any Pan-Slavic concepts. Pan-Slavism was used politically, first of all, in the Russophilic spirit during the 123 years of Russian occupation of Poland, as well as during the period of the Soviet-dependent People's Republic of Poland, and if this idea ever appeared outside of this

---

[5] Woźniak, A. (2021). '27 ćwiczeń najlepszych do kobiet', *Joga słowiańska, Wysokie Obcasy,* https://www.wysokieobcasy.pl/Instytut/7,163393,26969351,podkresla-kobiecosc-wzmacnia-cialo-uspokaja-nerwy-gimnastyka.html.

[6] Łazuga, W. (2013). *Kalkulować... Polacy na szczytach c.k. monarchii,* Poznań: Zysk i S-ka.

context, it was justified rather by a *raison d'État* than by any greater faith in it, and with even less enthusiasm.[7] The choice of organisations whose activities, goals, and concepts are discussed in this chapter was based primarily on the idea of presenting the two main schools of Polish Pan-Slavism (respectively the pro-Russian one and the Polish-centric concept of the *Intermarium*) and showing their most visible representatives from the past thirty years while, however, reaching earlier and presenting them as continuators of much longer historical lines. This chapter also aims to show the impact of this idea on mainstream Polish political discourse by indicating the electoral achievements of the parties representing this idea and showing in which currents in Polish political thought these ideas have appeared most often. Polish scientific monographs by Bogumił Grott (2010),[8] Jarosław Tomasiewicz (2003),[9] Maciej Strutyński (2014),[10] and Grzegorz Tokarz (2002)[11] have been of some help, but as there has been no comprehensive study devoted only to the presentation of Pan-Slavism in contemporary Poland, and so information about it must be extracted either from works dealing with the extreme right (as this is the most common carrier of the idea) or with Polish foreign policy or the foreign doctrine of other Slavic states.

Warsaw Between the East and the West

The key to the emergence of Polish Pan-Slavism has always been the idea of who in foreign policy terms Poland's main opponent is. Poland, placed in the twentieth century on the map between Germany and Russia, first of all chose—from the pool of these two countries—who to consider as the primary opponent. Thus, if a given political group saw the main threat in the German *Drang nach Osten*, then the likelihood of its use of the

---

[7] Wiśnicki, J. (2004). 'Rosja w myśli politycznej Narodowej Demokracji 1887–1915: zarys problematyki', *Annales Universitatis Mariae Curie-Skłodowska. Sectio F, Historia*, 59, pp. 37–52.

[8] Grott, B. (ed). (2010). *Różne oblicza nacjonalizmów*. Kraków: Polityka—religia—etos, Nomos.

[9] Tomasiewicz, J. (2003). *Ugrupowania neoendeckie w III Rzeczypospolitej*, Toruń: Wydawnictwo Adam Marszałek.

[10] Strutyński, M. (2014). *Neopogaństwo*, Kraków: WAM.

[11] Tokarz, G. (2002). *Ruch narodowy w Polsce w latach 1989-1997*, Wrocław: Wydawnictwo Uniwersytetu Wrocławskiego.

Pan-Slavic argument increased significantly. The twentieth-century divisions in Polish politics, regardless of what the parties brought to the fore, were largely based on this geopolitical choice,[12] which was additionally overlapped with ideological sympathies, making it even more difficult to establish an unambiguous and ideologically clear systematisation. When Russia presented tsarist, imperial, and religious—and thus ultraconservative—ideas, it gained the support of the right and far-right. And when the tsarist state was transformed into the Union of Soviet Socialist Republics and began exporting its revolution, part of the left began to support Pan-Slavic ideas. And it was among the representatives of the Polish far-right and the far-left where support of Pan-Slavic rapprochement was the biggest in the twentieth century.

For the latter, especially among communists, Pan-Slavism was a step towards achieving a classless European and global society within one workers' council state, and it also contained a propaganda and agitation dimension, pointing to the model of the workers' state being built by those close culturally and linguistically to Poles, the Russian people.[13] While in pre-war Poland these arguments from the communist side played a marginal role, they began to gain importance after 1945 when, as a result of decisions made between the superpowers at the Yalta Conference, Poland found itself in the pro-Soviet Eastern Bloc. At that time, certainly in propaganda and popular culture (Kurpiewski, 2017),[14] the issue of the unity of the Slavs, their cultural closeness, and their eternal friendship was raised as one of the pillars of Poland's cooperation with the USSR.[15] Motifs referring to a former Slavic unity appeared during the celebrations of the millennium of the Polish state in 1966 in the

---

[12] Eberhardt, P. (Ed.). (2008). *Problematyka geopolityczna ziem polskich*, Warszawa: Instytut Geografii i Przestrzennego Zagospodarowania PAN.

[13] Szczepański, T. (2009). 'Ruch zadrużny i rodzimowierczy w PRL w latach 1956–1989', *Państwo i społeczeństwo*, 4.

[14] Kurpiewski, P. (2017). *Historia na ekranie Polski Ludowej*, Gdańsk: Wydawnictwo Uniwersytetu Gdańskiego.

[15] Witkowski, P. (2021). 'Brunatny Dolny Śląsk. O czym jest ten serial (Odc. 2)', *Polityka*. https://www.polityka.pl/tygodnikpolityka/kraj/2119681,1,brunatny-dolny-slask-o-czym-jest-ten-serial-odc-2.read

studies by Kupriewski and Polniak[16,17] and films and TV series devoted to this period were created (including *Krzyżacy*, 1960; *Gniewko syn rybaka*, 1969; *Pierścień księżnej Anny*, 1970; *Bolesław Śmiały*, 1971; *Gniazdo*, 1974; and *Znak orła*, 1977). They depicted an age-old threat to Poland from Germany and the Germans' push towards the East and indicated that the Polish *raison d'état* was a search for allies in the East.[18] The atheist state also supported anti-clerical organisations, which were supposed to promote the idea of a secular state, for example the Society for the Promotion of Secular Culture (*Towarzystwo Krzewienia Kultury Święckiej*, TKKŚ), in which the progenitors of the post-war neo-pagan and Pan-Slavic revival in Poland, Bolesław Tejkowski and Jerzy Gawrych were active.

Polish nationalist formations traditionally faced with the dilemma of which state was more dangerous to the Polish nation, Germany or Russia, also clearly more often considered the former to be the greater problem, and so sought agreement with the latter—either in a spirit of political realism or in accordance with the ideal of Pan-Slavic friendship and cooperation, and certainly always because of Germanophobia. Paradoxically, it can be said that the support for Pan-Slavism by the founding father of Polish nationalism, Roman Dmowski (1864–1939) resulted from his deep admiration for the level of development of the German economy and culture and from his fascination with its technological development. On the other hand, however, he remained a Polish nationalist. Thus, all his admiration immediately turned into a deep fear. Since Germany had such political potential, technical development, and favourable demography, it would swallow the rest of the Polish lands at its first opportunity. And because they dominated culturally and materially, he had no doubts that Germanisation would take place there immediately. Seeing the Germany-Austria-Hungary-Turkey alliance emerging, he broke with the centuries-old Polish tradition of looking for the main

---

[16] Polniak, Ł. (2011). *Patriotyzm wojskowy w PRL w latach 1956-1970*, Warszawa: Wydawnictwo TRIO.

[17] Kurpiewski, P. (2017). *Historia na ekranie Polski Ludowej*, Gdansk: Wydawnictwo Uniwersytetu Gdańskiego.

[18] Białous. M. (2015). 'Społeczna konstrukcja filmów historycznych. Pamięć zbiorowa i polityka pamięci w kinematografii polskiej lat 1920–2010', Ph.D. thesis, University of Białystok, Białystok.

enemy in Moscow and sent a proposal for an alliance against the *Drang nach Osten* to Russia.

These observations from Dmowski's 1908 book *Germany, Russia, and the Polish Question*[19] are also at the root of the more than century-long tendency of Polish nationalists to look for an ally in Russia. This German 'Germaniser' with his factory, highway, sewage system, Deutsche Mark, and philosophy was for Dmowski the main enemy of the Polish nation. In the event, the October Revolution turned out to be a problem for building the alliance, with its overthrow of the monarchy and creation of a republic of workers' councils in Russia. In this case, however, the prewar nationalists suggested cold anti-German realism, and their attitude towards Germany did not change much.[20]

During the Polish People's Republic, the nationalist component was also strong, especially in satellite organisations around the ruling Polish United Workers' Party (*Polska Zjednoczona Partia Robotnicza*, PZPR)—such as the Pax Association, the priest-patriot movement, the Western Institute, the Patriotic Union 'Grunwald', and the Patriotic Council for National Salvation (Gasztold-Seń, 2012)[21]—and within the party itself (a group of supporters of Zygmunt Berling and Mieczysław Moczar).[22] Both circles strongly marked the unity of the Eastern Bloc in the face of the American-Germanic threat and drew generously from old Pan-Slavic myths, whether about Slavic cultural brotherhood[23] or about the role of Russia, which was great help against Germanisation or German-Jewish-American capital, researched by Szczepanski[24] and Walichnowski).[25]

---

[19] Dmowski, R. (2016). *Niemcy, Rosja i kwestia polska*, Warszawa: Wydawnictwo Capital.

[20] Koziełło, T. (2008). 'Stosunki polsko-radzieckie w myśli politycznej narodowej demokracji (1918–1939): zarys problematyki', *Historia i Polityka*, 7, pp. 59–78, http://dx.doi.org/10.12775/7836.

[21] Gasztold-Seń, P. (2012). *Koncesjonowany nacjonalizm. Zjednoczenie Patriotyczne Grunwald 1980-1990*, Warszawa: Instytut Pamięci Narodowej.

[22] Gasztold P. (2019). *Towarzysze z betonu. Dogmatyzm w PZPR 1980–1990*, Warszawa: Instytut Pamięci Narodowej.

[23] Szczepański, T. (2010). 'Działalność polityczna Bolesława (Bernarda) Tejkowskiego do roku 1989', In: Łętocha, R. (ed). (2010). *Religia, Polityka, Naród. Studia nad współczesną myślą polityczną*, Krakow: Nomos.

[24] Ibid.

[25] Walichnowski, T. (1968). 'Izrael-NRF a Polska', Warszawa: Interpress.

These concepts were promoted practically until the end of the Polish People's Republic and smoothly passed, after the transformation of 1989, to new organisations originating from the above-mentioned circles.

On the Return of Pan-Slavism

Pan-Slavism returned to Poland, first of all, in nationalist groups, including national Bolsheviks and national communists; in those nostalgic towards the period of the Russian Empire or the USSR (or towards both); and, geopolitically, among supporters of neo-Eurasianism. Additionally, the authorities of the USSR and later of Russia—to some extent as part of their 'portfolio diversification' and also to some extent as a choice from what was at their disposal—in Poland bet on very different ideological entities. There were times when an orientation towards Russia, also in the spirit of Pan-Slavism, was simultaneously proclaimed by both ultra-Catholic nationalists—seeking in fraternal Slavic Russia a defence against the liberal, Germanic-Jewish West[26]—and national communists, who saw the USSR as a proletarian state that had united in one bloc all the Slavic nations (including the Lusatian Serbs) and their proletariats—those formerly exploited by Germanic and Jewish capitalists.[27] Hence, there is some superficial confusion in discussions about whether the right or left in Poland are pro-Russian or, more broadly, Pan-Slavic. That is why Joseph Stalin's raising, especially during the Great Patriotic War, of the Pan-Slavic concept—or, more broadly, his making a certain synthesis of communist and nationalist ideas[28]—found fertile ground in Poland, which was quite strongly formed in a nationalist spirit, and this very approach, despite the passage of 65 years since the fall of Polish Stalinism, continues and operates among various formations, perhaps not as a permanent political formation but rather as a bundle of concepts and ideas.

At the same time, and especially after 1989, the idea of entering an alliance with the West (containing both the European Union and the United States of America) by joining NATO gained great popularity, strengthened by discouragement with the 'people's' system and

---

[26] Wielomski, A. (2012). 'Dlaczego uważam Putina za rosyjskiego katechona?', konserwatyzm.pl, https://konserwatyzm.pl/dlaczego-uwazam-putina-za-rosyjskiego-katechona/
[27] Walichnowski, T. (1968).
[28] Tomasiewicz, J. (2010). 'Osmoza komunizmu i nacjonalizmu w Rosji: geneza hybrydy', *Historia i Polityka*, 4(11), pp. 135–155.

the alliance with Moscow. Therefore, shortly after the transformation of 1989, it was difficult to find voices that would directly oppose the Zeitgeist and demand that the alliance with the USSR—and, after its collapse, with Russia—be maintained. Therefore, the figure of Bolesław Tejkowski deserves special attention. He created a unique combination of socialism, nationalism, and pro-Russian Pan-Slavism, which, especially in the early 1990s, had its fifteen minutes among Polish extremists. Tejkowski was a fairly known figure, politically active from the 1950s, when he started out as a student socialist opposed to Stalinism. Then, on the wave of the thaw in 1956, he failed to become a member of parliament. He studied sociology, and his unfinished doctoral dissertation was supervised by Zygmunt Bauman,[29] whose assistant he was at that time. The title of his thesis was 'The social function of bureaucracy'. The choice was not an accident, as Tejkowski had befriended the Trotskyist revisionists of the PZPR and later legends of the anti-communist opposition, Jacek Kuroń and Karol Modzelewski. He also helped them to edit their well-known texts, *Manifesto* and their *Open Letter to the PZPR*.[30]

However, Tejkowski also held a grudge against the left-wing part of the opposition at that time for, as he later claimed, their disregard of matters of religion and sovereignty. He also stood in solidarity with the Catholic Episcopate during its conflict with the authorities of the People's Republic of Poland over the millennium celebrations in 1966, and he paid an official visit to Primate Stefan Wyszyński and Cardinal Karol Wojtyla (later Pope John Paul II). Step by step, he moved towards nationalist positions. He believed that the Jews constituted a powerful mafia acting with premeditation for the destruction of Poland, and that the only salvation was the leader of the national communists in the PZPR, General Mieczysław Moczar.[31] In 1975, an officer of the SB (*Służba Bezpieczeństwa*, PRL), the secret police, stated of Tejkowski: 'The creed of action: the enemy of the revolution is the Jew (the internal enemy), the external enemy—the German, the friend—the Russian.' (IPN, BU 0247/905, pp. 301–302.).

---

[29] Szczepański, T. (2010). 'Działalność polityczna Bolesława (Bernarda) Tejkowskiego do roku 1989', In: Łętocha, R. (Ed.) (2010). *Religia, Polityka, Naród. Studia nad współczesną myślą polityczną*, Krakow: Nomos.

[30] Ibid.

[31] Kuroń, J. (1995). *Wiara i Wina: do i od komunizmu*, Wroclaw: Wydawnictwo Dolnośląskie, p. 286.

More and more isolated, he came to the conclusion that Poles, apart from religious ones, must also have purely national rituals.[32] He established contacts with the Circle of Światowid Worshipers, a neo-pagan religious group with roots dating back to the 1920s, led by Władysław Kołodziej and Jerzy Gawrych. 'Tejkowski wanted to strengthen his political idea,' said Gawrych, 'with religion. He claimed that Catholicism was a Jewish sect, and he could not base his idea of a national party [...] on the religion of spiritual Jews.'[33] In 1972, Tejkowski unsuccessfully tried to register his Slavic Society by submitting to the authorities a statute and a memorial for the full implementation of communism in Poland. In it he suggested that the effective construction of communism—the liquidation of the Church, the collectivisation of agriculture, the unification of the youth movement—required changes in culture, including the use of pre-Christian traditions (IPN, BU 0247/905, pp. 97–105).

Tejkowski continued his neo-pagan activity, working for the Society for the Promotion of Secular Culture. An SB employee reported on his activities: 'He does not give up thoughts about creating a Slavic organization.' Through the channels of the TKKŚ, he tried to reach as many people as possible, creating district circles of the TKKŚ, and also reaching the University of Warsaw. 'According to T.'s assumptions, the largest possible number of people with secular, pro-Soviet views should be organised, who can hold managerial positions to fight the Catholic Church, Zionists in Poland,' wrote the SB officer supervising him (Ibidem, p. 300). The authorities tested how nationalism and pagan traditions could be used. It seems that until the end of the 1970s, Tejkowski believed that there would be a kind of neo-pagan Pax (an organisation of Catholic nations supporting the Polish People's government). He even tried to contact the USSR embassy at that time.[34] It appears that his ultimate goal was to rely on nationalism in order to help revive Poland, claiming that Warsaw may be saved only if it entered in a federation with the states such as Latvia, Lithuania, and Slovakia (IPN, BU 0247/1064/1, p. 66).

---

[32] Tomasiewicz J. (2003). *Ugrupowania neoendeckie w III Rzeczypospolitej*, Toruń: Wydawnictwo Adam Marszałek.

[33] Łapiński, M. & Szczepański, T. (1992). 'Czciciele Polski Pogańskiej', *Karta*, 8.

[34] Szczepański, T. (2010).

During the transformation of 1989, Tejkowski formed the Polish National Community-Polish National Party (*Polska Wspólnota Narodowa-Polskie Stronnictwo Narodowe*, PWN-PSN) party. Their magazine *Myśl Narodowa Polska* was sent to kiosks. Despite the change of regime, Tejkowski's group remained in favour of close cooperation among Slavic states and an orientation towards the USSR and Russia. In August 1990, the Russian nationalist Milada Kovalkova came to Warsaw and met Tejkowski. As a result of the meeting, the PWN-PSN delegation was invited to St. Petersburg. They met with activists from the National Patriotic Front 'Memory' (*Pamiat*) and Vladimir Zhirinovsky's Liberal Democratic Party of the Soviet Union.[35] Tejkowski gave interviews, took part in demonstrations, and appeared on television. The organisation Slavic Congress, which was supposed to unite the Pan-Slavic movement, was then established. Tejkowski went to two more meetings. At the second one, in March 1991, as many as 88 organisations from Russia, Belarus, Ukraine, Kazakhstan, Poland, Czechoslovakia, Bulgaria, and Yugoslavia met. The head of PWN-PSN became one of the three vice presidents of the Slavic Congress. The board was chaired by the leader of the neo-Nazi group Russian National Unity, Alexander Barkashov.[36]

In a letter to Gennady Ziuganov, the leader of the Communist Party of the Russian Federation, Tejkowski wrote, 'We hope that your and our national programmes will make the Slavic Community a reality, constituting a comprehensive economic, political, and military alliance of the independent Slavic States.' Tejkowski also promoted Pan-European fascism, which practically was absent from other Polish nationalist groups of that period.[37] He preached national Bolshevism on economic issues, anti-Semitism and aversion to migrants on ethnic issues, and the unification of Europe in the spirit of Jean-François Thiriart's concept 'from Lisbon to Vladivostok', with Russia at the centre.[38] On 4 July 1991, when the largest Polish daily *Gazeta Wyborcza* published a long interview with him, he overnight became the most famous nationalist in Poland.

---

[35] Tomasiewicz J. (2003).

[36] Ibid.

[37] Jajecznik, K. (2011). 'Oblicze ideowe "Wspólnoty. Gazety Polskiej Wspólnoty Narodowej" w latach 1999–2005', In: Maj, Ewa; Dawidowicz, Aneta, (eds) 2011, *Prasa Narodowej Demokracji, t. 2: Od roku 1939 do początku XXI wieku*, Lublin: Wydawnictwo UMCS.

[38] Tomasiewicz J. (2003).

This did not, however, ensure his electoral success. His party managed to register lists in only two districts and won only 5,262 votes (0.05%) in the 27 October 1991 parliamentary election. However, his message reached one group very successfully: skinheads. They begin to pour into his organisation *en masse*.

On 15 February 1992, a PWN-PSN demonstration in Zgorzelec hit the headlines. A crowd of 400 skinheads left the train station, beating the Germans they encountered on the way, and headed towards the border, where they were stopped by the police and the anti-terrorist brigade. There they burnt the flag of Israel and abused the German one. The police forcefully pushed the skinheads back to the train station and arrested a dozen of them (Tomasiewicz, 2003).[39] Soon after, skinheads from the PWN-PSN picketed the consulates of West Germany and Israel and beat black students and supporters of marijuana legalisation.[40] Their leader was eventually arrested, and his party won only 14,989 votes (0.11%) in the 1993 elections. Controversial statements, financial embezzlement, inability to manage the party, and accusing countless enemies and former allies of Jewish origins caused his credibility among nationalists to quickly drop to zero. Nonetheless, in March 1998, Tejkowski emailed an appeal to all one hundred American senators, as well as to the Department of State and the White House, not to admit Poland to NATO, as this posed a threat not only to Poles and the Slavic nations but to the whole of Europe and the world.[41] In the parliamentary elections in 2001, the party ran as PWN-PSN, gaining 2,644 votes and 0.02% of the vote. To this day, at over 80 years of age, Tejkowski runs three organisations: the Polish National Community, the Polish-Russian Friendship Association, and the Polish Slavic Committee; however, they are currently limited to a maximum of a dozen members combined.

But when Tejkowski's star went out, another party appeared. Already in 1992, the National Social Union (*Unia Socjalno-Narodowa*, USN) was established. It was founded by Andrzej Wylotek and Antoni Feldon, who formed a very original duo. The former, until recently, had been the right hand of the hard-line anti-Semite Tejkowski. He published the bulletin *Żywioł* and ran the National Idea Study Group promoting neo-paganism,

---

[39] Ibid.
[40] Ibid.
[41] Jajecznik, K. (2011).

Pan-Slavism, and the new-right Third Position in the spirit of the French GRECE. The latter, on the other hand, is a Jewish political émigré, related to the wealthy families of bankers and industrialists from the times of the Second Polish Republic, the Lilpops and the Haberbuschs. He was also a secret collaborator of the SB, nicknamed 'Filel'.[42]

The USN published a magazine called *Miltaria: Reason of State*, as well as producing numerous leaflets, brochures, and stickers. Daniel Mider from the USN leadership declared: 'We are Polish National Socialists.'[43] The party's ideology is pro-Russian Pan-Slavism, anti-Germanism, and neo-pagan nationalism. The religious credo of the USN was the Confession of Polish Faith. Its core was what could be called a Volkish nationalist pantheism, where life is a struggle and a source of perfection, and work for the nation equals immortality. USN[44] tried to hook the neo-pagan message to the wave of alternative anti-clericalism of the early 1990s. The columns for the texts of the USN were opened, among others, by the Krakow ecological monthly *Zielone Brygady*. Feldon opposed the European Union and NATO. 'With our consent, bombs were sent to the capital of our friendly Slavic state,' he said during the NATO bombing of Serbia. In his opinion, Poland's ally should be Russia, a brotherly Slavic state fighting against the deluge of aggressive Islam.[45] He believed that his grouping was a cultural movement that was striving for a fundamental re-evaluation of the Polish logos and ethos. 'This is a long-term issue for intellectuals, not for short-sighted politicians who are completely absorbed in the realities of the here and now,' said Feldon in one interview.[46] He quoted Antoni Wacyk, the ideologist of nationalist neo-paganism, and recognised that everything Slavic and pagan was dear to him. He stated in an interview,

---

[42] Śpiewak, J. (2017). Ukradzione miasto kulisy afery reprywatyzacyjnej, Warszawa: Arbitror.

[43] Witkowski, P., (2018). 'Wielka Aryjska Lechia, Wielka Aryjska Lechia, czylinacjonali'sci-neopoganie', *Krytyka Polityczna*, https://krytykapolityczna.pl/kraj/wielka-aryjska-lechia-czyli-nacjonalisci-neopoganie/

[44] Witkowski, P., (2018). 'Wielka Aryjska Lechia'.

[45] Smoleński, P. (2001). 'Reduta Feldona', *Gazeta Wyborcza*, https://www.1944.pl/artykul/reduta-feldona,426.html

[46] Ibid.

It is from there that our spiritual roots grow. A Polish child should be a thousand times closer to the concept of Swarog than a foreign, Catholic Yahweh. As the child grows up, Swaróg will take the name of Will of Creation, then it will become in the Nation [...] today again, like a thousand years ago, Masław's message is carried on, and the Slavic world awakens. Our Slavic common faith, we from Lech, Siemowit, Krak, we do not want to know overseas messiahs, and the sign of Swarog is dear to us.[47]

However, Feldon did not care too much about his party, arguing with activists and dealing mainly with his own businesses. As a result, the USN dissolved itself in the fifth year of its existence, on New Year's Eve 1997. Remnants of its membership ended up on the lists of the Polish National Committee, Obywatelski 'OKO' or went on to the Self-Defence of the Republic of Poland (*Samoobrona RP*) party created by Andrzej Lepper. Mateusz Piskorski turned out to be the key link between these two circles.

The entire political biography of Piskorski is situated at the intersection of the extreme right, of former PZPR members, and the social left. These were united by pro-Russianism and anti-liberalism. Piskorski took his first political steps in the early 1990s in his hometown of Szczecin as co-founder of the Temple of the Full Moon and the Black Order, NSBM (National Socialist Black Metal) organisations. He published two zines with his friends, *Odala* and *Wadera*, inside of which could be seen Adolf Hitler, NSBM, Holocaust denial, esoteric National Socialism, Ariosophy, the Church of the Creator, anti-Semitism, and Pan-Slavism.[48] At that time, Piskorski collaborated with Blood & Honour groups. He co-founded the Polish branch of the New Right, the Niklot Association for Culture and Tradition, and became its vice president. In 2001, Mateusz Piskorski went to Moscow for the first time. There he met with Russian neo-pagan nationalists and Pavel Tulayeva from the neo-Nazi party Russian National Unity. Its members were uniformed and greeted each other with a Roman salute.[49] Meanwhile in Poland, the *Odala* Group joined the structures of the nationalist parties National

---

[47] Ibid.

[48] Witkowski, P., (2019b). 'Lider faszyzującej Falangi domaga się w Moskwie przyłączenia do Polski Lwowa', *OKO.Press*, https://oko.press/lider-faszyzujacej-falangi-domaga-sie-w-moskwie-przylaczenia-do-polski-lwowa

[49] Shenfield, S. D. (2001). *Russian Fascism: Traditions, Tendencies, Movements*, New York: M. E. Sharpe, pp. 113–189.

Party (*Stronnictwo Narodowe*, SN) and the League of Polish Families (*Liga Polskich Rodzin*, LPR), as well as the agrarian Polish People's Party (*Polskie Stronnictwo Ludowe*, PSL). 'The signed agreement is not a sensation but a testimony to the return to the national trend from which the people's movement originated. Introducing Slavic elements to the election campaign is to strengthen the national identity,' the leader of the Szczecin PSL, Jarosław Ościłowski explained to journalists. In order to emphasise these 'Slavic elements', the ceremonial signing of the contract was accompanied by the *Odala* group dressed as Slavic warriors.[50] However, the weekly *Wprost* magazine published a photo from this period, in which the members of Niklot/*Odala* make a fascist greeting. As a result, only one of them, Igor Górewicz, ran from the PSL lists, gaining only 246 votes. Ultimately, in 2002, the entire group went on to a new formation, Self-Defence, at that time on a rising tide. Górewicz and Piskorski become members of the Szczecin branch of this party and stood as candidates on its lists in local government elections.

Self-Defence was mainly the party of Andrzej Lepper, a charismatic people's tribune, known at the time for his loud protests—road blockades, dumping grain on tracks, presenting himself in the media as a defender of victims of the political transformation. In the back room of his organisation, however, one could find in the nineties many former members of the SB, national communists from the Patriotic Union 'Grunwald' (such as the film director Bohdan Poręba, the famous military aviator of the 303 Squadron from World War II, Stanisław Skalski, and Józef Kossecki) or nationalists oscillating around the PZPR, such as Leszek Bubel or Janusz Bryczkowski. As a result of the intersection of these circles, a national-social party in the spirit of pro-Russian Pan-Slavism was formed.

It was also the first party of this trend to break into the mainstream, and its support in elections oscillated between 2.78% (1993) and 11.41% (2005). After the 2005 elections, it was the third power in parliament with 56 MPs. There were also clearly explicated Pan-Slavic concepts in its programme. Self-Defence quite consistently emphasised that it attached great importance to Poland's relations with the Russian Federation. Tensions emerging in relations with that eastern neighbour were often considered the result of attempts to divide Warsaw from Moscow, aimed at cutting Poland off from trade and giving Russia's place to Western

---

[50] Witkowski, P. (2018b). 'Żywot Mateusza', *Krytyka Polityczna*, https://krytykapolityczna.pl/kraj/zywot-mateusza-witkowski-piskorski/

countries. It was often considered the party in parliament most favourable to the idea of Polish-Russian cooperation.[51] The party's deputy Bolesław Borysiuk proposed the development of trade treaties between the two countries, the entry of the prime ministers of both countries into a Joint Polish-Russian Commission for Trade and Economic Cooperation, cooperation at the regional level, the establishment of a Polish-Russian bank to finance trade, and a foundation dealing with, *inter alia*, economic information for interested entities from both countries.[52] According to the party, an important element in improving Polish-Russian relations should be ties in the field of culture and science, as well as references to common historical and ethnic roots emphasising the Slavic character linking Poland with its eastern neighbour. The same was emphasised in relation to Ukraine. The party supported close cooperation between Warsaw and Kiev, even suggesting the possibility of the joint accession of both countries to the EU. Self-Defence's position towards Belarus was a derivative of the party's belief that Poland's relations with its eastern neighbours needed to be normalised and economised. That is why Lepper's party often distanced itself from those political initiatives aimed at a negative assessment of the Belarusian authorities, for example in the context of allegations of violations of human and civil rights by the administration of President Alexander Lukashenka. Lepper recognised that negotiations with Lukashenka were facilitated by the fact of the Slavic community to which both nations belonged.[53] Apart from the postulate of de-ideologising and economising mutual relations, the points of the party's programme referring to Poland's relations with Slavic countries also contained some Pan-Slavic influences, manifested in its emphasising the common ethnic origin, cultural community, and similar historical experiences of these nations. Self-Defense protested in 1999 against the NATO attacks on Yugoslavia, recognising that in this case 'NATO rejected the mask of a defence pact and became a gendarme, guarding the interests of international finance'.[54]

---

[51] Piskorski, M. (2010). 'Samoobrona RP w polskim systemie partyjnym', Ph.D. thesis, Adam Mickiewicz University, Poznań, pp. 337–338.

[52] Ibid.

[53] Ibid., 337–339.

[54] Ibid., 340.

Piskorski also founded the European Centre for Geopolitical Analysis, a think tank writing about foreign policy from a pro-Russian perspective, publishing books, organising conferences, and running the portal geopolityka.org, as well as observing elections in pro-Russian self-proclaimed republics such as Transnistria and Abkhazia.[55] As a result, it found a good reception on the Russian side. On the website of Alexander Dugin, there is a post dated 26 September 2005, entitled 'Success of Polish Eurasians in the elections', in which he congratulated Piskorski on joining the Polish parliament 'despite the strong pressure of the current Atlantic pro-American regime in Poland'. Self-Defence was referred to here as 'the only pro-Russian party in Poland'. 'He is our politician and agent of influence in Poland'—such a statement about Piskorski by journalist Filip Leontiev was published by the portal of the Russian television o2TV.

When in 2011 Self-Defence found itself, after the death-by-suicide of its leader Lepper (accused of corruption, sex crimes, and embezzlement), on the margins of Polish politics, Piskorski[56] tried his hand at his own party, the nationalist-social party Change (*Zmiana*), which united former members of Self-Defence, some socialists, national socialists, and neo-fascists. However, the brilliant career of the most famous Polish Pan-Slavist, Piskorski, was finally interrupted in 2016 by his arrest by Polish counterintelligence.[57] He was accused of espionage for Russia and China, and the case is still pending before Polish courts.

A group called Falanga, led by Bartosz Bekier, the former vice-chairman of the Change party, can be considered a continuation of Change in the Pan-Slavic register. The Revolta publishing house associated with this group publishes books by Aleksander Dugin in Poland, and their website xportal.pl is the main seedbed of Pan-Slavic and pro-Russian ideas, as well as containing a large collection of texts in the spirit of Pan-European fascism, neo-Eurasianism, national Bolshevism, and the Third Position. The group was also quite eager to infiltrate the Polish army. At one point, the Falangists dominated the Rifle Unit No. 2039 in Kraków,

---

[55] Witkowski, P. (2018b). 'Żywot Mateusza', *Krytyka Polityczna*, https://krytykapolityczna.pl/kraj/zywot-mateusza-witkowski-piskorski/

[56] Pytlakowski, P. (2013). 'Seks bezterminowo odroczony', *Polityka* 06.2013 (2894) from 05.02.2013, p. 32.

[57] Witkowski, P. (2018b). 'Żywot Mateusza', *Krytyka Polityczna*, https://krytykapolityczna.pl/kraj/zywot-mateusza-witkowski-piskorski/

and several of them served in the 6th Airborne Battalion in Gliwice and the 23rd Silesian Artillery Regiment in Bolesławiec. Three members of this organisation were accused of terrorist activity in Ukraine, and their trial is still pending.[58] The map of Bekier and Falanga's connections is simple to systematise: all the forces in Europe and its vicinity are sympathetic to Russia: Assad, Serbian nationalists, Hezbollah, Donbas separatists, and Western neo-fascists. Speaking in the Russian Duma, Bekier called for Poland to leave NATO and the EU and to conclude a Polish-Russian alliance. He advocated forcing federalisation with Lithuania and territorial autonomy for the Vilnius Region, as well as the partition of Ukraine and the incorporation of Lviv into Poland.[59] Falanga is currently the most visible entity presenting pro-Russian Pan-Sovietism in Poland.

Multifacetedness of Pan-Slavism in Poland

Seeing Russia as the centre, although undoubtedly the dominant Polish Pan-Slavic concept, is not the only idea in the history of Polish political thought proposing the creation of a wider camp of Slavic states. There have also been ideas hostile to having the centre in Moscow, which focused on concepts for an anti-Russian Slavic alliance (Polish-Ukrainian, Polish-Belarusian, Polish-Czech), which in time developed into the concept of the *Intermarium*. Polish-centric or Pan-European Pan-Slavic concepts can also be found among nationalist neo-pagans, national socialists, fascists, and neo-Nazis, especially in the spirit of Ariosophic inquiries praising common heritage, not only Proto-Slavic but also Proto-Indo-European.

One of the first modern Pan-Slavic concepts aimed at uniting the non-Russian Slavic lands under the leadership of Poland was the nineteenth-century concept of the leader of the Polish conservative émigrés, Prince Adam Jerzy Czartoryski.[60] Czartoryski wanted to obtain French, British, and Turkish support for the restoration of Polish-Lithuanian statehood, federating additionally with the Czech lands, Slovakia, Hungary,

---

[58] Witkowski, P., (2019b). 'Lider faszyzującej Falangi domaga się w Moskwie przyłączenia do Polski Lwowa', *OKO.Press*, https://oko.press/lider-faszyzujacej-falangi-domaga-sie-w-moskwie-przylaczenia-do-polski-lwowa.

[59] Ibid.

[60] Eberhardt, P. (2010). 'Polscy prekursorzy idei zjednoczenia politycznego Europy, *Przegląd Geograficzny*, 82 (4), pp. 509–529'.

Romania, and all the southern Slavs. Poland would in such a formation mediate conflict between Hungary and the Slavs and between Hungary and Romania. Although the idea seemed to be implemented during the Spring of Nations, the lack of support from France and England; Hungarian conflicts with the Czechs, Slovaks, and Romanians; and the growth of German nationalism blocked its creation.[61] Some support among Poles also went to the Austro-Slavic and neo-Slavic concepts, especially at the beginning of World War I when the future dictator of Poland, Józef Piłsudski and his armed forces (the Polish Legions) sided with Austria-Hungary against Russia. He also developed the concept of the *Intermarium*, which can be considered a creative transformation of the German idea of *Mitteleuropa*.

The latter concept was formulated in the book *Mitteleuropa* in 1915 by the German political scientist Friedrich Naumann. According to its assumptions, Central Europe was to become an economic and political entity subordinate to the German state. In his programme, Naumann also supported the Germanisation and Magyarisation of the region. Demands were also put forward to create a German colonial state in Crimea and to colonise the Baltic states.[62] The Polish response to this concept was the idea of the *Intermarium*. Józef Piłsudski's strategic goal was to restore the Polish-Lithuanian Commonwealth and to weaken and disintegrate the Russian Empire, and later the USSR, on the basis of its ethnic differences. He also saw his concept as a counterweight to the imperialist tendencies of Russia and Germany. Piłsudski's plans were considered unrealistic by his allies in the Triple Entente, and Poland was to be limited to ethnically Polish territories. Indeed, the other nations of the former Kingdom of Poland did not express any interest in joining the federation. The chances of implementing Piłsudski's plan were additionally diminished by border conflicts between Poland and its neighbours, Lithuania, Ukraine, and Czechoslovakia. Then Piłsudski considered a federation or alliance of the Baltic and Balkan states. This union was to include Poland, Czechoslovakia, Hungary, Scandinavia, the Baltic states, Italy, Romania, Bulgaria,

---

[61] Eberhardt, P. (ed.). (2008). *Problematyka geopolityczna ziem polskich*, Warszawa: Instytut Geografii i Przestrzennego Zagospodarowania PAN.

[62] Brechtefeld, J. (1996). *Mitteleuropa and German Politics. 1848 to the Present*, London, UK: Palgrave Macmillan.

Yugoslavia, and Greece[63]; it would therefore extend not only between the Baltic Sea and the Black Sea, but also the Arctic Ocean and the Mediterranean Sea. This project also failed; Poland had tense relations with Lithuania and Czechoslovakia, and although contacts with the rest of the countries were positive, they themselves were often at odds with each other. The only outcome was the Polish-Romanian alliance.

The concept of a Central European Union between the Baltic, Black, Adriatic, and Aegean Seas was rejuvenated during World War II by the Polish government-in-exile. The first step towards its implementation were discussions in 1942 between the Greek, Yugoslav, Polish, and Czechoslovak governments-in-exile regarding the establishment of Greek-Yugoslav and Polish-Czechoslovak federations.[64] The idea of a federation was supported by the main Polish political parties (apart from the communists). The idea, however, met with opposition on the part of the USSR—and with indifference or hostility on the part of the other allies—and so the idea was finally ended by decisions made by the superpowers at the Tehran and Yalta conferences.

The idea of a Central European federation or at least a close block of cooperation with Poland in the central role would also continue after World War II, in the Cold War conservative-liberal idea of the Central European federation of Juliusz Mieroszewski and Jerzy Giedroyc[65] and in the political thought of the neo-Piłsudskian anti-communist opposition Confederation of Independent Poland (*Konfederacja Polski Niepodległej*, KPN),[66] as well as in the concept of 'Jagiellonian Poland'[67] adopted by the nationalist-Catholic Law and Justice (PiS) party (currently ruling in

---

[63] Świder, K. (2018). 'Europa Środkowa jako obszar projektowania geopolitycznego', *Studia Europejskie*, 2.

[64] Świder, K. (2018). 'Europa Środkowa jako obszar projektowania geopolitycznego', *Studia Europejskie*, 2.

[65] Urbańczyk, M. (2015). 'Idea ULB (Ukraina-Litwa-Białoruś) w myśli Jerzego Giedroycia i Juliusza Mieroszewskiego', in: Fiktus, Paweł; Marszał, Maciej; Malewski, Henryk (eds). *Rodzinna Europa. Europejska myśl polityczno – prawna u progu XXI wieku*. Wroclaw: Wydział Prawa, Administracji i Ekonomii Uniwersytetu Wrocławskiego, pp. 309–322.

[66] Szczepański T. (1993). 'Międzymorze. Polityka Środkowoeuropejska', *KPN*, Warszawa.

[67] Kubera, J. (2016). 'Polska "piastowska" vs "jagiellońska". Odmienność wizji relacji z Niemcami jako determinanta poglądów na polską politykę zagraniczną', *Acta Politica Polonica*, 4 (38).

Poland). It was the KPN milieu that had the greatest influence on the transfer of the idea of the *Intermarium* from the pre-war period to the Third Republic of Poland. Some former activists of this party joined the PiS, while some others radicalised and transferred the concept to neo-fascist circles.

The heritage of Bolesław Piasecki, the leader of the pre-war fascist National Radical Camp (*Obóz Narodowo-Radykalny*, ONR) and post-war collaborator with the Polish People's Republic and leader of the Pax Association, also had an additional impact on neo-fascist, Polish-centred Pan-Slavic concepts. During World War II, in the fall of 1942, Piasecki believed that after the peace conference, a Catholic Slavic Empire would be established from the Caucasus to the Neva Bay, from Rostock to Bratislava, and from the Carpathians to the Dniester basin between the Baltic, Black, and Azov Seas. The dominant political role in the empire would be played by the Poles.[68] The political thought of Jan Stachniuk, the so-called *zadrużny* nationalism had also an important impact on this current of Pan-Slavism. 'Zadruga' is a Polish Pan-Slavic neo-pagan national communist movement created in the interwar period, additionally enriched with elements of the 'cultural revolution' and fantasies of a national revival based on pagan beliefs. The goal of this movement was a hierarchically organised, disciplined, and Pan-Slavic supernation, creating a national-theocratic-Bolshevik state—the Slavic Empire.[69]

Thus, it is from the overlap of concepts from Piasecki, Stachniuk, and Piłsudski that we can derive the position of the Polish-centric Pan-Slavists of the fascist rite, with Tomasz Szczepański as its main representative. He is the leader of the Niklot Neo-pagan Association for Culture and Tradition, closely related to the Native Faith (*Rodzima Wiara*) religious association. Niklot members declare themselves to be enemies of liberalism, Americanisation, the mixing of people of different ethnic origins,

---

[68] Grott, B. (ed.) 2010, 'Różne oblicza nacjonalizmów', *Polityka—religia—etos*, Kraków: Nomos.

[69] Ibid.

and Christianity (Witkowski, 2018).[70] Niklot works closely with the neo-fascists associated with the magazine *Szturm*[71] and also has close contacts with the Ukrainian Azov Battalion. They think of themselves as the Polish equivalent of the New Right,[72] a French neo-pagan and neo-fascist intellectual formation led by the philosopher Alain de Benoist. The leader of Niklot, Tomasz Szczepański is a real political wanderer. He has successively been an anarchist, a Trotskyist, a founding member of the Polish Socialist Party, a member of the Civic Committee 'Solidarity', and then an activist in the KPN, where he became a member of its Political Council. He welcomed the year 1998 as a member of the nationalist-Catholic Movement for Reconstruction of Poland (*Ruch Odbudowy Polski*, ROP), then joined the Nationalist-Catholic LPR in 2001, and subsequently the nationalist National Movement (*Ruch Narodowy*, RN). Today he gives lectures under a flag with a *toporzeł* (an eagle-axe, a Polish neo-pagan, neo-fascist symbol) and the Slavic swastika, the *swarzyca*, praising apartheid and defending Janusz Waluś, who in 1993 killed Chris Hani, the leader of the communist party of the Republic of South Africa. Finally, Szczepański is the main organiser of the Ku Niepodległej festival, whose guests have often been neo-fascist and neo-Nazi bands. The event is sponsored by Keep it White (a racist fashion brand whose neo-pagan and neo-fascist clothing designs feature models tattooed with '18', '88', 'Blood and Honour', the Black Sun, and other Nazi symbols) and a publisher of neo-Nazi music, SS Records.[73]

For the issues discussed in this chapter, the key factor is Szczepański's long-term activity in entities fighting for the implementation of the *Intermarium* idea. Regardless of the party he represents, Szczepański has remained socially oriented towards the economy and, at the geopolitical

---

[70] Witkowski, P., (2018). 'Wielka Aryjska Lechia, czyli nacjonaliści-neopoganie', *Krytyka Polityczna*, https://krytykapolityczna.pl/kraj/wielka-aryjska-lechia-czyli-nacjonalisci-neopoganie/

[71] Witkowski, P., (2019). '"Europa będzie biała albo bezludna", czyli szturmowcy', *Krytyka Polityczna*, https://krytykapolityczna.pl/kraj/szturmowcy-przemyslaw-witkowski/

[72] Witkowski, P., (2018). 'Wielka Aryjska Lechia, czyli nacjonaliści-neopoganie', *Krytyka Polityczna*, https://krytykapolityczna.pl/kraj/wielka-aryjska-lechia-czyli-nacjonalisci-neopoganie/

[73] Witkowski, P., (2019). '"Europa będzie biała albo bezludna", czyli szturmowcy', *Krytyka Polityczna*, https://krytykapolityczna.pl/kraj/szturmowcy-przemyslaw-witkowski/

level, a supporter of the *Intermarium*. Already in the years 1986–1995, he was the founder of the Pomost Society and the editor of its opposition and anti-Soviet periodical *Międzymorze* (*Intermarium*). The aim of these entities was to popularise the idea of anti-communist and anti-imperial cooperation by the nations of the *Intermarium* region and to educate a team of people familiar with Central European issues who could in the future, after the already-expected overthrow of communism, work in the service of the state for this programme. A magazine was published and conferences and lectures were organised. The speakers were scholars to a greater or lesser degree sympathising with the opposition, as well as activists of the Belarusian and Ukrainian minorities. The members of the group in question were, among others, Paweł Cieplak, Michał Kurkiewicz, Tomasz Marek Leoniuk, Joanna Strzelczyk (all working at the Polish Ministry of Foreign Affairs after 1989), Paweł Kazanecki, Tomasz Szczepański (after 1989, at the Ministry of Culture and Art, Office for National Minorities), Tadeusz A. Olszański (after 1989, an employee of the Centre for Eastern Studies), Eugeniusz Wappa (after 1989, chairman of the Belarusian Union in Poland), Włodzimierz Pac (after 1989, journalist of the Belarusian section of Radio Polonia and a PR correspondent in Minsk), Jerzy Leszczyński (after 1989, a journalist in the Belarusian editorial office of Polish Radio in Białystok), and Mirosław Czech (after 1989, a member of the leadership of the Union of Ukrainians in Poland).[74]

At the beginning of the 1990s, his ideas penetrated the mainstream of Polish politics. Szczepański was a member of the leadership of the KPN, a party in the ruling coalition at the time. At KPN, he was in charge of the '*Intermarium* Department', a cell that served the party's contacts in Central and Eastern Europe. According to Szczepański, the core of *Intermarium* was to be around the axis Warsaw-Kiev, and coordinated actions by the *Intermarium* states should therefore prevent their vassalisation by a 'creature managed by bureaucrats from Brussels' and protect them from 'blurring national identification'.[75] Szczepański also published in the *Gazeta Polska* (1992–1997), published by the KPN, being a member of its editorial team and responsible for Central and

---

[74] Szczepański T. (2019). 'Powstanie i działalność Towarzystwa "Pomost" oraz pisma "Międzymorze" (1986–1990)', *Polityka Narodowa*, 21.

[75] Szczepański T. (1993). Międzymorze. Polityka Środkowoeuropejska *KPN*, KPN, Warszawa.

Eastern European issues. He co-organised the Second Congress of the League of the *Intermarium* Countries in Jarosław nad Sanem (9–11 June 1995), and he participated in the Third (Minsk, 1996) and Fourth (Kiev, Wodica Forest, 1997) Congresses.[76]

Starting in 1997 he published the quarterly *Trygław*. This periodical for 10 years (1997–2007) was the main publication of the Polish New Right. The following wrote for *Trygław*: Szczepański, Piskorski, the well-known Polish New Rightists Jarosław Tomasiewicz and Remigiusz Okraska, and—from the older generation—Antoni Wacyk. In addition to texts on archaeology and ethnography, you could find there Stachniuk's 'culturalism', the idea of *zadruga*, and ads for skinhead zines and the nationalist radio Szaniec. There, ideological articles mixed with scientific ones, and the latter acted to legitimise the former. At the same time, and to this day, Szczepański was active in the neo-pagan religious group Native Faith (*Rodzima Wiara*), educated nationalist youth, and was the mentor of the leader of the young generation of Polish neo-pagan neo-fascists, Grzegorz Ćwik.

Szczepański's friend from his religious association Native Faith, the *żerca* (neo-pagan priest) Adam Cieśluk, also known as 'Świaszczysław Afield', represents a slightly different Pan-Slavic, non-pro-Russian vision. When censorship was abolished in 1989, a large number of far-right zines were formed. *Poganin* was published in Olsztyn, *Odmrocze* in Inwrocław; in Bydgoszcz, *Błyskawica* and *Lechita*. Wrocław's satanic-neo-pagan *Menhir* was published by the future leader of the NSBM and star of the Graveland band, Robert Fudali (aka 'Rob Darken'), and *Barbaricum* by the archaeologist and nationalist Tymon Wojnicki (aka 'Wojgniew'). *Lechia Stragona* was printed by the Jarotan Association from Jarocin. At extreme right-wing concerts and rallies, you might buy *Watra*, *Wieszcz*, *Dla synów tej ziemi*, *Zryw*, *Gniew Ludu*, *Hedeby*, *Garazel*, *Przesilenie*, *Fimbrethil*, *Grom*, *Flame in Wolf Eyes*, *Phoenix*, *Cyclone* (later *Vril*), *Biały Głos*, *Wilczy Hak*, *Wehrwolf*, and many, many others.[77]

One of the groups editing this kind of magazine was Cieśluk's circle. In the 1990s, Cieśluk was a famous Nazi skinhead in Central Pomerania. In mid-1994, he and his friends founded the group Thule (then known

---

[76] Szczepański T. (2019). 'Powstanie i działalność Towarzystwa'.

[77] Tomasiewicz J. (2003). *Ugrupowania neoendeckie w III Rzeczypospolitej*, Torun: Wydawnictwo Adam Marszałek.

as Othala). They have published the zines *Antichrist*, *Securius*, *Jesteśmy* (later *Iron Cross*), and *Żerca*, mixing Nazism, paganism, Satanism, and anti-Semitism.[78] Cieśluk founded, with a group of sympathisers, the Order of Zadruga 'Northern Wolf' (*Zakon Zadrugi Północy Wilk*, ZZPW), whose official name would become the Świaszczyca Patriotic Youth Association. All members were uniformed in black, with combat boots, cargo pants, and a belt with an eagle-axe-shaped buckle. On the collar of black shirts, they wore patches: on the right, a *gammadion* (Greek swastika); on the left, the letters ZZ (for the Order of Zadruga) based on the runic badge of the SS men. During the several years of its activity, the organisation covered the territory of Pomerania from Szczecin to Gdańsk and from Darłowo to Szczecinek, with sections in Mazovia, Greater Poland, and England, with about 40–50 members. As for its goals, 'As racial patriots, Pagan Ario-Slavs, we cannot stand idly by the anti-Polish and anti-Slavic campaign in the West. [...] We are Polish, Slavic National Socialists,' they declared in their programme credo. They wanted to create.

> a racially pure nation of White People [...] believing that they themselves are demigods, heroes, because they have a part of this cosmic divine power, which is the Aryan Creator's Will. Whoever mixes his inheritance with another race, degrades the blood and spirit that were given to him, 'because' Jewry and other mentally weaker nations killed the White Man's life force. [...] In the face of the decay and multiracialism of the West, only a united Slav —the northern empire of the rising sun—is hope for the White Race.[79]

---

[78] Witkowski, P. (2018). 'Wielka Aryjska Lechia, czyli nacjonaliści-neopoganie', *Krytyka Polityczna*, https://krytykapolityczna.pl/kraj/wielka-aryjska-lechia-czyli-nacjonalisci-neopoganie/

[79] Filip, M. (2006). 'Zakon Zadrugi "Północny Wilk". Nacjonalizm jako pierwiastek konstruujący tożsamość współczesnych neopogan(istów) (rodzimowierców) polskich', M.A. thesis, Adam Mickiewicz University, Poznań.

Poland, the Czech Republic, and the Slovaks would create one pillar; the Southern Slavs, the second; and Russians, in a great continental alliance with India, the third.[80]
As a candidate for association with the Native Faith is the Whitefire Group (*Gromada Białożar*), which united the Warsaw neo-fascist neo-pagans of the younger generation with members like the journalists of the fascist *Szturm* magazine; its editor-in-chief, Grzegorz Ćwik; a doctoral student at the Jagiellonian University, Paweł Bielawski; Patryk Paterek (aka 'Jarowoj Mazowszanin'); and an associate of Richard Spencer, then leader of the American alt-rightists, Brandon Andrew Jackson (aka 'Aspir Befreier').[81] The Stormtrooper Movement (*Ruch Szturmowców*) to which Whitefire belongs forms the 'black block' at the Warsaw nationalist Independence March and is a new generation of Polish neo-fascists. Economically socially oriented, aggressive, and racist, they represent a specific type of Pan-Slavism. Their attitude combines the approaches of Szczepański and Ciesluk, and so the first circle of cooperation of a Pan-Slavic nature is Central Europe with Poland and Ukraine in the centre, then next the whole community of 'white' Indo-Europeans. The East is an important direction of cooperation for the Stormtroopers. Unlike most Polish nationalists, they sympathise with the Ukrainian nationalists. In Ukraine, the Stormtroopers cooperate mainly with the Azov National Corps and the Carpathian Sich. They maintain looser contacts with the Ukrainian Right Sector and Svoboda.[82] In the Czech Republic, the Stormtroopers cooperate with the national-socialist Workers' Party of Social Justice (*Dělnická Strana Sociální Spravedlnosti*, DSSS); neo-Nazis from the National Resistance (*Národní Odpor*) and their women's section, Resistance Women Unity; cells of the Radical Boys; and identitarians from Generace Identity. They also visit the Lukov March organised by the Bulgarian National Union (*Български национален съюз*) and dedicated to the memory of one of the ideologues of Bulgarian fascism,

---

[80] Ibid.
[81] Witkowski, P., (2019). '"Europa będzie biała albo bezludna", czyli szturmowcy', *Krytyka Polityczna*, https://krytykapolityczna.pl/kraj/szturmowcy-przemyslaw-witkowski/
[82] Ibid.

the minister of war during World War II and Nazi collaborator, Hristo Nikolov Lukov. In Russia, they cooperate with a wide range of anti-Putin nationalists—from the neo-Nazis from the MMA White Rex group, through the pagan neo-Nazi Pan-Slavists from Wotan Jugend and the eco-fascists in the Greenline Front, to the National Socialists from Wolnica and the terrorists from the NS/WP Nevograd.[83]

Conclusion

We can divide Polish Pan-Slavism into two main perspectives. First of all, the pro-Russian one, which is also part of a wider pro-Russian camp, is based on ideas other than Pan-Slavic ones, such as the vision of Moscow as the Third Rome, Vladimir Putin in the role of *katechon* of European civilisation, or simply the calculation of the current political interest. Here, Pan-Slavists mix in the pro-Russian camp with Catholic religious integralists, ultra-conservatives, and neo-Eurasians. Pan-Slavists focus in this context on the cultural and ethnic unity of the Slavic peoples, especially in opposition to Germany and, more broadly, to the entire West, an idea that adds to the Kremlin's soft power in the region.

The second current is the one focusing on the idea of the *Intermarium* and the close cooperation of Poland, Ukraine, and Belarus and, more broadly, of the countries of the entire region of Central and Eastern Europe, Russia excluded. In the broadest sense, as recognised by some neo-fascists and neo-Nazis, this Pan-Slavism extends to the idea that it is part of the unity of the 'white race' or of 'Aryans'—as opposed to non-European migrants, Muslims, Jews, or blacks—and basically ceases to be Pan-Slavism, although this aspect is also emphasised at this movement.

Regardless of which line of Polish Pan-Slavism is chosen, each of them represents a continuation of a line that goes back eighty to a hundred years or more. Nor do these lines appear likely to end soon. New groups and parties are emerging that develop these ideas, and to discuss these, a much longer text would be necessary. This indicates only the most important ideologically or most popularly endorsed Pan-Slavic groups in the

---

[83] Witkowski, P. (2019). 'Europa będzie biała albo bezludna, czyli szturmowcy', *Krytyka Polityczna*, https://krytykapolityczna.pl/kraj/szturmowcy-przemyslaw-witkowski/

last thirty years in Poland. Regardless, this overview should give an idea of how Pan-Slavic and related ideas are reflected in the modern history of Poland, how they still influence political thinking and discourse, what roles they play in political discourse, and what kinds of manifestations they find in the cultural sphere.

On Pan-Slavism, Identity, and Other Issues

A Distant Acquaintance: Reflecting on Croatia's Relationship with Pan-Slavism

Tin Puljić and Senada Šelo Šabić

INTRODUCTION

Pan-Slavist ideas in Croatia have little resonance. One reason is that Pan-Slavism, as a political thought and cultural identity, has never been a salient idea to Croats. Insofar as Pan-Slavism refers to a broad idea of the existence of cultural, linguistic, and historical commonalities among the Slavic peoples, who should share a bond of brotherhood expressible through political action, such ideation has carried little weight in Croatia.

It is worth noting at the start of this chapter that most of Croatia's relationship with ideas of Pan-Slavic unity has been in fact a relationship with South Slavism. As will be further elaborated, modern Croatian national thinkers appropriated ideas of South Slavic unity and applied them to Croatia's immediate surroundings, seeking to use these ideas and concepts as a gateway to political emancipation. One must keep in mind,

---

T. Puljić
Faculty of Political Science, University of Zagreb, Zagreb, Croatia

S. Š. Šabić (✉)
Institute for Development and International Relations, Zagreb, Croatia
e-mail: senada@irmo.hr

however, that there was little interaction, and that there are indeed very few contemporary echoes of Pan-Slavism in its broadest sense. Rather it was South Slavism that permeated the political space of Croatia, both historically and in contemporary times. It is the Yugoslav idea, the idea of a union of South Slavs—first as an expression of political imagination and later as a practical attempt at uniting several ethnic groups in Southeast Europe under one state—that is most salient in Croatian history. In some instances, such as in Serbia, an element of Pan-Slavism was added to the Yugoslav idea, but Pan-Slavic sentiment was never at its core. Croats certainly never equated Pan-Slavism and Yugoslavism. One reason for this lies partially in the fact that the country perceived as the cradle of Slavic identity—Russia—was never a centre towards which Croat people gravitated. Therefore, instead of Pan-Slavism—which we deem to be too broad and inapplicable to the Croatian context—we will primarily focus on South Slavism to refer to conceptions about the unity and commonality of South Slavic nations in particular.

This chapter will delve deeper into the utilisation of South Slavism in the history of the two Yugoslavias—first the Kingdom of Yugoslavia (originally named the Kingdom of the Serbs, Croats, and Slovenes) created after World War I and the dissolution of the Austro-Hungarian empire, and second the communist Yugoslavia created in the aftermath of the defeat of Nazism and the triumph of the People's Liberation Movement (the Partisan movement) in the Balkans. It will show that the motivation for a union among South Slavs was driven more by a desire for self-determination and freedom than for integration with other Slavs in Europe.

This chapter starts with an historical overview of the perceptions of South Slavism in the nineteenth- and twentieth-century history of the Croats, in both the pre- and post-Yugoslav periods. It will go on to present a more nuanced picture of the political, social, and cultural drivers of the tension that Croatia has experienced with South Slavism. This is primarily presented through an analysis of the violent dissolution of Yugoslavia in the 1990s, and of the Croatian experience and perception of this break-up. The chapter then further elaborates the post-war and post-independence development of Croatian foreign and other public policies, including education, as tools for national identity formation and as a path of differentiation from South Slavism. The primary theoretical approach used throughout the chapter is discourse analysis and thematic analysis; by analysing statements by relevant political officials, important national documents, and the representation of history in education and culture, we seek to locate and map consistent patterns related to perceptions of South Slavism in Croatia. We will discuss the types of language and symbolism used to refer to Croatia's recent past and explain how they structure discourse related to South Slavism and Pan-Slavism more broadly.

To support our claims, we use a wide array of sources and scientific papers. In describing contemporary Croatian political discourse, we reference prominent Croatian political scientists with expertise in Croatian history and nationalism more broadly,[1] as well as those with extensive knowledge of the geopolitics of the Balkan region in general[2] not forgetting foreign experts such as Paula Pickering, who focuses on democratisation in post-communist states, and Mark Baskin, who specialises in post-conflict administration and has participated in UN peacekeeping missions in the region.[3] When discussing historical myths and the sources they derive from, we refer to the works of multiple Croatian historians specialising in, among other areas, research concerning Croatia in Byzantine times and the Middle Ages[4] and the history of Catholicism in

---

[1] Cipek, T. (1995). 'Ideja seljaštva u političkoj misli Stjepana Radića', *Društvena istraživanja: časopis za opća društvena pitanja* 4(2–3), pp. 343–353.; Cipek, T. (2017). 'The Spectre Of Communism Is Haunting Croatia. The Croatian Right's Image of the Enemy', *Croatian Political Science Review* 54(1–2), pp. 150–169.; Đurašković, S. (2008). 'Politike povijesti: pregled razvoja discipline u Hrvatskoj i Slovačkoj', *Politička misao: časopis za politologiju* 45(3–4), pp. 201–220.

[2] Jović, D. (2011). 'Hrvatska vanjska politika pred izazovima članstva u Europskoj Uniji', *Politička misao: časopis za politologiju* 48(2), pp. 7–36.; Kasapović, M. (1996). 'Demokratska tranzicija i političke institucije u Hrvatskoj', *Politička misao: časopis za politologiju* 33(2–3), pp. 84–99.; Kasapović, M. (2018). 'Genocid u NDH: Umanjivanje, banaliziranje i poricanje zločina', *Politička misao: časopis za politologiju* 55(1), pp. 7–32.; Kasapović, M. (2019). 'Povijest, povijesni revizionizam i politike povijesti', *Časopis za suvremenu povijest* 51(3), pp. 939–960.

[3] Baskin, M. & Pickering, P. M. (2008). 'What is to be done? Succession from the League of Communists of Croatia', *Communist and Post-Communist Studies* 41(4), pp. 521–540.

[4] Gračanin, H. (2008). 'Od Hrvata pak koji su stigli u Dalmaciju odvojio se jedan dio i zavladao Ilirikom i Panonijom: Razmatranja uz DAI c. 30, 75–78'. *Povijest u nastavi* 6(11/1), pp. 67–76; Klaić, N. (1985). 'Najnoviji radovi o 29. 30. i 31. poglavlju u djelu De administrando imperio cara Konstantina VII. Porfirogeneta', *Starohrvatska prosvjeta* 3(15), pp. 31–60.; Margetić, L. (1977). 'Konstantin Porfirogenet i vrijeme dolaska Hrvata', *Zbornik Odsjeka za povijesne znanosti Zavoda za povijesne i društvene znanosti Hrvatske akademije znanosti i umjetnosti*, 8, pp. 5–88.

Croatia.[5] Furthermore, in discussing the educational system we cite works by authors with expertise in the teaching of history in the classroom, who have produced guidebooks for history teachers in primary schools and published articles in journals related to the teaching of history.[6] When analysing linguistic changes and the connection between language and culture, we call on Croatian linguists and literary experts such as Ivo Žanić, Lada Badurina, and Mate Kapović.[7]

As a small country of around four million people, and relatively young, Croatia is still building its international profile. It sees itself strongly embedded in the Western political, economic, and cultural circle, being a member both of the European Union and of NATO. Relations with other countries are pursued primarily through economic interests. However, reality is never just black or white. There are various grey shades in between, and it is in this area that we will try to bring to the surface an understanding of Croatia's relationship with Pan-Slavism and in particular South Slavism.

Historical Overview

Attitudes towards Pan-Slavism and ideas of South Slavic unity in Croatia are ambivalent, both at the highest echelons of political power (with different parties approaching the issue slightly differently) and among the broader citizenry. On the one hand, contemporary attitudes are strongly influenced by the (for some Croats) disquieting cultural and political experience of Yugoslavism. Croatia spent most of the twentieth century in Yugoslav unions, both of which emphasised a South Slavic

---

[5] Krišto, J. (1991). 'Hrvatsko katoličanstvo i ideološko formiranje Stjepana Radića (1893–1914)', *Časopis za suvremenu povijest*, 23(1–3), pp. 129–163.

[6] Švigir, D. (2018). 'Slika "drugoga": predodžbe o Srbima u hrvatskim udžbenicima povijesti za osnovnu školu od 1990. do 2012. godine', *Historijski zbornik*, 71(1), pp. 105–134.; Tomljenović, A. (2012). 'Slika Hrvata u srpskim i Srba u hrvatskim udžbenicima povijesti za osnovnu školu', *Povijest u nastavi*, 10(19), pp. 1–32.

[7] Badurina, L. (2015). 'Standardizacija ili restandardizacija hrvatskog jezika u 90-im godinama 20. stoljeća'. In: Pišković, Tatjana and Vuković, Tvrtko (ed.) *Jezične, kulturne i književne politike. Zbornik radova 43. seminara Zagrebačke slavističke škole*. Zagreb: Zagrebačka slavistička škola, pp. 57–79; Kapović, M. (2011). *Čiji je jezik?* Zagreb: Algoritam.; Žanić, I. (2003). 'Simbolični identitet Hrvatske u trokutu *raskrižje-predziđe-most*'. In: Kamberović, Husnija (ed.) *Historijski mitovi na Balkanu*. Sarajevo: Institut za istoriju u Sarajevu, pp. 161–202.

identity above (and often instead of) national identities. The 'integral Yugoslavism' of the first Yugoslavia and the 'brotherhood and unity' doctrine of the second not only sought to establish a common identity in place of individual ones, but were also at times used as tools of political oppression (especially as both Yugoslav regimes were authoritarian in nature). However, one must understand that the second Yugoslavia started with an internationalist outlook, as a federation of nations, and the Yugoslav constitutions underlined that the nations had united to form Yugoslavia. It was only in the later stages of the existence of the Yugoslav state that a higher level of unity among nations was encouraged through a concept of Yugoslav patriotism. While some Croats maintain a negative view of post-Second World War Yugoslavia, there is also a significant number who remember with nostalgia the 'old days' and highlight that during the existence of the Socialist Federative Republic of Yugoslavia, Croatia, like other Yugoslav republics, experienced significant economic, cultural, and social development.

Ideas and political conceptions of South Slavic unity have had a strong presence in the construction of a modern Croatian identity and in the political thought of many forefathers of the Croatian nation. Although ideas of South Slavic unity on the territory of modern Croatia can be traced back to the fifteenth and sixteenth centuries and the works of prominent authors such as Vinko Pribojević (*On the Origin and Glory of Slavs*), Mavro Orvini (*The Kingdom of the Slavs*), and Juraj Križanić (*Discussions on Rulership*), South Slavism truly rose to prominence during the process of constructing a unified and modern Croatian identity. The genesis of a Croatian national and political identity in the modern sense can be traced back to the early nineteenth century and the Croatian National Revival (*Hrvatski narodni preporod*), a political and cultural movement that not only laid the groundwork for wider national awareness, but also planted the early seeds of a burgeoning urban intelligentsia that would be the heart of Croatian national ideation for decades to come. It as well created a modern, codified language and orthography based on the Shtokavian dialect (*štokavski*), without which a nation in the sense of an imagined community of 'deep, horizontal comradeship'[8] could not have been established.

---

[8] Anderson, B. (1983). *Imagined Communities. Reflections on the Origin and Spread of Nationalism*. London: Verso.

This movement was deeply infused with Slavic ideas and conceptions. The most notable figures of the Revival such as Ljudevit Gaj and Janko Drašković united under the banner of the Illyrian Movement and sought to achieve linguistic, literary, and cultural unity among South Slavic peoples. The genesis of Croatian national identity therefore occurred within a wider framework of South Slavic commonality. The very name of the movement was intended to be a symbol of unity, implying that all South Slavs were direct descendants of the ancient Illyrians and thus shared a common destiny. The formation of the Illyrian Party in 1841 is often taken to represent the entry point of Croatian national ideation into the political sphere and therefore the birth of modern Croatian nationalism.[9] It is notable that the founding fathers of modern Croatian identity did not conceive of Croats as a separate entity outside of an overarching South Slavic identity—the birth of the Croatian nation occurred under the auspices of South Slavic brotherhood.

Ljudevit Gaj was strongly influenced by the writings of perhaps the most prominent ideologue of Pan-Slavism, the Slovak writer Ján Kollár. Kollár developed an idea of Slavic cultural mutuality, claiming that all Slavic languages were but dialects of one common language, and that there existed a primordial Slavic unity that Slavic peoples should strive to once [10] again reify. Gaj, who studied under Kollár in Budapest, echoed this conception in his seminal work titled *A Brief Foundation of Croat-Slavic Orthography* (*Kratka osnova horvatsko-slavenskoga pravopisanja*), which established the basis for the codification of a Croatian *lingua franca*. Gaj explicitly utilised the terms 'Pan-Slavism' (*Panslavismus*) and 'literary Slavness' (*literärischer Slaventum*) and called for the unification of 'all the dialects of our great people' (thereby conceptualising all Slavs as part of one cultural body) with the aim of having his orthographic reform adopted not just by Croats, but by all South Slavic peoples utilising the Latin script.[11]

---

[9] Benson, L. (2004). *Yugoslavia: A Concise History.* New York: Palgrave Macmillan.

[10] Stančić, N. (1997). 'Ideja o "slavenskoj uzajamnosti" Jana Kollara i njezina hrvatska recepcija', *Radovi Zavoda za hrvatsku povijest Filozofskoga fakulteta Sveučilišta u Zagrebu*, 30(1), pp. 65–76.

[11] Stančić, N. (1997), pp. 72–73.

Gaj attempted to operationalise his ideas and sought support for the Illyrian cause in Serbia and Russia, though to little avail.[12] A few decades later, the bishop Josip Juraj Strossmayer founded the Yugoslav Academy of Arts and Sciences as a means to bridge the differences between the Catholic and Orthodox Slavic peoples. Strossmayer hoped that South Slavic unity would pave the way for the federalisation of Austria-Hungary, granting Croatia its long-sought autonomy, as well as bestowing upon it the mantle of leadership among South Slavs. In a text written to commemorate Strossmayer, Lukas[13] references a document written by Strossmayer regarding the political system of a prospective South Slavic state, in which Strossmayer states that the 'most important goal of the common struggle of Croats, Serbs, Bulgarians, and Slovenes' should be the creation of a South Slavic state, but he also emphasises that all the comprising nations ought to be fully independent and free within the union, thus granting Croatia the liberty it did not enjoy as part of the Austro-Hungarian empire. Lukas also quotes a speech made by Strossmayer in 1884 regarding the Academy, in which the bishop states that 'in the holy faith and in arts and sciences there are no differences', emphasising the Academy's role in cementing Strossmayer's concept of a South Slavic union which would also serve as a vessel for Croatian political emancipation.

The early formative period of the Croatian language and national identity was thus steeped in Slavic (especially South Slavic) narratives. This pattern remained unchanged in the first half of the twentieth century. The unification of the South Slavic peoples into a single nation was strongly supported by prominent Croatian politicians such as Ante Trumbić and Frano Supilo, while one of the most prominent Croatian thinkers of the time, Stjepan Radić, was very much under the influence of Pan-Slavism. Inspired by Czech and Slovak writers such as Tomáš Masaryk and Pavel Josef Šafařík, Radić's writings called for the brotherly unity of Croats, Serbs, Slovenians, and Bulgarians. Radić claimed that Croats and Serbs

---

[12] Jonke, L. (1975). 'Ljudevit Gaj kao višestruki pobjednik', *Jezik: časopis za kulturu hrvatskoga književnog jezika*, 23(3–4), pp. 67–79.; Murray Despalatović, E. (1973). 'Ljudevit Gaj—Panslavist i nacionalist', *Radovi Zavoda za hrvatsku povijest Filozofskoga fakulteta Sveučilišta u Zagrebu*, 3(1), pp. 111–122.

[13] Lukas, F. (1926). *Strossmayer i hrvatstvo. Spomenspis povodom otkrića spomenika.* Zagreb: Matica hrvatska.

were but western and eastern denominations of a single people, the South Slavs, who comprised the four aforementioned nations.[14]

In the final days of the Austro-Hungarian monarchy, Radić supported the Austro-Slavic solution, a transition from dualism into trialism with the establishment of a third, South Slavic entity.[15] Although he would soon grow disillusioned with the newly created Kingdom of Serbs, Croats, and Slovenes, Slavic ideation would still play an important part (although implicit rather than explicit) in his political thought. As per Radić's *Constitution of the Neutral Peasants' Republic of Croatia (Ustav Neutralne seljačke Republike Hrvatske)*—written as a manifesto for and itinerary of the creation of an independent Croatian state—as well as his other works, a true and functional republic was to be constructed around the peasantry as the embodiment of the public interest. His conception of the peasantry was in turn moulded by the Russian *narodniks* and their understanding of the peasant as a just and virtuous man of the land whose unsullied soul provided an ideal foundation for political action.[16]

Even though ideas of Slavic unity did not represent a monolithic consensus within the Croatian political elite, they were still influential among some of the more prominent members of the political arena at the time. A few decades later, during World War II, swathes of Croats chose to seek a brighter future by joining the Partisan resistance led by the Communist party of Yugoslavia and its leader Josip Broz Tito, a movement which fervently espoused ideas of South Slavic unity. Many of these were not communists, but rather hoped that the antifascist resistance movement heralded a fairer and more equal South Slavic union to come after the war, one which would espouse social and political democracy among the nations and the working people instead of the oligarchic authoritarianism of integral Yugoslavism.[17]

It is important to point out that in none of the aforementioned modern examples was *Pan*-Slavism salient. At no point during and after the formation of a Croatian political identity did Croatian political representatives or the Croatian people more broadly strive towards the creation of a

---

[14] Krišto, J. (1991), pp. 134–136.

[15] Rychlik, J. (2016). 'The Brothers Antun and Stjepan Radić and the Croatian Peasant Party', *Zbornik Janković*, 1(1), pp. 91–99.

[16] Cipek, T. (1995), pp. 343–344, 348.

[17] Kisić-Kolanović, N. (1995). 'Proturječnosti hrvatskog partizanskog pokreta', *Časopis za suvremenu povijest*, 27(3), pp. 425–439.

wider Slavic union, nor was the idea of such unity prominent. Rather, ideas of *South* Slavic unity were selectively appropriated and applied to the political context of a given time in order to serve as a tool of national emancipation.

South Slavism and Yugoslavia

How, then, does one explain Croatia's contemporary detachment from ideas of South Slavic unity and cooperation? A common pattern in all the aforementioned historical examples is the use of South Slavism, and to some extent Pan-Slavism, as an anti-hegemonic ideology of liberation; it was used as a framework and foundation for crafting political alternatives to a bleak *status quo* of subservience, be it under the Habsburg crown or under Axis tyranny. The proximate cause of Croatian alienation from Pan-Slavic conceptions was the perceived transformation of Yugoslavism/South Slavism into a tool of political oppression and identity erasure in both the Kingdom of Yugoslavia and in socialist Yugoslavia (with the latter having substantially more influence as it is the more recent and therefore more vivid component of the current collective political memory).

It must, however, be said that the two Yugoslav unions were fundamentally different. Unlike the first Yugoslavia, where any form of national emancipation was metaphorically thrown out the window, the second Yugoslavia allowed for a certain level of national self-determination and identity. Its roots lay in the antifascist Partisan resistance, which created independent national antifascist councils (the Croatian version being ZAVNOH), which then transformed into (relatively) autonomous socialist republics within the newly formed Yugoslav union. The Yugoslav constitution of 1974 not only explicitly affirmed a right to self-determination for all the constituent nations, but also granted them the right to secede.[18] Despite all of this, national freedoms and identity were limited in socialist Yugoslavia. Indeed, even as the new constitution was unveiled in 1974, Tito was purging hundreds of reformists who had demanded those very amendments from the party.[19]

---

[18] Ustav Socijalističke Federativne Republike Jugoslavije. Ustav Socijalističke Republike Hrvatske (1974). Zagreb: Narodne novine.

[19] Benson, L. (2004), pp. 122–123.

In Croatia, the reformist movement was first known as MASPOK (short for *masovni pokret*, 'mass movement') and later as the Croatian Spring (*Hrvatsko proljeće*). It was led by reformist communists such as Savka Dabčević-Kučar and Miko Tripalo, who agitated for wider autonomy for the federal states within Yugoslavia as well as for broader reforms to the political system. Even though the movement succeeded in pushing for some reform, it was ultimately defeated and its proponents purged.[20] This remains one of the reasons why the period of socialist rule is a significant source of cultural trauma in Croatia and is seen by many to be a period of identity suppression.

On the cultural level, socialist Yugoslavia also pushed for supranational unity. As per the Novi Sad Agreement of 1954, Serbs and Croats shared a common language in communist Yugoslavia. The document claimed that Serbian and Croatian were one language with two distinct dialects and scripts; as per the document, Croats did not speak Croatian, they spoke Serbo-Croatian or Croato-Serbian[21] To counter this, a group of Croatian linguists published the 'Declaration on the Name and Position of the Croatian Literary Language' (*Deklaracija o nazivu i položaju hrvatskog književnog jezika*), advocating for a stronger position for the Croatian language within the Yugoslav union. This antagonised the regime; the Central Committee of the Croatian Communist Party attempted to prevent the document's publication, and its signatories were expelled from the party and/or dismissed from the public positions they held.[22] For many Croatian citizens, the aforementioned linguistic rebranding constituted nothing but an attempt at artificial cultural unification and the erasure of a Croatian identity historically tied to the existence of an independently developed language, as well as to the preservation of cultural heritage and intergenerationally transmitted national memory via the Croatian language.[23] However, one has to bear in mind that there is no language, in particular a language of a small and young nation, which developed independently in a vacuum. In that respect, the Croatian

---

[20] Kasapović, M. (1996), p. 86; Baskin, M. and Pickering, P. M. (2008), p. 524.

[21] Batović, A. (2010). 'Zapadne reakcije na objavu Deklaracije o nazivu i položaju hrvatskoga književnoga jezika 1967. godine', *Časopis za suvremenu povijest*, 42(3), pp. 579–594.

[22] Batović, A. (2010), pp. 584, 587.

[23] Piskač, D. and Sršen, A. (2012). 'Hrvatski nacionalni identitet i Europska Unija', *Slavia meridonalis*, 12, pp. 159–171.

language developed under the influence of Austrian, Hungarian, Italian, Yugoslav, and other cultural milieus, and Croatian writers have used different variants of what we today call the Croatian language. Nevertheless, the aggressive reaction of the Yugoslav regime to demands for linguistic parity helped further entrench Croatian resentment.

Dissolution of Yugoslavia in the 1990s

The Croatian War of Independence (commonly referred to as the Homeland War, *Domovinski rat*) is seen by many, especially those who were affected and victimised by the war, as a struggle against both the aggression of the Yugoslav army and the Croatian Serb uprising from within Croatia's own territory—leading to the establishment of a self-proclaimed Serb state on Croatian territory (the Republic of Serbian Krajina)—and also simultaneously a struggle against Yugoslav and communist ideology. This war created an anti-communist and anti-Yugoslav perception among the Croatian people.

By the time the war had broken out, SFR Yugoslavia existed only nominally: full control of the state apparatus and the military had been assumed by the leader of the League of Communists of Serbia, Slobodan Milošević, who instrumentalised it in pursuit of Serb nationalism. In Croatian public discourse, however, Milošević was but a continuation of communist oppression, and the war of the 1990s is often framed within the political sphere and in popular culture as the emancipatory act of Croatian resistance against a communist and dictatorial regime. The collective memory of the dissolution of Yugoslavia is therefore defined by an inextricable triangular link between (Yugo)slavism, communism, and the horrors of war, which is a framework utilised within the Croatian political narrative.

The contemporary Croatian right wing strategically evokes these memories for the purpose of political mobilisation. The image of the enemy in the ideology of Croatian right-wing parties—including the current ruling party, the HDZ (*Hrvatska demokratska zajednica*, Croatian Democratic Union)—is constructed around the belief that communists, Yugoslavs, and Serbs are still a credible threat to Croatian democracy and independence, with the three elements most often intertwining into one singular notion of the enemy. A former deputy prime minister, Tomislav Karamarko explicitly blamed communists ('commies') for the negative consequences of the process of democratic and market transition in Croatia, while droves of war veterans protesting from October 2014 until April 2016 against Predrag Matić, the Social Democratic Party's minister for veterans' affairs at the time, claimed they were 'fighting against Communists and Yugoslavs'.[24] The Croatian right wing seeks to equate its political opponents on the left with a pre-existing historical and political trauma in order to demonise them.

It needs to be said, however, that although the left's position on Croatia's twentieth-century history is not as unambiguous as that of the right, it would be quite a stretch to claim that there is any strong influence of communism or even socialism on the contemporary Croatian left. The most popular nominally left-wing party, the SDP (*Socijaldemokratska partija Hrvatske*, the Social Democratic Party of Croatia) is best described as centrist, and while the newly formed political platform *Možemo!* (Yes, we can!)—whose candidate Tomislav Tomašević recently won the mayoral elections in Zagreb—is indeed a green-left progressive party, they are far removed from communist ideology. Furthermore, ideas of South Slavic unity are not represented on the Croatian left; its representatives are largely pro-EU and Atlanticist in their advocacy.

However, insofar as the concept of a Yugoslav/Serb/communist conspiracy is still alive in the minds of the Croatian right wing, and insofar as this image is perpetuated as part of electoral campaigns, Yugoslavism is likely to be seen not as a dangerous symbol of oppression, but also as a potential present and future danger. It is important to emphasise that such conceptions are not only facilitated through overt political action, but through the Croatian national broadcaster, the media, and through policies and patterns concerning commemoration, including monuments, memorials, and national holidays and related celebrations (such as the annual Victory Day ceremony in Knin) that tend to be quite subjective and exclusionary towards victims from the Serbian side,[25] and as such contribute to the perpetuation of the beliefs described herein.

---

[24] Cipek, T. (2017), pp. 155–157.

[25] Banjeglav, T. (2012). 'Sjećanje na rat ili rat sjećanja? Promjene u politikama sjećanja u Hrvatskoj od 1990. godine do danas', In: Banjeglav, Tamara, Govedarica, Nataša and Karačić, Darko (ed.) *Re:vizija prošlosti. Službene politike sjećanja u Bosni i Hercegovini, Hrvatskoj i Srbiji od 1990. godine*. Sarajevo: ACIPS & Friedrich-Ebert-Stiftung, pp. 91–161.

Post-Independence Politics

Given the factors analysed so far, we posit that there is a strong sense of enmity towards ideas of South Slavic unity and common destiny in the minds of majority of the Croatian people, as well as a powerful effect of path dependence,[26] which compels the highest echelons of political power in Croatia to perpetuate this belief, having constructed much of their political legitimacy on that very basis. We shall therefore further two sets of claims.

Firstly, we claim that the country's contemporary detachment from South Slavism has had a strong, if not overpowering effect on Croatian foreign policy. After having achieved international recognition and the reintegration of occupied parts of its territory, Croatian foreign policy has focused almost exclusively, and with absolute priority, on Euro-Atlantic integration and accession to NATO and the European Union. Former Special Advisor to the Croatian President and current international relations professor at the Faculty of Political Sciences in Zagreb, Dejan Jović posits that Croatia has pursued a single-goal foreign policy, focusing most of its efforts on becoming a full-fledged member of the political West. Croatia's strong desire to join NATO and the EU was not motivated solely by material benefit but also by a yearning for a 'return to Europe',[27] in other words, by the belief that Croatia's rightful place is not in the Balkans alongside other South Slavic nations but rather in the cultural circle of Western Europe and *Mitteleuropa*. To the extent that Euroscepticism has existed and continues (to a relatively significant extent) to exist, it is driven by a fear of losing sovereignty anew after having won it through bloodshed, and thereby potentially succumbing to a 'new Yugoslavia'.[28] Indeed, Article 135 of the Croatian constitution explicitly forbids any and all forms of interstate relations which would or may lead to the

---

[26] In economics, path dependence refers to a situation where an outcome is a result of a sequence of past actions in the sense that a set of conditions established by past actions necessitates a certain present outcome. In this context, it is used to explain how previous political action affects that in the present.

[27] Jović, D. (2011), p. 10.

[28] Jović, D. (2011), p. 11.

creation of a Yugoslav or Balkan multinational union.[29] This constitutional decree was added as an amendment in reaction to the rise of the 'Western Balkans' as a geopolitical concept.

In the 1990s, EU institutions and policies related to the region began increasingly to refer to the 'Western Balkans', a term meant to encompass all ex-Yugoslav countries except for Slovenia and with the addition of Albania. In EU documents such as the *Regional Approach for the Western Balkans*, Croatia was considered part of a larger regional whole, a single geographic unit which was to be the target of multiple facets of EU foreign and enlargement policy.[30] This prompted a reaction from the then-HDZ government, which amended the constitution with the aim of putting a final stop to any political action leading in any way whatsoever to a South Slavic union.

Croatia's most recent strategic document on national security[31] emphasises that Croatia 'belongs to a group of developed democratic countries, with which it shares common European values', as well as underlines its Central European identity and commitment to the trans-Atlantic partnership with the United States of America. This same document highlights that Croatia considers the presence of NATO and the EU to its immediate south-east to be of the utmost importance. Croatia has shown a strong commitment to the Europeanisation of its foreign policy and demonstrates (at points unwavering) loyalty to the European Union, examples of which most recently can be seen in the Croatian response to the COVID-19 crisis. This does not mean that Croatia is not trying to develop relations with the Russian Federation or other Slavic nations. However, these relationships are based on economic ties and, in the case of countries also belonging to the EU and NATO, function within the frameworks of cooperation of these organisations. Therefore, there is no pro-Slavic thought driving relations with countries inhabited by Slavs.

---

[29] Zakon.hr (2021). 'Ustav Republike Hrvatske', https://www.zakon.hr/z/94/Ustav-Republike-Hrvatske. Accessed on 2 October 2021.

[30] Slukan Altić, M. (2011). 'Hrvatska kao Zapadni Balkan – geografska stvarnost ili nametnuti identitet?' *Društvena istraživanja: časopis za opća društvena pitanja*, 20(2), pp. 401–413.

[31] Narodne-novine.nn.hr. (2017). 'Strategija nacionalne sigurnosti Republike Hrvatske', https://narodne-novine.nn.hr/clanci/sluzbeni/2017_07_73_1772.html. Accessed on 2 October 2021.

Secondly, we claim that anti-South Slavic narratives have strongly impacted Croatian internal affairs. Multiple spheres of cultural and social life have been impacted by the attempts of the political and intellectual elite to differentiate Croatia from other South Slavic nations. A primary locus of identity politics is language: numerous words and phrases used in everyday speech have been replaced by new ones considered 'more Croatian'. Elements of language considered Serbisms were removed *en masse*, while new words were crafted alongside new Croatian-Serbian dictionaries published to highlight the differences between the two languages and to decouple them from one another. Many of those changes were highly illogical, and some of them paradoxically led to replacing perceived Serbian linguistic influence with that of other Slavic languages such as Czech.[32] A clear example of such effort is the publication of a dictionary of differences between the Serbian and Croatian languages (*Razlikovni rječnik srpskog i hrvatskog jezika*) authored by Vladimir Brodnjak, the publisher being Školske novine. In the same year, the same author and publisher issued a paperback edition in an effort, as described in the preface, to make the Dictionary accessible to the largest number of readers.

The conceptual link between Serbs, Yugoslavs, and communists lives on in political narratives. There is a general tendency to emphasise differences between Croatia and other South Slavic states and to demonise South Slavism as a source of woe and trauma. Although negative references to Pan-Slavism specifically are few and do not occupy significant space in public discourse, negative perceptions of South Slavism/Yugoslavism have created a strong disincentive to foster positive beliefs towards Pan-Slavic ideas. We will attempt to provide a comprehensive analysis of how the politics of history in Croatia has shaped Croatia's relationship with Pan-Slavism, and how, insofar as detachment is facilitated instead of leaning in, this acts as a perpetuating mechanism for Croatian foreign policy.

Although there have been individual studies dealing with particular aspects of Croatia's complex relationship with (South) Slavic ideation, many of which are referenced in this text, no relevant study has to our knowledge attempted to provide a broad and comprehensive overview of

---

[32] Kapović, M. (2010).

this topic at a general level, covering both historical aspects and contemporary internal affairs as well as foreign policy. We therefore aim to further deepen the understanding of this issue through the analysis presented in the next section.

DIFFERENTIATION FROM SOUTH SLAVISM THROUGH EDUCATION

One of the most insightful ways of determining the ideological course a society is pursuing is to closely inspect its educational system, particularly the way it teaches history. The way a country presents itself, its past challenges, and the context in which it envelops these are all tied to its ideology and are the building blocks of identity construction. Ever since the creation of an independent Croatia, the educational system has been instrumentalised as a tool of decoupling the notion of a Croatian identity from any form of South Slavic ideation. The perceived connection between Yugoslavism and South Slavism has played a pivotal role in this process. The Homeland War raged parallel to a battle on a more intellectual battlefield, the one over the construction of identity.

Croatian politics of history have had a strong influence on educational curricula. History textbooks have consistently been a tool for the construction of national identity and of the Other: multiple studies have analysed reductionist patterns equating Serbian history with perpetual plans of establishing a Greater Serbia, as well as representing Yugoslavia primarily as a smokescreen for Serbian oppression.[33] Švigir analyses Croatian history textbooks to find that Serbs and Croats are consistently presented as being in a perpetual conflict, in which Croats are presented as victims of Serbs.[34] A 1992 history textbook described the problems of socialist Yugoslavia as being generated by the Serbian leadership, which 'attempted to centralise Yugoslavia to realise its hegemonic, Greater Serbia interests and ambitions.... It was clear that such expansionist politics had one goal: either to transform Yugoslavia into expanded Serbia or to create a Greater Serbia'.[35]

---

[33] Đurašković, S. (2008). Tomljenović, A. (2012).

[34] Švigir, D. (2017), p. 117.

[35] Švigir, D. (2017), p. 113.

All of this has helped to create a perception that the history of Croatia is a history of a centuries-long struggle for independence and sovereignty, a struggle in which the enemies are Croatia's Slavic neighbours to the east. What is important to keep in mind is that history textbooks, particularly those used by younger children, necessarily present a simplification of history. They extrapolate figures and names deemed to be most important and craft a broad storyline around them, removing numerous elements of context. This allows for a relatively effortless inculcation of ethnocentric historical narratives and the association of positive or negative attributes with historical actors, even with entire nations. Although some improvement has occurred over the years, biased perceptions of history have lived on in textbooks well into the 2000s; a large number of textbooks devote a significantly larger amount of time to Serbian misdeeds than to Croatian ones, while trying to relativise responsibility for the latter, as well as simplistically assign sides in conflicts to entire ethnic groups while ignoring factual nuance.[36]

Even though there is no pertinent discussion of Pan-Slavic ideas in Croatian public discourse, nor are such ideas espoused by any relevant public figure or organisation, if those ideas were to appear, it is likely that Croatia's relationship with South Slavism would offer infertile ground for this type of ideation. Given the aforementioned enmity towards Serbs perpetuated through the educational system, and the connection between this enmity and negative perceptions of Yugoslav unitarism (which utilised conceptions of South Slavic unity in its symbolism, as evident in the name itself), it is also likely that negative connotations would apply to anything bearing the 'Slavic' name, as this would evoke memories of historical and political trauma.

The active desire of the political elite in Croatia to define the nation as naturally belonging to Central Europe in a political and cultural sense is also reflected in the representation of earlier Croatian history. Numerous history textbooks emphasise the role of Croatia as the 'bulwark of Christendom' (*predzide kršćanstva/antemurale Christianitatis*) in the face of the Ottoman threat,[37] thereby also implying a geographical narration of 'us' versus 'them': Croatia is assaulted by ruthless invaders and conquerors

---

[36] Tomljenović, A. (2012), pp 11–13.
[37] Jurić, F. (2013). 'Balkan u hrvatskim udžbenicima povijesti za osnovnu školu', *Povijest u nastavi*, 21(1), pp. 23–44.

from the outside (from the Balkans), while beyond her borders lies the civilised Christian lands of Europe. This perception is not limited to formal education; rather, it has been explicitly endorsed by the highest echelons of political power. A former high-ranking Croatian diplomat, Miomir Žužul, referred to Croatia's future NATO membership as a renewal of 'the historical duty to act as the bulwark of Christendom', while the former president Franjo Tuđman evoked the aforementioned motif on multiple occasions.[38]

Tuđman's party (and Croatia's current ruling party), the HDZ, continues to draw from the same symbolic repositories in constructing their political discourse, thereby perpetuating and reinforcing it, and presents itself as the founder of the Croatian state. In general, the framing of Croatian independence from Yugoslavia as a ticket 'back into' Central Europe and away from the Balkans—where, supposedly, Croatia never belonged—has been deeply entrenched in education, in the media, and in political communication.[39] Croatia, in short, aims to distance itself from the European east and southeast and position itself in the European centre and west—i.e. away from the geographical nexus of Pan-Slavic ideas and tendencies.

Given the structural tendency of the educational system, and of the wider political sphere, to renounce the Balkans as a part of Croatian identity, as well as to advance an ethnocentric framing of historical events that fosters antagonism and enmity towards the idea of Yugoslav political unity, there is little fertile ground for ideas of Pan-Slavic unity in Croatia. The first and second Yugoslavias (and, by extension, the Balkans, since both Yugoslav states were essentially unions of Balkan nations) are seen to be synonymous with war, oppression, and a loss of political as well as personal agency. The Yugoslav states (especially socialist Yugoslavia) strongly appropriated the linguistic and symbolic register of South Slavism not just in their very name but also in most other elements of their political identities; therefore, insofar as the idea of Yugoslavia and Yugoslavism represents a taint on Croatian history, this taint has spilled over, as a corollary, onto Pan-Slavic ideation more broadly. Insofar as the educational system continues to perpetuate these beliefs, it is unlikely that the situation will change. This is particularly true given that Pan- and South

---

[38] Žanić, I. (2003), p. 192.
[39] Jurić, F. (2013).

Slavism do not prominently feature in textbooks or classrooms. Students perceive them in a political and ideological sense through the lens of Yugoslavism, therefore strengthening the already existing conflation of the two concepts.

Detachment from but also Occasional Nostalgia for Yugoslavia

Lastly, in the context of Croatia's relationship with Pan-Slavism, it is important to analyse the dominant politics of history in Croatia, embodied particularly in its politics of commemoration and usage thereof in identity construction.

In the immediate post-war years, the new political leadership systematically erased references to Yugoslav history from public life. Numerous monuments commemorating the antifascist struggle of the Partisan movement were destroyed, removed, neglected, or damaged. Official discourse often recalls the Yugoslav period as a time when it was 'forbidden to call oneself a Croat'.[40] The Yugoslav state is equated with an absolute denial of identity; in other words, South Slavic unity devoured the individual national identity of Croatians. This belief was not exclusive to the post-war years: it continues to the present day. In 2016, a Croatian deputy prime minister, Tomislav Karamarko, openly evoked the aforementioned structures of remembrance and blamed the 'children of communism' for all issues plaguing the state.[41] In this rhetoric, Tuđman was mistaken in not having effectively purged the offspring of former communist officials and members of the Communist Party from the political and social arena, for by not doing so, he allowed them to infiltrate the political system and undermine 'true Croatian values'.[42]

Again, not only are Croatian values and the notion of Croatianness directly counterposed to the history of the South Slavic union, but those who supported Yugoslavia are made out to be actively hostile to the Croatian state. Even though there is no direct discussion of Pan-Slavism, the

---

[40] Đurašković, S. and Jušić, L. (2017). 'Politike povijesti u Estoniji i Hrvatskoj: Drugi svjetski rat kao "prošlost koja nikad neće proći"?. *Anali Hrvatskog politološkog društva: časopis za politologiju*, 14(1), pp. 125–142.

[41] Đurašković, S. and Jušić, L. (2017), p. 134.

[42] Đurašković, S. and Jušić, L. (2017), p. 134, quoted per Hudelist, Darko (2015).

notion of South Slavic unity has been irrevocably connected to negative memories and narratives. Although not tainted in and of itself, it would be reasonable to posit that any wider discussion of Pan-Slavic ideation would be tainted by proxy.

Finally, it has to be noted independently of the politics of commemoration that intergenerationally transmitted memory, particularly memory related to past trauma, is a powerful source of incentives and disincentives for political behaviour. As per Đurašković, it is exactly the memory of failed Slavic political unions that helped install right-wing nationalist governments not just in Croatia, but also for instance in Slovakia after the dissolution of the Czechoslovak state.[43] Their respective unions had pursued the establishment of their political subjectivity through union rather than independence, and the failure of these unions, which is alive in the collective memory of their population, has served as empirical proof that Slavic unity is an ill-fated concept best left in the worn-out pages of history books.

It is important to note that discourse regarding Croatia's recent past is not monolithic. Many reputable historians such as Damir Agičić and Hrvoje Klasić actively criticise the way history is portrayed in classrooms and advocate for curricular reform. There is also no clear consensus on the politics of remembrance: the renaming of Zagreb's Marshal Tito Square (*Trg maršala Tita*) to the Square of the Republic of Croatia (*Trg Republike Hrvatske*) was preceded by long and intense public debate. Annual memorials are held for the victims of Jasenovac and are regularly attended by Croatian government officials. However, in recent years commemorations by national minority communities (Jewish, Serbian) have taken place separately from the state's, reflecting a rift between national minorities and the state as a result of more forceful nationalistic political rhetoric. The political arena is also far from uniform. Not only has HDZ moved towards the political centre in recent years, with the ambition of transforming itself into a modern Christian Democratic party, but there are also relevant centre-left political actors, including the Social Democratic Party and the newly formed green-left platform Možemo!, whose political narrative is not focused on anti-Yugoslavism but rather on ideas of civic democratic participation, the environment, and local development. Lastly, younger generations tend to be either more conservative or the complete

---

[43] Đurašković, S. (2008), p. 205.

opposite, embracing progressive ideas of tolerance and openness while shedding the skin of nationalism.

It is also worth noting that one may encounter a fair amount of nostalgia towards the socialist Yugoslav state among some sections of the older population, particularly among those who were not ideologically at odds with the regime or strongly affiliated with an exclusively Croatian identity. This nostalgia will most often take the form of lamenting the social security citizens enjoyed during the former Yugoslav regime (secure employment, secure pensions, etc.), as well as the loss of an idealised conception of 'brotherhood and unity' between Yugoslav nations, as many people will have had close friends or acquaintances from other federal states. It could be said that, in this form, South Slavism continues to live on in Croatia, albeit not assuming any relevant political form or expression.

Conclusion

This chapter presents a historical and political review of Croatia's perception of and engagement with ideas of Pan-Slavism and, more specifically, South Slavism. In the nineteenth and the early twentieth centuries, Croatian writers and political actors embraced and advanced ideas of South Slavic unity as a way for nations in the Balkans to emancipate and liberate themselves from Austro-Hungarian rule, while ideas of Pan-Slavism were never strongly salient among Croatian thinkers. The formation of the two Yugoslavias, after the First and Second World Wars respectively, served as attempts to implement ideas of South Slavic unity in practice. However, the failure of these two states, in particular the violent break-up of socialist Yugoslavia, imprinted onto modern Croatian political thought the notion of distance and the active negation of any possibility of future union among South Slavs.

Official political narratives actively seek to distance Croatia from Yugoslavia and, in effect, from South Slavism. Since the war in the 1990s, Croatian political leadership has been actively shaping national identity on the ideological basis of Croatia's rightful place in Central and Western Europe, in the European Union, and in an active partnership with the United States. Identity formation through nationalist discourse is pursued via official rhetoric, media, public policies, and education.

History textbooks still, albeit less explicitly today than in the early 1990s, attach negative connotations to Yugoslavia in general and to Serbs specifically. The trauma of a war in which the Yugoslav army, controlled by the then-Serbian leadership, was an aggressor on Croatian territory and actively supported an insurgence by Croatian Serbs strongly influences negative Croatian views of any union among South Slavs.

However, as years pass and the democratic culture develops, Croatia's perceptions of Yugoslavia, its own politics and actions in the 1990s, and of its relations towards Serbia, become less polarised. All this means that Croatia's relationship with (South) Slavism is nuanced, and may yet change over time. For now, however, the echoes of the past described in this chapter remain strong and are the key determinant of Croatia's complex relationship with Pan-Slavist ideation.

On Pan-Slavism(s) and Macedonian National Identity

Cvete Koneska

Introduction

This chapter investigates the role and impact of Slavophilia (and related narratives about belonging to larger, pan-national Slavic families) on recent domestic and foreign policy discourses in Macedonia. In particular, the focus is on post-independence domestic discourses about Macedonian national identity, tracing the influence of Slavophile arguments in the struggle to reshape and redefine national identity after the end of communism and the break-up of the Yugoslav federation. While these debates predominantly take place within the domestic political sphere, they are shaped by broader regional and geopolitical contexts. Therefore, geopolitical developments indirectly affect domestic political and social debates, increasing or decreasing the appeal and persuasive power of different narratives of belonging, such as that Macedonians belong to democratic Europe and the EU, or alternatively that they are part of an Orthodox Christian, Slavic space.

C. Koneska (✉)
St Antony's College, Oxford, UK

Drawing on literatures on national identity formation and foreign policy narratives, and following a three-layered approach to examining how Slavophile ideas have evolved and become incorporated in domestic politics over the past several decades, the chapter investigates how ideas about a shared Slavic past and identity permeate the public arena in Macedonia today. From popular culture and its expressions in traditional and social media as well as in the arts, through the political debates between decision-makers at the policy level, to strategic thinking on long-term foreign policy objectives concerning NATO and EU membership, I identify how notions about Slavic identity and affiliation with other Slavic nations shape policy and strategic outcomes.

The findings suggest that since 1991 the narrative about the Slavic nature of Macedonian identity has become increasingly questioned. Domestically, the 'Yugoslav' ideas about a South Slavic union of nations became discredited. The independent statehood of the former constituent republics of the Yugoslav federation triggered a rethinking of the master narrative of national identity and history away from the prevailing argument about the 'brotherhood and unity' of Yugoslav nations. Additionally, ethnic diversity in Macedonian society and a growing recognition of the need to include minority communities, especially ethnic Albanians, in a broader Macedonian civic identity further undermined the appeal of the Slavic roots of the Macedonian nation. Externally, aspirations to align with the West and obtain membership in regional organisations, such as the European Union and NATO, have meant that narratives about belonging to a Slavic family of nations distinct from other, especially Western European communities, have lost traction in domestic deliberations about strategic alignment in international politics.

However, beneath these three broad trends, many pan-Slavic ideas and beliefs persist, both among the general population and among the political and cultural elites. Such ideas appear to be particularly flexible and durable, not necessarily as a coherent political, ideological, or cultural movement, but most often as disparate and often paradoxical beliefs that serve to articulate the incomplete hegemony of the pro-EU and pro-democratic discourses. As such, Slavophile ideas and arguments are very plastic and have evolved to fit with both left-wing and far-right conservative ideas and policies in domestic politics, conveying both nostalgia for the Yugoslav past and frustration over the lack of progress in EU integration.

The chapter is divided into four sections. It starts with a brief overview of the key theoretical arguments that underpin the main research question, reviewing the most relevant concepts from the literature of national identity and historical narratives, along with a few insights into the links between foreign policy and national identity. The next section provides historical context, surveying the history of pan-Slavic ideas and movements in Macedonia and their role in shaping national identity over the past few decades. These legacies are critical to contemporary discourses on Macedonian national identity, providing fuel for discursive struggles and serving as counterpoints to the dominant historical narratives. The third section considers the evidence for Slavophilia in Macedonian political debates about national identity over the past two decades. Looking across popular, policy, and strategic levels, it examines how notions of Slavic national roots and of belonging to the 'Slavic world' impact how national identity is imagined and articulated. Finally, the last section discusses the findings against the broader research question. It reflects on the importance of these findings for understanding Macedonian politics, as well as more generally for studying and understanding pan-national movements and ideas in today's international politics.

NATIONAL AND PAN-NATIONAL IDENTITIES

All nations are imagined. Whether the narrative about the nation's roots and origins stretches back for centuries into early human civilisation or only reaches back to Early Modern times, it always serves a similar purpose: not to provide scientifically sound evidence about the history of a specific group of people but rather to act as a binding tissue for a large group of people, most of whom do not and will not know each other personally, yet nevertheless believe they belong to the same group—their nation.

Narratives about a nation and its origins are rooted in history, as historical legitimacy is critical to building a credible argument about a group's shared destiny, ideals, and aspirations. However, history is used selectively, with some persons, places, and events featured more prominently than others in dominant accounts of national history. History is adapted to support a story about the nation and its people, often following a common three-pronged model of (1) a 'Golden Age' in the past, which was unjustly taken away, leading to, (2) the nation's (un)deserved suffering in the present, to make sure past mistakes are not repeated, and (3) its bright future and recovery of the national glory of the past. These three elements are equally important in providing a unifying story about a nation and its past, present, and future. The more coherent and compelling this narrative is, the more successful a nation-(re)building project is likely to be, as it will resonate strongly with group (nation) members and their perceptions of the world.

The latter applies not only to building new national identities, which at present is a very rare occurrence, but also—and perhaps more importantly—to rebuilding or recalibrating existing national identities, of which the past few decades have presented many instances. For example, the break-up of large socialist federations such as Yugoslavia and the Soviet Union between 1989 and 1992 triggered rethinking of national identities by their constituent units as the unifying narrative that had legitimated each group identity was discredited. The appeal and credibility of competing narratives about the newly independent states and their nations were essential to reaching a broad new consensus on what the nation was and who belonged to it. For some, such as the Baltic states, this was a relatively smooth process, as pre-existing counter-narratives about the nation were quickly revived and elevated as the new dominant stories about these nations and their histories. For others, such as Macedonia, this was a more contentious process, and one that—as competing narratives about the people, history, their place in the world, and relations to other nations continue to vie for popular support and acceptance—remains unfinished.

As such, the case of Macedonian national identity is a particularly good case to examine. It provides insight into how different components of group identity and history are combined and built into new and revised versions of national identity. Since those debates are rooted in the specific political, economic, and social contexts through which the Macedonian people and their political elites see themselves and the world around them, this is not purely an exercise in historiography. Rather, debates over national identity also reflect the current fears and aspirations of the Macedonian people and their political leaders, adding geopolitical, economic, and regional layers to arguments about their national origins. It is in this overlap between history, regional relations, and geopolitical concerns that the question of Slavophilia in Macedonian politics becomes most relevant. As this chapter will outline, unresolved questions about the Macedonian nation and in its members engender arguments about their place in the world, with narratives on pan-Slavic unity competing with those about

Macedonia as a member of a democratic and prosperous European family of nations.

If nations are imagined, there is no reason why other communities, perhaps composed of several different nations, cannot also be imagined. Indeed, social group theory suggests that most group identities are constructed, and that the successful building of in-group identity and group affiliation is not contingent on any 'real' shared past, features, or personal identity markers. The same logic, therefore, can be applied to supranational and pan-national identities. Shared histories, language, geography, and other markers can be used to construct a broader group identity—for example, a supranational European identity (as is often debated in relation to European Union member nations) or a pan-Slavic identity encompassing all Slavic-speaking nations in Europe. Indeed, such identities may be easier to imagine given the recent, modern nature of most European nations and the resulting shared histories of many ethnic groups that used to be part of larger states and empires.

In this sense, national and pan-national identities are related concepts. When discussing 'Slavic identity' or a belonging to a Slavic group of nations, we are effectively extending the nation-building logic to a larger entity but otherwise keeping within the same methodological approach, using shared history (events, individuals, dates), common language, religion, and other markers of identity to construct a larger group identity. These broader identities are not antithetical to national identities. On the contrary, they are often predicated on the existence of different nations within the broader 'family', and stories about how different nations have helped (or betrayed) each other in the past are central to their narratives. For example, Russian support for Serbia and Bulgaria in their struggles for independence from the Ottoman Empire in the nineteenth century is central to Slavophile arguments in the region. That the Soviet Red Army also led the liberation of Belgrade in the Second World War, and post-1989 Russia continued to support Serbia in international politics concerning the status of Kosovo, only reinforces arguments about solidarity among (certain) Slavic nations—regardless of whether Russian or Serbian actions were motivated by loyalty or affinity towards related Slavic nations or not.

However, it would be misleading to see pan-national identity as an extension of national identity. One key difference is the role the state plays in building and maintaining national identity, which is missing in the case of pan-national identities. Although state and national boundaries tend not always to overlap neatly, many states today do tend to have one main constituent nation, as civically or otherwise defined. This means that national identity is tightly linked to the state and its official policies, tools, and institutions, and is supported by them. Indeed, the symbiotic nature of the state-nation relationship is fundamental to several theories about nations and national identity. As Anderson has highlighted, nation-building projects are essential to building efficient, modern states. Without the mass education and communication systems of the state, unified modern nations would have been less successful over the past two centuries.

In the case of pan-national identities, there is no direct champion of the pan-national community with comparable power, commitment, and resilience. Most pan-national identities tend to be conceived as academic or cultural projects, lacking the institutional and administrative apparatus of nation-states to support their mass appeal and to inspire loyalty towards them. As a result, they rarely enjoy the popularity and loyalty of national identities. Moreover, even in cases where supranational identities have been explicitly endorsed and promoted by a state, such as in the case of Yugoslavia, they seem to fail to gather as much popular affiliation as (ethno-)national identities do. In Yugoslavia, data from the 1981 census indicates that only 5.4% of the population identified as Yugoslav.[1] Yugoslav citizens predominantly identified with the narrower identities of their ethno-national groups. The situation is similar in more established states with longer histories of promoting pan-national identities, such as the United Kingdom, where fewer people identify as solely British than they do as English, Scottish, Welsh, or Irish.

Nonetheless, while it is not as powerful in mobilising mass loyalty and affiliation, pan-national projects remain relevant to domestic and foreign policies. Domestically, elements of pan-national ideologies and projects tend to feature in the building and redesign of national identities and the narratives that support them. In particular, the narratives about a nation's place in the region and world are often woven into official national histories and cultural and educational policies. In addition, pan-national ideas and projects tend largely to play out in the inter-state arena and in geopolitical realignments. Therefore, from an analytical perspective, they are

---

[1] 1981 Census Data in 1985 Statistical Yearbook of SFRJ. In *Statitsicki Godišnjak Jugoslavije 1982*. Republicki zavod za statistiku Republike Srbije.

most salient to foreign policy and most visible in states' behaviour towards other nations in- and outside the pan-national group. Therefore, this chapter will reflect on both the domestic and the external expressions of pan-nationalism—Slavophilia in particular—in Macedonian politics.

Pan-Slavism and Macedonian National Identity

Ideas about Slavic, and specifically South Slavic, origins and belonging are central to narratives about Macedonian national identity. From the earliest discourses on Macedonians as a separate people with their own language and history in the late-nineteenth century to today's debates among leading politicians and intellectuals in the country, the Slavic nature of Macedonian identity is integral to thinking about the Macedonian nation.

Historically, two strands of Pan-Slavic thought have shaped Macedonian thinking on national identity: (1) earlier Pan-Slavic theories and arguments, promoted by Macedonian émigré students in Russia in the mid- to late-nineteenth century; and (2) Yugoslavism, the South Slavic variety of Pan-Slavic thinking, focusing on the South Slavic nations that comprised Yugoslavia from 1918 to 1991. These two lines of thought were not fully independent but rather often interacted, and at times were used in conjunction with each other. Nonetheless, it is worth disentangling their roots and content, and tracing how they evolved over the decades.

Although broadly based on the same pan-national thinking about group identities, Pan-Slavism and Yugoslavism came to represent two different arguments about Macedonian national identity. Since Yugoslavism was tightly linked to the Yugoslav state, especially the socialist federation of 1945–1991, its view of the Macedonian nation was closely aligned with its wider paradigm about Yugoslavia and its constituent nations. Macedonia's territory, language, and history were cast as compatible with the overall ideological, political, and administrative structures of the Yugoslav state.

However, earlier thinking about Macedonians as a separate nation, based on Pan-Slavic arguments, saw Macedonians as a separate nation, not necessarily closer to the other Yugoslav nations than to other Slavic groups generally. Predicated on the romantic ideas about nationhood spreading through Europe and its peripheries in the nineteenth century, early thought about Macedonian nationhood revolved around issues of language, history, and cultural revival. They also advocated for the independence or autonomy of Macedonia from the Ottoman Empire as a necessary condition for, and outcome of, the national revival process.

The legacies of these two lines of pan-Slavic thought can still be traced in present Macedonian politics. They continue to reverberate through current political discourses and engage with each other through the arguments of political parties on both sides of the political spectrum in Macedonia.

Pan-Slavism in Early Takes on Macedonian National Identity

As Pan-Slavism emerged and evolved across the Russian Empire in the nineteenth century, its influence on émigré intellectuals and students from other Slavic lands gradually increased. Pan-Slavic ideas, along with nationalist thought, influenced emigrants' thinking about their own lands and peoples, and shaped the ideas they then articulated, published, and disseminated at home. While initially such activities were centred on language and literature, literary circles and their publications often acquired political overtones and engaged with contemporary political debates. Thus, pamphlets and books published abroad often included a mix of poetry and literature alongside discussions on national culture, identity, and statehood.

In the Macedonian case, among the most influential was the circle of students and intellectuals around Dimitrija Chupovski and Krste Petkov Misirkov in St. Petersburg during the early 1900s. This group was the first to clearly articulate arguments about a distinct Macedonian nation. Their periodical publication *Makedonski Golos*, though published in the Russian language, was instrumental to the articulation of ideas about Macedonian national identity, language, and culture.

The group around Chupovski and Misirkov in St Petersburg was influenced by Pan-Slavic thinking. Since its foundation in 1903, the Macedonian Scientific and Literary Society, as they were known, was sponsored by the Charitable Slav Society in St. Petersburg.[2] The latter is unlikely to have directly interfered with or influenced the content of Chupovski or

---

[2] Constitution of the Slav-Macedonian Scientific and Literary Society in Saint Petersburg. 16 December 1903. (Museum of Macedonia, Skopje).

Misirkov's writing; nonetheless, the Charitable Slav Society operated on broadly Pan-Slavic principles, providing support to the Slavic nations in the Austro-Hungarian and Ottoman Empires, studying Slavic culture, and supporting publications and learning among Slavic diasporas in Russia.[3] The establishment of the Macedonian Scientific and Literary Society was endorsed by several influential Slavophile figures at the time, including political and religious leaders.[4]

The key ideas underlying the Society's work are best illustrated in its Constitution and its publication *Macedonian Voice*. The Constitution outlines a programme that is a mix of linguistic, ethnographic, and political projects, a mix common in nationalist and Pan-Slavic thinking at the time. For instance, Article 2 summarises well this politico-cultural mix of activities:

'a) Organising meetings and lectures
b) Reading paper, stories, and poems, etc.
c) Collecting works of folk literature (folklore) and works of historical interest from Macedonia
...
e) be helping develop interrelations with other Slav societies and circles, as well as individual Slav activists.'

Perhaps the most explicit link to pan-Slavism is referenced in Article 13, which stipulates:

'In order to disseminate the idea of solidarity and the spiritual unity of all Slavs, regardless of religion and nationality [...], the Society allows the former to read essays and conduct discussions during its meetings only in Russian – the only Pan-Slavic language.'[5]

The above clearly links the purpose of the Macedonian Scientific and Literary Society to Pan-Slavism as a project to promote Slavic unity and solidarity. That the primary aim of the Society was to build and promote

---

[3] Zdravkovski, A., (2011). *The Macedonian Scientific and Literary Society in St. Petersburg, 1902–1917* (MA Thesis, Budapest: Central European University).

[4] Among those were the influential Slavicist Vladimir Karlovich Sabler and Foreign Minister Lambsdorf.

[5] Constitution of the Slav-Macedonian Scientific and Literary Society. Quoted in Zdravkovski (2011), p. 27.

Macedonian national identity clearly positions the two ideas in alignment. Indeed, it appears that for the Society, promoting Macedonian national 'revival' was only possible within the larger frame of Pan-Slavism.

Macedonian Voice was published by the Society in eleven editions in 1913–14, visibly departing from the scientific and literary nature of its activities. Its contents were intended to shape a public discussion on the 'Macedonian question' and put it on the political and public agenda in Russia and abroad. Chupovski was the most prolific contributor, as well as editor, of the periodical, advocating the independence of Macedonia as a state for Macedonians *qua* a separate Slavic nation. Similar arguments were advanced in *Vardar*, another publication of the Macedonian émigrés in Russia, edited by the co-founder of the Society, Krste Petkov Misirkov.

The writings in both publications inevitably reflected the political and social context of the time. With the Balkan Wars ongoing in 1913–14 and the withdrawal of the Ottoman Empire from the Balkans, the status and future of Macedonia—both as a territory and as a nation-building project—had become a topical issue, both in diplomatic circles and among students of Slavic languages and culture. Therefore, Chupovski and Misirkov's writings mostly reflect the immediate issues and arguments of the day.

Nonetheless, their work and ideas did not become irrelevant once the 'Macedonian question' was resolved after the end of the Balkan Wars and World War I. Although the Society was disbanded in 1917, the ideas that it promoted and developed did not become obsolete. On the contrary, Chupovski's and, especially, Misirkov's work have become some of the most influential ideas at the core of the narrative of Macedonian nationhood. In 1903, Misirkov published *Za Makedonckite Raboti* in Sofia, a text that is the cornerstone of Macedonian national identity, setting out the key parameters that have marked Macedonian identity since the early 1900s.[6]

Misirkov's work is cited often in contemporary debates about Macedonian national identity. *Za Macedonckite Raboti* remains the paragon against which alternative ideas and arguments are measured. His ideas are deeply rooted in how the Macedonian nation is seen by Macedonians

---

[6] Misirkov, K. P., (1969). *Za makedonckite raboti*.

today. His work is rarely questioned or critiqued, while potential Pan-Slavic origins and influences are seen as peripheral to his argument, if raised at all.

Yugoslavism and Macedonian National Identity

Yugoslavism was a regional response to the larger Pan-Slavic project in Southeastern Europe. Constructed on similar premises concerning historical, cultural, and linguistic ties among the Slavic nations in the Balkans, Yugoslavism was one of the key cultural and intellectual drivers of the creation of the first Yugoslav state after the end of World War I in 1918. Rooted in broader Pan-Slavic ideas (as well as regional varieties, such as the Illyrian movement, which developed in the 1830s and 1840s in the Austro-Hungarian empire; and the Yugoslav movement, which operated in the early 1900s), the ideas of linguistic and cultural similarities between the South Slavic nations provided a background against which to launch political initiatives to create a new, Yugoslav state in Southeastern Europe.[7]

This early Yugoslavism which culminated in the creation of the Kingdom of Serbs, Croats, and Slovenes—and from 1929 the Kingdom of Yugoslavia—did not directly contribute to the development of Macedonian national identity. Indeed, Macedonians were not recognised as a constituent or separate nation within the Yugoslav kingdom. Despite the work of the Macedonian intellectuals in Russia and within the region (Chupovski and Misirkov both spent time in Belgrade and Sofia), their ideas about the Macedonians as a separate nation in the Slavic family did not become part of the official Yugoslav project. Instead, after the end of the Balkan Wars and World War I, the Macedonian territories that were incorporated into the newly founded Kingdom of Serbs, Croats, and Slovenes became de facto part of Serbia. The official policy of the Yugoslav state at the time considered Macedonians as (South) Serbs. The Macedonian language was not recognised, and educational and administrative initiatives were introduced to build Serbian identity among the population.

---

[7] Djokić, D., (2003). *Yugoslavism: Histories of a Failed Idea, 1918–1992*. London: Hurst. Troch, P., 2010. "Yugoslavism between the World Wars: Indecisive Nation Building." *Nationalities Papers*, 38(2), pp. 227–244.

This approach did not result in any significant adoption of Serbian national identity among Macedonians. Instead, resistance towards the Yugoslav state and its authorities grew, along with clandestine nationalist organisations seeking Macedonian independence or even unification with Bulgaria. This culminated in the assassination of the Yugoslav King Aleksandar I Karadjordjevic in 1934 by a Bulgarian terrorist, Velichko Kerin (also known as Vlado Chernozemski)—*ostensibly* over the status of Macedonia within Yugoslavia.[8]

From an analytical perspective, however, this assassination was a response to growing Serbian nationalism within Yugoslavia rather than an expression of emerging Macedonian nationalism. The incident highlights the tensions between nationalisms and pan-national projects, particularly in cases where national boundaries and identities are fluid and contested, as was the case with the Macedonian nation *vis à vis* its Serbian (and Bulgarian) neighbours. Consequently, the ultimate impact of the early Yugoslavism was that the Macedonian nation-building project diverged from its previous trajectory. Instead of developing alongside other South Slavic nations, it evolved in opposition to Serbian nationalism. The legacies of these early articulations of Macedonian nationhood in relation to its neighbours are still present in the political discourse today.

Socialist Yugoslavia and 'Brotherhood and Unity'

Yugoslavism evolved and persisted after 1945, when the socialist federation of Yugoslavia with six constituent republics was established. Socialist Marxist ideology underpinned most official thinking and policy after 1945, which meant that the pre-war Yugoslavism was altered and adapted so as to be compatible with official socialist ideology in the country.[9] Some features of early Yugoslavism were kept, such as the unity between the South Slavic nations that had become the constituent nations of the

---

[8] The assassination of King Aleksandar I Karadjordjevic was unlikely to have actually been motivated by plans for Macedonian independence or efforts to get Macedonians recognised as a nation. Kerin worked with three Croat nationalists in planning and carrying out the assassination.

[9] Adamson, K. and Jović D. (2004). "The Macedonian–Albanian political frontier: the re-articulation of post-Yugoslav political identities." *Nations and Nationalism*, 10(3), pp. 293–311.

federation, and which were titular groups in each of the six republics of the federation.

In some other respects, post-war Yugoslavism added and expanded to the existing Pan-South Slavic project. For instance, to the arguments about shared origins, history, and culture, claims about shared ideology were added.[10] The joint legacies of the *partizan* resistance movement of World War II were elevated as fundamental to the shared history and destiny of the six Yugoslav nations that comprised the socialist Yugoslav state. The state, at the federal and republic levels, invested substantial resources (via official historiography and educational and administrative policies) in promoting the narrative of Yugoslavia as unifying frame for the six related Slavic nations. Employing tools usually applied by nation-states to build and promote national identity, Yugoslavia promoted a pan-national narrative about the brotherhood and unity of the Yugoslav nations and nationalities.[11]

However, in many important respects, this second Yugoslavism diverged from its predecessor. Most importantly for the Macedonians, they were recognised as a separate and constituent nation in the Yugoslav federation. This meant that the Macedonian Republic became de facto the nation-state of the Macedonian nation. Moreover, within Yugoslavia, the Macedonian language and alphabet were codified and recognised.[12] Despite the relatively late codification of the language, official Yugoslav history linked these post-1945 developments to the medieval creators of the Cyrillic alphabet, Cyril and Methodius, and to their disciples, Clement and Naum, who lived and taught in lands that now belonged to the Macedonian Republic. Similarly, Macedonian histories written after 1945 promoted a narrative of the ancient roots and continuity of the Macedonian nation, through medieval and Ottoman times, until it finally joined the other Yugoslav nations in a joint state.

---

[10] Constitution of SFRY, (1974). Preamble.

[11] Yugoslav nationalities (minority groups) were the non-Slavic ethnic communities. As listed in the 1974 Constitution, Yugoslav nationalities were Albanians, Hungarians, Italians, and Turks.

[12] The Macedonian language was codified immediately after the establishment of the Yugoslav federation and of Macedonia as a constituent federal unit within it. Key works by Blaze Koneski: *Gramatika na makedonskiot jazik* (1952), *Pravopis na makedonskiot jazik* (1945).

Another significant departure from pre-war Yugoslavism was the governing political elite's substantial efforts to suppress ethno-nationalisms, especially those of the largest nations in Yugoslavia.[13] As a result, Serbian nationalism ceased being the existential threat to Macedonian national identity that it had been between the wars. Macedonian and Serbian official histories were aligned, with controversial events and personalities omitted from the official narratives. This allowed Macedonian intellectual and political elites to develop and establish the Macedonian nation-building project in a relatively safe context, without overt challenges from the larger neighbouring nation.

However, outside of Yugoslavia, Macedonian nationhood remained contested, most fiercely by Bulgaria, which remains the main challenger to Macedonian national identity narratives to this day. And yet, until the break-up of Yugoslavia in 1991, Yugoslav foreign policy and its relative status in the international arena were such that Bulgarian challenges were never seriously regarded either as a potential for future conflict or as an opportunity for compromise. Bulgaria's close alignment to the USSR, from which Yugoslavia had forged an independent trajectory beginning in the 1950s, disincentivised Yugoslav leaders from engaging with their Bulgarian counterparts. Within Macedonia, the authorities saw any affinity towards Bulgaria as suspicious and potentially undermining of Macedonian nationhood. Perhaps engagement with Bulgarian arguments during Yugoslav times would have helped resolve some outstanding issues and mitigate mutual animosity, but that is a counterfactual. As it happened, once Macedonia declared independence in 1991, its nationhood and key markers of identity (language, history, and culture) were contested by Bulgaria (and Greece), and this dispute has remained unresolved.

In summary, by the time Macedonia became an independent state in 1991, its national identity had been developing within the protective frame provided by the regional pan-Slavic project promoted by the Yugoslav socialist state. The benefits of this set-up were two-fold. First, socialist Yugoslavism had neutralised Serbian nationalism, which between the wars had posed a major threat to Macedonian nation-building efforts. Second, Yugoslavia provided additional protection from external adversaries of Macedonian nationhood, such as Bulgaria. As

---

[13] Guzina, D. (2003). Socialist Serbia's Narratives: From Yugoslavia to a Greater Serbia. *International Journal of Politics, Culture, and Society*, 17(1), pp. 91–111.

a result, Macedonian elites successfully established and promoted their narrative about the Macedonian nation, as distinct from—but related to—the other South Slavic nations within the joint Yugoslav state.

This narrative comprised the core of Macedonian national identity until 1991. However, once the Yugoslav state fell apart, it became increasingly difficult to maintain the idea of South Slavic unity. The violent reality of the Yugoslav conflicts suggested there was little unity and shared interest among the Yugoslav nations. And as other Yugoslav nations renounced Yugoslavism and revived pre-war nationalist projects, the consensus around Macedonian national identity also became increasingly weaker.

Contemporary Debates on Macedonian Identity: New Myths, New Supranational Projects

The regional and international geopolitical context which Macedonia entered as a newly independent state in the 1990s was quickly changing and radically diverging from the bipolar world pre-1989. In addition to the challenges of managing the political transition to multi-party democracy and of building state institutions, Macedonian political elites faced an urgent need to legitimate the new state domestically and internationally. This implied, on the one hand, recalibrating the domestic discourse in order to forge a new consensus about the Macedonian state and nation; and on the other, negotiating the geopolitical arena to boost its status regionally and build alliances.

With the socialist Marxist ideology that had underpinned Yugoslav ideology delegitimised, Macedonian elites were pressed to seek alternative narratives in the post-communist world. While many post-communist states resorted to earlier constitutions or narratives about their nationhood, this was not a readily available avenue for the Macedonian leadership to pursue. Having only achieved recognition and statehood within the Yugoslav federation, resorting to pre-communist statehood and national identity concepts would be challenging. Moreover, in the uncertain times during the fall of communism and the break-up of the Yugoslav state, most political leaders were disinclined to seek radical changes to national identity. Therefore, their initial response was to maintain the existing narratives as far as possible, adapting where needed to accommodate the new political and social contexts.

Nonetheless, over the past thirty years since independence, the issue of Macedonian national identity and of the stories about the origin, belonging, and destiny of the Macedonian nation have not abated. It remains central to Macedonian politics and continues to be negotiated among domestic political subjects, as well as with neighbouring states like as Bulgaria and Greece. Elements of pan-Slavic thinking continue to recur in these deliberations. Inevitably, such ideas have evolved over the intervening century and now have somewhat different political and geopolitical projects attached to them. In particular, pan-Slavic thinking continues to be articulated in partial opposition to Western liberalism and rationalism, but it does not seem to provide a platform for nation-building by young Slavic nations, as was the case in the late-nineteenth and early-twentieth centuries. Instead, since most Slavic nations have achieved statehood, pan-Slavic thinking predominantly centres on geopolitical and social agendas. Central among these is the rivalry between Russia and the West, and between the respective sets of values each represents in international and domestic politics.

In the Macedonian case, this entails arguments over Macedonia's membership in Western institutions, such as NATO and the European Union, as opposed to the potential alternative geopolitical alignment with Russia and other international powers. Domestically, debates over Macedonian national identity are where arguments about Macedonians' Slavic roots are opposed to alternative ideas about the nation's more ancient origins. Yet, these arguments are not strictly pan-Slavic: they lack the consistency and unifying objectives of pan-national movements. They are used and adapted to local political circumstances by political actors depending on their project—sometimes in paradoxical ways. Nonetheless, the Slavophile tone—the affinity to Slavic culture and Orthodox Christianity, and the weariness towards Western liberal values—tends to resonate across domestic and foreign policies. The sections below outline the evidence for the debate on the ancient vs. Slavic nature of Macedonian national identity, and for the interrelated discussion on EU integration.

The Long Road to EU Integration

European Union integration has been the main foreign policy priority of consecutive Macedonian governments since the mid-1990s, when

Macedonia first established diplomatic relations with the EU.[14] As an integrative project, the ideas at the heart of the EU are reminiscent of those of pan-national movements: the uniting of nations around a set of shared values, history, and worldviews.[15] However, as a supranational institution, the EU is different from Pan-Slavic and other pan-national movements in entailing the creation of joint institutions and policy instruments to replace nation-state powers in specific policy areas.

When it comes to national identity over the past three decades in Macedonia, debates have largely revolved around history and belonging. With the removal of Yugoslavia as the larger community of nations to which Macedonia belonged, there was an implicit need to 'belong' somewhere else. The European Union was the obvious choice. It was the union of choice for most former communist states in Eastern Europe, and its democratic, liberal, and collaborative values strongly resonated with the population in Macedonia, especially given the uncertainty and violence in the immediate region. Arguably, EU enlargement projects have been as much about spreading 'European' values to the European peripheries as they have been about economic and political interests; and conversely, the appeal of EU membership to candidate states is both about identifying with a union of values and about access to EU institutions and budgets.[16]

The post-communist quest for belonging is not specific to Macedonia and is in line with what some international relations theories posit about the behaviour of small states in the international arena, as well as with the arguments of several European integration theories.[17] What has made belonging more difficult to achieve for Macedonia is the lack of previous statehood and strong opposition to its statehood and national identity by neighbouring Greece and Bulgaria. Specifically, Macedonian

---

[14] Koneska, C. (2014). Policy consensus during institutional change: Macedonian Foreign Policy since Independence. In *The foreign policies of post-Yugoslav states* Eds. S.Keil and B.Stahl. (pp. 97–121). Palgrave Macmillan, London.

[15] For an overview of the intellectual and historical origins of the EU integration project, see: Dedman, M. (2009). The Origins & Development of the European Union 1945–2008: A History of European Integration. Routledge.

[16] Sjursen, H. ed., (2007). Questioning EU enlargement: Europe in search of identity (Vol. 3). Routledge.

[17] See 'bandwagoning theory' in Waltz, K. N. (2000). Structural Realism after the Cold War. *International security*, 25(1), pp. 541. Also, Bailes, A. J. and Thorhallsson, B. (2013). Instrumentalising the European Union in small state strategies. *Journal of European Integration*, 35(2), pp. 99–115.

efforts to join the EU as a full member have been repeatedly thwarted by Greek and Bulgarian vetoes in the EU on grounds that broadly concern national identity issues.[18] Thus, Macedonia's efforts to join the EU have been explicitly linked to its national identity narratives. Not only was Macedonia expected to adapt European values and norms in a new, Europeanised version of its identity, but Greece and Bulgaria also demanded specific changes in how Macedonians defined and perceived their nation and history.[19]

These demands, coupled with the large power gap between Macedonia and the EU, have made 'belonging to the EU' and building a European national identity difficult to achieve. At the most immediate level, it meant that EU membership—as the recognition of a nation's belonging to Europe and it values—was not possible because of formal vetoes against Macedonia in EU institutions. However, after a decade of vetoes, the domestic consensus on the desirability of EU membership has also weakened, so that belonging to the EU is not seen as unambiguously good for Macedonia or its people. The sacrifice of the state (and nation's) name, and the prospect of compromising over its history and language to appease neighbouring states, are not unanimously viewed as a price worth paying to gain EU membership.[20]

As a result, over the past decade Slavophile rhetoric has gradually resurfaced in Macedonian politics. While EU integration remains a firm priority, alternative geopolitical projects have become more appealing.

---

[18] Greece objected to the name 'Macedonia' for 25 years between 1992 and 2018, claiming it implied territorial claims, historical inaccuracies, and the theft of 'Greek' history. The two countries signed an agreement in 2017 to end the name dispute, and Macedonia changed its name to North Macedonia. See summaries and arguments in: Kalampalikis, N. (2020). A Lasting Symbolic National Threat: The Dispute Over the Name Macedonia. Ivanovski, H. 2013. The Macedonia-Greece dispute/difference over the name issue: mitigating the inherently unsolvable. *New Balkan Politics*, 14, pp. 48–80. Bulgarian governments, however, continue to object to the existence of a Macedonian language, history, and nationhood.

[19] Balalovska, K. (2004). Between 'the Balkans' and 'Europe': a study of the contemporary transformation of Macedonian identity. *Journal of Contemporary European Studies*, 12(2), pp. 193–214.

[20] See, for example, Džankić, J. and Keil, S. (2019). The Europeanisation of contested states: comparing Bosnia and Herzegovina, Macedonia and Montenegro. In *The Europeanisation of the Western Balkans* (pp. 181–206). Palgrave Macmillan, Cham. Runcheva Tasev, H., 2020. European Perspectives of North Macedonia: EU Enlargement Challenges. *TEPSA Briefs*.

Among those, closer alignment with Russia is one of the main alternatives to EU membership.[21] Inevitably, such arguments are accompanied by Slavophile rhetoric about shared Slavic culture and roots, shared Orthodox Christian religion, and traditional family values reminiscent of earlier Pan-Slavic rhetoric.[22] These are often supplemented with more recent examples of Russian support for Macedonia, such as Russia's recognition of Macedonia under that name, while the EU and NATO used the provisional reference 'Former Yugoslav Republic of Macedonia'. The final component of the new Pan-Slavic narrative is usually reference to the threat posed by ethnic Albanians (both the domestic community and that in neighbouring Kosovo and Albania), which in the popular imagination are seen as the favourites of the West in the region, and from which Russia is more likely than the West to protect ethnic Macedonians.

Thus conceptualised, this new Slavophile rhetoric is less a coherent political or cultural project than it is a response to rejection by the EU. It provides a release for the growing frustration of Macedonian political elites and the population alike with an EU reluctant to recognise their national identity. Surrounded by EU member states, and with no meaningful economic links to Russia, Macedonia is unlikely to gain much by aligning itself closer to Russia. Regardless of its impracticality, the persistence of the idea illustrates the resilience of pan-Slavic ideas and their versatility in adapting to new geopolitical contexts.

Domestically, Slavophile ideas are endorsed and promoted by rightwing, nationalist, and conservative political actors. This is not unexpected, given the nationalist-conservative focus on the ethno-cultural markers of national identity. In Macedonia, the opposition conservative VMRO-DPMNE has been the main proponent of pro-Russian rhetoric, having over its years in government (2006–2017) hardened its stance against Greece, Bulgaria, and the EU. Paradoxically, however, DPMNE did not fully subscribe to ideas about Macedonians' Slavic roots, promoting

---

[21] Bazerkoska, J. B. and Spasov, A. (2019). Challenging the West by (ab) Using the Vacuum: The Case of the Russian Influence in Republic of North Macedonia. *Iustinianus Primus L. Rev.*, *10*, p. 1. See also on Russia's broader regional influence: Wiśniewski, J. (2017). Russia ups its game in the Balkans, but the West should avoid responding in kind. *LSE European Politics and Policy (EUROPP) Blog*.

[22] On primordialisation and traditionalisation of Macedonian politics, see: Vangelov, O. (2017). Stalled European Integration, the Primordialization of Nationalism, and Autocratization in Macedonia Between 2008 and 2015. *Intersections. East European Journal of Society and Politics*, 3(4), pp. 17–40.

instead the idea of Macedonians as the descendants of Alexander the Great, an argument that only escalated the dispute with Greece.[23] It was the centre-left Social Democrats, on the other hand, who maintained the Slavic origins of Macedonian nation, yet it was they who were also seeking EU membership and compromise with Greece (and Bulgaria).

Specifically, during the eleven years it governed the country (2006–2017), the nationalist VMRO-DPMNE-led coalition undertook an ambitious initiative to rewrite the official history, including the 'foundational myths' of the origins and belonging of the Macedonian nation. In what became known as the 'antiquisation project'—with its most tangible output, the 'Skopje 2014' redecoration of the capital city—the government tackled a few fundamental questions related to the roots of the Macedonian nation:

- **Competing narratives about the origin of the Macedonian nation.** Contrary to the established narrative about the Slavic origins of Macedonians, the VMRO-led government promoted alternative arguments about a distinctive Macedonian identity from ancient times, as distinct from the ancient Greeks. While to many, especially abroad, this appeared to be a completely fabricated reinterpretation of history, the government—as Vangeli (2018) argues—only recycled existing but peripheral narratives in circulation since the mid-nineteenth century. Thus, for the first time since independence, there was a debate in the public domain about Macedonian national history that questioned the established wisdom of Yugoslavism and the Macedonians' Slavic origins.

  Spearheaded by historians and archaeologists, the new discourse was fully endorsed by the leading politicians. As documented in Vangeli (2018) and Georgievska-Jakovleva (2014), the costs and extent of the Skopje 2014 project were such that full government support and planning were crucial. Both the prime minister at the time, Nikola Gruevski, and the president, Gjorge Ivanov, provided explicit support for the arguments favouring a revised national history of the Macedonians, including a more prominent role for their ancient as opposed to Slavic roots.

---

[23] Vangeli, A. (2011). Nation-building ancient Macedonian style: the origins and the effects of the so-called antiquization in Macedonia. *Nationalities Papers*, 39(1), pp. 13–32.

- **Revision of the official historiography** to include omitted figures, events, and interpretations of national history. Between 2008 and 2016, the government erected monuments to individuals and organisations that had been edited out of official histories during the Yugoslav period. Presumably the government intended to disrupt the consensus view of Macedonian history inherited from Yugoslav times by re-evaluating the roles of controversial historical figures, some of whom had acted against the incorporation of Macedonia into the Yugoslav federation after 1945.[24] Beyond revising the roles of specific individuals and organisation, this move also probed the consensus historical narrative based on Yugoslavism. Historical figures deemed incompatible with the Yugoslav version of Macedonian national history were re-introduced to provide alternative interpretations of Macedonian history.

  Ultimately, this was an attempt to displace the Pan-(Yugo)Slavic foundation on which Macedonian national identity had been constructed. It questioned the narrative of their belonging to a larger Slavic family of nations, seeking to introduce an alternative (and 'glorious') past, drawing on figures such as Alexander the Great and his father, Philip of Macedon.

- **The link between Macedonia's Slavic origins and its foreign policy focus**. The VMRO-DPMNE governments (2006–2017) definitively rebutted the assumption that support for the theory of the ancient origins of the Macedonian nation was in opposition to pursuing a pro-Russian foreign policy. Such an assumption as was never explicit in Macedonia, as post-war Yugoslavism had been constructed partially in opposition to broader, Russian-centred Pan-Slavism following Yugoslavia's split from the Soviet bloc in the early 1950s. In Yugoslavia, pan-Slavism meant Yugoslavism, and it was in response to the latter that Gruevski's government sought to redefine Macedonian national identity.

  Therefore, turning towards Russia after relations with the West had deteriorated from 2009 on, following Greek vetoes in the EU and NATO, was not a politically difficult manoeuvre. In fact, the nationalist VMRO's insistence on the ancient, pre-Slavic origins of

---

[24] This includes individuals such as Todor Aleksandrov, Vancho Mihajlov, Andon Kjoseto, and others, who in Yugoslav Macedonia were deemed 'anti-Macedonian' and thus excluded from official historiography.

the modern Macedonian nation fitted well with Russia's policy in the region, which in this case entailed support for Macedonia's constitutional name at the time (the Republic of Macedonia).[25]

Indeed, paradoxically, it appeared that Russia supported the anti-Slavic stance of the conservative government in the 'name dispute' with Greece.

This all suggests that current Slavophile ideas are somewhat removed from original arguments about shared Slavic culture, languages, and history. Rather, they tend to primarily serve geopolitical purposes, and are used instrumentally by domestic and foreign political entrepreneurs seeking to capitalise on the continued resonance of myths about common Slavic origins, culture, and languages.

More broadly, Pan-Slavism in Macedonian politics remains tightly linked to Yugoslavism and its legacies, while geopolitical concerns are of secondary importance. This is unsurprising given the geographic proximity and former shared statehood of the other ex-Yugoslav states. In addition, unlike some neighbouring states such as Serbia or Bulgaria, Macedonia's historical links with Russia are rather thin, as it has never played a central role in achieving either Macedonian statehood or foreign policy goals.

Conclusion

Pan-Slavism and Yugoslavism (the South Slavic regional pan-national variant) played a major role in articulating and recognising Macedonian national identity during the twentieth century. Pan-Slavic ideas influenced early thinking about nationhood among Macedonian émigré intellectuals and students in Russia in the early 1900s. Their work, publications, and activism promoted the idea of a separate Macedonian nation, equal to the other Slavic nations, which remains the core of Macedonian national identity to the present day.

Yugoslavism's role was more complex. Early, inter-war Yugoslavism did not recognise the existence of a Macedonian nation, despite relying on pan-Slavic ideas in the construction of the Yugoslav narrative. Serbian nationalism within inter-war Yugoslavia undermined both the recognition

---

[25] Metodieva, A. (2019). Russian narrative proxies in the Western Balkans. *German Marshall Fund of the United States*, pp. 1–20.

of Macedonian national identity and the appeal of Yugoslavism among Macedonians in the Kingdom of Yugoslavia. However, post-war socialist Yugoslavism did provide a nurturing environment for the development and growth of the Macedonian nation and its aspirations to statehood. Socialist Yugoslavism reined in Serbian nationalism, aligning Macedonian and Serbian official histories and national identity narratives while also protecting Macedonian nation-building from external, antagonistic nationalisms.

The influence of the two pan-national (pan-Slavic) projects and their ideas have waned over the past three decades since the break-up of the Yugoslav federation and the turn towards European and NATO integration among the former communist states in Eastern Europe. Nonetheless, the failure of Macedonia to make progress with EU integration over the past decade has allowed for a renewed appeal of Slavophile ideas and rhetoric in domestic political debates. This has been amplified by the continuing domestic conversations around the nature of Macedonian national identity that were triggered by the delegitimisation of Yugoslav ideology and internal interethnic disputes.

However, these findings suggest that today's Slavophile ideas and thinking tend to serve a primarily geopolitical purpose, and are not consistent with the original pan-Slavic ideals. Specifically, in the Macedonian case, pro-Russian foreign policy and views on the Slavic origins of the Macedonian nation are held by parties at the opposite sides of the political spectrum. This incongruence suggests that Slavophile ideas about common origins, language, and culture are more often used instrumentally, for domestic or foreign policy purposes, and at present do not actually advocate pan-national projects or institutions. As such, they are only superficially pan-national, however they do demonstrate the resilience and versatility of pan-Slavic ideas beyond their initial design and objectives.

Invented 'Europeanness' Versus Residual Slavophilism: Ukraine as an Ideological Battlefield

Mykola Riabchuk

Introduction

On September 17, 2004, Ukraine's President Leonid Kuchma signed Decree #1096, 'On the Day of Slavonic Literacy and Culture', establishing an annual celebration, on a regular, state-sponsored basis, of the 'significant historical and educational contributions of the Slavonic enlighteners [Saints Cyril and Methodius] to national culture'.[1] The document was arguably adopted at the initiative of local authorities, civic and religious organizations, and the National Academy of Sciences. It was not clear, however, why none of them had raised the initiative earlier, during the previous thirteen years of Ukraine's independence, or whether they indeed cared much about it.

---

[1] *Про День слов'янської писемності і культури* [On the Day of Slavonic Literacy and Culture] Decree of the President of Ukraine no. 1096/2004. (2004, September 17). Retrieved from https://www.president.gov.ua/documents/10962004-1882.

M. Riabchuk (✉)
Institute of Political Science, Kyiv, Ukraine

University of Warsaw, Warsaw, Poland

© The Author(s), under exclusive license to Springer Nature Switzerland AG 2023
M. Suslov et al. (eds.), *Pan-Slavism and Slavophilia in Contemporary Central and Eastern Europe*,
https://doi.org/10.1007/978-3-031-17875-7_12

This question may become less enigmatic when one remembers that, in a month and a half's time, Ukraine was to hold the first round of its highly contested presidential election. The incumbent president, dogged by domestic scandals and ostracized internationally, needed desperately to promote his hand-picked successor, the incumbent Prime Minister Viktor Yanukovych. And the only way to achieve this was to mobilize his core Pan-Slavonic, pro-Russian, pro-Soviet, and anti-Western electorate— people with largely congruent ideological orientations. For probably the same reason, the authorities organized a large-scale celebration of the 60th anniversary of the liberation of Kyiv from the Nazis, staging a pompous military parade (never held on that date before or indeed ever again afterwards), with Vladimir Putin as the special (and only) foreign guest. Remarkably, the celebration occurred on October 28, one week before the actual date of the liberation of Kyiv but, crucially, three days before the scheduled elections.[2]

Ultimately, Messrs. Kuchma and Yanukovych lost the election, but the power of seemingly outdated symbols and discourses remained significant, as well as the temptation to instrumentalize them for political purposes. Five years later, on the eve of the next presidential election, Patriarch Cyril of the Russian Orthodox Church held a grand tour in Ukraine that many considered an attempt to mobilize Yanukovych's electorate.[3] And in 2014 the whole set of propagandistic discourses, including pro-Russian and Pan-Slavonic (alongside anti-Western and 'anti-Nazi') at their core, was employed to justify the annexation of Crimea and intervention in the Donbas.

The appeal of those discourses might appear 'natural' if one believed in a primordial unity of the Ukrainian and Russian peoples, in their virtual 'sameness' (as Vladimir Putin insists),[4] but this hardly explains why the great Slavonic idea did not work per se—not in 2004, when electoral fraud was employed to assist, nor in 2014, when a military invasion was

---

[2] Radio Liberty. (2004, October 28). 'Україну звільнили від нацистів в середині листопада, а не 28 жовтня' [Ukraine was liberated from Nazis in mid-November, not on October 28]. Retrieved from https://www.radiosvoboda.org/a/922065.html.

[3] Voice of America. (2009, August 3). 'Візит Кирила в Західну Україну розпочався зі скандалу' [Cyril's visit to Western Ukraine started with a scandal]. Retrieved from https://ukrainian.voanews.com/a/a-49-2009-08-03-voa9-86912317/223113.html.

[4] President of Russia. (2021, July 12). On the Historical Unity of Russians and Ukrainians. Retrieved from http://en.kremlin.ru/events/president/news/66181.

needed to promote the alleged 'unity'. It also does not explain why political party after political party with the seemingly attractive word 'Slavonic' in their titles and/or programmes has failed to make any noticeable electoral advance at either the national or local level.[5]

The only arguably 'pro-Russian' and 'Pan-Slavonic' party to attain some success at the national level was the oligarchic Party of Regions (2002–2014), but it made no specific 'Slavophile' references in its programmatic documents. Rather, it styled itself as a 'centrist' and 'pragmatic' party, committed to 'multi-vector politics' and mutually beneficial relations with both Russia and the West. This was hardly new, as such politics had been pursued in 1994–2004 by President Leonid Kuchma. It reflected the preferences of both the ruling elite and of the population at large. The oligarchic elite benefited from this proverbial 'multi-vectorism', as it allowed them to continue in murky business to the east (and at home), but also to maintain good relations with the West (and with Western banks). The people at large benefited from 'multi-vectorism' in their own way, as it absolved them, at least temporarily, from a difficult choice between the West and the East, a choice framed as both civilizational and existential. Well into the early 2010s, the majority of Ukrainians (up to two-thirds of respondents according to various opinion surveys) wished to join *both* the EU *and* some sort of a post-Soviet ('Eurasian' or 'East Slavonic') Union led by Russia.[6] When pressed with a tougher question, however—to choose either one union or the other—the majority or at least a plurality of respondents opted for the East.[7]

East Slavic sentiments in this situation, and in related connections, became rather a mixed blessing for the ruling elite. On the one hand, it provided a tool for the political mobilization of the more conservative, pliable, and manipulable parts of the electorate. It was an asset in allowing this elite to fence off their interests from the Westerners demanding more

---

[5] Karamzina M. (2006). 'Партійний вимір російського націоналізму в Україні' [The party dimension of the Russian nationalism in Ukraine], *Political management* 6, pp. 29–44; also, 'В Україні зареєстровано 14 проросійських партій' [14 pro-Russian parties registered in Ukraine] (2013, May 21). *Ukrainsky tyzhden*, Retrieved from https://web.archive.org/web/20190504195419/http://mobile.tyzhden.ua/News/79989.

[6] *Українське суспільство: моніторинг соціальних змін* [Ukrainian society: monitoring of social changes] (2018). Kyv: Institute of Sociology of NASU, p. 430.

[7] National Security and Defense. (2016). 'Ukrainian Identity Changes, Trends, Regional Aspects. p. 45 '. Retrieved from https://razumkov.org.ua/uploads/journal/ukr/NSD 161-162_2016_ukr.pdf.

rule of law, transparency, and curbs on corruption. It also allowed them to keep at bay the pro-Western democratic opposition at home, who were raising the same demands even more vociferously. Yet, on the other hand, the ruling elite also had to keep a safe distance from the 'Slavonic' idea so as not to overplay their hands or undermine their own legitimacy and power *vis à vis* the former metropole.[8] This task was increasingly difficult as Moscow, under Vladimir Putin, revitalized the idea and made it into a powerful tool of East Slavonic/Eurasian integration. None of the post-Soviet leaders were eager to follow that way, despite all their verbal commitment to 'integration'.

It was one thing to flirt occasionally and opportunistically with the 'Slavonic' idea, something different to embrace it fully. This is why neither President Kuchma nor his arguably pro-Russian successor Viktor Yanukovych ever featured the 'Slavonic' idea as part of their (or their groupings') political doctrines. Occasionally some member of their teams would make references to 'Slavonic (or East Slavonic) brotherhood', but then only rhetorically, without further conceptualization. In most cases, these references were tailored carefully to specific electoral needs and adjusted to suit regional peculiarities.

By 2012, however, supporters of Ukraine's western versus eastern integration had attained parity in number, and in 2013 the 'westernizers' slightly numerically prevailed—for the first time since Ukraine's independence.[9] One may speculate as to what brought about the change—the public debates on the Association Agreement with the EU, which had enhanced the salience of that issue; the European football championship hosted in major Ukrainian cities; or the growing authoritarian tendencies of Yanukovych's regime, its alarming concessions to Russia in various fields, and Moscow's apparent desire to take more and more. Most likely, though, these factors played only a secondary, 'catalysing' role, while the process itself had been driven by much stronger, structural factors: the same that had determined the fall of the ineffectual communist system

---

[8] The title of Leonid Kuchma's book 'Ukraine Is Not Russia' (2004) was nearly as bold, under circumstances, as a recent Volodymyr Zelensky's quip at Putin's obsessive claim that Russians and Ukrainians "are the same people". "If Ukrainians and Russians were one people, then hryvnia, most likely, would circulate in Moscow, and a yellow-blue flag would fly over the State Duma," Zelensky was quoted as saying. See 'Putin's Ukraine Complex Again Makes Itself Felt' (2021, July 1). *Russia Monitor*. Retrieved from https://warsawinstitute.org/putins-ukraine-complex-makes-felt/.

[9] 'Ukrainian Identity', op. cit., p. 45.

in Eastern Europe and the westward drive of its captive nations in the pursuance of catch-up modernization. The soft power (and attractiveness) of the liberal democratic West appeared much stronger (and more acceptable) than the harsh power of the totalitarian Soviet Union or of Putin's increasingly authoritarian Russia.

The real question is not why the idea of Slavonic (primarily East Slavonic) unity did not work in Ukraine as a basis and driver of post-Soviet, Russian-led political integration, but rather why the idea has persisted for so long and still retains some influence on certain people and groups, despite its explicitly reactionary and implicitly anti-Ukrainian character.

SLAVOPHILES INTO UKRAINIANS

Ironically, modern Ukrainian nationalism evolved, in its early stages, within the discursive and institutional framework of Russian imperial Slavophilism, under the strong influence of Herder's ideas of *Kulturnation* and his passionate praise for Slavonic (Ukrainian in particular) cultures and languages. As a semi-peripheral reaction to European modernity, Herder's ideas provided East European intellectuals with a convenient tool to raise their cultural self-esteem and to find in an idealized native past some resources (and hopes) for a brighter future.[10]

At the time these ideas arrived in Russia, Ukrainians were not considered a separate nationality but rather a subgroup of the 'Russian' (Ruś-sian) people: 'Little Russians'. Their Cossack autonomy had gradually shrunk throughout the eighteenth century and, in 1764, was completely abolished; the Cossack gentry was assimilated into the imperial nobility, while the peasantry was enserfed and placed under the supervision of the Russian Orthodox Church. What Ukrainians retained was a nostalgic memory of past Cossack glory, a recollection of their rights and privileges in the Polish-Lithuanian Commonwealth, and an unabating

---

[10] I discussed the issue in more detail in Riabchuk M. (1996). 'The Nativist/Westernizer Controversy in Ukraine: The End or the Beginning?' *Journal of Ukrainian Studies*, 21(1–2), pp. 27–54.

interest in historical manuscripts and other documents that confirmed their honourable provenance.[11]

For nearly two decades, Russian Slavophiles looked rather favourably, even paternalistically, at Ukrainians' literary activity, considering it part of an 'all-Russian' cultural process, and so willingly published and reviewed in their journals works in what they believed to be a 'Little Russian' dialect. They did not foresee that the same historical force, the same set of ideas that awoke Russian romantic nationalism and mobilized Ukrainian ('South Russian') regionalism in its service, would cause irreversible changes in the minds of the obedient and, since Peter's times, fully domesticated 'Little Russians'.

Like any nativists, the Ukrainian Slavophiles seemed to be strongly committed to all things local, native, and 'traditional', while also duly hostile to things alien and imposed by foreigners. It very soon appeared that the 'native' things the Ukrainians felt proud of were not in fact the same as were dear to the Russians (and, in some cases, were actually their opposite, such as, for instance, their visions of the pre-Petrine past, which Ukrainians preferred to centre not in the despotic Muscovy but in their own—'republican'—Cossackdom). On the other hand, it also appeared that quite a few 'alien' things rejected by Russians as inappropriate were embraced by Ukrainians, such as 'traditional' (valued arguably since Cossack times) notions of *liberté, égalité,* and *fraternité*.

The moment of truth came in 1847, when the secret Ukrainian Saints Cyril and Methodius Society was uncovered in Kyiv. Its members were arrested, imprisoned, and sent into exile. The incident deeply shocked Russian Slavophiles, who condemned the Ukrainian 'heresy' and distanced themselves from the 'conspirators'. Aleksei Khomiakov, one of the leading Russian Slavophiles, argued in a letter to Iu. Samarin that.

> 'when the social question has only just been formulated and when it is not only unresolved but not even approaching resolution, people who are supposed to be intelligent take up politics! I don't know to what extent

---

[11] On the early Ukrainian nationalism, see an illuminating book by Plokhy, S. (2012). *The Cossack Myth. History and Nationhood in the Age of Empires.* Cambridge University Press.

the poor Little Russians' delusion was criminal, but I know that their wrongheadedness is very clear'.[12]

Indeed, Ukrainian Slavophiles had gone far beyond the permissible limits: they had begun 'to think that their culture was worth promoting for its own sake, not merely for the prospect of enrichment that it offered to Russian culture'. They had begun 'setting Ukraine in the context of the Slavic world as a whole' and had 'advocated a federation of Slavic peoples'.[13] The 'political fever' that affected the students of Kiev University had a dangerous symptom: it had evoked, in the minds of the conspirators, the really 'wrongheaded' idea of how to transform an absolutist monarchy into a constitutional state—an idea that was rather Decembrist and, essentially, more Westernizing than Slavophile.

All in all, the Ukrainian version of Slavophilism differed notably from its contemporary Russian counterpart in its radical tone. Ukrainians, in Johannes Remy's apt observation, 'were familiar with the Slavophile ideas circulating in Russia and among the Western Slavs.... On the whole, however, the Society's West Slavic inspiration and contacts were more important'. He notes that 'Lelewel's theory of ancient Slavic democracy and his emphasis on the voluntary nature of the Polish-Lithuanian union' were close to the ideas of the Society's members; that their recognition of the tsar was conditional (as no Slavic federation was actually possible without a constitution); and that they were 'neutral on religious matters' and tried to dissociate national identity from the Orthodox faith.[14] The latter probably reflected not only their awareness of the multi-confessional character of the Slavonic world (assigned presumably to federalization) but also of the confessional differences between the Ukrainians themselves—Orthodox in the Russian empire and mostly Greek Catholics ('Uniates') in Austria-Hungary.

In summary, nineteenth-century Ukrainian Slavophilism can be seen as an interesting attempt to combine modernity and tradition: to express modern nationalistic demands in the traditional form of local patriotism that presumably did not subvert supranational ('all-Russian') unity.

---

[12] As quoted in Saunders, D. (1985). *The Ukrainian Impact on Russian Culture. 1750–1850*. Edmonton: Canadian Institute of Ukrainian Studies, p. 250.

[13] Ibid., pp. 231, 233, 245.

[14] Remy, J. (2005). 'Panslavism in the Ukrainian National Movement from the 1840s to the 1870s'. *Journal of Ukrainian Studies. 30*(2), pp. 34–47.

The Slavophiles strove to achieve the maximum of what was possible, given the horizon of expectations of Ukrainian (at the time still mostly 'Little Russian') society. In practice it also meant gradually broadening and transforming that horizon. The 'Slavonic federation' that they envisioned was apparently not a mere extension of 'all-Russian' dynastic unity, and Ukraine as a member of the federation was not merely a set of 'Little Russian' *gubernias*.

The Empire, predictably, had no need of Ukrainians' assistance in 'unifying the Slavs' under the tsar's auspices at the cost of their cultural (at the least) emancipation. Even less was it interested in any kind of federative union of 'equal and fraternal Slavonic nations'. The Empire's response to the Ukrainian challenge was harsh but rational and, from the Empire's perspective, justifiable. The Ukrainian version of Slavophilism could not satisfy either 'all-Russian' (imperial) or 'Little Russian' (Ukrainian) patriots. The former had been shifting towards Great Russian supremacism and imperialism, while the latter had been embracing modern Ukrainian nationalism. No compromise nor reconciliation between the two was possible. They could co-exist in a pre-modern, pre-nationalistic world as two different sorts and levels of patriotism, a state one and a local one, but they came into deadly collision as soon as new forms of identity, new 'communities of spirit' had evolved from the former dynastical, estate-hierarchical, and religious identities and communities.

By the end of the 1870s, Ukrainian Slavophilism—as a distinct and influential intellectual trend—had been virtually extinguished. On the one side, the Empire had discerned—however belatedly—the subversive potential of the ostensibly loyalist 'Little Russian' cultural movement and responded with enhanced restrictions, bans, and persecutions of activists. This forced many Ukrainian intellectuals to emigrate and/or to shift their cultural activity abroad, primarily to Habsburg-ruled Galicia, which had actively, and not without the influence of Dnieper Ukraine, been discovering its own Ukrainian identity.[15]

[15] The 'Slavophile' movement or, actually, *movements* in Western Ukraine had their own distinct history, left beyond the scope of this study. In brief, the Ukrainian national project, imported from the Dnieper Ukraine, had ultimately won in the region. By the end of the nineteenth century, the Austrian 'Rusyns' recognized their close affinity with Ukrainians ('Little Russians') in the Russian empire and accepted all the founding symbols and myths of Ukrainian identity developed by the Kyiv and Kharkiv intellectuals (with an important compromise on the religious issue). The story is comprehensively covered in

On the other side, the Russian version of Slavophilism had been increasingly imbued with imperial ideology and subordinated to the political goals of imperial expansion and dominance. What had emerged in the 1830s as a backward-looking, nostalgic-utopian, cultural-cum-ethical doctrine was transformed into a highly reactionary, militantly anti-Western, and aggressively jingoistic Pan-Slavist project. To outsiders, the Russian version of Slavophilism had become more of a threat, an imperial 'Trojan Horse', than any kind of attraction. And its domestic versions had become merely obsolete and redundant, giving way to the more straightforward, appealing, and politically pragmatic ideology of modern nationalism.

Persistent Ambivalence

The 'Slavonic' idea had lost its lustre by the twentieth century but did not fade away. In Ukraine it retained its positions in two fields. First, it remained an essential component of the imperial Pan-Slavism that still promoted its narratives in the heavily Russified Ukrainian cities.[16] And secondly, it remained an important element of the Orthodox Christian creed, deemed the only officially sanctioned version of Christianity in the Empire, including in Ukraine as its arguably 'canonical' territory.

The Bolshevik revolution changed some dimensions of that idea, and modified narratives, but did not dismiss it completely. The Russian Orthodox Church lost its state blessing and coveted status as a major stakeholder in the ideocratic state, but it retained the state-sponsored monopoly over the whole 'canonical' territory that effectively precluded the existence of any alternative (Ukrainian in particular) Christian

---

Sereda, O. (2012). *Between Polish Slavophilism and Russian Pan-Slavism. Reception and Development of the Slavic Ideas by Ukrainian (Ruthenian) Public Activists of Austrian Galicia in the 1860s*. Lviv: Institute of Ukrainian Studies NASU. See also an insightful article on the perplexities of the Ukrainian identity-building in Galicia by Himka, J. P. (1999). *'The Construction of Nationality in Galician Rus': Icarian Flights in Almost All Directions'*, in Suny, R. and Kennedy, M. (eds.), *Intellectuals and Articulation of the Nation*. Ann Arbor: University of Michigan Press, pp. 109–154.

[16] This peculiar ideology seems to attain afterlife today in two Russia-occupied ('secessionist') regions of Ukraine, the 'Donetsk' and the 'Luhansk People's Republics'. See Machitidze, I. (2020). *'Popular Imagery, Competing Narratives and Pan-Slavism: the Case of Ukraine's Break-away Regions'*, The Journal of Cross-Regional Dialogues. Special Issue, https://doi.org/10.25518/2593-9483.139.

church. As a secular ideology, Pan-Slavism was dissolved initially into the more universalistic doctrine of 'proletarian internationalism', centred also in Moscow, but soon re-emerged in the modified form of 'East Slavonic brotherhood'. This doctrine promoted the primordial unity of Ukrainians, Russians, and Belarusians; praised their teleologically inevitable 're-unification'; and (predictably) charged the 'great Russian people' (as the most 'advanced' and 'progressive') with the role of an 'older brother' within this triad.

This doctrine would hardly have survived the end of communism and the collapse of the Soviet empire if the notion of the tripartite East Slavonic nation had not been fused at a deeper cognitive and emotional level with an archaic quasi-religious idea of the Orthodox brotherhood—an imagined community of true believers, *Slavia Orthodoxa*—in a loose analogue to the Muslim *ummah*. Derived originally from Kyivan Ruś but appropriated and instrumentalized eventually by Moscow,[17] the concept provided a powerful symbolism to the rather crude notion of three 'brotherly' nations. It facilitated not only the unquestioned acceptance of that idea (which should not be a problem in a totalitarian state) but also its profound internalization—unreflective, unproblematic, and self-evident as a common piece of wisdom or, rather, as a common faith.

'Wisdom', however 'common', is malleable: it may yield to the pressure of facts, arguments, and social reality. 'Faith' is beyond logic and rationality; it merely 'is' and, like any myth, cares little about the facts. It does not necessarily reject them but, rather, places them into a parallel reality to avoid contradictions. This might be the only plausible explanation for Ukraine's persistent ambivalence as revealed again and again in various sociological surveys throughout the three decades of its independence.

The earliest evidence of this can probably be derived from the results of the 1991 national referendum on independence as contrasted with the results of the presidential election held on the same day. While national independence was approved almost unanimously (by 90% of voters), the votes on the future president split remarkably: more than

---

[17] Plokhy, S. (2006). *The Origins of the Slavic Nations: Premodern Identities in Russia, Ukraine and Belarus.* Cambridge, Cambridge University Press, 2006. See also insightful article by Edward Keenan (1994). '*On Certain Mythical Beliefs and Russian Behaviors*', in S. Frederick Starr (ed.), *The Legacy of History in Russia and the New States of Eurasia.* Armonk, NY: M. E. Sharpe, pp. 19–40.

two-thirds supported the incumbent head of state, the former communist apparatchik Leonid Kravchuk, and only one quarter cast their ballots for the non-communist candidate, the former political prisoner Viacheslav Chornovil—a possible but improbable Ukrainian analogue of Vaclav Havel or Lech Walesa. The results can be read as a popular vote on the essence and type of their newly acquired independence.[18] One quarter of Ukrainian voters apparently wished for a radical break with the communist past and the former empire, while two quarters preferred a post-communist continuity, with all the political, cultural, and institutional implications that this entailed.

Certainly, there could have been some other factors determining Ukrainians' seemingly incoherent vote—for instance, a high percentage of ethnic Russians and Russified Ukrainians eager to benefit from putative economic prosperity under independence but not to jeopardize their privileged social position, their primarily cultural and linguistic preponderance in the new independent state. This might have been *a* factor but certainly not *the* factor. In 1991, ethnic Ukrainians made up 73% of Ukraine's population, and most of them (62% of the country's inhabitants) declared Ukrainian as their native language.[19] The residual, deeply internalized attachment to an imaginary East Slavonic community of 'ours' is a more plausible explanation for the ambiguous 1991 vote as well as for a great number of other seemingly inexplicable behavioural and voting twists that eventually occurred.

Social ambivalence looms large in various sociological surveys, especially those related to identitarian issues, and is often misinterpreted as a sign of a 'weak', 'yet unformed' national identity—as if coherence is the only parameter of national identity and the only determinant of its 'strength'. 'East Slavonic belonging' is an important, constitutive part of Ukrainian identity, however residual and unreflective. People are attached to this identitarian complex variously: some fully share in its founding

---

[18] "Independence—over 90% vote yes in referendum; Kravchuk elected president of Ukraine" (1991), *The Ukrainian Weekly*, 8 December. See also: Solchanyk, R. (2000). *Ukraine and Russia: The Post-Soviet Transition.* Lanham, MD: Rowman & Littlefield, 2000, p. 100.

[19] Gunn, J. (2014). 'Ethnicity and Language in Ukraine'. *RUSI*, 12 March, Retrieved from https://rusi.org/explore-our-research/publications/commentary/ethnicity-and-language-ukraine; Stebelsky, I. (2009). *'Ethnic Self-Identification in Ukraine, 1989-2001: Why More Ukrainians and Fewer Russians?' Canadian Slavonic Papers* 51.1, pp. 77–100. Retrieved from http://www.jstor.org/stable/40871355.

myths and narratives, some have been completely emancipated from its spell, and yet others retain (very loosely and incoherently) its more casual elements—at the level of ideological memes rather than thought-out concepts.

Back in 2005 Stephen Shulman singled out two alternative types of Ukrainian ethnic identity, or what he called 'national identity complexes'. He called one of them, tentatively, 'ethnic Ukrainian' and the other, 'Eastern Slavic', the latter of which being also 'Ukrainian' but with an emphasis on the common East Slavic culture, history, and heritage as basic unifying features for all Ukrainians. This entails an understanding of Ukrainian and Russian cultures as basically similar, their histories amicably intertwined, identities complementary, and geopolitical stances mutually positioned against the West as the main 'Other'.[20]

This puts the proponents of 'East Slavic' identity at odds with holders of Ukrainian 'ethnic identity' who prioritized Ukrainian language and culture, considered the 'common history' to be more colonial than amicable, emphasized Russian-Ukrainian dissimilarities (most conspicuously in political culture), and stressed Ukraine's alleged 'European belonging' *vis à vis* Russia as the main 'Other'. Such radical, value-based differences between the two major types of national identity might have resulted in a profound schism and fracture in society were they not merely Weberian 'ideal types' distinguishable in the abstract but blurred, diffused, hybridized, and dispersed in reality.[21] Additionally, the salience of 'East Slavic' identity was rather low and gradually declining, thus its utility for political mobilization was also in decline. This might be the reason why proponents of 'ethnic Ukrainian' identity were able to promote their 'nationalistic' agenda against the will of the more numerous but also more passive supporters of the 'East Slavonic' orientation. What for the former group was a matter of existential significance, of 'survival', was for the latter group merely a matter of convenience.

Sociological surveys carried out in Ukraine since the early years of national independence graphically illustrate the numerical preponderance

---

[20] Shulman, S. (2005). 'National Identity and Public Support for Political and Economic Reform in Ukraine', *Slavic Review* 64(1), pp. 68–69.

[21] "The researchers agree that Ukrainian society is split, but in their opinion this split is very indistinct, as a rule not accompanied by a sense of profound ethnic boundaries separating groups—even at a time of emerging interstate war". Onuch, O. and Hale, H. (2018). 'Capturing Ethnicity: The Case of Ukraine', *Post-Soviet Affairs* 34(2–3), p. 106.

Table 1 Ukrainians' changing attitudes toward Russia, Russian leadership, and the project of the Russian-led East Slavonic Union, with the 2014 as the turning point

	1998	2012	2013	2015	2017
What is your attitude toward the Russian Federation? (positive/negative, %)	nd	85/9	82/10	34/51	37/46
What is your attitude toward the president of the RF Vladimir Putin? (positive/negative, %)	nd	53/32	47/40	16/75	10/81
Would you like Ukraine to join the union with Russia and Belarus? (yes/no, %)	61/21	56/25	49/29	22/62	20/62

Ставлення населення України до Росії [The attitude of Ukraine's population toward Russia] (2021, March 2). Kyiv International Institute of Sociology. Retrieved from http://kiis.com.ua/?lang=ukrampcat=reports&id=1015&page=1
Attitudes of Ukrainians towards world leaders (2019, 11 November). Rating Sociological Group. Retrieved from http://ratinggroup.ua/en/research/ukraine/dinamika_otnosheniya_ukraincev_k_mirovym_lideram.html
Українське суспільство [Ukrainian Society], op. cit., p. 430

of the post-Soviet holders of the 'East Slavonic' identity and, therefore, a much higher quantitative support for the related values and attitudes. At the same time, they show the slow but steady decline of this group and of its political influence, which then plummeted dramatically in 2014, after 'Euromaidan' and the Russian military invasion (Table 1).

Cultural changes, meanwhile, have been remarkably slower and less radical. In 2007, only 20% of respondents recognized Western 'values, norms, and traditions' as being closer to them than the East Slavonic, whereas 47% declared the opposite affinities, and 33% failed to answer. By 2018, the number of self-proclaimed 'Westerners' reached 35% but the number of 'Easterners' did not change that much, falling to 40% in 2014–2018.[22]

The firm stability of the 'East Slavonic' option is particularly striking when seen against the precipitous drop in Russian ethnic self-identification between 2013 and 2015 (pre-war and wartime results, respectively) and the accompanying significant rise in ethnic Ukrainian and 'European' self-identifications:

[22] Ibid., p. 431.

Perhaps most revealing in connection with this Ukrainian/East Slavonic ambiguity would have been a yes/no answer to an explicit question about whether Ukrainians and Russian are 'the same people'. Such a question is recurrently posed in Russia by the Levada Centre, with mostly affirmative answers, while in Ukraine, for some reason, nobody put it to a survey until 2016. Two minor exceptions can hardly be seen as representative. One is a survey held in 2009 in Crimea, in which 56%, predictably, responded in the affirmative, while 35% denied their sameness.[23] The other survey, also conducted in 2009, was held nationwide but covering only young people. In this case, the positive/negative answers tied at 48%.[24] We may assume, therefore, that the number of people in Ukraine who then shared the view that Ukrainians and Russians are 'the same people' (whatever that may mean) must have been between 56 and 48%, i.e. lower than in the Crimea but higher than among the young (Table 2).

The first survey that posed this question explicitly, from 2016, largely confirms the assumption: 42% of respondents agreed that Ukrainians and Russians are 'the same', and 48% disagreed.[25] As the Russo-Ukrainian war proceeded, 55% of respondents denied Russo-Ukrainian 'sameness' in 2021, but 41% still agreed with the statement, and 4% declined to answer.[26] The notion of 'brotherhood', however, remained almost unshaken: in 2014, 62% of Ukrainian respondents agreed that Ukrainians and Russians are 'brotherly people'; by 2016, after two thousand people had been killed and a million and a half displaced, 51% still held to the

---

[23] *Росіяни та українці—це один народ (соціокультурна спільнота) чи два різні народи?* [Are Ukrainians and Russians the same people (one social-cultural community) or two different peoples?] (2009). Razumkov Center. Retrieved from http://www.razumkov.org.ua/ukr/journal.php/files/category_journal/poll.php?poll_id=471.

[24] *Громадська думка молоді України, Азербайджану та Росії* [Public opinion of young Ukrainians, Azeris and Russians] (2010). Democratic Initiative Foundation. Retrieved from http://dif.org.ua/modules/pages/upload/file/molod.doc.

[25] *Украинцы и русские* [Ukrainians and Russians] (2016). Research & Branding Group, unpublished results in the possession of the author.

[26] *Суспільно-політичні настрої населення* [Social and political attitudes of the population] (2021). Rating Sociological Group, July 23–25, p. 20. Retrieved from http://ratinggroup.ua/en/research/ukraine/obschestvenno-politicheskie_nastroeniya_naseleniya_23-25_iyulya_2021.html.

Table 2 People variously define themselves in different categories. To what degree you feel that you are: Source: Quantitative Surveys on Ukrainian Regionalism (2013–2015). University of St. Gallen, Center for Governance and Culture, 2017, https://www.uaregio.org/en/surveys/methodology/

		Definitely no (%, year 2013/2015)	Rather no	Difficult to say	Rather yes	Definitely yes	Average (5-point scale)
1	An ethnic Ukrainian	2.5/1.9	4.5/2	7.2/5.4	31.4/26.5	54.4/64.3	4.31/4.49
2	An ethnic Russian	45.6/67.6	22.9/14.4	12.1/8.3	11.2/6.3	8.2/3.5	2.13/1.63
3	A member of the East Slavonic community	26.4/25.6	16.0/16.9	23.6/25.6	25.1/22.8	8.9/9.5	2.74/2.73
4	A European	22.4/19.6	22.4/17.5	23.7/24.4	21.9/27.0	9.8/11.6	2.74/2.93

notion, while the number of those disagreeing slightly increased, from 28 to 34%.[27]

Indeed, the idyllic idea of 'brotherhood' bizarrely co-exists in peoples' minds alongside the sober notions that Russia is an 'aggressor state' (71% agree, 22% disagree),[28] that it was Russia who started the war (60% agree, 21% disagree),[29] and that it still is the main threat to Ukraine (74% agree, 15% disagree).[30] It seems as if Ukrainians were living in two different realities. One of these is that of their daily experience, informed not only by

[27] 'Consolidation of Ukrainian Society' (2016). *National Security and Defense* 7–8, p. 71. Retrieved from https://razumkov.org.ua/uploads/journal/ukr/NSD165-166_2016_ukr.pdf.

[28] *Суспільно-політичні настрої населення* [Social and political attitudes of the population] (2021, March 23–24), Rating Sociological Group, p. 34. Retrieved from http://ratinggroup.ua/en/research/ukraine/obschestvenno-politicheskie_nastroeniya_n aseleniya_23-24_marta_2021.html.

[29] *Чи ковтають українці фейки та пропаганду* [Do Ukrainians swallow fakes and propaganda] (2020, October 5), Democratic Initiative Foundation. Retrieved from https://dif.org.ua/article/chi-kovtayut-ukraintsi-feyki-ta-propagandu.

[30] *Суспільна підтримка євроатлантичного курсу України* [Popular support for Ukraine's Euro-Atlantic integration] (2021). Razumkov Center, p. 12. Retrieved from https://razumkov.org.ua/uploads/article/2021-nato-ukr.pdf. Notably, the view is

the news media but also by personal encounters with various people—veterans, volunteers, their relatives, and acquaintances—who have had first-hand knowledge of the ongoing war, reportedly 'low-intensity' but with nearly daily casualties.

The other 'reality' is largely virtual, based on a broadly shared and deeply internalized ideological myth about the primordial and eternal 'brotherhood' of Slavonic (East Slavonic) people, which defies both modern scholarly knowledge and the grim reality of the war. The 'Slavonic idea' seems to play an important role in this myth, and so deserves to be scrutinized in this connection more in detail.

Ambient Slavophilism?

At first glance, the 'Slavonic idea' should not have played a significant role in Ukrainians' public consciousness inasmuch as it has a very limited currency in media discourse, political programmes, intellectual debates, and cultural imagery.

All the parties that had tried to exploit the Slavonic idea in their names and programmes performed dismally and had, by 2015 vanished thoroughly. The unreformed Communists retained their core electorate throughout the 1990s, but they draw their strength not so much from their occasional references to the 'Slavonic' idea as from the nostalgic 'Sovietophilia' of elderly people. The oligarchic successors to all these groups—primarily the Party of Regions (eventually rebranded as the Oppositional Platform)—abandoned clear ideological markers and styled themselves as pure 'pragmatists', committed only to common sense and the people's interest.[31] This implied, *inter alia*, laissez-faire in language and cultural politics, and the policy of 'multi-vectorism' in international relations. In reality, they have pursued pro-Russian ('Kremlin-light') policy, but their explicit rhetoric is usually equivocal and remarkably void of any references to 'Slavophilism'.

predominant even in the allegedly 'pro-Russian' East: 54% of the respondents consider Russia the main threat, versus 28% who deny it.

[31] See: 'Передвиборча програма Партії Регіонів' [Electoral program of the Party of Regions] (2007, August 4). *УНІАН*. Retrieved from https://www.unian.ua/politics/57393-peredviborcha-programa-partiji-regioniv.html; *Предвыборная программа политической партии "Оппозиционная платформа—за жизнь"* [Electoral program of the party Oppositional platform—for life] (2019). Retrieved from https://zagittya.com.ua/en/page/programma.html.

A peculiar form of Ukrainian Pan-Slavism (or rather Dugin-style Pan-Eurasianism, with the dominant role assigned to Ukraine) was developed by a leader of the fringe far-right group Bratstvo, former paramilitary UNA-UNSO, Dmytro Korchynsky, who is broadly perceived as either a Russian *agent-provocateur* or a maverick, political-cum-artistic performer. In any case, his narcissistic exercises and messianic statements are not taken seriously, and his occasional role in some TV-shows is typically that of a jester.[32]

The same can be said about the marginal 'neo-pagan' movements, in particular the followers of RUN-vira ('Native Ukrainian Faith') that evolved in Ukraine during the 1990s, having been imported thence from the Ukrainian diaspora in Canada and the USA. They share Slavophile views, to a certain degree, but usually place Ukraine at the top of this world, as the most authentic and genuinely 'Slavonic'. Russians are typically excluded from this group as arguably 'Finno-Ugric', 'Mongolian', or generally 'non-Aryan'.[33]

The 'neo-pagans' pair, in a way, with another fringe group that promotes Ukraine as the cradle of all Aryan, Indo-European civilization.[34] The group operates at a para-academic level, finding support for their ideas in ethnology, archaeology, and comparative linguistics

---

[32] See: Korchynsky, D. (1998). *Викликаю вогонь на себе* [Calling fire on myself]. Kyiv, p. 27. Notably, the 2021 nationwide survey revealed that not only 41% of Ukrainians tend to agree with Vladimir Putin's claim that Ukrainian and Russians are virtually "one people", but also that the odd view is shared by 10% of supporters of the allegedly "nationalistic" party European Solidarity and 12% of supporters of the ultra-nationalist Svoboda (*Social and political attitudes*, July 2021, p. 21). It is very unlikely that they considered Ukrainians a split group of Russians, in Putin's way. Rather, they tended to see Russians a split group of Ukrainian people—the only true heirs of Ancient Rus.

[33] See Ivakhiv, A. (2005). 'In search of deeper identities Neopaganism and "Native Faith" in contemporary Ukraine', *Nova Religio: The Journal of Alternative and Emergent Religions* 8(3), 7–38; Ivakhiv, A. (2005) 'The Revival of Ukrainian Native Faith', in Strmiska, M. (ed.), *Modern Paganism in World Cultures: Comparative Perspectives*. Santa Barbara CA & Oxford UK: ABC Clio, pp. 209–240; Lesiv, M. (2009). 'Glory to Dazhboh (Sun-god) or to All Native Gods? Monotheism and Polytheism in Contemporary Ukrainian Paganism', *The Pomegranate*, 11(2), pp. 197–222; Shnirelman, V. (2002). "Christians! Go home": A Revival of Neo-Paganism between the Baltic Sea and Transcaucasia', *Journal of Contemporary Religion*, 17(2), pp. 197–211.

[34] E. g. Shilov, Yu. (2005, January 27). 'Скільки тисячоліть слов'янській державності?' [How many millenniums the Ukrainian nationhood has?] *Українська газета* [Ukrainska gazeta], Retrieved from https://samumray.in.ua/skilki-tisyacholit-slo vyanskij-derzhavnosti.

(amateurishly applied). They are not especially interested in Slavonic unity or uniqueness since their ambitions are greater, but occasionally they do overlap with the fringe neo-pagans and the Pan-Ukrainian 'Slavophiles' when confronting together 'malicious Christianity' or a sinister 'Jewish-Masonic conspiracy'.[35]

In fact, the only practical venue for Slavophile ideology (or rather imagery) in Ukraine is the Orthodox church of the Moscow patriarchate that operates legally, even though it explicitly promotes the Kremlin agenda in many areas.[36] Until 2014, it was the largest church in Ukraine, with the greatest number of parishes inherited from Soviet times. This playing field was barely level since, for nearly three hundred years, it was the only officially recognized and legally permitted Orthodox church in Ukraine. Hence, by 2009, 41% of Ukrainian believers claimed to belong to this church, while the split Ukrainian Orthodox Church of the Kyiv Patriarchate had the support of only 27% of believers.[37] In 2013, the picture was largely the same, but a year later it had changed radically, probably for two reasons.

Firstly, a notable part of the Ukrainian population (up to 10%), being on Russia-occupied territories, fell beyond sociological scrutiny. And secondly, quite a few sympathizers of the Moscow Patriarchate broke with the Russian church in dissatisfaction with its pro-Kremlin position. Additionally (and partly as a response to these changes), a new option for confessional self-identification—'just Orthodox'—was introduced into

---

[35] Shakurova, O. (2019). 'Apologetics and Criticism of Pseudoscientific Hypotheses of the Ukrainian Ethnogenesis', *Ukrainian Studies 3*, 86–103; Halushko, K. (2008) 'Битий шлях від археології до нацизму, або які "теорії" ми обговорюємо' [The beaten track from archeology to Nazism, or what "theories" we are discussing], in: *Новітні міфи та фальшивки про походження українців* [The new myths and falsehoods on Ukrainians' origin]. Київ: Tempora. C. f., Laruelle, M. (2008). 'Alternative identity, alternative religion? Neo-paganism and the Aryan myth in contemporary Russia', *Nations and Nationalism*, 14(2), pp. 283–301.

[36] The data analysis proves that the adherents of the Moscow church are much more supportive for Russian policies and, more generally, East Slavonic values framed as anti-Western, than the adherents of any other confession in Ukraine. See: *Українське суспільство: моніторинг соціальних змін* [Ukrainian Society: monitoring of social changes] (2020). Київ: Institute of Sociology of NASU, pp. 252–265.

[37] *Українське суспільство 1992–2013. Соціологічний моніторинг* [Ukrainian Society 1992–2013. Sociological monitoring]. (2013). Київ: Institute of Sociology of NASU, p. 554.

questionnaires. Hence, the number of supporters of the Moscow Patriarchate plummeted to 21% in 2016,[38] down further to 17% in 2020. Support for the Kyiv Patriarchate (now the Orthodox Church of Ukraine) remained almost the same—26% in 2020, which means that the newly rubricated group of 'just Orthodox' (52% of the surveyed) accrued its members primarily from the Moscow Patriarchate's dissenters.[39]

Still, whatever might be the influence of the Russian church, it does not explain the persistence of Slavonic imagery in broad strata of the Ukrainian population—far beyond just the supporters of the Moscow Patriarchate, let alone active churchgoers. The impact of Russian media and local pro-Russian outlets does not hold sufficient explanatory power, either. First, their accessibility is variously restricted because of the war,[40] and secondly, their credibility remains rather low even in the presumably 'pro-Russian' regions of Ukraine.[41] Social media play a more important role and, as experts have observed, are increasingly filled with anti-Ukrainian disinformation. And yet, remarkably, there are virtually no appeals to 'Slavonic unity', 'brotherhood', or other relics of Pan-Slavic imagery. This imagery might offer a convenient space for specific propagandistic messages, but there are few attempts to overtly activate it and realize this. The messages typically convey the notion of Ukraine as a 'failed state' mismanaged by 'nationalists', and of the rotten, greedy, and cynical West striving to subjugate Ukraine and exploit it. (Occasionally the West is charged with attempts to undermine Russia, but virtually no references are made to 'Slavonic unity' or 'brotherhood' as their propagandistic appeal in Ukraine has become highly dubious.) All these messages are densely peppered with conspiracy theories, with the clear

---

[38] *Ukrainian Society* (2018). op. cit., p. 523.

[39] *Ukrainian Society* (2020). op. cit., p. 544.

[40] I discuss the issue in more detail in Riabchuk M. (2020). '*A Difficult Trade-Off: Freedom of Speech and Public Security during the 'Hybrid War','* Harriman Magazine, Spring, pp. 16–23. Retrieved from http://www.columbia.edu/cu/creative/epub/harriman/2020/spring/a_difficult_trade-off_freedom_of_speech_and_public_security_during_the_hybrid_war.pdf.

[41] *Opposition to Russian Propaganda and Media Literacy: Results of All-Ukrainian Opinion Poll. Analytical Report* (2018). Kyiv: Detector Media, pp. 18–19.

intent of distorting and confusing rather than promoting any coherent description of events.[42]

The Slavonic imagery is certainly not a product of these narratives, but rather their facilitator and precondition, a catalyst that makes their spread and uncritical acceptance smoother. One should not confuse this imagery with a sheer Russophilism that may stem from quite rational roots: ethnic or linguistic affinity, cultural, or religious attachment, political sympathy for imperial greatness and tough authoritarian rule, or feeling of cultural superiority *vis à vis* the indigenes who failed to appreciate the empire's *mission civilisatrice*. Such a stance has always had some currency in Ukraine but was never dominant—and certainly is not today. A recent survey found that only 5% of respondents claim they are definitely not 'patriots of Ukraine',[43] while only 6% feel themselves to be 'ethnic Russians'—even as 22% still declare Russian as their native language.[44]

If support for the Kremlin-sponsored concept of *Russkii mir* ('the Russian World') can be any indicator of 'Russophilia' in Ukraine, it is incomparably lower than latent Slavonic sympathies and attachments. The reason is rather simple: Slavophilia operates at the level of cultural-cum-historical myth and quasi-religious imagery; it transcends political reality and places the people into the comfortable glow of *ur*-brotherhood. Russophilia is increasingly political and attached to reality, and the Moscow-promoted concept of *Russkii mir* only makes it more real, political, and unpalatable.[45] At the end of 2014, belonging to the *Russkii mir* was felt marginally in Ukraine, even in the most Russified southeastern regions: only 12% of respondents in Odesa and Kharkiv 'strongly agreed' with the proposition that their region 'belongs to the *Russkii*

---

[42] Pomerantsev, P., et al. (2021). *Why Conspiratorial Propaganda Works and What we can Do About It: Audience Vulnerability and Resistance to Anti-Western, Pro-Kremlin Disinformation in Ukraine*. London School of Economics, p. 10.

[43] *Defender's Day of Ukraine* (2020). Rating Sociological Group, October 14, p. 4. Retrieved from http://ratinggroup.ua/en/research/ukraine/fbb3f3c52d452cdd16 46d4a62b69dba5.html.

[44] *Ukrainian Society* (2020). op. cit., pp. 542–543.

[45] Laruelle, M. (2015). *The "Russian World". Russia's Soft Power and Geopolitical Imagination*. Washington DC: Center on Global Interests; Wawrzonek, M. (2016). *"Russkiy mir": A Conceptual Model of the "Orthodox Civilization"*, In M. Wawrzonek, N. Bekus and M. Korzeniewska-Wiszniewska (Eds.), *Orthodoxy Versus Post-Communism? Belarus, Serbia, Ukraine and the Russkiy Mir*. Cambridge Scholars Publishing, pp. 37–70.

mir'. In Kherson and Zaporizhzhia, 6% strongly agreed, in Dnipro 3%, and in Mykolaiv 0% [sic].[46] So much for the 'Russian Spring' promoted throughout the whole year by Russian troops, paramilitaries, and media-fighters.

The distinction seems obvious: as long as the notion of East Slavonic proximity revolves around common culture and history (ethnographic levels), up to 40% of Ukrainians may agree with Putin's notorious claim about Ukrainians being with Russians virtually 'one people'. Yet as soon as political aspects are introduced into the question, the notion of proximity crumbles. Only 12% of Ukrainian respondents agreed with Putin's claim that there was no reason for Ukrainians' (or Belarusians') separate existence, that they were merely 'invented' by the Bolsheviks (70% definitely disagreed); only 7% agreed that Ukraine 'owes' Russia some territories (76% disagreed)[47]; and only 8% agreed that Russia is a legitimate heir of Ancient Rus (75% believe instead that Ukraine is).[48]

Perhaps most remarkable are the results of a 2015 nationwide survey in which Ukrainians were asked about the values they presumably shared with Russia and with the West, respectively. They could mention a few particular features from an offered list, out of which they compiled two fundamentally different lists. Predictably, cultural and historical features prevailed on the 'Russian' list: 46% of respondents felt Ukraine shared with Russia 'history and traditions', 26% mentioned 'culture', 18% 'ethnicity', 15% 'religion', and 12% 'language'. Conversely, the 'Western' list consisted almost entirely of civic/political characteristics: 28% of respondents claimed that Ukraine shared with the West 'rights and liberties', 27% mentioned 'democracy', 14% 'rule of law', 14% 'respect for the

---

[46] O'Loughlin, J., Toal, G. and Kolosov, V. (2016). *'Who Identifies with the "Russian World"? Geopolitical Attitudes in Southeastern Ukraine, Crimea, Abkhazia, South Ossetia, and Transnistria', Eurasian Geography and Economics.* 57(6), p. 757.

[47] *Оцінка громадянами України головних тез статті В. Путіна "Про історичну єдність росіян та українців"* [Ukrainians' assessment of the main theses of Putin's article "On the Historical Unity of Russians and Ukrainians"] (2021, August 11). Центр Разумкова, Retrieved from https://razumkov.org.ua/napriamky/sotsiologichni-doslidzhennia/otsinka-gromadianamy-ukrainy-golovnykh-tez-putina-pro-istorychnu-iednist-rosiian-ta-ukraintsiv.

[48] *Суспільно-політичні настрої населення* [Social and political attitudes of the population] (2021, July 23–25). Rating Sociological Group, p. 18.

people', and 12% 'economic development'.[49] It is not that Ukrainians believed they were on par with the West in terms of full-fledged democracy, and even less so in 'economic development' or 'rule of law'; rather they declared their normative preferences, values they wished to be cherished in Ukraine according to the Western template rather than the Russian. And since Ukraine was conceived as a political nation, and firmly reiterated this status in 2014, it is very unlikely that *Blut und Erde* can make Ukrainians 'one people' with Russians (as Putin believes)—especially in the absence of 'rights and liberties', 'rule of law', and 'democracy'.

This implies that whatever we hear or read about the Ukrainian-Russian 'proximity' (and, more generally, the East Slavonic 'brotherhood' at its core), we need to scrutinize, time and again, which particular 'Russia' is in question: that of redundant Slavonic imagery, of the tripartite East Slavonic 'brotherhood', or of the real Russia as shown in the concrete words and deeds of its leaders and citizens. In each case, we need to examine how Ukrainians understand the notions of 'same' or 'almost the same' or 'brotherly' people, and, crucially, examine how all these notions correlate with their ability to perceive and adequately assess the reality on the ground. So far, we observe that this ability has been steadily growing since 2014, while the Slavonic imagery has been dissipating—but much more slowly.

The dynamics of that growth (and of many other changes in Ukrainian society) are not particularly impressive, but it is quite steady and sustainable insofar as it is driven by generational changes and the spread of information ('enlightenment'). As the data in Table 3 indicate, the younger and better educated people are more likely to be pro-Western, whereas the older and less educated people tend to be more attached to East Slavonic values. Importantly, these changes are evolving in the same direction (albeit at different scales and intensities) in all Ukraine's regions and among all ethnic and ethnolinguistic groups.[50] This keeps Ukrainian

---

[49] *The current situation in the Ukrainian society* (2015). Kyiv International Institute of Sociology, May, p. 34. Retrieved from http://www.kiis.com.ua/?lang=rus&cat=reports&id=529&page=1.

[50] I discuss the process in more detail in Riabchuk M. (2020). *'Between the "Victory" and "Betrayal": Transformation of Ethnic and Civic Identities in Ukraine since the Revolution of Dignity'*, In V. Voynalovych, (Ed.), Ethnopolitical factors of consolidation of today's Ukrainian society. Kyiv: Institute of Political and Nationalities' Studies NASU.

society quite diverse and, by default, pluralistic but, at the same time, precludes it from an antagonistic split and break-up (Table 3).

On the other hand, the very persistence of 'East Slavonic' imagery makes us recognize that it is not merely a product of Soviet or even tsarist propaganda. It apparently grows out of the much older quasi-religious imagery of *Slavia Orthodoxa*, from its early confrontations with the Catholic world, eventually projecting that essentially religious imagery upon the ethnic and newly discovered 'national' relations.[51] Both the nineteenth-century Pan-Slavism and the twentieth-century 'tripartite brotherhood' drew on that ancient concept and covered it like a palimpsest with new ideological ornaments. But essentially it was the same—about the community of true believers united by blood and God's (or History's) blessing.

To discard such a myth is a difficult task since it functions at an irrational, pre-logical level—performative rather than informative. It is produced and reproduced daily more or less like Michael Billig's 'banal nationalism'. In an insightful article on today's situation in religion and churches in Ukraine, Catherine Wanner and Viktor Yelensky have introduced the notion of an 'ambient faith' as a form of feeling 'just Orthodox' or as a 'believer without a confession', i.e. not aligned with a specific denomination. 'Ambient faith is a mode of being and a mode of belonging that centres on how faith is lived and experienced, as opposed to how religion is practiced'.[52] The authors connect it with the notion of 'Orthodox imagery' that facilitates people's membership in an imagined community based on an imagined shared religious and cultural heritage that conceptualizes all the national churches as one.

'This imagery...allows believers to minimize and transcend confessional boundaries among 'national' churches by imagining them into one.... The

Retrieved from https://ipiend.gov.ua/publication/etnopolitychni-chynnyky-konsolidatsii-suchasnoho-ukrainskoho-suspilstva/. See also Riabchuk, M. (2015). 'Two Ukraines' Reconsidered: The End of Ukrainian Ambivalence? *Studies in Ethnicity and Nationalism*. *15*(1), pp. 138–156, https://doi.org/10.1111/sena.12120.
[51] Kohut, Z. (2011). *Making Ukraine: Studies on Political Culture, Historical Narrative, and Identity*. Toronto & Edmonton: Canadian Institute of Ukrainian Studies.
[52] Wanner, C. and Yelensky, V. (2019). 'Religion and the cultural geography of Ukraine', In U. Schmid, and O. Myshlovska, (Eds.), *Regionalism without regions: reconceptualizing Ukraine's heterogeneity*. Budapest & New York: Central European University Press, pp. 277–278.

Table 3 Support for the two competing systems of values among the major social and demographic groups (%) (*Source* Українське суспільство: моніторинг соціальних змін. 2014 Випуск 1(15). Том 1, pp. 125–132. http://nbuv.gov.ua/UJRN/ukrsoc_2014_1%281%29_14)

System of values	Respondents by age			By education		By region		By ethnicity		By native language	
	younger	middle	older	lower/middle	higher	West/Center	East/South	Ukrainian	Russian	Ukrainian	Russian
Western	23	51	26	70	30	79	21	95	4	85	15
East Slavonic	15	49	36	76	24	34	66	80	17	53	45

'Orthodox imagery' is an adaptive strategy that Ukrainians have devised in order to grapple with Orthodoxy as they would like it to be (unitary, ambient, and depoliticized), rather than how it is (divided, competing for believers, money and state privileges, and increasingly used as a pawn in geopolitical struggles)'.[53]

In our case, a similar notion of 'ambient Slavophilism' can probably be applied alongside the 'Slavonic imagery' to indicate 'an adaptive strategy' that Ukrainians have devised to grapple with the Slavonic world as they would like it to be, rather than how it is. It helped them to reconcile their Ukrainian identity with imperial loyalty in both the Russian and the Soviet empires, but it has become increasingly difficult—virtually impossible—to accommodate their East Slavonic sentiments, however residual and ambient, to the post-imperial reality of nation-states.

It seems to be even more difficult to reconcile the East Slavonic type of Ukrainian identity with the challenges of catch-up modernization, inasmuch as that type of identity was informed by a strong opposition to Western values and a strong conformity to the archaic, pre-modern values of *Slavia Orthodoxa*, contaminated eventually by the highly reactionary values of Pan-Slavism and today's *Russkii mir*. Slavophilia in this context is hardly an asset, as it reinvigorates an attachment not merely to the imaginary East Slavonic/Orthodox Christian community of 'ours' but also, implicitly, to the whole set of conservative values upon which that community was constructed.[54]

---

[53] Ibid., pp. 279–280.

[54] Stephen Shulman found out a strong correlation between the type of national identity ('Ukrainian ethnic' versus 'East Slavonic') and public support for political and economic reform in Ukraine. Adherence to an Eastern Slavic identity, in his view, "is likely to inhibit support for democracy and capitalism. Elite proponents of the identity argue that ethnic Ukrainians and ethnic Russians, whether in Ukraine or Russia, have extremely close and harmonious historical and cultural ties and that the worldview of these "brotherly" peoples is substantially different from that found in Europe, which is the primary "Other" for this identity". (…) Consequently, we would expect that advocates of the Eastern Slavic identity are less likely to support liberal democratic and capitalistic values and institutions, as they are allegedly historically and culturally estranged from both the preferred core internal group (Eastern Slavs: Ukrainians and Russians) and the key foreign nation with which this identity compares Ukraine (Russia). (Shulman, op. cit., pp. 69–70).

Conclusion

Ukrainian Slavophilism emerged in the mid-nineteenth century within the cultural and intellectual framework of Russian Slavophilism, but it evolved very soon into a distinct ideological movement increasingly incompatible with imperial politics and ideology. Ukrainian Slavophiles appropriated Western ideas of democracy, constitutionalism, and federalism as allegedly natural and traditional for Ukraine, and thus laid the groundwork for modern Ukrainian nationalism. Its new adherents felt no need for Pan-Slavonic ideas, particularly after they were appropriated by Russian imperial expansionism.

Subsequently, Ukrainian Slavophilism as a distinct ideological movement ceased to exist. This did not mean, however, disappearance of Slavophilia in Ukraine insofar as Russian Slavophilism retained its position in the province (and, eventually, in the Soviet 'republic'), supported variously by imperial institutions and dominant discourses. While Ukrainian nationalism strove for a mental emancipation of its flock from the empire, Russian Slavophilism sought to prevent such an emancipation and promoted the idea of the primordial unity of the tripartite Russian nation (transformed eventually into the doxa of the 'brotherhood' and the 'near sameness' of the three East Slavonic nationalities).

The political and ideological struggle between these two projects did not come to an end with the dissolution of the Soviet Union but, rather, acquired peculiar new forms. It appeared that Ukrainians are not clearly divided into supporters of one or the other project but demonstrate different levels and forms of attachment to both projects—incoherent, selective, and controversial. And since the two ideological projects are politically (and, even more so, axiologically) incompatible, mixed attachments have produced the high level of social ambivalence discernible from the early days of Ukraine's independence.

Some interpret this as a sign of an allegedly 'weak' national identity, which, in fact, is not 'weaker' than elsewhere in Europe by all measurable parameters—apart from its internal integrity. Quite a few Ukrainians are still variously attached, often unconsciously, to some elements (images, narratives, linguistic clichés, mythical beliefs) of 'East Slavonic' ideology. The sporadic, unconscious, and non-participative character of that attachment largely prevents Ukrainians from a serious ideological-cum-political schism, but it does also complicate the process of their emancipation from the redundant 'East Slavonic ideology' or, rather, 'imagery'. The main problem is not that Ukrainians too deeply internalized that ideology within both the Russian and Soviet empires, but instead that 'Slavophilia' merely overlaid much deeper structures of pre-national, essentially confessional ('Slavic-Orthodox') mentality. Today those structures have lost any relevance and coherence, but they still support some archaic imaginary and fuel 'East Slavonic ideology' with quasi-religious, 'civilizational' rationales.

This chapter has defined these remnants of Slavophile ideology as 'ambient Slavophilia'—a mode of being and of belonging that strives to reconcile local Ukrainian patriotism with residual Slavophile sentiments. It eclectically combines the new state-inculcated ideology with mental matrices and discursive clichés, deeply internalized in the collective unconsciousness and still operating at the level of 'banal Slavophilism'. In some cases, this 'ambient Slavophilia' finds a hybrid expression in eccentric and marginal movements of neo-paganism, or white supremacism, or even Ukraine-centric Pan-Slavonic neo-imperialism. More often than not, however, it resurfaces in the highly ambiguous attitudes towards things Ukrainian and Russian, Western and Pan-Slavonic, 'modern' and 'traditional'. The mythical character of these beliefs makes their rapid disappearance unlikely. At the same time, they have been gradually fading away since 1991, especially since 2014. This makes Ukraine's prospects for catch-up modernization far better than Russia's, where the 'Slavonic' idea assumes an increasingly larger and programmatically retrograde role.

On Pan-Slavism, East vs. West Divide, and Orthodoxy

ND
Bulgaria's Backlash Against the Istanbul Convention: Slavophilia as the Historical Frame of Pseudo-Religious Illiberalism

Nevena Nancheva

INTRODUCTION

Ten years old already at the time of writing, the Council of Europe's Convention on Preventing and Combating Violence against Women and Domestic Violence is a major European human rights treaty establishing a comprehensive legal standard for ensuring women's right to be free from violence.[1] Despite this laudable goal—and to the amazement of the Secretary General of the Council of Europe,[2] the United Nations High

---

[1] Council of Europe Key Facts about the Istanbul Convention. Available at https://www.coe.int/en/web/istanbul-convention/key-facts [accessed 1st July 2021].

[2] In a joint statement to mark UN International Women's Day (2021), German Federal Minister for Family Affairs, Senior Citizens, Women and Youth Franziska Giffey and Council of Europe Secretary General Marija Pejčinović Burić. Available at https://rm.coe.int/final-version-8-march-joint-statement/1680a1a5dc [accessed 1st July 2021].

N. Nancheva (✉)
Kingston University London, London, UK
e-mail: n.nancheva@kingston.ac.uk

Commissioner for Human Rights,[3] and the European Parliament[4] (not to mention liberal public opinion in Europe)—Bulgaria vociferously rejected the treaty. The President, Constitutional Court, Bulgarian party elites, intellectuals, the church, media, and the public pointed to traditionalist national and family values, faith, and the national sovereignty of the state to justify their position. What became known as the Istanbul Convention was regarded as the 'spiritual death of our people'[5] and an assault on 'traditional Orthodox values rooted in a millennium of historical and cultural development'.[6]

How did Bulgarians suddenly remember these traditional values, given that only around 4% of them practise Bulgaria's traditional religion, Orthodox Christianity, and more than 58% declare that religion does not play a leading role in their lives?[7] What explains the surfacing of such polarising public reaction to an otherwise celebrated human rights development, banning violence against women? In order to explore some answers to these questions, we will delve into Bulgaria's narrative search for a national and geopolitical identity which suits both its position as a Slavic country with one of the oldest historical legacies of sovereign

---

[3] In an End of Mission Statement after Official visit to Bulgaria, 14–21 October 2019 by United Nations Special Rapporteur on violence against women, its causes and consequences, Dubravka Šimonović. Available at https://www.ohchr.org/EN/NewsEvents/Pages/DisplayNews.aspx?NewsID=25173&LangID=E [accessed 1st July 2021].

[4] European Parliament resolution of 28 November 2019 on the EU's accession to the Istanbul Convention and other measures to combat gender-based violence 2019/2855(RSP). Available at https://www.europarl.europa.eu/doceo/document/TA-9-2019-0080_EN.html [accessed 1st July 2021].

[5] Holy Synod of the Bulgarian Orthodox Church (2018) Official Statement on the Istanbul Convention of 22nd January 2018. Available at https://old.bg-patriarshia.bg/m/news.php?id=254101 [accessed 1st July 2021].

[6] Open Letter of Bulgarian Academics on the Istanbul Convention. 25th January 2018. Available at http://www.nbp.bg/nbp/%D0%B1%D1%8A%D0%BB%D0%B3%D0%B0%D1%80%D1%81%D0%BA%D0%B8-%D0%B0%D0%BA%D0%B0%D0%B4%D0%B5%D0%BC%D0%B8%D1%86%D0%B8-%D1%81-%D0%BF%D1%80%D0%B8%D0%B7%D0%B8%D0%B2-%D0%B2%D1%80%D0%B5%D0%BC%D0%B5-%D0%B5-%D0%B4/ [accessed 1st July 2021].

[7] Minchev, O. (2017). Interview for Goran Blagoev on 11th November 2017. Bulgarian National Television. Available at https://bnt.bg/bg/a/blgarite-vyarvat-v-bog-no-ne-khodyat-na-tsrkva-zashcho-11112017 [last accessed 1st July 2021].

statehood in Europe[8] and as the poorest member state of the European Union.[9]

We argue that one way to better understand this development is by unpacking the historical significance of Slavophilia in Bulgaria, which will reveal some of its central elements in the polarised public discussion we are exploring. This is not necessarily linked to the subject at hand: Turkey, Hungary, the Czech Republic, and Slovakia (among others) also registered strong objections to the Istanbul Convention, framing them differently. But overlaying the historical significance of Slavophilia onto the Bulgarian case allows us to identify and understand the geopolitical implications and uncertainty of the identitarian search we explore here.

Why Slavophilia?

We see the backlash against the Istanbul Convention as a search for a (truer) identity more befitting the uncertain domestic and geopolitical context Bulgaria finds itself in. Showcasing Bulgaria's unique sovereign legacy in Europe, rooted as it is in Orthodox Christianity and a shared Slavic culture, this search reflects Bulgaria's history of balancing (though not infrequently falling on the losing side) at the geopolitical fault line between the Eurasian East and the European West. By disentangling some of the narratives in the public discussion on the subject at the levels of political and intellectual elites, decision-makers, and the general public, we point to broader nationalistic and geopolitical discourses which previously appeared as elements of Bulgaria's historical relationship with Slavophilia. They sustain iterations of identity which go well beyond the modest confines of Bulgaria's current sovereign borders.

As we will see from the exploration that follows, aspects of Pan-Slavism seem to resurface every so often in such identitarian claims, only to categorically submerge again, back to the realm of the nineteenth- and twentieth-century history of the modern Bulgarian state where they belong. However, the legacy of Pan-Slavism remains palpable as a background to the nationalistic and geopolitical narratives that populate

---

[8] Dating back to the seventh century. See Bulgarian Academy of Sciences (1981). History of Bulgaria. Volume II. [Istoriya na Balgariya].

[9] Eurostat (2020). Volume Indices GDP per capita. Available at https://ec.europa.eu/eurostat/statistics-explained/index.php?title=GDP_per_capita,_consumption_per_capita_and_price_level_indices [last accessed 1st July 2021].

Bulgaria's current identitarian search, bringing forth discursive elements which do not otherwise fit popular discourses. In order to frame this elusive discursive presence, we refer to the term Slavophilia proposed in this volume.

'Slavophilia' is useful here in that it captures the incoherent 'coalescence of ideas, emotions, visions, and metaphors' (see the Introduction) which reflects Bulgaria's uneasy position between the Eurasian East and the European West, fully at home neither here nor there, and combines easily with the populist, illiberal discourses resurgent throughout Europe. Slavophilia expresses, all at the same time, a peculiar resentment towards 'Europe' as an imposing external Other, a nebulous emotional attachment to the Orthodox East as a civilisational choice, and a desire to find an independent path which (more) truly reflects Bulgaria's own vision of itself amidst the troubles of the present.

What we observe as an identitarian search here does not fit neatly into nationalist rhetoric inasmuch as it speaks of civilisational choices that go beyond the national Self: it calls upon values and imagery which are part of a larger geopolitical discourse juxtaposing 'Us' and 'Them' (the latter here embodied by the Euro-Atlantic West and its norms). In this juxtaposition, the geopolitical identity that Bulgaria chooses for itself does contain elements of the same populism visible across Europe. However, it also brings back imagery of a past connecting Bulgaria to the Slavic world in its struggles for national emancipation and political independence, while also adapting it to the dilemmas of the present: namely, an inability to fit properly into the requirements of its new geopolitical place.

Having lost the links with the Slavic world that sustained it in its past struggles, Bulgaria still looks beyond its own borders in search of a civilisational identity more closely aligned with its own vision of the Self. In doing so, it borrows discursive elements from its Pan-Slavic past, without necessarily naming them, and patches these onto its current visions of the Self, even though they no longer fit. In our exploration of Bulgaria's embattled position on the Istanbul Convention as a case study here, we will see an inward search for family values and traditional gender stereotypes, glorification of national culture and history, the significance of national sovereignty, as well as the rediscovery of religious tradition as a response to liberal secularity, which all clash with its official geopolitical choices and declared national identity in obvious ways.

While not always explicitly named, Slavophilia captures the pan-nationalist historical background which enables such imagery. Based on presumed commonality and an imagined historical community of values beyond the state, it also points to an uncomfortable geopolitical choice between the European West and the Eurasian East. For Bulgaria, this historical background frames a contemporary geopolitical identity which is fully neither 'here' nor 'there'. Slavophilia is also useful because it describes, and not only in Bulgaria, the peculiar position of the 'weak': as a populist pan-nationalist expression of the exclusion felt across the continent by the numerous groups left behind by the global hegemony of 'the West' (personified in Europe by the European integration project), illiberal populism is critical of 'Brussels' and the supranationalisation of sovereign power which it represents, so it seeks to re-enact an historical sovereign legacy preceding that. The incongruence engendered by populist pan-nationalist narratives and liberal democracy within the Euro-Atlantic geopolitical space explains the polarised public discussion on the ratification of a human rights treaty protecting women against violence and the paradoxical iterations of identity emerging from it in the Bulgarian public space of the past decade.

The notion of Slavophilia frames some of the key positions in that narrative battle, drawing from a mixed pan-nationalist palette contrasting with the European West, a rich cultural tradition dipped in Orthodox Christianity but claiming its own (often pagan) authenticity, with a palpable political uncertainty rooted in disenchantment with EU membership, the democratic transition in general, and with the peculiarly opaque brand of market economy which has characterised the post-communist decades.

In what follows, we contextualise Bulgaria's dynamic historical relationship with Slavophilia and the Slavic idea as a cultural-civilisational and political-ideological choice by outlining three main phases: from the beginning of Bulgaria's national revival to the country's political autonomy from the Ottomans in 1878; the period of the Third Bulgarian Kingdom lasting until the Second World War; and the period of communist rule lasting until 1989, when the Euro-Atlantic choice was made. Against this background, we then present and unpack the case of Bulgaria's backlash against the Istanbul Convention.

Bulgaria's Slavic Connection

When it comes up at all, the so-called Slavic Question, which was at the centre of the nineteenth-century romantic ideology of Slavophilia, seems to have been settled once and for all with the accession to the European Union of most of the Slavic states: the geopolitical role of the Slavs—their future in world politics—has been largely re-aligned with that of the Euro-Atlantic West.[10] Bulgaria was among those Slavic states (albeit one of the poorest and most reluctantly admitted to the 'Club'), and its Euro-Atlantic future seemed to have been sealed.

It was not always so: Bulgaria's Eurasian pagan heritage, its Slavonic culture, its Eastern Orthodox faith, and the territory it occupied on the Balkan peninsula at the very edge of the European mainland all mean that it has navigated a geopolitical space of civilisational clashes. Most decidedly in its modern history—and for nearly 500 years before that—this was the realm of the Ottoman Empire. What distinguished the Bulgarians as one of the many religious minorities under Ottoman rule were Christianity, the Old Slavonic used (to this day) in Bulgarian church services, and the spoken and written version of the Slavic language later codified into modern Bulgarian through the Cyrillic alphabet.[11] In the nineteenth century, during the period of national revival, these became the bases for Bulgaria's claim for religious autocephaly within the Ottoman Empire—and the first steps towards its national independence. In our exploration of debates on the Istanbul Convention, we will see the resurgence of some of these cultural narratives stripped of their inherently religious rationale but still carrying over a pseudo-religious traditionalism from these earlier centuries.

National Revival

The role of Slavic heritage during the Bulgarian national revival is central, as Bulgaria saw its place within the Slavic world as one of leadership. The symbolic beginning of this period is linked to a historiographic manuscript written by Paisius of Hilendar around 1762 entitled *Slaveno-Bulgarian History*, which clearly ascribes the Bulgarian people a leading role among the Slavs:

---

[10] Anchev, P. (2010). Slavs and Slavophilia. Is unification of the Slavs possible in the postmodern world? In Literaturen sviat. Issue 21. June 2010. Available at https://literaturensviat.com/?p=30983 [accessed 1st July 2021].

[11] Old Slavonic and Old Bulgarian were not quite the same languages but were apparently similar in many ways, see Georgiev, E. (1984). Studies in the History of Slavic Literature, Part I. Science and Art: Sofia. [Ocherki po istoria na slavyanskite literaturi].

'Of all the Slavic people, most glorious have been the Bulgarians: they have called themselves kings first, they have had a patriarch first, they have christened themselves first, they have conquered the most lands.'[12]

Among other things, Bulgaria's leadership claim as a Slavic enlightener is based on the warm reception by the old Bulgarian kings[13] of the disciples of St Cyril and St Methodius (who created in the ninth century the alphabet for the Old Slavonic language to be used in Christian worship), some of whom may have been Bulgarians. Their missionary work in what had at various times been Bulgarian lands has been celebrated as proof of Bulgarians' Enlightenment role:

'[...] we have also given something to the world [...],
To all Slavs—the Book to read.'[14]

In the period of revolutionary struggle for independence from the Ottomans, this prominent Slavic heritage aligned with Russia's foreign policy of Pan-Slavism and its Slavophilic ideology and played a key part in Bulgaria's liberation in the 1876–78 Russo-Turkish War.[15] Russia at this time was seen as a 'Liberator', and the Russians were fondly addressed as *bratushki* (brothers). In many ways, Bulgarian Slavophilia often aligns with Russophilia as a result of this decisive Russian role in Bulgarian independence. The fact that Russia supported a large Bulgarian state in the Peace Treaty of San Stefano (which remained the Bulgarian national ideal of sovereignty in the decades that followed) helped to reinforce this image and strengthen the notion of Slavic brotherhood in Bulgaria. This was especially significant in terms of the Western 'Great Powers', who were hostile to the idea of a large Russophile outpost in the Balkans and prevented a San Stefano Bulgaria in favour of a partitioned one, formally vassal to the Sublime Porte.

---

[12] Paisius of Hilendar (1760–62) History of the Slovene-Bulgarians. Available at https://chitanka.info/text/3746-istorija-slavjanobylgarska [accessed 1st July 2021].

[13] During the First Bulgarian kingdom 681–1018.

[14] This is part of an epic poem by one of the leading Bulgarian intellectuals of the post-independence years Vazov, I. [1893], Paisius in Epic of the Forgotten [Epopeya na zabravenite]. Narodna mladezh: Sofia. 1962.

[15] Andreev, A. (2014) The Russian Slavic Committees in Bulgaria (1857–1878). Abagar: Sofia. [Ruskite slavyanski komiteti v Balgariya].

Independent Statehood

In our study of the debates around the Istanbul Convention, we will once again notice at times this overlap between Slavophilia and Russophilia as a civilisational choice, for example in the warm reception of the Russian Orthodox patriarch. But Bulgaria's complex, often strained relationship with Russia prevents us from fully aligning the two notions. Indeed, Slavophilia appears closer to the civilisational narratives underpinning these debates because these aim to circumvent the dominance of external Others and re-install a more befitting vision of the Self.

In this sense, it is important to note that Pan-Slavism underscored and supported Bulgarian nationalism in the period leading up to Bulgaria's autonomy in 1878, while after that the two began to gradually clash as Bulgaria's monarch and its political elite sought to assert greater independence from the Russian 'Liberators'. Especially resented seems to have been Russian meddling in the affairs of the new state during the reign of its first monarch, Prince Alexander Battenberg, which ultimately led to his abdication from the throne.[16] This set the tone for Bulgaria's search for an independent political path (guided by macro-nationalism and a desire for territorial unification), away from external influences.

There is a palpable detachment from Pan-Slavic affinity at this time, more so after a war with neighbouring Serbia over contested territory and the unification of Bulgaria with Eastern Rumelia, which alienated Russia even further. Addressing then-Prime Minister Stoilov and Bulgaria's political elite, a leading statesman from the period (Stefan Stambolov) summarised the reasons for this alienation:

> '[...] we are grateful to our brotherly Russian people [but] the Russian government does not want an independent Bulgaria! [...] It wants the south, the warmth, a passage for its navy through the Black Sea. Pursuing these interests excludes respecting ours.'[17]

---

[16] Andreev, A. (1997). Bulgarian Exarch and the Russian Plans for Destabilising Bulgaria (1887–1894). In Special Issue on 120 anniversary of the Lovech Metropolitan Joseph's election for Bulgarian Exarch. Bulgarian Patriarchate, Lovech. [Balgarskiyat ekzarh i ruskite planove za destabilizirane na Balgariya].

[17] Tsankov, I. (1915). Stefan Stambolov and Bulgaria's present state. Sofia: Y.T. p.42. [Stefan Stambolov i dneshnoto polozhenie na Balgariya].

Nevertheless, this is still a period of significant popularity for the Slavic idea in Bulgaria, as evidenced by the activities of influential Slavic organisations. Founded in Bulgaria under the model of the Russian Slavic Committees, they were originally meant to support fellow Bulgarians still living under Ottoman rule, then later to advance Slavic kinship and cooperation.[18] The most prominent were the association Slavic Talks, founded in 1880, and the Slavic Association of 1899.[19] Despite their efforts to distance themselves from the political ideology of Pan-Slavism, they were inevitably influenced by the geopolitics of the time. The Slavic associations played an active part in Bulgaria's intellectual and political life. And while their primary functions were the development of cultural ties with the rest of the Slavic world and support for Bulgarians abroad, the associations also engaged in charitable work for the benefit of Russia and, after the 1917 Revolution, of Russian émigrés seeking refuge in Bulgaria.[20]

It is notable that the Slavic idea during this time was closely linked to Orthodox Christianity as a shared faith, thus nurturing relations overwhelmingly with the Southern Slavs (although strong cultural exchange was also developed with the Catholic Czechs). It was, however, also intrinsically linked to Bulgaria's struggle for the national unification of lands inhabited by Bulgarians but remaining in neighbouring countries.[21] These two goals often pulled in opposite directions, creating an inherent paradox at the heart of Bulgaria's relationship with Slavophilia. Both kinship and betrayal characterised this relationship, and provide an insight into Bulgaria's shifting political allegiances during the Balkan Wars

---

[18] Encyclopaedia Daritelstvoto. Slavic Association in Bulgaria. [Slavyanskoto druzhestvo v Balgariya]. See http://daritelite.bg/slavyansko-druzhestvo-v-balgariya/ [accessed 1st July 2021].

[19] State Archives Sofia, Fund Number 1318 K. Association 'Slavic Talk'. [Druzhestvo Slavyanska beseda]. See https://www.archivesportaleurope.net/ead-display/-/ead/pl/aicode/BG-00000021357/type/fa/id/25559 [accessed 1st July 2021].

[20] Chumachenko, V. et al. (2013). The White Emigrants in Bulgaria: Memories. [Beloemigranti v Bolgarii. Vospominaniya]. Synergy and Andreev, A. (2009) Orthodox and Slavic Ideas against Bulgarian-Russian Relations during fifteenth-nineteenth centuries. In Ivan Stoyanov (ed.). Collected Volume 130 Years of Modern Bulgarian Statehood. Veliko Tarnovo. [Pravoslavnata i slavyanskata idei na fona na balgaro-ruskite otnosheniya prez XV-XIX vek].

[21] Nyagolova, M. (2017). Slavophile Ideas in Bulgaria during the 1920s. Slavonic Voice Review. Shumen University Ep. Konstantin Preslavski. Issue 2. pp. 284–300. [Slavyanofilskite idei v Balgariya prez 20-te godini na XX vek].

(1912–13), the First World War, and in the interwar period leading up to its alignment with the Axis powers during World War II (in hope of fulfilling its ideal for the unification of Bulgarian lands). The value of faith and a desire for geopolitical emancipation are also visible in Bulgaria's present-day relationship with Slavophilia as an alternative civilisational discourse, as we will see below.

Communist Period

Ultimately, Bulgaria fell within the Soviet sphere of influence after 1945 and entered a 45-year-long period of totalitarian rule under a communist regime. During this time, a new Slavic Committee[22] was established, but its activities were entirely guided by the needs of communist state propaganda. Interestingly, the Slavic Committee reinvented itself as an organisation looking to establish connections with Bulgarian émigrés (mostly in North America but also across the world), and was supported in its functions by the Foreign Ministry, the Bulgarian Academy of Sciences, the Committee on Church Issues, and the state media. It was understandably mistrusted by Bulgarians abroad (most of whom had escaped precisely that regime which now supported the Slavic Committee), even after it was refashioned explicitly into a Committee for Bulgarians Abroad in 1982 and, after the fall of the communist regime, into an official state Agency for Bulgarians Living Abroad (a nebulous administration existing to this day). In the identitarian discourse, we explore here, this outreach element of Bulgaria's Slavophilia is not so visible, but it still calls upon an external geopolitical commonality of value which is more inward-looking and confrontational.

We can find the roots of this shift in the country's forty-five years of totalitarianism, when the two most prominent elements in Bulgaria's Slavophilia—its irredentist ambitions and its Orthodox faith—were largely subdued. Bulgarian nationalism turned inwards towards the domestic Others (most visibly the large Turkish minority[23]) as the state came to

---

[22] Established 1945. See https://bgemigration.com/project/state-agency/ [accessed 1st July 2021].

[23] Stoyanov, V. (1998). Bulgaria's Turkish Population between the Extremes of Ethnic Politics. Sofia: Lik. [Turskoto naselenie v Bulgariya mezhdu polyusite na etnicheskata politika].

terms with its existing territorial borders, while religious practice gradually declined in the face of communist persecution and an atheistic cultural policy. (The years of state-led atheism may explain the pseudo-religious traditionalist revival which later came to replace the secular liberalism of the Euro-Atlantic West.) What remained of cultural and political significance of Bulgaria's outward calls for belonging were a faith-based kinship across the borders of the Orthodox world and an emotional closeness with the Russians (the Russian language was embedded in the national school curriculum), underlain with suspicion and resentment of the Russian state as the former metropolitan master.

We will see this nuanced love-and-hate relationship re-emerge in the post-communist years in the form of geopolitical nostalgia, especially when disenchantment with the new Euro-Atlantic orientation of the Bulgarian state surged in the face of prolonged economic crises and widespread corruption. It is in such a volatile political climate that Bulgaria's narrative search for a truer identity began to turn away from the liberal secular values of the 'West' and towards the (quasi-)religious, conservative, and traditionalist narratives of a past closely linked to the Slavic world, yet never fully in unison with it.

How Bulgaria Misunderstood the Istanbul Convention

Tying such non-liberal narratives of identity around public discussions of the Istanbul Convention is a useful way to put together a clearer picture of Bulgaria's shifting geopolitical belonging of the past decade. Caught between a Euro-Atlantic membership which had largely failed to hold political party elites to account and a South-Eastern Slavic heritage which never fully supported its national emancipation, Bulgaria seemed to be straddling the geopolitical fault line between West and East with unease. Its gradual embrace of illiberal populism, which testifies to this, is well illustrated by the backlash against the Istanbul Convention.

Long in the making, the Council of Europe's programme to combat violence against women culminated in the text of a convention opened for signature in May 2011.[24] Still a recent EU member state (it had joined

---

[24] Council of Europe. Text of the Convention. Available at https://www.coe.int/en/web/istanbul-convention/text-of-the-convention [accessed 1st July 2021].

only in 2007 and was awaiting the lifting of the last transitional restrictions in 2012), Bulgaria at this time was governed by a prime minister elected on a strongman's agenda: this was Boyko Borisov's first term in power.[25] Cashing in on his *machista* image (as a former private security guard and chief of the Interior Ministry), Borisov epitomised the search for 'law and order' by a Bulgarian public fatigued from two decades of post-communist transition. But disappointment with his rule—and with the whole political system—erupted in massive protests throughout 2013.[26] Across the country and over several months, at times ending in violent clashes with police, the protests indicated a public dissatisfied with its leadership and looking for radical change. The fact that such change was not possible—Borisov remained in power for two further mandates until May 2021, provoking further protests in 2020—suggests a deep-seated rift between the Bulgarian public and its leadership. It is exactly this rift which allowed for competing and contesting narratives of identity to gain salience.

Albeit not among the first signatories, during Borisov's second government, Bulgaria did finally sign the Istanbul Convention in April 2016 (two years after it had entered into force), and during his third government, he initiated the domestic legal process of ratification by the end of 2017 through a legal strategy led by the Ministry of Justice.

'Gender' as the Focal Point of Identity Iterations

It is within the ensuing public discussion that the notion of 'gender' entered the Bulgarian discursive space and dramatically polarised it over the course of the following year.[27] It is precisely this notion, not quite fitting into the vocabulary of the Bulgarian language, which uniquely pulled in the identitarian narratives of a state at the geopolitical fault line

---

[25] Boyes, R. (2009). Election victory of ex karate coach brings strongman tactics to Bulgaria. In The Times. 6th July 2009. Available at https://www.thetimes.co.uk/article/election-victory-of-ex-karate-coach-brings-strongman-tactics-to-bulgaria-9zcqdb7xtrr [accessed 1st July 2021].

[26] Investor. 2013. 2013: The Year of Protests. In Investor of 30th December 2013. Available at: https://www.investor.bg/nachalo/0/a/2013-g-godinata-na-protestite-164114/ [accessed 1st July 2021].

[27] Deutsche Welle. 2019. How Bulgarian Society Fell in the Trap of Gender. In Deutsche Welle of 23rd October 2019. Available at: https://p.dw.com/p/3Rki9 [accessed 1st July 2021].

between the Euro-Atlantic West and Slavophile East. From homophobia to Roma-hatred, the term 'gender'—untranslatable into the Bulgarian language—seemed to translate into everything that was wrong with the country and its policies, while channelling public backlash against the Convention into populist uproar (Figs. 1 and 2).

Opposition to ratifying the convention was so staunch that the Constitutional Court was brought in to rule on the compatibility of the text with Bulgaria's foundational law. Ultimately in the summer of 2018, the Court ruled that the text clashed with core values embedded in Bulgaria's constitution, in particular concerning legal discrepancies which could ensue as a result of the difference between the notion of gender (as employed in the Convention) and that of biological sex (as employed in Bulgarian legislation), which effectively stalled the ratification:

> 'Defining gender as a social construct relativises the boundaries between the two sexes—the male and the female—as biologically determined. But if society loses its ability to distinguish between male and female,

Fig. 1 Visual for the 'Petition against the EU's accession to the Istanbul Convention', run by the organisation Rod International (*Source* https://rod-bg.com/articles/petition-against-joining-of-eu-in-ic.html)

Fig. 2 Protest against the Istanbul Convention depicting a slogan which reads 'Save Children from Debauchery (*Source* BGNES for Bulgarian National Radio on 11th Jan 2018. Available at: https://bnr.bg/vidin/post/100918948/vredna-za-balgarskoto-obshtestvo-li-e-istanbulskata-konvencia)

combating violence against women remains as a formal but unachievable commitment.'[28]

---

[28] Constitutional Court of the Republic of Bulgaria. 2018. Decision Number 13. Available at http://www.constcourt.bg/bg/Acts/GetHtmlContent/f278a156-9d25-412d-a064-6ffd6f997310 [accessed 1st July 2021].

Thus, it was the notion of gender which seemed to have triggered the profound, discursive soul searching visible in Bulgaria's public discussions on the Istanbul Convention during 2017–18 and after. As a link between the legal protection of human rights and the liberal agenda of secular tolerance and freedom of choice, gender captures some of the deep-seated ontological assumptions of Bulgarian public discourse which seemed to have been disturbed by the new meanings that the Convention was seen to introduce. While not explicitly coated in the language of Slavophilia, the debates on the incompatibility of 'gender' with the Bulgarian psyche and law were sustained by some of the pan-nationalist narratives of Slavophilia which we highlighted above, making the notion pertinent and useful.

Political Iterations of Pan-Nationalist Identity Against 'Gender'

It is not coincidental that the earliest opposition to the Convention came from the side of the Bulgarian nationalist party outfits[29]: naturally affiliated with traditionalism, their populist rhetoric fit well the illiberal reaction against 'Europe' as an imposition. At a public discussion on the topic hosted in the main aula of the University of Sofia in January 2018, they expressed concern (met with applause) that the ratification of the convention would result in 'such ruination of morals and values that soon there will be no one to make children'.[30]

The nationalists took issue with the Council of Europe's term 'gender' and demanded legal definitions of the notions of 'social sex' and 'sexual identity' as opposed to it. They pointed to the traditionally unequivocal meanings and roles attached to these terms in Bulgarian society and national culture, raising the alert against the construction of a 'third gender', same-sex marriages and adoptions, and the reception of transgender refugees. Linking such a wide range of issues to the notion of 'gender' as used in the Istanbul Convention, they called upon a much stronger discursive opposition than their argument can logically summon.

---

[29] These are the VMRO-Bulgarian National Movement's Krasimir Karakachanov and National Front for the Salvation of Bulgaria's Valeri Simeonov, as well as the VMRO-BNM's offshoot Revival political party.

[30] Public Discussion on the Istanbul Convention, 23rd January 2018. Sofia University St Kliment Ohridski. Available at https://www.youtube.com/watch?v=-J_FTCafhhg [accessed 1st July 2021].

The discursive success of this strategy was evidenced by a pollster in February 2018, who showed that 30% of Bulgarians actually did believe that the ratification of the Convention would result in legalising a 'third gender', gay marriage, and adoption for gay parents,[31] outcomes that went against 'our Motherland' and the '125-year history of [the party] representing the deep-rooted traditions and ways of the Bulgarian people'.[32]

It is interesting that the Bulgarian Socialist Party—a large and established player in Bulgarian politics—also condemned the Convention vocally. Given the socialists' discursive association with Russophilia and the geopolitical East, this may not be too surprising. Despite the rift this position created with the Party of European Socialists (whose president and former BSP leader Sergey Stanishev even suggested the exclusion of the BSP from the European socialist family[33]), the party leadership in the person of Kornelia Ninova defended their stance vehemently:

> 'I believe [the rejection of the ratification] is a victory of the Bulgarian people in defending its identity, national, and family values.'[34]

In her consistent opposition to the Istanbul Convention, Ninova relied on a revealing discursive binary of 'us' and 'them' (also illustrating the pan-nationalist proclivity to antagonisms), in which the 'authentic', 'traditional family home' was existentially threatened by the 'foreign': 'an

---

[31] According to the pollster Sova Haris as reported by Bulgarian National Radio on 23rd February 2018. Available at https://news.bg/bulgaria/30-ot-balgarite-smyatat-che-s-konventsiya-se-vavezhda-treti-pol.html [accessed 1st July 2021].

[32] The name of the party Internal Revolutionary Macedonian Organisation speaks to the period of struggles for independence and carries strong 'patriotic' associations. As reported by Desislava Andonova for News BG on 27th July 2018 at https://news.bg/politics/patriotite-gordi-che-sa-se-vazprotivili-na-istanbulskata-konventsiya.html [accessed 1st July 2021].

[33] Staridolska, E. (2018). Why BSP voted against the Istanbul Convention. For Capital of 15th January 2018. Available at https://www.capital.bg/politika_i_ikonomika/bulgaria/2018/01/15/3112666_zashto_bsp_shte_glasuva_sreshtu_istanbulskata/ [accessed 1st July 2021].

[34] Panayotova, D. (2018). Ninova welcomes the decision of the Constitutional Court. In News BG of 27th July 2018. Available at: https://news.bg/politics/ninova-privetstva-reshenieto-na-ks-za-istanbulskata-konventsiya.html [accessed 1st July 2021].

ideology foreign to our society and family'.[35] This stance was maintained fiercely, even against accusations of being 'anti-European, nationalist, fascist'[36]: such accusations could be waved off without any argumentation because they came from 'foreign [actors]'.[37]

The president, Rumen Radev (a former major-general who was elected in 2016 with the support of the BSP and, not unlike his political nemesis Borisov, represents the strongman figure) also spoke against the Istanbul Convention. In his opposition he emphasised another element of populist anti-Europeanism found in Bulgaria's use of Slavophilia: the centrality of national sovereignty. Without engaging with the narratives around the traditional family or social authenticity, he spoke directly on the importance of sovereign independence:

'We cannot accept declarations from the heart of Europe that we will ratify this convention, without first hearing our own Parliament on the issue. [...] We cannot sign *(sic)* a document which has not been debated fully and profoundly here.'[38]

Radev also used the situation to take a swipe at his political rival Borisov:

'I suggest the Prime Minister was less attentive to voices outside Bulgaria.'[39]

Besides the nationalist and the socialist parties and the president, the case against the Istanbul Convention was also taken up by an array of public figures and intellectuals. A group of senior academics formulated

---

[35] Duma. 2018. Ninova welcomes the decision on the Istanbul Convention. In Duma of 30th July 2018. Available at https://duma.bg/ninova-privetstva-reshenieto-na-ks-za-ist anbulskata-konventsiya-n172118 [accessed 1st July 2021].

[36] Ibid.

[37] Ibid. ('чуждите').

[38] Kostadinova, V. (2018). Now is not the time for the Istanbul Convention. In News BG of 24th January 2018. Available at: https://news.bg/politics/sega-ne-e-momentat-za-istanbulskata-konventsiya-smyata-radev.html [accessed 1st July 2021].

[39] Kostadinova, V. (2018). The president recommends that the prime minister listened... In News BG of 15th February 2018. Available at: https://news.bg/pol itics/prezidentat-preporacha-na-borisov-da-slusha-po-malko-glasovete-izvan-balgariya.html [accessed 1st July 2021].

an open letter from a religious-conservative standpoint, evoking Bulgaria's history as 'embedded in traditional Orthodox values of millennium-long development'.[40] This is relevant, as such religious reference points are usually completely absent from Bulgarian intellectual discourse: their emergence in this context suggests larger sets of narratives embedded in the public domain, beyond the everyday.

Pan-Nationalist Iterations of Religious Identity Among a Non-Practising Public

Amidst the vehement public discussions about the 'third gender' and homosexuality, the Bulgarian Orthodox Patriarchy understandably also leaned in to reaffirm the Church's official position on the matter. The Synod provided a broad analysis of its opposition to the Convention, agreeing both that the Bulgarian legal system could not accommodate a misalignment between sex and gender and that the latter concept did not even exist in the vocabulary of the Bulgarian language (which, incidentally, is true and one of the reasons why 'gender' could appear as a floating signifier able to carry all meanings). The Synod rejected 'the ideas embedded in the Convention about intersex relations, attitudes towards religion, tradition, custom, and education, as incompatible with the deep-seated understanding of the Bulgarian people of faith, ethnicity, morality, dignity, honour, upbringing, family'.[41] We see in this statement that the issue is linked explicitly to more than just religion: the mention of ethnicity and honour invite us to search for a more multi-layered discursive realm of geopolitical identity and role.

On an official visit for the commemoration of 140 years since the liberation of Bulgaria from the Ottomans, Kirill, the Russian Patriarch of Moscow and All Russia fully supported the position of the Bulgarian Patriarchy on the issue. In an interview for Bulgarian national media, he explained that 'the Convention expects gay partnerships to be treated as families',[42] which the Church could not accept. The timing of his visit and

---

[40] Open Letter of Bulgarian Academics on the Istanbul Convention. 25th January 2018.

[41] Holy Synod of the Bulgarian Orthodox Church. 2018. Official Statement.

[42] Topnovini. 2018. Russian Patriarch Kiril. In Topnovini of 1st March 2018. Available at: https://topnovini.bg/novini/785673-ruskiyat-patriarh-kiril-iskame-tsarkvata-da-pomogne-za-svobodata-na-choveka [accessed 1st July 2021].

the media uptake of his comments pointed to the deep-rooted cultural links with Russia which we mentioned above.

Ultimately, it did not matter much that the subject matter of the Convention was a serious human rights issue—violence against women—and one that Bulgaria had not been able to address meaningfully. It also did not matter that the Convention did not actually deal with matters of homosexuality, gay marriage, or adoption of children by gay partners (among other claims). The prime minister, who officially expressed embarrassment[43] at the inability of his cabinet to ratify the Convention and at the public 'misinformation campaign'[44] which completely hijacked debates on the issue,[45] did not manage to counter the dominant narratives.

That such narratives appealed to the Bulgarian public, who embraced them with readiness,[46] suggests their compatibility with deep-seated ideas, emotions, and visions of belonging not quite suited to the secular liberalism incidentally epitomised by the Council of Europe's convention combating violence against women. Disenchanted with the results of the geopolitical choices made during the post-communist transition, the Bulgarian public showed a readiness to look for a geopolitical space of belonging away from and beyond the Euro-Atlantic liberal West. Their identitarian search delved into forgotten images, legacies, and traditions, captured here by the frame of Slavophilia, which do not necessarily reflect the reality of Bulgarian public life but rather indicate a desire for change. It is this uneasy geopolitical position which is revealed in the vehement public opposition to the Istanbul Convention, expressed in narratives of pan-nationalist populism.

---

[43] News BG, 2018. Borisov is embarrassed at the failure.

[44] European Parliament resolution of 28 November 2019.

[45] Svobodna Evropa. 2020. The European Parliament and the Noise around the Istanbul Convention. 9th October 2020. Available at: https://www.svobodnaevropa.bg/a/30884308.html [accessed 1st July 2021].

[46] Public comments on the debate: https://www.dnevnik.bg/analizi/2020/10/09/4124791_evroparlamentut_i_shumut_okolo_istanbulskata/ [accessed 1st July 2021].

Conclusion: The Discursive Legacy of Slavophilia in Bulgaria's Current Geopolitics

Bulgaria's unexpected resistance to the ratification of a human rights instrument protecting women from violence may surprise those less familiar with the country's deep-seated geopolitical discourses and the inherent clashes within them. But a closer look at the text of the convention concerning the notion of 'gender', as well as the dominant (mis)interpretations thereof in Bulgarian public life, reveals quasi-religious, conservative, and traditionalist narratives of identitarian origin, which the term Slavophilia frames usefully. While these narratives do not necessarily explicitly refer to Slavophilia as an ideology, they speak directly back to Bulgaria's past, within which Slavophilia played a crucial role, as the first part of this chapter has demonstrated. Placing an emphasis on the historical traditions of a culture suspicious of 'Great Power' encroachment and steeped in Russophilia and an irredentist vision of national sovereignty, and embedded into conservative visions of society which is not necessarily religious, 'Slavophilia' captures the coalescence of ideas, visions, and emotions which guide Bulgaria's search for an independent geopolitical path. While this is not necessarily the most obvious framework analysing for the identitarian quest that prompted this exploration, we also see that a similar reaction in neighbouring Turkey has not led to any such calls for civilisational commonality and geopolitical closeness. Indeed, it is not necessarily the issue at hand but rather the kind of narratives that are pulled together that point to the subtle relevance of Slavophilia as a frame of reference in this case.

Bulgaria's search for a truer civilisational choice may not have been necessary if its public had felt more at ease with the geopolitical choices of the post-communist period. The Euro-Atlantic membership it embraced, however, did not fully deliver on the issues which mattered most to Bulgarians. Somewhat disenchanted with their leadership and unable to enact meaningful changes in terms of the rule of law and economic prosperity, Bulgarians embarked upon a decade of political unrest constrained by an absence of political alternatives. It is this uneasy situation which provoked a renewed search for an independent geopolitical path on the basis of the legacies of pan-nationalism and the toolbox of right-wing populism.

True to its pan-nationalist nature, Slavophilia thus emerges indeed as a 'weapon of the weak' (see Introduction), those who are antagonised and uncomfortable in their current state. Its discursive power helps to reject external and internal Others: in this case, what is seen as an imposition from 'Europe' embraced domestically by unprincipled godless 'liberals' indifferent to traditional values. It fits comfortably into pan-nationalist agendas and skilfully appropriates such populist devices as misinformation, fake news, and demagogic rhetoric. But what such a geopolitical discourse overlooks is that the proposed pan-nationalist identity leaves Bulgaria in an internal conflict with its own geopolitical choices: between an unfulfilled Slavic past and an unhappy Euro-Atlantic present.

Instead of harking back to traditional family values and faith in a society which overwhelmingly does not practise religion, a more honest identitarian narrative would be to recognise the problem actually at hand: violence against women is something Bulgaria has not been able to curb on its own terms for reasons not unrelated to dominant interpretations of gender. Without deflecting discussion of these off into ideological nostalgia, Bulgaria could use to their full potential all geopolitical partnerships it has at its disposal. In doing so, it may actually find the independent path it seems to be looking for.

Montenegrin Squaring of the Circle: Between Russophilia, Pan-Orthodoxy, and Competing Nationalism

Vladimir Vučković and Miloš Petrović

INTRODUCTION

Russia has traditionally been engaged in Balkan political affairs, perceiving the region through a prism of cultural proximity and as a strategically important domain. Two aspects—Eastern Orthodoxy and Slavic heritage—represent functional bonds with nations like Montenegro. Montenegro's traditionally Russophile population ranks it among a few other Slavic-Orthodox nations like Serbia and Bulgaria perceived as 'bear huggers'.[1] Slavic Orthodoxy has been deployed as a supranational idea spanning the vast geographical distance from Russia and encouraging further transnational contacts (through the Serbian Orthodox Church [SOC] and its Metropolitanate of Montenegro and the Littoral [the

---

[1] Milo, D. (2021). The Image of Russia in Central & Eastern Europe and the Western Balkans-Russia: Mighty Slavic Brother or Hungry Bear Next-Door? Report. Bratislava: GLOBSEC, available at: https://euagenda.eu/upload/publications/image-of-russia-mighty-slavic-brother-or-hungry-bear-nextdoor-spreads.pdf. [Accessed 29th October 2021].

V. Vučković (✉)
Faculty of Social Studies, Masaryk University, Brno, Czech Republic
e-mail: vuckovic@mail.muni.cz

Metropolitanate/MML]). However, contrary to reductionist depictions of Russian-Montenegrin relations in the 'brotherhood' narrative, their ties have been more nuanced and ambiguous throughout recent history[2].

Nationalism and religion have historically been coupled in the Balkans.[3] Part of the canonically recognised SOC and the country's largest religious denomination, the Metropolitanate considers itself the only legitimate representative of the Orthodox-Christian community, Serbs and Montenegrins alike.[4] In contemporary historical terms, such a dominant position originates from the Ecumenical *Tomos* (1922), which recognised the merging of individual Orthodox units across the new Yugoslav state with the SOC.[5] The Metropolitanate considers itself the guardian of Montenegro's Orthodox heritage, while its organic relationship with the SOC influences its policies and perceptions. Officially, the SOC favours the 'unity' of Serbs and Montenegrins, nurturing narratives about their shared origins and affinities. A statement by the previous SOC patriarch, Irinej was illustrative: 'Serbs and Montenegrins are one people … although divided, they are not split'.[6] Interestingly, similar discourses exist in fellow Slavic-Orthodox countries. The Russian Orthodox Church (ROC) patriarch Kirill found earlier that 'Russians and Ukrainians were the same people', appealing to them not to 'sacrifice their values' in favour

---

M. Petrović
Institute of International Politics and Economics, Belgrade, Serbia
e-mail: milos.petrovic@diplomacy.bg.ac.rs

[2] Kusovac, M. (2013). 'Odnos Crne Gore i Rusije', *Matica Crnogorska*, 2013/2014, pp. 53–72.

[3] Šistek, F. (2011). 'Clericalization of Nationalism, Interpreting the Religious Rivalry between Serbian and Montenegrin Orthodox Churches, 1989–2009', In: Andras, M. T. and Rughinis C. (eds.), *Spaces and Borders: Current Research on Religion in Central and Eastern Europe*, Berlin/Boston, Walter de Gruyter GmbH & Co, p. 129.

[4] Šljivić, D., and Živković, N. (2020). 'Self-Ruled and Self-Consecrated Ecclesiastic Schism as a Nation-Building Instrument in the Orthodox Countries of South Eastern Europe', *Genealogy*, 4(2), pp. 1–36.

[5] Ibid.

[6] RTV. (2018). Irinej: Srbi i Crnogorci jedan narod, iako podeljen, nismo razdeljen, available at: https://www.rtv.rs/sr_ci/drustvo/irinej-srbi-i-crnogorci-jedan-narod-iako-podeljen-nismo-razdeljen_958232.html. [Accessed 30th June 2021].

of Europe.[7] While anti-Western and conservative sentiments dominate in the Russian political and religious arena, the SOC is also exposed to those ideas through, *inter alia*, cooperation with the ROC. Some researchers, such as Alice Forbess, argue that the SOC primarily represents Serbs and 'pro-Serbian minorities'.[8] Perceptions of Serbo-Montenegrin relations, also influenced by religious bonds, range from a horizontal logic of 'brotherhood' to a vertical concept of the primacy of Serbian over Montenegrin identity (based on macro-nationalist considerations of Montenegrins as a sub-branch/derivative of Serbs). Petar Vlahović, a renowned ethnologist associated with the Serbian and Montenegrin academies of sciences and arts, considered identity in Montenegro to be historically dualistic, arguing that even when declaring as Montenegrins, that did not imply that individuals would not also profess Serbian self-awareness.[9]

Identitarian complexities may be additionally interpreted through a Montenegrin 'situational nationalism', characterised by high exposure and responsiveness to external influences.[10] These authors argue that the fluidity of Montenegrin identity correlates with the changed geopolitical circumstances since the early 1990s. That period was marked by the collapse of socialism, as well as the forceful nationalist decomposition of the former Yugoslavia. While most republics demanded independence, political elites in Serbia (led by Slobodan Milošević) and Montenegro (headed by Milo Đukanović, Momir Bulatović, etc.) initially chose to retain Yugoslavia. Đukanović nurtured cordial relations with Metropolitan Amfilohije, the top-ranking and highly conservative religious personality, aiming to secure SOC support in internal political struggles against rivals like Momir Bulatović. Since then, Đukanović has grown into the most influential and long-lasting Montenegrin politician, famous for his

[7] Bigg, C. (2009). Russian Patriarch's Visit Creates Storm in Ukraine, available at: https://www.rferl.org/a/Russian_Patriarchs_Visit_Creates_Storm_In_Ukraine/1789959.html. [Accessed 20th July 2021].

[8] Forbess, A. (2013). 'Montenegro versus Crna Gora—The Rival Hagiographic Genealogies of the New Montenegrin Polity', *Focaal—Journal of Global and Historical Anthropology*, 67, pp. 47–60.

[9] Vlahović, P. (1995) 'Srpsko poreklo Crnogoraca', *Srpsko pitanje na Balkanu*, pp.157–168.

[10] Jenne, E., and Bieber, F. (2014). 'Situational Nationalism: Nation-Building in the Balkans, Subversive Institutions and the Montenegrin Paradox', *Ethnopolitics*, 13(5), pp. 431–460.

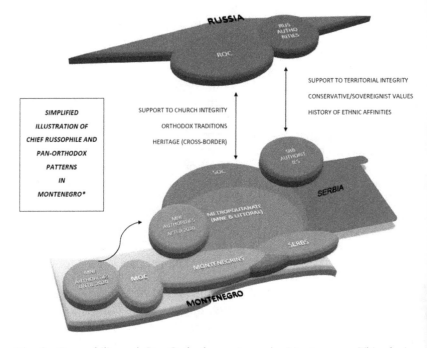

Fig. 1 Russophilic and Pan-Orthodox patterns in Montenegro. This depiction primarily intends to provide a contextual overview of the said patterns. Map items' positions, correlations, and sizes are broadly presented and not based on quantitative data but rather ideological, ethnic, and other proximities. Abbreviations are used consistently throughout this chapter

adjustable views, ideologies, and actions over time, from openly pro-Yugoslav and SOC-supportive, to pro-Montenegrin and anti-SOC—and recently also anti-Kremlin (Fig. 1)

The Changing Dynamics of the Montenegrin-SOC-Russian Triangle

The end of socialism enabled a *rapprochement* between church and state authorities. Greater SOC presence has contributed to the consolidation of post-Cold War Serbian identity. Simultaneously, a separate phenomenon occurred: Montenegrin identity started eroding. The statistical share of ethnic Montenegrins dropped, while the Serbian community increased. Likewise, Montenegrin self-awareness became increasingly associated with the secessionist movement, whereas local Serbs remained pro-union.[11] These variations represented a manifestation of the fluid Montenegrin identity, which has always been prone to external influences, including those related to Serbia/the Serbs.[12] Such changeableness between identity layers was additionally facilitated by their common traits: allegiance to the SOC/Metropolitanate, shared language/traditions/customs, and other bonds.

The position of the SOC as a unifying actor strengthened due to (1) the collapse of socialism and (2) the decision to preserve the Serbo-Montenegrin union. These events were marked by the rise of Serbian nationalism, which also employed Christian-Orthodox arguments (especially regarding Kosovo). Circulation of these ideas in Montenegro was facilitated by the pro-Milošević course of the leading Democratic Party of Socialists (DPS) throughout most of the 1990s.[13] The DPS remained in power until 2020. There was also a third reason for the greater prominence of the SOC in Yugoslavia: democratic developments like the reintroduction of religion to the public sphere, the reconstruction of religious objects/institutions, greater media presence, the return of nationalised property, state financial support/fiscal deductions, etc.[14] Metropolitanate-State relations had long been evolving (until their recent demise). For instance, the state co-financed the construction of the largest Montenegrin cathedral, Podgorica's Temple of the Resurrection of Christ. After twenty years, its opening in 2013 was personally attended by top state representatives, as well as by international guests like ROC Patriarch Kirill; some observers even 'identified' Milo Đukanović's likeness in one of the frescoes.[15]

---

[11] Ibid, pp. 448–450.

[12] Džankić, J. (2014). 'Reconstructing the Meaning of Being "Montenegrin"', *Slavic Review*, 73(2), pp. 347–371.

[13] Hilton Saggau, E. (2019). 'Kosovo Crucified—Narratives in the Contemporary Serbian Orthodox Perception of Kosovo', *Religions*, 10(578), pp. 1–18.

[14] Vukomanović, M. (2016). 'Srpska pravoslavna crkva, desekularizacija i demokratija', *Poznańskie Studia Slawistyczne*, 10, pp. 269–279.

[15] RTS. (2014). Đukanović na fresci u podgoričkoj crkvi?, available at: https://www.rts.rs/page/stories/sr/story/11/region/1507287/djukanovic-na-fresci-u-podgorickoj-crkvi.html. [Accessed 22nd July 2021].

Apart from the Serbophile narratives, the SOC/Metropolitanate also nurtured affinities towards the ROC. Their cooperation has widened since the 1990s also due to their shared concerns about the respective requests they faced for ecclesiastical independence; the statement by a Montenegrin Orthodox Church (MOC, the second largest, canonically unrecognised Orthodox community) official that autocephalous status for the Ukrainian Orthodox Church would also resonate in Montenegro highlights these worries.[16]

Metropolitan Amfilohije may have played a critical role in consolidating Milo Đukanović's power and dominance over his pro-Milošević rivals during late 1990s.[17] The metropolitan's anti-Milošević attitude might be illustrated by his participation in Belgrade's student protests in 1996–1997. Either way, in 1997 Đukanović, with implicit approval from the Metropolitanate, won his first presidency, defeating the pro-Milošević (and Russophile) Bulatović. As a consequence of this 'understanding' between the religious and state authorities, 'political Orthodoxy' became a powerful and lasting phenomenon in Montenegrin politics, also providing space for Russophile influences.[18]

During the 1990s, the Serbo-Montenegrin federation and Russia started to re-discover their Slavic-Orthodox affinities and deepen previously underdeveloped cooperation. In the political domain, the two sides' views regarding the Yugoslav wars converged. 'Brotherly Russia' vetoed a United Nations Security Council resolution (UNSCR) that attempted to authorise intervention against Yugoslavia during the Kosovo conflict in 1999, meaning the subsequent bombing campaign was undertaken without UN support; likewise, it also secured the adoption of UNSCR 1244, which nominally maintained Kosovo's status within Serbia.[19]

---

[16] MINA. (2018). Autokefalnost Ukrajinske crkve uticaće i na CG. Available at: http://www.rtcg.me/vijesti/drustvo/214771/autokefalnost-ukrajinske-crkve-uticace-i-na-cg.html. [Accessed 20th July 2021].

[17] Janković, S. (2020). Amfilohije Radović: Mitropolit molitve i kletve, available at: https://www.slobodnaevropa.org/a/mitropolit-amfilohije-in-memoriam/30919884.html. [Accessed 20th July 2021].

[18] Nikolaidis, A. (2020). *Političko_pravoslavlje_Crnu_Goru_vodi_put_Srbije_i_Rusije*, available_at: https://balkans.aljazeera.net/opinions/2020/8/8/politicko-pravoslavlje-crnu-goru-vodi-put-srbije-i-rusije. [Accessed 20th July 2021].

[19] Schwabach, A. (1999). 'The Legality of the NATO Bombing Operation in the Federal Republic of Yugoslavia', *Pace International Law Review*, 11(2), pp. 405–418.

Afterwards, Russia pragmatically maintained close relations with both republics. Political alienation between Belgrade and Podgorica progressed during the late 1990s due to Montenegrin dissatisfaction with poor federal management and their international pariah status. Montenegrin authorities began presenting their state as more progressive, liberal, and a 'hostage' of the Belgrade autocracy.[20] The 1999 NATO bombing campaign completely disrupted the economic and political foundations of the union.[21] Additionally, while Serbian-Russian ties have since been centred around defending Belgrade's clam on Kosovo (which was greeted as traditional inter-Slavic solidarity), Montenegrin authorities started to distance themselves from that dispute.

Discontent in Montenegro continued even after the pro-Western turn in Serbia in 2000, which marked the beginning of its European integration process. No longer the sole political favourite, Đukanović's DPS widened its requests for a dissolution of the Serbo-Montenegrin union, which was devolved in 2003. However, these sovereignty debates didn't disrupt Russophile attitudes, as investments from Russia boomed. By 2006, Montenegro had recorded the highest share of Russian FDI in the entire CEE/SEE.[22] Metropolitan Amfilohije later stated that 'had there not been Russian money, Montenegrin sovereignty wouldn't have been achieved'.[23] Russia became the first UNSC member, and among the first countries internationally, to recognize the Montenegrin sovereignty vote. Moreover, according to a *Kommersant* source, Russia facilitated the independence efforts, considering EU mediation to be 'rigid towards Montenegro'.[24]

---

[20] Džankić, J., and Keil, S. (2017). 'State-sponsored Populism and the Rise of Populist Governance: The Case of Montenegro', *Journal of Balkan and Near Eastern Studies*, 19(4), pp. 403–418.

[21] Morrison, K. (2018). *Nationalism, Identity and Statehood in Post-Yugoslav Montenegro*. London & New York: Bloomsbury Academic, pp. 100–101.

[22] Rojec, M., Mrak, M., Szemlér, T., and Novák T. (2007). 'The Russian Economic Penetration in Montenegro', In Briefing Paper (Brussels: Directorate General xternal Policies of the Union, European Parliament).

[23] Politika. (2020)._Amfilohije:_Da_nije_bilo_Rusa,_Đukanović_ne_bi_bio_predsednik, available_at: http://www.politika.rs/sr/clanak/448952/Amfilohije-Da-nije-bilo-Rusa-Dukanovic-ne-bi-bio-predsednik. [Accessed 24th July 2021].

[24] Jovićević, B. (2006). Rusija već priznala crnogorsku državu, available at: https://www.slobodnaevropa.org/a/672395.html. [Accessed 20th July 2021].

As for the Metropolitanate, during the independence campaign, it remained largely silent and passive, with the metropolitan himself later stating that he valued the 'sacredness of Montenegrin statehood'. The Metropolitanate's reserved stance could perhaps be attributed to some 'understanding' with the authorities regarding the preservation of SOC competencies and privileges.

In an internationally backed referendum in 2006, a majority of the population voted for independence, which cemented further dominance of the DPS-led sovereigntist bloc. In contrast, the pro-unionist bloc, centred around the 'pro-Serbian parties' (with the support of Belgrade's intellectual elite and other circles) and having previously campaigned against independence, have increasingly started to be perceived—and politically depicted—as permanent opponents of Montenegro's sovereignty. This simplistic division has been very skilfully exploited by the DPS. The largest opposition party, the 'pro-Serbian', catch-all conservative Democratic Front (DF), has been frequently accused of being financed by 'international enemies'.[25] Pro-Serbian opposition actors were generally portrayed as traitors by the populist DPS, exploiting the identity rift in Montenegro (internally) and distinguishing foreign policy from Serbia and its Russian partner (externally).

Domestically, the Đukanović leadership cult gradually became associated with Montenegrin sovereignty/identity, whereas in practice, DPS presence in the domains of the economy, politics, social life, and media—as well as in criminal and corruption allegations—steadily increased. These tendencies contributed to feelings of resentment among the increasingly fragmented Montenegrin opposition, which long attempted to unite against the DPS.[26] These include the pro-Serbian parties that constitute the DF: New Serb Democracy (NSD), the Democratic People's Party (DPP), and partially also United Montenegro. Their affinities towards Serbia and the SOC/Metropolitanate and their conservative, anti-NATO, and occasionally anti-EU views have facilitated their image as anti-Montenegrin/anti-sovereignty actors. Conversely, their reliance on Orthodox, sovereignty, and Russophile ideas has been *politically opportunistic* in two aspects: (1) they received affection from the SOC and

---

[25] Komnenić, P. (2016). 'Marković: Jasno je ko finansira crnogorsku opoziciju', *Radio Slobodna Evropa*, 14 September, available at: https://www.slobodnaevropa.org/a/dusko-markovic-izbori/27987680.html. [Accessed 10th June 2021].

[26] Morrison, K. (2018), pp. 169–172.

Russia; and (2) such a programme has resonated well with the conservative elements of society. In the institutional domain, these ideas were manifested in criticism of governmental policies. Opposition MPs heavily criticised the economic and social consequences to investment and the tourism sector caused by distancing from Russia and Serbia. While the DPS used state resources and took a pro-Western course in the context of Montenegrin nationalism, the SOC and pro-Serbian actors countered it with Russophile and conservative manifestations.

Although Russia didn't oppose its independence, growing Montenegrin disengagement from Serbian/SOC claims on Kosovo, coupled with country's pro-Western course, began to increasingly alienate the two sides. Conversely, the SOC became the main non-state Russophile actor, not only in the spiritual-cultural domain but also politically, due to Russia and the ROC's support for the preservation of its Christian heritage in Kosovo, while its cross-border competencies in Montenegro and Bosnia-Herzegovina provided a platform for a spillover of influences. Willingly or not, the SOC has grown into a reliable lever for Russian influence, while the preservation of cooperation with both the ROC and the Russian state has been beneficial for all actors.

Sovereign Montenegro was enabled to: (1) define and pursue its Euro-Atlantic course and (2) distance itself from Serbia's high-political issues. Nevertheless, dissociation also followed on in aspects of identity, i.e., Slavic-Orthodox bonds with Russia and Russophile practices, in favour of a pro-Western international image.[27] Consolidation of a separate state identity included both symbolic aspects (national symbols, language/script, etc.) and systemic changes.[28] Since the 2000s, the system has encouraged participation by the Albanian, Bosniak, and Croatian minority communities in the political process, as part of its constituent, civic-state changes. In practice, DPS-led governments have

---

[27] Forbess, A. (2013). 'Montenegro versus Crna Gora, The rival hagiographic genealogies of the new Montenegrin polity', *Focaal—Journal of Global and Historical Anthropology*, 67, pp. 47–60.

[28] Đukanović, D. (2014). '„Identitetska pitanja" i linije unutrašnjih podela u Crnoj Gori', *Međunarodni problemi*, 66(3–4), pp. 395–422.

'instrumentalised' minorities, applying a narrative of multi-ethnic inclusiveness to attract both their and international support.[29] However, these developments caused feelings of exclusion among local Serbs. According to the 2007 Constitution, Montenegrin became the official language, while Serbian remained officially used (Article 13). Additionally, marginalisation of the Metropolitanate grew more evident, especially as the Montenegrin Government regulated the position of the Catholic (2011), Jewish (2012), and Islamic (2012) communities, leaving the legal position of the SOC unsettled. Since then, the unregulated status of the SOC, combined with the marginalisation of the Serbs, also disturbed cooperation with Moscow, whose officials frequently voiced concern over those issues.

Montenegrin recognition of Kosovo's unilaterally declared independence in 2008 further aggravated the situation. The Montenegrin president backed the act as an 'obvious condition' for the Euro-Atlantic path, although it ultimately didn't bring any direct benefits.[30] The move provoked large demonstrations; the SOC, whose spiritual seat is in Kosovo (at Peć, Metohija region), called on the government to revoke it. Metropolitan Amfilohije praised the two-week hunger-strike by the Serbian People's Party (SNS) leader Andrija Mandić, cursing the government for the recognition and referring to it as 'shameful treason'.[31,32]

The recognition not only fundamentally disrupted SOC-DPS relations but also triggered a rearrangement in the opposition ranks. It represented a key turn for the former Milošević allies, the Socialist People's Party of Montenegro (SNP), who used the situation to attract patriotic voters, all while simultaneously relabelling itself as a modern social-democratic grouping and accepting Euro-Atlantic priorities in an effort to reclaim opposition leadership.[33] Andrija Mandić also sought to modernise his engagement by guiding most of the SNS party infrastructure to merge

---

[29] Džankić, J., and Keil, S. (2017). 'State-sponsored Populism and the Rise of Populist Governance: The Case of Montenegro', *Journal of Balkan and Near Eastern Studies*, 19(4), pp. 403–418.

[30] Morrison, K. (2018), p. 141.

[31] Ibid, pp. 140–141.

[32] RSE. (2008). Amfilohije prokleo sve koji će priznati Kosovo, available at: https://www.slobodnaevropa.org/a/870801.html. [Accessed 18th July 2021].

[33] Morrison, K. (2018), pp. 141–144.

with the People's Socialist Party into the 'New Serb Democracy' grouping under his leadership. NSD later became a constituency of the DF, the chief opposition actor.

POLITICAL ALLIANCE WITH RUSSIA IS MORE ATTRACTIVE AND PROMISING THAN THE 'EUROPEAN DREAM'

Contemporary manifestations of Russophilia and related ideas are predominately noticeable in Montenegro in the political and cultural spheres, specifically through the active roles of the political party coalition DF and the SOC. These actors have strongly supported conservative and traditional patterns in the domain of politics and religion in line with the regulation of these areas in Russia. Transmitting and glorifying Russophile sentiments to its worshippers and believers—particularly by emphasising a deep connection between the Montenegrin and Russian peoples through the existence of common history, tradition, culture, and religion—remain the main ideological characteristics and patterns of behaviour of the DF and SOC in the modern political development of the state.

Having asserted this, three main manifestations point to the strong existence of Russophilia in Montenegro, playing an important role in domestic political discourse as such: (1) the institutionalisation of relations through the establishment of closer cooperation between Serbian nationalist right-wing parties in Montenegro and the Russian state in order to prevent its entry into NATO; (2) activism towards revoking recognition of independent Kosovo; and (3) the preservation of the canonical unity of the ROC and SOC on its territories.

Revival of Russophile discourse, its ideas, and visions during the past decade has been predominately emphasised by right-wing nationalist pro-Serbian political parties such as NSD and the DPP through their support for improving bilateral relations between Montenegro and Russia. Based on their ideology, these Serb parties in Montenegro are defined as nationalist, conservative, right-wing populist political groupings whose constituents openly support pro-Russian foreign policy ambitions in the Balkans.[34] As a part of the wider political block called the DF, NSD and the DPP have advocated stronger political, economic, and cultural ties

---

[34] Bieber, F. (2020). The Rise of Authoritarianism in the Western Balkans, Palgrave MacMillan, Cham.

with Russia in the form of a strategic partnership since their foundation in 2009 and 2014, respectively. These two parties perceive Moscow as the most important foreign ally in implementing their political and national programmes, especially after Montenegro received a formal invitation to join NATO.[35] Strengthening traditional and fraternal relations between the Russian and Serbian parties culminated in May 2016 with the signing in Cetinje of the Lovćen Declaration of Mutual Cooperation between United Russia and the DPP in Cetinje, with the blessing of Metropolitan Amfilohije of Montenegro and the Littoral. This political document specified the need for an improvement in political and economic relations, for support for an alliance of militarily neutral countries, and for holding a referendum on Montenegro's eventual accession to NATO.[36] A step towards the implementation of their party programmes started to materialise when United Russia, Rodina, NSD, and the DPP signed the Declaration of Mutual Cooperation in June 2016.[37] This being said, cooperation was further strengthened through the establishment of political relations with the Serbian far-right nationalist Alliance of Independent Social Democrats from the Republika Srpska (BiH) and the populist Serbian Progressive Party (SPP). The main aim of these parties' cooperation remains the preservation of Orthodox spiritual values and Christian shrines as well as the protection of traditional, historical Slavic ties between the Serbian and Russian nations, despite the growing influence of 'grotesque' Western values.[38]

These populist parties have gathered around the main idea of preserving Slavic unity by nurturing Orthodox sentiments, values, and memories and protecting the centuries-old traditions, history, and culture

---

[35] Nova srpska demokratija (NSD). (2021). *Program*, available at: http://www.nova.org.me/stranica.php?id=2&tip=stranice. [Accessed 12th July 2021]; Demokratska narodna partija Crne Gore (DNP). (2021). *Program*, available at: http://www.dnpcg.me/program/. [Accessed 12th July 2021].

[36] Komnenić, P. (2016). Lovćenska deklaracija—potpis bliže Rusiji, available at: https://www.slobodnaevropa.org/a/lovcenska-deklaracija-potpis-blize-rusiji/27724013.html. [Accessed 12th July 2021].

[37] Vijesti. (2016a). Nova potpisala sporazum sa Jedinstvenom Rusijom, available at: https://www.vijesti.me/vijesti/politika/139094/nova-potpisala-sporazum-sa-jedinstvenom-rusijom. [Accessed 4th June 2021]; DNP. (2016a). *DNP potpisuje memorandum o saradnji sa Rodinom*, available at: http://www.dnpcg.me/dnp-potpisuje-memorandum-o-saradnji-sa-rodinom/. [Accessed 4th June 2021].

[38] NSD. (2021). *Program* (DNP). (2021) *Program*.

characterised by the connection between South and East Slavs. In geopolitical terms, the preservation of close Orthodox bonds with Russia might also serve as a political deterrent against the pro-Western strategic course undertaken by Montenegro in recent years. Politically affiliated as Eurosceptic, the DF's manifestos from 2012 and 2016 reflect an anti-Western orientation, highlighting that the newly elected DF government will abolish the sanctions on Russia and rectify 'many historical foreign-policy errors and omissions, caused in the last two decades, which directly contradict the national interests of Montenegro'.[39] For them, Slavdom represents a thesis about a threat to the survival of global Orthodoxy, in which the West seeks to destroy the remnants of the unity between the South Slavs (for instance, Montenegro) and East Slavs (such as Russia) that was built centuries ago. Based on this ideological-political postulate, the EU and the United States intend to undermine Slavic roots, tradition, history, and religion, but perhaps far more importantly, also destroy the remnants of unity among Southern Slavs, as the current situation between Serbia and Montenegro might illustrate. From the Russian perspective, the politics of the West is based on the principle *divide et impera* and affects not only Montenegro (and Serbia) but the Balkan relations as a whole, consequently causing a strong ethnic and religious polarisation between South Slavic nations. Moscow perceives these political divisions and the creation of permanent crises as part of international attempts to westernise Eastern European authorities and societies. Therefore, it is not surprising that the call for Slavic unification was enthusiastically accepted by DF leaders during their visit to Moscow in 2016, when the deputy chairman of the Russian Duma, Pyotr Tolstoy said that the dream of an alliance with Russia was more beautiful and promising than the 'European dream', and that it was a dream of returning to oneself and one's roots and origins, as well as an alliance and sincere dialogue with Russia.[40]

Worsening relations between the two countries were influenced by the Montenegrin decisions to align with the EU sanctions against Russia imposed following the annexation of Crimea in 2014 and to join NATO on 5 June 2017. Consequently, the foreign policy of Montenegro has

---

[39] Vučković, V. (2016). 'The Europeanization of Political Parties in Montenegro,' *Romanian Journal of European Affairs*, 16 (3), pp. 36–55.

[40] DNP. (2016). Tolstoj sa DF-om: San o savezu sa Rusijom ljepši i perspektivniji od "evropskog sna', available at: http://www.dnpcg.me/tolstoj-sa-df-om-san-o-savezu-sa-rus ijom-ljepsi-i-perspektivniji-od-evropskog-sna/. [Accessed 26th July 2021].

been perceived by Moscow as hostile, which is reflected in declining political and economic cooperation. Before Montenegro's NATO accession, Russia mainly used soft power mechanisms to divert the country's attention from joining the alliance. Examples range from strong political allegations disseminated by high-ranking political officials, such as the Russian deputy prime minister, Dmitry Rogozin (founder of the right-wing political party Rodina), saying that Montenegro would regret joining NATO, or the Russian Foreign Ministry's warning not to travel to Montenegro, presenting the state as highly corrupt and insecure.[41]

At the domestic level, Montenegro's formal invitation to join NATO, received in December 2015, influenced the DF to launch a 'No to NATO' campaign. Speakers—among others, the presidents of NSD and the DPP, respectively Andrija Mandić and Milan Knežević—stressed that Montenegro must remain consistent with the concept of a 'Balkan Alliance of Neutral Countries' (together with Serbia, BiH, and North Macedonia); the very same document was accepted by DF and United Russia party officials during continuous meetings on this particular issue.[42] Bishop Amfilohije took part in the anti-NATO protest organised by the DF, cursing the DPS-led government also for imposing sanctions on Russia: 'Whoever was not faithful to a monolingual, one-blooded Russia, may the living flesh fall away from him, cursed three times and 3,000 times by me'.[43] Protesters also called for a referendum on the issue of Montenegro's willingness to join NATO, referring to views of the member of the Committee of the State Duma of Russia for International Affairs, Sergey Zelezak, as well as to the decision to deploy Montenegrin soldiers in Kosovo as members of the NATO-KFOR (Kosovo

---

[41] Conley, A. H., and Melino, M. (2019). 'Russian influence in Montenegro: The Weaponization and Exploitation of History, Religion and Economics', *Center for Strategic & International Studies* (May), pp. 1–5; Center for the Study of Democracy. (2018). 'Assessing Russia's Economic Footprint in Montenegro,' *CSD*, Policy Brief no. 73, available at: https://csd.bg/publications/publication/policy-brief-no-73-assessing-russias-economic-footprint-in-montenegro/. [Accessed 16th July 2021].

[42] DNP. (2016). Podrška Balkanskom savezu neutralnih država, available at: http://www.dnpcg.me/podrska-balkanskom-savezu-neutralnih-drzava/. [Accessed 16th July 2021].

[43] Balkan Insight (BIRN). (2016). Montenegro Anti-NATO Activists Stage New Year Party, available at: https://balkaninsight.com/2016/01/13/montenegro-s-nato-foes-celebrate-orthodox-new-year-eve-01-12-2016/. [Accessed 18th July 2021].

Force) mission.[44] Consequently, this situation was directly affected by the sharp increase in pro-Russian sentiments among Serbian nationalists in Montenegro, who carried Russian and Serbian flags, portraits of Vladimir Putin and Tsar Peter the Great, icons and frescoes from monasteries and churches of the ROC, etc., demanding from the pro-Western government an urgent withdrawal of the decision to join NATO.[45]

The strong echo of the anti-NATO protest in Montenegro at the end of December 2015 showed the strength and depth of the relationship between the DF and the Russian state. DF leaders used every opportunity in their public appearances to emphasise the importance of maintaining traditional relationships aiming to nurture the Orthodox achievements of civilisation through the preservation of the cultural, linguistic, and religious proximity of two nations. This being said, when DF leaders Mandić and Knežević attended a luncheon organised by Serbian president Aleksandar Vučić on the occasion of Vladimir Putin's visit in January 2019, the Russian president was told that the people of Montenegro perceive him as their true leader, because the Principality and Kingdom of Montenegro had seen the Russian tsar as their own.[46] Also, the NSD vice president, Strahinja Bulajić, who was also elected vice president of the Montenegrin parliament after the 2020 parliamentary elections, has continuously demonstrated his pro-Russian and anti-Western narrative in public discourse, which often coincides with ideological postulates about the superiority of the Russian and Serbian nations over other nations. In this regard, Bulajić claimed that both the Montenegrin and Ukrainian nations are by-products of communist ideological experiments in the twentieth century. According to him, the first Serbian state and church were created on the territory of Montenegro, as was the case with

---

[44] Morrison, K. (2018). pp. 157–159; DNP. (2017). Jedinstvena Rusija podržala Narodni referendum u Crnoj Gori, available at: http://www.dnpcg.me/jedinstvena-rusija-podrzala-narodni-referendum-u-crnoj-gori/. [Accessed 15th July 2021].

[45] Vijesti. (2019). Rusi pomažu crkvu, medije i političare, available at: https://www.vijesti.me/vijesti/politika/412899/rusi-pomazu-crkvu-medije-i-politicare. [Accessed 17th July 2021].

[46] Blic. (2019). Mandić i Knežević prenijeli Putinu pozdrave Srba iz Crne Gore, available at: https://www.blic.rs/vesti/politika/mandic-i-knezevic-preneli-putinu-pozdrave-srba-iz-crne-gore/rbj15f6. [Accessed 21st October 2021].

Russia, where the first Russian state and church were created on the territory of Ukraine.[47] Interestingly, this kind of identitarian populism was also noticeable even after the NSD became part of the newly formed government established in December 2020, despite the defined strategic pro-Western course of the state being also confirmed by an agreement between the leaders of the three winning party-coalitions (Coalition for Future Montenegro, Democratic Montenegro, and United Reformed Action), primarily referring to the assumption of all international obligations arising from NATO membership, the continuation of the EU integration process, and the unquestioned recognition of Kosovo.[48]

Finally, Marko Milačić, the president of the nationalist party True Montenegro and an MP, is a glaring example of an advocate of Russophile policy and Pan-Orthodoxia in the Balkans. Milačić's views largely coincide with Russia's foreign policy preferences for Montenegro. At a time when Russia was advocating for Montenegro's military neutrality, Milačić organised in 2014 the so-called 'Movement for Neutrality', in which he sought to demonstrate a positive example of Serbia as an anti-militarised country that did not call into question traditionally good relations with Russia. However, Montenegro's formal invitation to join NATO in December 2015 was a turning point for further strained relations with Russia. At the same time, Milačić abandoned the concept of neutrality and started pursuing a strong anti-NATO campaign by organising a so-called 'Referendum caravan' in nine EU countries and finally burning the NATO flag on Independence Square in Podgorica.[49] Milačić and his party are profiled as political actors directly responsible to Moscow in order to

---

[47] Novosti. (2020). Crna Gora je zemlja čuda, available at: https://www.novosti.rs/vesti/planeta.300.html:848748-Dr-Strahinja-Bulajic--Crna-Gora-je-zemlja-cuda. [Accessed 21st October 2021].

[48] BBC. (2020). Parlamentarni izbori u Crnoj Gori: Izabrana nova Vlada, prvi put bez DPS-a predsednika Mila Đukanovića, available at: https://www.bbc.com/serbian/lat/balkan-55186317. [Accessed 11th July 2021].

[49] Vijesti. (2017). Krenuo "referendumski karavan": Od Podgorice do Brisela, available at: https://www.vijesti.me/vijesti/politika/92739/krenuo-referendumski-karavan-od-podgorice-do-brisela. [Accessed 21st October 2021]. RSE. (2017). U Podgorici spaljena NATO zastava, bez reakcije policije, available at: https://www.slobodnaevropa.org/a/29860937.html. [Accessed 21st October 2021].

strengthen Russophilia and instal loyal Orthodox subjects in key positions in Montenegro.[50] As a result, this open anti-NATO rhetoric imposed by conservative right-wing nationalist parties and supported by radical conservative Orthodox clerics greatly contributed to the homogenisation of the Serbian national population in Montenegro. This is one of the chief reasons why the Serbian minority community felt threatened and vulnerable, not only because of the 'repressive' pro-Montenegrin government and its imposed identity policies, but also because of the proclaimed state foreign policy course towards Euro-Atlantic integration. On the other hand, demonstration of pro-Russian affiliation among Serbian political elites and their supporters has led up to flare-ups of existing interethnic divisions, and nation- and statehood disputes between Serbs and Montenegrins. Montenegro's membership in NATO, the position of the SOC, recognition of the Montenegrin language, and adoption of the new state symbols have all greatly contributed to the Serbian minority's rejection of Montenegro as their homeland. The claims of NSD and the DPP that Serbians and Montenegrins are part of wider Serb nation, and therefore that Montenegrin national identity does not exist, has triggered a political revolt by the ruling DPS to strengthen Montenegrin identity, even in some cases quite artificially.[51]

The SOC as Protector and Preserver of Orthodox Unity and Pan-Slavic Ideology in Montenegro

Apart from the political arena, contemporary expressions of Pan-Orthodoxia are observable in the cultural and religious spheres in Montenegro, predominately in the strong role of the SOC in domestic socio-political life. This is the case with the Metropolitanate, an eparchy of the SOC, with its active role and interference in internal political processes and developments, mostly in the post-independence period, when issues of nationhood, statehood, and national identity still play an important role in political divisions between Montenegrins and Serbs. The late Metropolitan Amfilohije was considered one of the strongest Russophiles

---

[50] Digitalni forenzički centar (DFC). (2021). Uloga Rusije na Balkanu: Slučaj Crne Gore. Podgorica, DFC, pp. 20–22.

[51] Vučković, V. (2021). Europeanizing Montenegro: The European Union, the Rule of Law, and Regional Cooperation. New York & London: Lexington Books, pp. 22–24.

in the Balkans, presenting an image of a hard and conservative Orthodox priest nurturing nationalist pro-Serbian discourse and advocating the strengthening of Pan-Slavic connections between Montenegro and Russia and the ROC. Maintaining close ties with Russia, promoting a positive image of the Kremlin and the Russian contribution during the Second World War have all certainly been behind his receiving a large number of Russian decorations, such as the Order of Lomonosov (2001) and honorary doctorates from the Moscow Spiritual Academy (2014) and the Spiritual Academy in St. Petersburg (2016).[52] During the turbulent 1990s, for instance, Metropolitan Amfilohije often used nationalist narratives and ethnically intolerant rhetoric instead of spiritual, and celebrated war criminals such as Radovan Karadžić—even inviting the Serbian paramilitary leader Željko Ražnatović ('Arkan') to come and protect the Cetinje Monastery from MOC supporters who had gathered during Christmas Day on King Nikola Square.[53] Political opponents of Metropolitan Amfilohije accused him of spreading fear and hatred in Montenegro, but also of being nationally and religiously exclusive, propagating a 'Great Serbia' ideology and trying to undermine the state's intention to integrate into the Atlantic alliance. Amfilohije also defended his faithful and the religious and social positions of the SOC by directing profanity towards his enemies, especially the DPS-led government and the MOC, as well as their families and descendants.

Concerning the requests by the canonically unrecognised MOC to gain autocephaly, the political conflict between the SOC and the government and MOC escalated after Montenegro gained independence and later requested of the ownership of Montenegro's religious buildings and properties.[54] The MOC began to renew its request for the return of more than 650 churches in Montenegro that had switched hands in 1920, when religious properties in Montenegro were handed over to the management of the SOC. Consequently, the MOC began taking over some of the churches, believing and arguing they were only looking for

[52] DFC. (2021), pp. 48–49.
[53] Morrison, K. (2018), p. 87.
[54] Morrison, K. (2018), p. 87.

what had previously belonged to them.[55] Although initially neutral, the government increasingly favoured MOC property restitution requests, especially after Amfilohije stated that Montenegrins were 'communist bastards' and the SOC openly politically supported the nationalist pro-Serbian DF following the anti-NATO protest of December 2015.[56] Also, the state began actively supporting MOC activities by providing free plots of land for building churches and monasteries in Podgorica, while on the other hand, SOC priests, originally citizens of Serbia, were exposed to detailed checks of regulated residence-based papers.[57]

However, the political conflict between Montenegrin state authorities and Metropolitan Amfilohije culminated with the adoption of the Law on Religious Freedom in December 2019. This controversial law has established the property rights of the state over religious buildings that represent the cultural heritage of Montenegro built over the centuries and from state funds. The law stipulated that all religious buildings representing cultural heritage and having been the property of the state of Montenegro before its loss of independence on 1 December 1918 (i.e., when the Kingdom of Montenegro was annexed to the Kingdom of Serbia in the creation of the Kingdom of Serbs, Croats, and Slovenes), and which did not later become the property of a certain religious community in an appropriate legal manner, would be registered as state property. And if any religious community had evidence that it had become the owner of any property in past or present times, the state would recognise and respect it.[58]

---

[55] Deutsche Welle (DW). (2020). Crnogorska kvadratura (crkvenog kruga), available at: https://www.dw.com/bs/crnogorska-kvadratura-crkvenog-kruga/a-52024528. [Accessed 18 July 2021].

[56] RSE. (2020). *Mitropolit Amfilohije in memoriam*, available at: https://www.slobodnaevropa.org/a/mitropolit-amfilohije-in-memoriam/30919884.html. [Accessed 19th June 2021].

[57] Vijesti. (2020b). *SO Podgorica: CPC dobija zemljište od Glavnog grada za izgradnju hrama*, available at: https://www.vijesti.me/vijesti/politika/495761/mikic-nece-lekcije-o-crnogorstvu-drzati-dps-i-djukanovic-koji-su-mitraljezima-isli-na-liberale. [Accessed 22nd June 2021].

[58] Balkan Insight (BIRN). (2019). Montenegrin Parliament Adopts Religion Law Amid Furious Protests, available at: https://balkaninsight.com/2019/12/27/montenegrin-parliament-adopts-religion-law-amid-furious-protests/. [Accessed 16th June 2021].

The law was adopted despite fierce opposition from the SOC and the right-wing nationalist DF; the latter caused a major incident in the Parliament of Montenegro, with eighteen MPs being consequently arrested for obstructing a parliamentary session.[59] As the law was viewed as discriminatory and targeted against the SOC, the Church itself immediately—with the assistance of the DF, the clergy and monks, and lay members—organised massive public protests, so-called street church liturgies, in order to influence the government into withdrawing the disputed law.[60]

The adopted law was also the subject of great interest not only in the region but also by the Russian state and the ROC—i.e., by the main promoters of Pan-Slavic ideology. Immediately after its adoption, the Russian Ministry of the Foreign Affairs raised serious concerns over the adoption of the conversion legislation, claiming that the law allowed the DPS-led government to seize over 650 religious facilities belonging to the SOC, thus opening the possibility of their being delivered to the 'schismatic' and unrecognised MOC, which would consequently increase administrative pressure on the SOC, leading to its being pushed out completely from Montenegro. That the adopted law would not only infringe on the interests of the SOC made this topic an international issue, as 'the unity and cohesion of the Orthodox world and the preservation of its centuries-old traditions are a guarantee of the normal development of society'.[61]

Bearing in mind shared Slavic and Orthodox bonds, perhaps it is not unusual that Russia used different tools to influence the internal political and religious affairs of Montenegro. The strong connection between the Russian state and the ROC was also relevant in the case of Montenegro,

---

[59] Reuters. (2019). Montenegro's parliament approves religious law despite protests, available at: https://www.reuters.com/article/us-montenegro-lawmaking-protests-idUSKBN1YV0WT. [Accessed 19th June 2021].

[60] Reuters. (2020). Thousands in Montenegro march against religious law, available at: https://www.reuters.com/article/us-montenegro-protest-religion-idUSKBN20N0LL. [Accessed 11th June 2021].

[61] Ministry of Foreign Affairs of Russian Federation. (2019). Comment by the Information and Press Department on the adoption of the law on religious rights in Montenegro, available at: https://www.mid.ru/ru/foreign_policy/news/-/asset_publisher/cKNonkJE02Bw/content/id/3988667?p_p_id=101_INSTANCE_cKNonkJE02Bw&_101_INSTANCE_cKNonkJE02Bw_languageId=en_GB. [Accessed 21st June 2021].

where Moscow protected Slavic ideas by preserving Orthodox unity. The ROC was the first to begin the process of establishing a strong connection with the Russian state in response to increased cultural threats coming from the West. When Putin came to power in 2000, the ROC became one of Moscow's most important soft power instruments for influencing the views of believers about the need to preserve Orthodox unity and Slavic heritage and, at the same time, for showing sympathy for Putin's neo-expansionist policies in Georgia and Ukraine. Such Orthodox expansionism has become an important element both in Montenegro and in the wider Balkans in strengthening the concept of Russophilia, which aims to unite supporters of the 'Russian world' abroad, who are expected to be loyal defenders of Slavdom.[62] When Patriarch Kirill of Moscow publicly supported Putin's candidacy for the presidency of Russia during the 2012 elections, the state in return glorified Orthodoxy as a national idea aiming to unite Russian citizens under one national umbrella. Thus, the Kremlin has used the Orthodox Church as a foundation for its geopolitical ambitions in the East and the Balkans, considering that ROC has cross-border competencies and influence (as with the SOC) outside Russia itself. The synthesis of church-state relations had a strong impact on the definition of Russian foreign policy priorities, where the Kremlin has (mis)used Orthodoxy as a tool to make an explicit claim on Orthodox states in the Balkans: in the case of Montenegro, Russia's expansionist policy is reflected in the protection of the interests and legal rights of the SOC while neglecting the SOC's encroaching on historical realities by creating conditions leading to disunity among believers.[63]

The primary objective of the Pan-Slavic idea advocated by both the Russian state and the Church is the preservation of the unity of Eastern Orthodoxy and Slavic heritage. There is strong mutual support between the ROC and SOC regarding the issue of 'autocephaly' (gaining the autonomy of a canonical church) for the UOC and MOC. Following the current religious affairs, demands for autocephaly in Ukraine and Montenegro (although they are different cases) according to the canonical laws of Orthodox Christianity have been dismissed by the Mother

---

[62] DFC. (2021), p.44.

[63] Ibid. Vijesti. (2016b). Pravoslavna crkva—moćno oružje Putina, available at: https://www.vijesti.me/svijet/evropa/146389/pravoslavna-crkva-mocno-oruzje-putina. [Accessed 21st July 2021].

Churches in Russia and Serbia.[64] In the dispute that erupted after the Ecumenical (Constantinople) Patriarchate recognised the autocephaly of the UOC, the SOC resolutely sided with the ROC.[65] The same logic was applied by the ROC when the position of the SOC was endangered in Montenegro by the adoption of the law on freedom of religion, with the Church calling the legislation 'an act of supporting schism by weakening the canonical Church and trying to put it in a humiliating and dangerous dependence on the state—all the more unjust because Montenegro is a secular state'.[66]

The issue of autocephaly remains a political issue per se in Montenegro, as religious and political components are traditionally interconnected in Slavic countries. Although the autocephaly request from the MOC has resulted in a substantial deterioration of political relations between Montenegro and Serbia, this religious claim has been used as an important political instrument for strengthening Montenegrin national identity, integrity, and political cohesion. Consequently, the intra-Orthodox conflict between the SOC and MOC over autocephaly has spilled over into political conflict over identity, nationhood, and statehood in Montenegro. Both Orthodox Churches have been largely connected with nationalism, as religious institutions actively involved in domestic politics often align with patriotic political parties or governments that advocate ethnically homogeneous states. In so doing, the Churches have become symbols of nationality being substantially linked to ethnic-religious identity and thereby politicised.[67] Autocephaly demands in Montenegro have deep historical roots. After the MOC was de facto abolished by decree of King Alexander I in 1920 following the creation of the Kingdom of Serbs, Croats, and Slovenes, and then uncanonically re-established during the 1990s, the cornerstone of the SOC-MOC political conflict is the issue

---

[64] Veković, M., and Jevtić, M. (2019). 'Render undo Caesar: Explaining Political Dimension of the Autocephaly Demands in Ukraine and Montenegro,' *Journal of Church and State*, 61(4), pp. 591–609.

[65] BBC. (2018). SPC i raskol izmedju Carigarda i Moskve: kome se privoleti carstvu, available at: https://www.bbc.com/serbian/lat/srbija-45887109. [Accessed 23rd July 2021].

[66] Glas Amerike. (2019). Srpski patrijarh o situaciji u CG, oglasile se ruska crkva i vaseljenski patrijarh, available at: https://www.glasamerike.net/a/srpski-patrijarh-o-situaciji-u-cg-oglasile-se-ruska-crkva-i-vaseljenski-patrijarh/5224843.html. [Accessed 3rd July 2021].

[67] Morrison, K. (2018), p. 83.

of autocephaly, as it remains a question of Montenegro's national identity, with one side advocating a separate Montenegrin identity, language, and church, and the other considering Montenegro to be partially or even fully part of the Serbian world.[68]

Demands for autocephaly represent a significant challenge to achieving greater unity in the Slavic and Orthodox world. Montenegrin authorities have attempted to manage the Church and its religious properties more independently on their territory, leading to an escalation of national and religious tensions, placing the issue of national affiliation in the foreground. Since the autocephaly demands in Montenegro need to be approved and supported by another canonically recognised church such as the SOC, it is evident that, due to several reasons—above all, status issues, identity aspects, and politics—there is substantial opposition by the Mother Church to providing autocephaly prerogatives to the MOC. However, demands for the creation of an autocephalous Montenegrin Orthodox Church does not come from the Mother Church, but rather from the government and domestic political leadership. Hence, it is no wonder that Milo Đukanović, the president of Montenegro and the DPS, has initiated the formation of the Orthodox Church of Montenegro as a national prerogative that will supposedly resolve the divisions between Orthodox believers in the state.[69] Political support for autocephaly remains an issue as domestic political elites are supporting a church that is de facto non-canonical, and therefore directly influencing Montenegrin domestic and international politics.[70] Governmental initiation of a unique Orthodox Church in Montenegro is driven by political interests, as it disregards canonical laws and rules by directly interfering in church-related affairs.

On the other hand, there is a clear interest on the part of domestic political elites in preventing foreign political interference in state affairs and strengthening Montenegrin national identity, nationhood, and statehood. While SOC and ROC aim to preserve the brotherhood and unity of the Slavic nations under the auspices of Pan-Orthodoxia, both churches are characterised as Eurosceptic and strongly opposed towards

---

[68] Ibid, p. 84.

[69] RSE. (2020c). Đukanović: Ako SOC odbije dogovor, formiraćemo pravoslavnu crkvu u Crnoj Goru, available at: https://www.slobodnaevropa.org/a/djukanovic-crna-gora-spc-pravoslavna-crkva-kriza/30619177.html. [Accessed 13th July 2021].

[70] Veković, M., and Jevtić, M. (2019), p. 597.

Montenegro joining NATO. Even though the SOC, nominally speaking, is not in opposition to the EU integration processes of either Montenegro or Serbia, it does consider NATO membership damaging. The state also provides political support for establishing a national church due to national security reasons, regarding this as a key condition for maintaining peace and stability in the Balkans.[71] This is why President Đukanović, after losing the last parliamentary elections, claimed that—unlike in the supposed 2016 coup attempt, when Russia had to control its operation with Russian agents from Belgrade—this time it had applied a more sophisticated version of hybrid war to Montenegro 'with the help of a new partner, originally non-political, and in essence an extremely political player—the Serbian Orthodox Church'.[72]

Conclusion

The authors argue that the Slavophilic concept in Montenegro does not exist in its classical form. Instead, several intertwining manifestations that blend into Serbophile, Russophile, and Pan-Orthodox attitudes are being connected more with ethno-religious and political affinities, rather than with genuinely 'pro-Slavic' ones. Some Pan-Slavic ideas are embedded in Slavic-Orthodox ideology, deployed by the Serbian Orthodox Church with the support of its Russian fellow church in portraying itself as the guardian of Christian tradition in Montenegro. However, Christian-Orthodox symbolism is also politically (ab)used, especially between competing Serbian and Montenegrin nationalisms. Among the pro-Serbian population, Orthodox-Slavic arguments are used as an auxiliary instrument for backing Serbophile or Russophile practices and narratives.

We have observed these manifestations in three mutually overlapping domains: (1) the social: shared Serbo-Montenegrin identity traits, perceptions, and practices; (2) the political: use of conservative ideology and anti-Western patterns; and (3) the religious: Orthodox Slavdom as a phenomenon surrounding Serbophilia and Russophilia. Given the prominent role of the SOC in Montenegro, the authors consider that

---

[71] Ibid, p. 605.

[72] RTS. (2020). Đukanovic: Srpska pravoslavna crkva znacajan politički igrač u Crnoj Gori, available at: https://www.rts.rs/page/stories/sr/story/11/region/4182432/milo-djukanovic-srpska-pravoslavna-crkva-rusija.html. [Accessed 24th July 2021].

welcoming a greater Russian role in the religious domain inevitably spills over into the others. For example, the DF—the second largest party—in praising Orthodox traditions and ties to the Russian Orthodox Church also uses conservative, sovereignist, and anti-Western rhetoric resembling those used by Russian authorities. Rather than representing a mere reflection of Russophilia, such discourses are also populist-driven: similarities between the two sides are cherished and even idealised (by reaffirming traditional friendship with Russia) in order to paint a suitable ideological backdrop and obtain greater prestige among the local population. Faced with growing animosity from the authorities, Russophilia has been used as an instrument both by pro-Serbian political parties and the SOC in order to counter their marginalisation and discrimination in Montenegro.

Although Slavic identity and Orthodox bonds do represent useful references in political speeches, they constitute a minor rather than a prevailing argument in explaining current mutual affinities. Issues like the position of Serbs in neighbouring countries, the Montenegrin Orthodox Church's request for autocephaly, and the unregulated functioning of the SOC all draw support for the Russian state and Serbian religious institutions. Moreover, the multidimensionality of the Kosovo dispute—which straddles both legal-political (international law, the status of the Serbian community, etc.) and cultural-religious (its being a seat of the SOC) domains—constitutes an important element in understanding Montenegrin political developments, which are significantly more layered than originally meets the eye.

Instead of Slavophilia, we consider that there is significant Russophilia in the ethnic, religious, and political domains, especially on the pro-Serbian spectrum in Montenegro, which has relied on the 'Russian card' to consolidate its unfavourable position. Politically speaking, conservative, sovereignist, and anti-Western logic match Russia's international preferences. These aspects have been countered by the seemingly liberal, internationally and pro-Western oriented Montenegrin governments before 2020 by (1) reducing cooperation with Russia; (2) questioning the status of the SOC; and (3) systemically encouraging the rift between Montenegrins and Serbs.

Hence, revival of Pan-Orthodoxy and Slavic heritage in modern times was accomplished particularly through the active participation of the pro-Serbian nationalist coalition DF and the traditional SOC in domestic political processes and changes. These aimed to strengthen anti-state, conservative, and occasionally retrograde policies in order to undermine

Montenegro's integration into Euro-Atlantic structures. The identitarian issue has played a significant role in the polarisation and division of Montenegrin society. Both the DF and SOC have capitalised on identity disputes, statehood, and nationhood problems (such as anti-NATO protests), and autocephaly issues, which have greatly burdened relations between ethnic Montenegrins and Serbs, creating a fertile ground for Russian political interference in the country.

The SOC's position has become dominant in Montenegrin sociopolitical life especially after the adoption of a controversial law on religious freedom. The direct political involvement of the SOC in the last parliamentary election not only led to the demise of the DPS after three decades but also strengthened the Political Orthodoxy phenomenon in Montenegro, bringing into question the scope of state sovereignty and its civic and secular character. With the support of the DF, ROC, and Serbian and Russian actors, the SOC has succeeded in positioning itself as a major political player, consequently influencing not only the revision of religious freedom laws but also the election of new government members who are loyal to the church and its ethnophyletic ideology. Therefore, Montenegro's position seems to be unique in the light of the existence of strong Russophilic sentiments, beliefs, and behaviours, as well as a religiously motivated 'Pan-Orthodoxia', rather than of Slavophilia *per se*.

Pan-Slavism and Slavophilia in the Czech Republic Within the Context of Hybrid Threats

Miroslav Mareš and Petra Mlejnková

Introduction

The political spectrum in the Czech lands is traditionally divided into pro-Western and pro-Russian segments. These different attitudes towards the foreign policy orientation of the country have deep historical roots. Some have recently been misused by both external and internal illiberal actors within the context of so-called *hybrid threats*. The rejection of modern Western democratic values in the recent era is usually connected with expressions of sympathy towards the regime of Vladimir Putin. In support of these activities, ideas of Pan-Slavism and Slavophilia are also propagated in specific forms. This chapter will analyse the role of these ideas in the politics of hybrid threat actors in the Czech Republic.

M. Mareš (✉) · P. Mlejnková
Department of Political Science, Faculty of Social Studies, Masaryk University, Brno, Czech Republic
e-mail: mmares@fss.muni.cz

P. Mlejnková
e-mail: mlejnkova@fss.muni.cz

© The Author(s), under exclusive license to Springer Nature Switzerland AG 2023
M. Suslov et al. (eds.), *Pan-Slavism and Slavophilia in Contemporary Central and Eastern Europe*,
https://doi.org/10.1007/978-3-031-17875-7_15

The conceptual framework of an interconnection between pan-nationalism and hybrid warfare/hybrid campaigns will first be described, including a short summary of the state of the art in this field. Then the historical legacies of the interconnection between Pan-Slavism/Slavophilia and some radical and extremist streams of Czech politics will be explained. Several campaigns and events in the Czech Republic with a presence by Pan-Slavism and Slavophilia will be analysed. The recent Pan-Slavic and Slavophilic spectrum and its political strategy and tactics will be characterised. The authors will also present a short case study of the so-called Vrbětice case, which is the most serious crisis in Czech-Russian relations of the 'hybrid war' ongoing between Russia and the West since 2014. A general assessment of the researched phenomenon will be included in the conclusion.

This chapter continues in the footsteps of previous research, and its added value is a new framing of the issue. The role of Pan-Slavism and Slavophilia has already been mentioned in a publication researching hybrid campaigns within the context of Czech-Russian relations,[1] without, however, the deeper actor-analysis. The impact of Pan-Slavism on political extremism in the Czech Republic has been assessed in several publications,[2] and their findings can be used for reframing within an approach focused on hybrid warfare. Contemporary ideas of Pan-Slavism within the context of hybrid warfare have also been analysed in different regions, particularly in the Western Balkans.[3] The limit of our

---

[1] Mareš, M., Holzer, J. and Šmíd, T. (2020). 'The Hybrid Campaign Concept and Contemporary Czech–Russian Relations', In: Holzer, J. and Mareš, M. (eds) *Czech Security Dilemma: Russia as a Friend or Enemy?* Cham: Palgrave Macmillan, pp. 15–53.

[2] Mareš, M. (1999). 'Slovanství a politický extremismus v České republice', *Středoevropské politické studie*, 1(1), pp. 19–36, Pospíšil, I. (2001). 'In Margine tzv. Slovanství. Na okraj studie Miroslava Mareše Slovanství a politický extremismus v České republice', *Středoevropské politické studie*, 1(3). Available from: https://journals.muni.cz/cepsr/rt/printerFriendly/3849/5432 and Mareš, M. (2006). 'Panslawismus im ideologischen Hintergrund der radikalen und extremistischen Strömungen in der Tschechischen Republik', In: Backes, U. and Jesse, E. (eds) *Gefährdungen der Freiheit. Extremistische Ideologien im Vergleich*. Göttingen: Vandenhoeck & Ruprecht, pp. 359–369.

[3] Kuczyński, G. (2019). *Russia's Hybrid Warfare in the Western Balkans*. Warsaw: The Warsaw Institute, see also DeDominicis, B. E. (2017). 'Pan-Slavism and Soft Power in Post-Cold War Southeast European International Relations: Competitive Interference and Smart Power in the European Theatre of the Clash of Civilizations', *The International Journal of Interdisciplinary Civic and Political Studies*, 12(3), pp. 1–17.

study is fixed by the lack of clear data about real, official Russian direction of Pan-Slavic and Slavophile groups in the Czech Republic; however, the activities of many of these groups can be subsumed under the specific category of hybrid threats due to their political outputs.

Hybrid Threats, Pan-Nationalism and Illiberal Actors: A Conceptual Framework

The fight against so-called hybrid threats is an inherent part of the recent security and defence policy of the Czech Republic. They are countered also at the EU and the NATO levels. The EU and the NATO established in 2017 the European Centre of Excellence for Countering Hybrid Threats (Hybrid CoE) with its seat in Helsinki.[4] The concept of hybrid war and interconnected issues (hybrid warfare, hybrid campaigns, hybrid threats, etc.) has been developed in various contexts in Western military thought since the 1990s. However, it took on a new dimension in 2014 thanks to the Russian and separatist activities in Ukraine and various subversive actions against Western countries.[5] Some authors have also used the hybrid war concept to label the activities of China, the so-called Islamic State and other actors.[6]

The broad spectrum of activities which can be subsumed under the label 'hybrid threats' makes it difficult to elaborate and adopt a commonly accepted definition thereof. In general, we can define hybrid threats as a mixture of conventional and non-conventional activities aimed at the weakening and potential elimination of an adversary's power centre in times when no conventional war exists on its territory. The general aim of a hybrid campaign is centrally designed and controlled,[7] however, it can also count on the involvement of various autonomous and spontaneous activities to aid the achievement of its main goals.

[4] Centre of Excellence. (2020). *Hybrid Threats as a Concept*. Available from: https://www.hybridcoe.fi/hybrid-threats-as-a-phenomenon/

[5] Stojar, R. (2017). 'Vývoj a proměna konceptu hybridní války', *Vojenské rozhledy*, 26(2), pp. 44–55.

[6] Bachmann, L. (2020). *Hybride Bedrohungen. Ein Resilienztest der österreichischen Wehrverfassung*. Weilerwist: Velbrück Wissenschaft.

[7] Maas, J. (2021). 'Hybrid Threat and CSDP', In: Rehl, J. (ed) *Handbook on CSDP: The Common Security and Defence Policy of the European Union*. Vienna: Federal Ministry of Defence of the Republic of Austria, pp. 131–136.

Individual countries can define their particular interest in countering hybrid threats. This is the case of the Czech Republic, which adopted its National Strategy for Countering Hybrid Interference in 2021. Hybrid interference, according to the strategy,

> 'involves both covert and overt actions by state- as well as non-state actors (perpetrators of hybrid interference), which target vulnerable elements of democratic states and societies. The perpetrators' aim is to disrupt the working of democratic institutions, rule of law processes, and internal security. They utilize political, diplomatic, information, military, economic, financial, intelligence, and other tools. Hybrid interference also makes use of legal and seemingly legitimate instruments to achieve hostile objectives and undermine the interests of the Czech Republic.'[8]

Recent hybrid threats to the Czech Republic are mostly caused by the activities of actors linked to the present regime in Russia. The term 'hybrid interference' is used in official documents in place of the term 'hybrid warfare', which is however current in media and academic debates.[9] Terms like 'hybrid war', 'hybrid threats', etc., have served to mobilise the Czech public and raise awareness of Czech policy in relation to the new security constellation; some authors even see the mass spread of these concepts in official policy as being inadequate.[10]

If hybrid warfare can be described as a situation in which militant and violent hybrid actors manifest either their readiness to use violence or this actual violence directly (an example could be the situation in Crimea in 2014), then the Czech Republic is under the influence of permanent hybrid interference with sporadic elements of violence (mostly the Vrbětice case—see below) and activities by actors with a violent potential (mostly pro-Kremlin non-state paramilitary groups). As we will show, however, hybrid interference is not typical only of the post-2014 era;

---

[8] Ministry of Defence of the Czech Republic. (2021). *National Strategy for Countering Hybrid Interference*. Prague: Ministry of Defence of the Czech Republic. Available from: https://www.mocr.army.cz/assets/informacni-servis/zpravodajstvi/national-strategy---aj-final.pdf.

[9] See Mareš, Holzer, Šmíd (2020).

[10] Daniel, J. and Eberle, J. (2018). Hybrid Warriors: Transforming Czech Security Through the 'Russian Hybrid Warfare' Assemblage. *Sociologický časopis/Czech Sociological Review*, 54(6), pp. 907–932.

a similar strategy (albeit without the strong impact of modern social networks) was also used in a previous era.

Slavophilia and Pan-Slavism are much older phenomena than the concept of hybrid threats. However, these have been used by various actors in their hybrid campaigns, mostly within the context of Russian and pro-Russian interference. Finding clear evidence of Russian governmental involvement in pro-Slavic activities in the Czech Republic is difficult in many cases (On the other hand, intelligence sources can confirm individual cases; see below). And of course many activities are autonomous and grow directly out of the domestic Czech Pan-Slavic and Slavophile scene. However, this activism—even when unintentional—serves Russian governmental interests, and it has been possible to conceptualise it within the framework of hybrid threats since the mid-1990s.

It is also important to mention that in recent times representatives of Czech groups with strong Slavic identities usually reject the Pan-Slavic label, using instead the term 'Slavic mutuality' (*Slovanská vzájemnost*) to characterise themselves.[11] We also distinguish between the traditional political concept of formalised Slavic cooperation—in its traditional form, under Russian leadership (Pan-Slavism)—and freely-structured activities focused on achieving subjectively defined Slavic interests (Slavophilia). These and similar terms (such as Slavic mutuality) were, and continue to be, discussed during the historical development of cooperation among the Slavic nations.[12]

HISTORICAL ROOTS OF PAN-SLAVISM IN CZECH EXTREMIST AND ILLIBERAL POLITICS

In the historical development of the Slavophilic spectrum, we can find various currents of Pan-Slavism and Slavophilia, in particular cultural and political ones. Of course, these have in various ways been strongly interconnected. Slavic culture and art have been used in political propaganda, and vice versa: Slavic literature, theatre, songs, etc., frequently reflect political motives. This interconnection is typical at the Czech national level as well as at the international ('inter-Slavic') level.

---

[11] Mareš (1999), p. 21.
[12] Lemberg, H. (2009). 'Hej Slované! Die Slawische Idee bei Tschechen und Slowaken', *Osteuropa* 59(12), pp. 20–39.

If we focus on the political side of the historical and contemporary Slavophilic spectrum, it is important to distinguish between three categories of actors according to their relation to the use of Slavic ideas. First, we can observe a general impact of Pan-Slavism and/or Slavophilia on the politics of broadly oriented political actors (e.g. political parties like National Democracy or individual politicians like Karel Kramář). Second are those who emphasise the Slavic name within, however, the broad scope of political interests in real politics (e.g. the Slavic Fascist Community of the late 1930s). In this context, it is important to mention that in the nineteenth and first half of the twentieth centuries, the 'Slavic' name also served to distinguish ethnic Czechs from Germans living on Czech territory (typically by the Czecho-Slavic Social Democratic Party). And thirdly, there are monothematic Slavophilic groups with a dominant focus on the politicisation of Slavic ideas. Among these, there can also be more specialised actors, such as the Slavophilic Czech supporters of the Lusatian Sorbs.

Regarding the relationship of Slavophilia and Pan-Slavism to illiberal politics, we can observe their large overlap with authoritarian and anti-democratic segments of the Czech political spectrum both historically (mostly in the twentieth century) and in the contemporary era. On the other hand, there are also liberal and pro-democratic Slavic political concepts (such as Masaryk's progressive Slavic politics during and after the First World War), and some Pan-Slavic politicians have played at least temporarily positive roles in the development of Czech/Czechoslovak democracy (e.g. Karel Kramář; see below).

Slavic identity was an important element of the Czech National Revival of the nineteenth century. At that time, Pan-Slavism was thematised by various actors in Czech cultural and political life. Pan-Slavic ideas were typical of Jan Kollár (1793–1852), a Slovak poet who had a strong impact on Czech writers and politicians. In 1848, the first international Slavic Congress was organised in Prague with strong engagement by Czech protagonists of national renewal, for example, the historian František Palacký (1798–1876) and the journalist Karel Havlíček Borovský (1821–1856). This congress was connected with progressive ideas at the time, including the guarantee of freedom for nations as well as for individuals.[13]

---

[13] Hugh, L. A. (2008). *Češi a země koruny české*. Praha: Academia, p. 183.

Havlíček, a liberal journalist and strong opponent of absolutism, is also connected with the first important clash between liberal and illiberal political forces in relation to Pan-Slavism and Russian rule. Havlíček was originally under the influence of Kollár, a strong supporter of Pan-Slavism; after visiting Russia in 1843–1844, Havlíček lost his illusions about Russian culture and politics, and he rejected Pan-Slavic ideas in the sense of Russian rule over the Slavic nations. However, he also criticised the Hapsburg monarchy and kept own Slavic identity. He published the journal *The Slav* (*Slovan*).[14]

A large part of the Czech political spectrum emphasised Slavic identity in the second half of the nineteenth century and at the beginning of the twentieth. Extreme nationalists used these Slavophilic and Pan-Slavic ideas in their intolerant politics. On the other hand, ideas about liberal and democratic Slavic cooperation were propagated by the foundational forces of Czech humanist and liberal politics, including Tomáš Garrigue Masaryk (1850–1937). They tried to reject 'naive' Russophilia and connect Slavic identity to a pro-Western orientation.[15] A specific goal was propagated by Karel Kramář (1860–1937), who belonged originally to Masaryk's 'realist stream' of Czech politics; however (due, among other factors, to his personal ties to the Russian environment) he later proposed establishing an All-Slavic constitutional monarchy under the rule of the Russian tsar. Nevertheless, this idea was not itself a priori illiberal, despite the fact that it was only illusory and that Kramář later turned to authoritarian nationalism.

If we take into account the extreme left wing of Czech politics under the Hapsburg monarchy, we can also see an interesting overlap between Czech anarchism (a relatively marginal phenomenon, however) and Slavophilia. The interconnection between anarchist and Slavophilic ideas was not atypical in Eastern Europe at that time, as shown by the visit by the Russian anarchist Bakunin to the Slavic congress in Prague

---

[14] Černý, V. (1995). *Vývoj a zločiny panslavismu.* Praha: Institut pro středoevropskou politiku a kulturu, pp. 27–29.
[15] Vlček, R. (2010). 'Rusko v politických koncepcích T. G. Masaryka a K. Kramáře. (80. léta 19. století – 1918/1919)', In: Prokš P. et al. (eds) *České země a moderní dějiny Evropy. Studie k dějinám 19. a 20. století.* Praha: Historický ústav Akademie věd České republiky, pp. 59–74.

(and his plans for a Slavic federation),[16] or by the mix of ideas about South Slavic cooperation and anarchism in the mind of Gavrilo Principle (the assassin in Sarajevo in 1914).[17]

In the Czech context, we can mention the case of one of the first homegrown small groups with nationalist, and perhaps also primitive anarchist ideas, called the Agency from Blaník (*Jednatelství z Blaníka*).[18] Their members attacked the building of the Police Presidium in Prague with a grenade in 1869. The group's political goals were the liberation of Bohemia and the unification of the Slavic nations.[19] On the other hand, another important and serious segment of the workers' and social democratic movement in the Czech lands supported the idea of Austromarxism, which struggled for non-extremist social and economic changes to all the nations (including the Slavic nations) of the Austro-Hungarian monarchy. Due to this fact, Slavic Czech Austromarxists rejected Pan-Slavism, though they could cooperate in some way with the Austroslavists[20] in supporting a solution to the 'Slavic Question' within the context of the Hapsburg monarchy.[21]

After the establishment of an independent Czechoslovakia in 1918, the concepts of Czech Austromarxism, Austroslavism and the connection of anarchism with Czech separatist ideas all lost their *raison d'être*. On the other hand, Masaryk's ideal of a democratic Slavic identity was still alive. The most important representative of Czech Pan-Slavism, Karel Kramář, became the first prime minister of Czechoslovakia in 1918. He

---

[16] Lavrin, J. (1966). Bakunin the Slav and the Rebel. *The Russian Review*, 25(2), pp. 135–149.

[17] Vojinovic, M. (2018). 'Political Ideas of Young Bosnia: Between Anarchism, Socialism and Nationalism', In: Höpken, W. and van Meurs, W. (eds) *The First World War and the Balkans: Historic Event, Experience, Memory/Der Erste Weltkrieg auf dem Balkan: Ereignis. Erfahrung und Erinnerung 53. Internationale Hochschulwoche der Südosteuropa-Gesellschaft in Tutzing 6.-10. Oktober 2014*. Frankfurt am Main: Peter Lang, pp. 162–193.

[18] Blaník is a Czech hill, in which—according to the legend—are sleeping knights who should wake up and save the Czech nation in case of crisis.

[19] Liška, P. (1992). *Osudné výstřely. Atentáty v českých dějinách*. Praha: Víkend, p. 10.

[20] Urban, O. (1996). 'Der tschechische Austroslavismus nach dem österreichisch-ungarischen Ausgleich', In: Moritsch, A. (eds) *Der Austroslavismus. Ein verfrühtes Konzept zur politischen Neugestaltung Mitteleuropas*. Wien: Böhlau Verlag, pp. 36–43.

[21] Grigorieva, A. A. (2009). 'Pan-Slavism in Central and Southeastern Europe', *Journal of Siberian Federal University. Humanities & Social Sciences*, 1(3), pp. 13–21. Available from: https://core.ac.uk/download/pdf/38633132.pdf

was a strong opponent of Bolshevism and struggled for the establishment of an All-Slavic democratic federation.[22] During the 1920s and '30s, however, Kramář turned to authoritarian nationalist politics. He initiated a political movement in 1934 called National Unification (*Národní sjednocení*), which sought to establish a 'Slavic-Romanian' international bloc (including also fascist Italy) and a strong Czech Slavic nation.[23]

Slavic identity was important also for a set of small anti-Semitic groupings at the beginning of the 1920s. They tried to connect anti-Jewish propaganda to criticisms of German influence (Jews were considered a German-linked, anti-Slavic element) and of Bolshevism (anti-Semitic arguments were also employed in anti-communist rhetoric). The weekly *Old Slav* (*Staroslovan*) or the Slavic Anti-Jewish Party (*Slovanská strana protižidovská*) are typical examples.[24] Pan-Slavic ideas connected with anti-democratic and anti-Semitic propaganda were typical also of the Czech fascist movement, which was represented mostly by the National Fascist Community (*Národní obec fašistická*, NOF) and its leader Radola Gajda (1892–1948). Gajda was former general of the Czechoslovak legions in Siberia during the civil war in Russia, and he held close ties to 'white' Russian émigrés in Czechoslovakia and abroad. He was allegedly selected as the leader of the fascists of All-Slavic nations,[25] however, such an international structure was never established. Parties split off from the NOF also emphasised Slavic identity, as in the cases of the Union of Slavic Fascists (*Svaz slovanských fašistů*), the Slavic Fascist Community (*Slovanská obec fašistická*) and the White Brotherhood—Slavic Unity (*Bílé Bratrstvo – Slovanská jednota*).[26]

---

[22] Hájková, D. (2013). 'Vražda v hotelu Metropol. Mohla Masayrkova smrt zamezit rozpadu Rakouska-Uherska?', In: Hájková, D. et al. (eds) *Historie na rozcestí. Jak mohly dopadnout osudové chvíle Československa?* Brno: Barrister & Principal, pp. 23–57.

[23] Rataj, J., Dlouhý, M. and Haka, A. (2020). *Proti systému! Český radikální konzervatismus, fašismus a nacionální socialismus 20. a 21. století.* Praha: Auditorium, p. 52.

[24] Sulitka, A. and Soukupová, B. (2018). Memorandum Svazu Čechů-židů v Republice československé postoupené vládě během přípravy národnostního statutu v roce 1938. *Právněhistorické studie*, 48(2), pp. 115–130.

[25] Klimek, A. and Hoffman, P.: *Generál Radola Gajda. Vítěz, který prohrál.* Praha, Litomyšl: Paseka, p. 222.

[26] Pejčoch, I. (2011). Fašismus v českých zemích. Fašistické a nacionálně-socialistické strany a hnutí v Čechách a na Moravě 1922–1945. Praha: Academia, pp. 111–113, 188–193.

Despite the fact that the dominant attitude of Czech fascists towards Germans during the first Czechoslovak republic was negative, after the occupation of the Czech lands, many of them started to collaborate with German Nazis. Some activists in this situation also declared Slavic identity as a part of the Aryan race concept. Of course, Pan-Slavism was rejected by them inasmuch as they accepted a 'New European Order' under German leadership. They were, however, only marginal. Their most important representative was a small group called the National Socialist Guard of Slavic Activists in the Greater Germanic Reich (*Nacionálně socialistická garda slovanských aktivistů v rámci Velkoněmecké říše*).[27]

Real Pan-Slavism and Slavophilia played a much more important role on the side of the anti-Fascist resistance. These were used mostly by communist and pro-communist forces specifically after the start of hostilities between Nazi Germany and the Union of Soviet Socialist Republics in 1941.[28] The All-Slavic ideas served to interconnect the communist tendency and the broader spectrum of sympathisers of the concept of a patriotic war between Slavic nations and Germans.

In Moscow, a Slavic congress was held in 1942, and the All-Slavic committee was founded under the supervision of the Soviet communists. It published the journal *Slaviane*, which was translated into several languages, including Czech.[29] Slavic ideas were propagated among the Czechoslovak foreign and domestic resistance. Names with Slavic motives were used by various resistance groupings. In Brno, there even operated a small organisation called the Pan-Slavists (*Panslavisté*) in 1941.[30]

The positive effect of antifascist mobilisation was accompanied by the controversial, uncritical indoctrination of Czech antifascists into the values of Stalin's empire. This legacy has been used to this day by illiberal communist and leftist nationalist forces in the Czech Republic. During the first years of the post-war period, various groupings tried to continue

---

[27] Pejčoch (2011), pp. 340–345.

[28] Kohn, H. (1952). 'Pan-Slavism and World War II', *The American Political Science Review*, 46(3), pp. 699–722.

[29] Szumski, J. (2019). 'The USSR's Politics of History Toward the Slavic Countries of the Eastern Bloc: Formal and Institutional Frameworks: 1945–1989', *Kwartalnik Historii Nauki i Techniki*, 64(4), pp. 61–81.

[30] Kopečný, P. (2018). *Deprese a naděje. Protinacistický odboj v letech 1939–1945 na Brněnsku*. Brno: Šimon Ryšavý, p. 99.

with Slavophilic or even Pan-Slavic activities, such as the organisation the Federation of Slavic Nations (*Federace slovanských národů*).[31] However, this strong role of Pan-Slavism and Slavophilia in Czechoslovakia as well as in the Eastern bloc in general was abandoned step by step by the end of the 1940s. The clash between the Soviet Union and Yugoslavia broke the illusion of Slavic communist unity. And due to the struggle to win over non-Slavic nations to communist ideas, proletarian internationalism and national liberation were officially propagated, not Pan-Slavism or Slavophilia. The international All-Slavic committee ended its existence in 1962.[32] The Slavic identity of Czechs and Slovaks was of course emphasised in the cultural dimension, however, the political importance of Slavophilia declined in the 1960s–1980s.

Hybrid Campaigns and Pan-Slavism and Slavophilia in the Czech Republic After 1993

The re-establishment of a pluralist political spectrum after the fall of communism in 1989 and the dissolution of the Czechoslovak federation in 1992 offered new opportunities for the renewal of Slavophilic and sometimes also Pan-Slavic ideas in the Czech lands. These were in large part expressed by political actors from illiberal ends of the spectrum, and they were also used in subversive propaganda campaigns, such as can be labelled hybrid campaigns in contemporary terminology. Of course, not all demonstrations and proclamations of Czech Slavic identity can be subsumed under this heading, and indeed various extremist or other illiberal uses of Slavic ideas are not always connected to organised hybrid campaigns; nevertheless, the activities of these groupings have served overall to subvert and destabilise the liberal democratic political order of the Czech Republic.

If we look at the perceptions of historical legacies in post-1989 development, we can see the various impacts of different eras and events on the politics of specific subjects on the extremist and illiberal political spectra. The most politically important current is that connected with the Communist Party of Bohemia and Moravia (*Komunistická strana Čech a*

---

[31] Ministerstvo vnitra ČSR. (1946). *Federace slovanských národů*. Located in: Archiv bezpečnostních složek, Praha.

[32] Szumski, J. (2019), p. 99.

Moravy, KSČM) and its satellite organisations, as well as more extreme communist splinter parties (like the Party of Czechoslovak Communists). The use of Slavophilia is connected mostly with the legacy of the common antifascist struggle of the Slavic nations against 'German Nazism' in the Second World War, as well as with positive images of social life in the 'socialist era', during which the socialist 'Slavic countries' cooperated (including of course the USSR) and the strong role of Russian culture.

The KSČM was originally established in 1990 as the Czech wing of the Communist Party of Czechoslovakia. It gained a relevant position in the Czech pluralist party system, in which it played an anti-system opposition role. It is considered a non-reformed dogmatic party in the international context.[33] Its members and sympathisers were also active in various intermediary groups attempting to connect the party to a broader swath of the population.[34] Leftist patriotism and Slavophilia played a part in these activities, utilising the rise of nationalism typical of Eastern Europe in the 1990s.

The first monothematic organisation was the Slavic Union (*Slovanská unie*), which was founded in 1991 by the writer Alexej Pludek (1923–2002). He had become well known as a writer in the communist era. He propagated leftist ideology; however he was also labelled as an anti-Semitic activist by Michal Mazel, a researcher on extremism, in the 1990s.[35] Pludek cooperated with the right-wing extremist Association for the Republic-Republican Party of Czechoslovakia (*Sdružení pro republiku-Republikánská strana Československa*, SPR-RSČ) on the one hand, and with communist organisations on the other.[36] The Slavic Union won only a minimum of attention at the time.

A new and more influential organisation was established in relation to the Slavic congress in Prague in 1998. This event was organised by activists from the hard-line communist wing, and they founded the

---

[33] Mannewitz, T. (2012). *Linksextremistische Parteien in Europa nach 1990 Ursachen für Wahlerfolge und -misserfolge.* Baden Baden: Noms Verlag.

[34] Fiala, P., Holzer. J., Mareš, M. and Pšeja, P. (1999). *Komunismus v České republice. Vývojové, systémové a ideové aspekty působení KSČM a dalších komunistických organizací v české politice.* Brno: Masarykova univerzita.

[35] Mazel, M. (1998). 'Oponenti systému. Přehled radikálních a extremistických organizací v České republice', In: Fiala, P. (ed) *Politický extremismus a radikalismus v České republice.* Brno: Masarykova univerzita, pp. 117–277.

[36] Ibid.

Slavic Committee of the Czech Republic (*Slovanský výbor České republiky*). Participants from several countries criticised the enlargement of NATO and the alleged division of the Slavic nations.[37] The International Slavic Committee, with its headquarters in Minsk, was also founded, and it organised Slavic congresses in other countries in the following years. The Belarussian President Alexander Lukashenko was elected honorary chair of this committee in 2005.[38]

The Slavic committee of the Czech Republic has kept close ties to the communist party. In 2006 a new, more nationalist group (however with sympathies towards the Soviet era) was founded under the name Czech-Moravian Slavic Union (*Českomoravský slovanský výbor*), with links to pro-Kremlin lobbying structures.[39] The marginal Moravian Slavic Committee has also existed since the year 2000. It promotes Moravian autonomist ideas with an emphasis on the Slavic identity of the Moravian nation.[40]

Besides these Marxist-Leninist and leftist-patriotic groupings with ties to the communist wing, Slavophilia also played a specific role in part of the far-right wing. The small neo-Fascist movement was inspired by Gajda's Pan-Slavic ideas, as in the case of the association Patriotic Front (*Vlastenecká fronta*). Quasi-religious Slavic paganism was incorporated into the policy programme of an obscure group called the National Front of Castists (*Národní front Castistů*), from the Latin *castus* meaning'- clean'.[41] On the other hand, Czech neo-Nazis have also propagated the shared German, Celtic and Slavic roots of the Czech nation, even as also they cooperated with Russian neo-Nazis.[42]

---

[37] Účastníci Slovanského sjezdu. (1998). 'Manifest Všeslovanského sjezdu 1998', In: Hoření, Z. (ed) *Všeslovanský sjezd Praha 1998. Zpráva o čtyřech dnech v dejvické pyramidě (2. – 5. června)*. Praha: Slovanský výbor ČR – JUDr. Jaroslav Weber.
[38] Mlejnecký, V. (2005). 'Ze sjezdového zápisníku', In: Hoření, Z. (ed) *Devátý všeslovanský sjezd*. Praha: Slovanský výbor and Orego, pp. 10–15.
[39] Bastl. M., Mareš, M., Smolík, J. and Vejvodová, P. (2011). *Krajní pravice a krajní levice v ČR*. Praha: Grada, p. 45.
[40] Mareš, M. (2002). 'Evropská politika moravistických organizací', *Středoevropské politické studie – Central European Political Studies Review*, 4(4). Available from: https://journals.muni.cz/cepsr/article/view/3920/5359.
[41] Mareš (1999), pp. 20–29.
[42] Holzer, J., Laryš, M. and Mareš, M. (2019). *Militant Right-Wing Extremism in Putin's Russia. Legacies, Forms and Threats*. London: Routledge, pp. 229–231.

If we assess the importance of Slavophilic groupings from the point of view of hybrid threats, the communist and leftist-patriotic organisations and factions have played the most important role. Only in some cases (such as in the anti-NATO campaign during the Yugoslav Crisis) have the far-right organisations also become relevant to disinformation campaigns and other subversive activities.

The main characteristics of the original Slavophilic and Pan-Slavic spectrum at the turn of the century was described in the governmental report on extremism as follows:

> 'On the basis of this historical and political interpretation of 'pan-Slavonic' orientation, they assess positively 'the world socialist system headed by the Soviet Union' and the communist regimes introduced in the Slavonic countries after World War Two. On the contrary, they evaluate the current development in former socialist countries very negatively, and they reject pluralistic democracy and the principles of the market economy, calling them capitalism directed, in their opinion, against Slavonic interests. The national principle is superior to civil society, and their attitudes include not only strong xenophobia and chauvinism, mainly in relation to the German nation, but also in some cases anti-Semitism.'[43]

Of course, the Slavophilic activists rejected this 'extremist labelling', and blamed the security agencies for their alleged misuse of power.[44]

The ideas mentioned above were used to politically mobilise the Slavonic political spectrum against the official governmental line with the goal of weakening or even disturbing the pro-Western orientation of Czech politics. Propaganda is interconnected with demonstrations and with the struggle to use disloyal governmental officials to advance Slavophilic anti-regime goals. The most important topics have been criticism of the dissolution of the Czechoslovak federation, fearmongering about Sudeten Germans, rejecting NATO enlargement and membership (or, recently the very existence of the NATO as such), criticism of the use of force by NATO against Yugoslavia, agitation against the planned building of a US radar station in the Czech Republic, rejection of EU

---

[43] Ministry of Interrior of the Czech Republic. (2000). *Report on the Issue of Extremism in the Czech Republic in 1999*. Prague: Ministry of Interrior of the Czech Republic, p. 21.

[44] Svoboda, M. (1999). 'Protislovanské cejchování', *Slovanská vzájemnost*, 2(13), p. 3.

membership, support for regimes in Russia and Belarus, and support for pro-Kremlin separatism in Ukraine.[45]

The Contemporary Pan-Slavic and Slavophilic Spectrum in the Czech Republic

The Slavophilic scene in the Czech Republic step by step partially changed its structure during the 2010s. The decline in importance of the Communist Party of Bohemia and Moravia on the one hand, and the rise of new pro-Kremlin actors on the other, caused a 'new distribution' of Slavic ideas within the illiberal spectrum. 'Old organizations' like the Slavic Committee of the Czech Republic and its splinter groups still exist, however, new organisations have also been founded. The image of a strong authoritarian Russia under the Putin regime as the protector of Slavic values against Western progressivism is typical of the propaganda from these organisations.

They are usually also supporters of President Miloš Zeman, who was elected in 2013 (and re-elected in 2018). He is considered a 'friend' of leftist-patriotic and Slavophilic groupings (Looking back in history to 1998, Zeman—at the time the chair of the Chamber of Deputies of the Czech parliament—sent his greeting to the All-Slavic congress, while liberal President Václav Havel distanced himself from it[46]).

While the traditional organisations worked mostly as broadly focused groups, organising rallies and publishing journals, we can identify specific profiles of several newly founded organisations. The Institute of Slavic Strategic Studies (*Institut slovanských strategických studií*), founded in November 2013, operates as a quasi-academic think tank critical of Western values.[47] Its members participated in workshops organised in the Czech parliament in the mid-2010s thanks to its good relations with

---

[45] Mareš, Holzer and Šmíd (2020).
[46] Mareš (1999), p. 31.
[47] Veřejný rejstřík a Sbírka listin. (2021). Institut slovanských strategických studií. Výpis ze spolkového rejstříku. Available from: https://or.justice.cz/ias/ui/rejstrik-firma.vysledky?subjektId=763019&typ=UPLNY

the far-right party Freedom and Direct Democracy (*Svoboda a přímá demokracie*, SPD).[48]

Several non-state paramilitary groupings with pro-Kremlin and 'all-Slavic' attitudes are active in the Czech Republic. The strongest of these groups, the National Home Guard (*Národní domobrana*), was initiated by the party National Democracy (*Národní demokracie*) and later became independent of the party. This marginal party proclaims a connection to Kramář's interwar national democratic party (including its Slavophilia) and is mostly known thanks to the anti-Semitic excesses of its leader Adam Bartoš.[49]

A new field for activities by Slavophiles is the esoteric and (quasi-) religious pagan scene. While much of this scene is not connected to political beliefs or hybrid campaigns, a role in such campaigns is played by part. Fake news and disinformation about various societal, political, cultural and (quasi-) scientific issues (including healthcare) are widespread on the communication channels of this scene. The main message undermines belief in official information among the broader public. For example, overpriced goods offering protection from the COVID-19 pandemic were sold by a company called Health from Slavs (*Zdraví od Slovanů*).[50]

An interesting development is exhibited by the Slavic Union. After the death of Alexej Pludek in 2002, the group was at first marginalised, then started new visible activity thanks to new chair Vojtěch Merunka in the second half of the 2010s. Merunka is an academic who together with colleagues founded a new Interslavic language.[51] He was elected in 2014 as chair of the Czech-Moravian Slavic Union, which has recently

---

[48] Novotný, J. (2016). Ruská propaganda proniká do sněmovny. *Euro*, 20. June 2016. Available from: https://www.euro.cz/politika/ruska-propaganda-pronika-do-ceske-snemovny-1298385

[49] Vejvodová, P., Janda, J. and Víchová, V. (2017). *The Russian Connections of Far Right and Paramilitary Organisations in the Czech Repiublic*. Budapest: Political Capital. Available from: https://www.politicalcapital.hu/pc-admin/source/documents/PC_NED_country_study_CZ_20170428.pdf

[50] Svoboda, V. (2021). E-shop nabízí přípravky ‚proti nanobotům ' z covidové vakcíny. Řeší ho inspekce i český lékový ústav. Irozhlas, 19. July 2021, https://www.irozhlas.cz/zpravy-domov/e-shop-zdravi-od-slovanu-leky-doplnky-stravy-coronavirus-covid-19-mrna-vakcina_2107190627_vis

[51] Steenbergen, J. van and Merunka, V. (2018). 'The Interslavic Language: An Opportunity for the Tourist Branch', In: Canbey-Özgüler, V., Çabuk, S. N. and Zibel, A. (eds) *Proceeding Book of the International Symposium on Advancements in Tourism, Recreation*

been cooperating with the All-Slavic Committee, founded in 2010 and registered in Prague.[52] However, due to his criticisms of anti-Ukrainian statements, Merunka was suspended by the pro-Kremlin faction.[53] He then left the ČMSS and restarted the Slavic Union. Under his leadership the organisation promotes moderate politics and criticises the anti-Christian tendencies of part of the neopagan Slavic movement. (The Slavic Union mostly promotes Orthodox Christianity.[54])

This anecdote shows that the Slavophilic scene in the Czech Republic is not a homogeneous entity, and that levels and forms of 'illiberalism' can be different. All said, the majority of their activities serve the interests of contemporary official Russian politics, and many members of Slavophilic groups are linked to structures of Russian influence.[55] Slavophilia has been able to have an impact on relevant political processes mostly due to favourable views of it by parliamentary parties, however recently this has mostly been in only a subsidiary role. This can be demonstrated with the help of a case study on the so-called Vrbětice Case.

CASE STUDY: THE VRBĚTICE AMMUNITION DEPOT EXPLOSION AND GRU INVOLVEMENT

On April 17 2021, Czech Prime Minister Andrej Babiš and interior minister Jan Hamáček publicly disclosed information about well-grounded suspicions of involvement by officers of the Russian intelligence service GRU in the explosion of an ammunition depot in the Vrbětice area in October 2014. Eighteen Russian embassy staff, identified as

---

and Sport Sciences. Podgorica: GSI Publication, pp. 164–175. Available from: http://int erslavic-language.org/doc/crnagora-2018-clanok.pdf

[52] Všeslovanský výbor. (2021). O nás. Retrieved from http://vseslav.eu/o-nas

[53] Ševela, V. (2015). *Pod dozor Moskvy se dostávají i české slovanské spolky*. Echo 24, 9 February 2015. Retrieved from https://echo24.cz/a/iq3G5/pod-dozor-moskvy-se-dos tavaji-i-ceske-slovanske-spolky.

[54] Slovanská unie (2015). *Slovanská unie z.s. – symbolika*. Retrieved from http://slo vane.org/ruzne/155-slovanska-unie-symbolika/

[55] Kadlec, M. (2017). *Naše slovanská elita a její kremelští loutkovodiči*. *Echo 24*, 29 November 2017. Retrieved from https://www.forum24.cz/nase-slovanska-elita-a-jeji-kre melsti-loutkovodici/

secret service personnel, were ordered to leave within 48h.[56] Others followed in May. Czech police said they were searching in connection with serious criminal activity for two men carrying Russian passports in the names of Alexander Petrov and Ruslan Boshirov, the same two individuals whom British prosecutors had charged with the attempted murder of Sergei Skripal in Britain in 2018. The case has had a serious impact on Czech-Russian relations. The Russian government expelled twenty Czech embassy staff in retaliation and placed the Czech Republic on its official enemies list.

The original case was a part of Russia's aggressive politics accompanying its hybrid campaign and conventional war in Eastern Ukraine. The attack itself was not connected with Slavic ideas. However, some reactions by Slavophilic elements in the Czech Republic to official countermeasures against Russia established their ties to the propaganda campaign within the broader context of Russian hybrid interference. The Communist Party of Bohemia and Moravia propagated a very strong narrative that evidence of GRU involvement did not exist, rejecting official information as 'hallucinations that could hardly be believed by those who are not captivated by ubiquitous Russophobia and anti-Slavic propaganda and who use the brain'.[57]

The case was also covered by the journal of the Slavic Committee of the Czech Republic *Slavic Mutuality* (*Slovanská vzájemnost*), which characterised it as an attack on Pan-Slavism. It was not considered as an attack from the Russian side, however, but from the Czech Republic, which 'stabbed a dagger in the back of Pan-Slavism'[58] as one issue described it. The journal repeated the narrative that evidence of GRU involvement did not exist and depicted the official Czech position as betrayal and perfidy in relation to Russia and Slavs, and as a fanning of anti-Russian hysteria. In this context, several images were offered to readers. Firstly, of the Czech government betraying the country that had liberated Czechoslovakia at the end of World War II; secondly, because the whole case was

---

[56] Reuters. (2021). *Czechs Expels 18 Russians Envoys, Accuse Moscow Over Ammunition Depot Blast*. Available from: https://www.reuters.com/world/czechs-expel-russian-embassy-staff-pm-says-suspected-russian-link-ammunition-2021-04-17/

[57] KSČM, Facebook page of KSČM, 19 April 2021.

[58] Nickelli, J. J. (2021). 'Dýka do zad slovanské vzájemnosti', *Slovanská vzájemnost*, 255(24), pp. 1–2.

interpreted by the journal only as an attempt to destabilise Slavic togetherness, of the Czech government as puppets or hostages of NATO, the American administration, and of all who hate Slavs; and thirdly, of Russia as generous in not further escalating the issue. The journal expressed an understanding attitude towards Russia and its reaction to the case—in which the Russian government had placed the Czech Republic on its official enemies list.[59]

Conclusion

The traditional tension between liberal and illiberal orientations in Czech politics is also mirrored by the employment of the Slavic identity of the Czech nation. Despite the existence of liberal concepts of Slavic politics, recent use of Slavophilia is connected with the illiberal legacies of Pan-Slavism and inter-Slavic cooperation. Various radical and extremist groupings promote ideas opposed to the official Western liberal orientation. These groupings and ideas play a specific role also within the hybrid campaigns led by the current Russian regime. It is difficult to find direct evidence about everyday coordinated and synchronised action from the Kremlin, however, the illiberal Slavophilic and Pan-Slavic spectrum as a whole does contribute to the general hybrid campaign on sensitive issues such as the Ukrainian crisis, the Serbia-Kosovo question, relations with Belarus, etc. (And, recently, trust in the government during the pandemic crisis can also be mentioned). The established illiberal Slavophilic wing acts according to Russian official interests even without direct instructions from Moscow. Russia can utilise non-state actors to manipulate public opinion also in topical crises, as the Vrbětice case has shown. The role of Pan-Slavism and Slavophilia in Russian hybrid campaigns in the Czech Republic will be visible also in the future due to the fact that illiberal and anti-Western tendencies are and will continue to be relevant parts of the Czech political spectrum and society, and the legacies of illiberal Slavophilia serve to support anti-Western propaganda arguments.

---

[59] ČTK and Jan Jelínek. (2021). 'Kde jsou důkazy o zapojení ruských agentů?' *Slovanská vzájemnost*, 254(24), pp. 1–3, ČTK and jel. (2021). 'Vyhoštění z ruské ambasády odcestovali do vlasti', *Slovanská vzájemnost*, 255(24), p. 1, Nickell, J. (2021). 'Dýka do zad slovanské vzájemnosti', *Slovanská vzájemnost*, 255(24), pp. 1–2.

Slovakia: Emergence of an Old-New Pseudo-Pan-Slavism in the Context of the Conflict Between Russia and Ukraine After 2014

Juraj Marušiak

Introduction

The relevance of the question of 'Slavicness' in geopolitical debate has been raised twice in post-1989 Slovakia. The first time was in the second half of the 1990s, during Vladimír Mečiar's third government, when this was presented as a potential alternative to Slovakia's integration into the EU and NATO. The issue re-emerged again in the context of the Ukraine crisis of 2013–2014, which soon changed from an internal Ukrainian

---

This chapter falls within the framework of the grants "This is not true But it could be": Conspiracy theories and hoaxes in the modern development of Slovakia in the European context (APVV-20-0334) and the Image of the "Other" in the post-1989 Slovak politics (VEGA 2/0046/19)

J. Marušiak (✉)
Institute of Political Science, Slovak Academy of Sciences, Bratislava, Slovakia
e-mail: juraj.marusiak@savba.sk

© The Author(s), under exclusive license to Springer Nature Switzerland AG 2023
M. Suslov et al. (eds.), *Pan-Slavism and Slavophilia in Contemporary Central and Eastern Europe*,
https://doi.org/10.1007/978-3-031-17875-7_16

political conflict to a conflict between Russia and the West. This crisis ultimately resulted in the Russian Federation's military aggression against Ukraine on 24 February 2022. This conflict was accompanied by a sudden surge in the popularity of pro-Russian narratives. While during the first stage of this conflict (2013–2015), these narratives were mainly present in the language of extremists and spread mainly through so-called conspiratorial or disinformation Internet media,[1] in later years they gradually penetrated the language of the decisive political parties and political leaders. Only rarely, however, can we speak of Pan-Slavism as a 'pure', coherent ideological platform.

It is precisely the fragmentary nature of Slavophilia and its problematic influence on the spheres of domestic and foreign policy that make some authors, for instance, Stefan Troebst,[2] prefer to speak rather of *Post-Pan-Slavism*, since the notion of Slavicness is often intertwined with other geographic-cultural framings, such as Eastern Europe or the former USSR, etc. The idea of Slavicness itself is practically absent at the level of interstate relations. Pan-Slavism can be examined at the level of supreme politics as a geopolitical doctrine, the essence of which is a programme of cooperation between Slavic states. However, such a doctrine is usually based on discourse in academic and intellectual circles and thus includes not only concerns such as building alliances and partnerships or participating in military and economic blocs, but also the debate on the civilisational belonging of Slovakia as a country lying between the East and the West. By this, we mean the choice of values on which the internal policy of the state is to be based. As a rule, the values attributed to the West are associated with the model of liberal democracy, while the 'Eastern' orientation not only includes the concept of close cooperation with the Russian Federation at the military, security or political level, but also values most often associated with the negation of the Western model of development, i.e. the rejection of globalisation, liberal individualism, independence of the state from any religion or ideology, the primacy of

---

[1] Gerulata Technologies. (2022). Top Pro-Russian Sources in Slovakia. Retrieved from https://www.gerulata.com/docs/gerulata_top_pro_russian_sources.pdf

[2] Troebst, S. (2014). 'Post-Panslavism? Political Connotations of Slavicness in 21st Century Europe', In: Gąsior, A., Karl, L., Troebst, S. and Helm, W. (eds) *Post-Panslavismus. Slavizität, Slavische Idee und Antislavismus im 20. und 21. Jahrhundert*. Gottingen: Wallstein Verlag, pp. 17–21.

the rule of law and recognition by the state of civil society as a legitimate political actor. In this respect, the current revival of the rhetoric of Pan-Slavism represents an identitarian and civilisationist response to the liberal version of globalisation and European integration, appealing to tradition and belonging on the basis of the linguistic and constructed cultural proximity of Slavic peoples in opposition to Western, non-Slavic peoples.

Ján Kollár, born in Slovakia, formulated the idea of Pan-Slavism as a cultural concept, which did not, however, translate into his practical political activity. On the other hand, another Slovak, Ľudovít Štúr formulated in his work the idea of Pan-Slavism as a model of social order based on idealised 'Slavic'—or more precisely Russian—traditions, while at the same time rejecting Western liberalism, individualism, private property and the overall Western concept of civilisation as a set of impersonally defined norms and institutions. At the same time, however, he also formulated Pan-Slavism as a foreign policy doctrine with the aim of building a Slavic empire under the domination of Russia and the Orthodox Church.[3] His rejection of the West can also be seen as an attempt to formulate a specifically Slovak (Slavic) *Sonderweg*, the consequence of which would be 'the severing of ties with [Slovakia's] traditional cultural and civilisational space'—with the West.[4]

Even Štúr's close associates were not unequivocally convinced that Slavic reciprocity had to be realised under Russian domination (e.g. Michal M. Hodža or Samo Chalupka), suggesting rather within the Austrian monarchy or in cooperation with the Polish national movement. However, these attitudes did not gain a wider resonance, and so Slovakia is an example of a country in which Slavophilic discourse has amalgamated with pro-Russian discourse, as manifested not only in a positive attitude towards Russia and its culture, but also to a large extent in political sympathies for the Russian regime and support for its foreign policy activities. Particularly in the context of Russia's military aggression against Ukraine, this discourse is also intertwined with a discourse hostile to Ukraine and even with Pan-Russianism,[5] which to varying degrees questions Ukraine's

---

[3] Štúr, Ľ. (1993). *Slovanstvo a svet budúcnosti*. Bratislava: SIMŠ.

[4] Bombík, S. (1993). 'Das Slawenthum... ako Štúrovo odmietnutie Západu', In: Štúr, Ľ. (ed) *Slovanstvo a svet budúcnosti*. Bratislava: SIMŠ, pp. 7–22.

[5] Nemenskyi, O. (2011). 'Panrusizm', *Voprosy Nacionalizma*, 7(3), pp. 34–43.

right to choose its own model of development. In the case of Slovakia after 1989, Slavophilic discourse is thus primarily reflected in relation to the Russian Federation and, to a lesser extent, with Serbia. Slovakia, in terms of its relationship to 'Slavicness' and its belonging to the Slavic world as perceived in this way, represents a specific case among Central European states and states that historically belong to the region of Central Europe, dominated by Western Christianity.

The aim of the present chapter is to identify traces of Pan-Slavism in Slovak political discourse and what impacts on the current form of Slovak domestic and foreign policy these have. Belonging to 'Slavicness' has been one of the important parts of Slovakia's self-identification in relation to other international actors. Therefore, it is legitimate to identify to what extent the idea of Pan-Slavism has contributed to the manner of Slovakia's integration within 'international society'[6] after 1993. By this term, I understand not only inclusion in the international system in the form of membership in international organisations, but especially the construction of a self-image and a perception of the 'other' through values, symbols and meanings. When we speak of the fragmented character of Slavophilic discourse, this means that it enters into interactions with a number of other discourses in Slovak society, and these either enter into a symbiotic relationship or, on the contrary, define themselves in relation to each other. Therefore, it is not enough to deal with Slavophilic discourse alone but also with the discourse of its carriers in the broader context of political and intellectual life in Slovakia and with the individual thematic areas of Slavophilic discourse in Slovakia. Unlike authors who analyse Slavophilic discourse primarily in the context of Russian soft power,[7] my research focuses mainly on an analysis of domestic discourse.

Heritage of the Historical Disputes

Although the early medieval 'Slavic' state of Great Moravia is not defined in the preamble of the Constitution of the Slovak Republic, adopted in

---

[6] Ejdus, F. (2017). 'Conclusion', In: Ejdus, F. (ed) *Memories of Empire and Entry into International Society: Views from the European Periphery*. London: Routledge, pp. 58–164.

[7] Shekhovtsov, A. (2017). *Russia and the Western Far Right. Tango Noir*. Abingdon: Taylor Taylor & Francis Group; Solik, M. (2020). 'Social-Conservative Russian Soft Power: A Traditional Agenda and Illiberal Values as a Source of Attraction or Coercion? A Case Study of Slovakia', *Revista UNISCI – UNISCI Journal*, 18(54), pp. 107–148.

September 1992 as the basis of present Slovak statehood, this founding document of the Slovak Republic refers to its 'historical legacy' and to the 'spiritual bequest of Cyril and Methodius'.[8] As the Slovak political scientist Jozef Bátora stressed, the foreign policy of independent Slovakia after 1993 has also referred in various ways to the heritage of Great Moravia, i.e., of a state in close contact with Byzantium and subject to its cultural influence as materialised in the mission of St Cyril and Methodius, but at the same time part of the West.[9] Slovakia thus perceives itself as a 'rogue state' in an area where the influences of different great powers and civilisational concepts intermingled.

Slovak political thinking after 1989 is to a large extent framed by the rivalry of the ideological heritage of two important Slovak writers and intellectuals from the second half of the twentieth century, Dominik Tatarka and Vladimír Mináč. While Tatarka embodied a civic and non-ethnic vision of the nation, Mináč advocated an ethnic conception of Slovakness.[10] Tatarka espoused continuity with the cultural and political values of the West, while Mináč remained loyal to the communist regime and its ideology. His essays can be described as a successful domestication of communist ideology, incorporating national traditions into official ideology. Later, his ideas were also one of the sources of inspiration for a large number of political actors and intellectuals from the so-called nationally oriented camp. According to Mináč, the romantic features of the Slovak national character—'an oscillation between humility and defiance, between patience and outburst, and a kind of deadly seriousness in the conception of life'—brought Slovaks closer to the East than to the West.[11] In his case, however, one can speak of Russophilia, which

---

[8] *Constitution of the Slovak Republic*. Bratislava: Office of the President of the Slovak Republic. Retrieved from https://www.prezident.sk/upload-files/46422.pdf

[9] Bátora, J. (2017). 'Slovakia's Layered into International Society and the Possibilities of Its Exit', In: Ejdus, F. (ed) *Memories of Empire and Entry into International Society: Views from the European Periphery*. London: Routledge, pp. 138–157.

[10] Bátorová, M. (2015). *Dominik Tatarka: The Slovak Don Quixote*. Frankfurt am Main: Peter Lang; Zenderowski, R. (2007). *Nad Tatrami błyska się... Słowacka tożsamość narodowa w dyskursie politycznym w Republice Słowackiej (1989–2004)*. Warszawa: Wydawnictwo UKSW, p. 212.

[11] Mináč, V. (1976). *Súvislosti. Eseje – state – rozhovory*. Bratislava: Slovenský spisovateľ, p. 88.

he referred to as Slovakia's 'most essential tradition',[12] rather than of Slavophilia. Even Slovak dissent, however, was not united on the question of Slovakia's belonging. The Catholic dissident Ján Čarnogurský remained faithful to the idea of a bridge between East and West, or of a pan-European concept of which Russia should become a part.[13] Eventually, however, Milan Šimečka openly referred to the Soviet model of communism as a 'Russian ideology' and spoke of the continuity of Stalinism with Russian messianic thinking, demanding automatic gratitude from other nations.[14]

These controversies influenced the first years of the democratic transformation and existence of the independent Slovak Republic established in 1993. The new authorities were consensually committed to a programme of European integration, and the idea of joining the EU and NATO was shared by the second government of Vladimír Mečiar, who in 1992 held talks with the Czech representation on the division of the Czech and Slovak Federative Republic. Developments in Russia itself after 1991 were also viewed negatively and with concern. In the 1990s, however, the dominant discussion among Slovak political elites was not so much about a 'Slavic' orientation of foreign policy but rather about the dilemma between a pro-Western, Euro-Atlantic orientation and the development of close relations with Russia, not on the basis of the multilateral principle of several Slavic states but on the basis of bilateral relations. A possible Slavic orientation of foreign policy was hinted at by Mečiar at the adoption of the Declaration on the Sovereignty of the Slovak Republic on 17 July 1992 in the National Council of the Slovak Republic. As the Czechoslovak state still existed, he addressed 'the Czech brothers' and then turned 'to our Slavic brothers, when for centuries our ancestors addressed all the world and called for unity and for the understanding of Slavs'. In this context, he called for a halt to the fighting in Yugoslavia and a search for understanding. He then turned to foreign Slovaks and only

---

[12] Daniška, J. and Majchrák, J. (2014, December 13). Naši rusofili. *Týždeň.sk*. Retrieved from https://www.tyzden.sk/casopis/16780/nasi-rusofili/

[13] Čarnogurský, J. (1997). *Videné od Dunaja*. Bratislava: Kalligram, p. 66.

[14] Šimečka, M. (2000). 'Ztráta skutečnosti', In: Šimečka, M. and Kusý, M. (eds) *Veľký Brat a Veľká Sestra*. Bratislava: Nadácia Milana Šimečku, pp. 131, 150.

in the next sequence to neighbouring states with a call for cooperation, recognition of borders and protection of national minorities.[15] Later the possibility of an Eastern orientation for Slovakia was hinted at by Mečiar, who threatened that 'if they don't want us in the West, we will turn to the East'.[16] However, such an alternative programme of an 'Eastern' or a 'Slavic' foreign policy orientation for Slovakia was not conceptualised. The intensification of cooperation with the Russian Federation in the economic and security spheres compensated for the deterioration in relation to the West. As a result of the increasingly authoritarian elements of the rule of the third Mečiar government (1994–1998), Slovakia was not invited in 1997 to join the first wave of NATO enlargement (unlike its neighbours, the Czech Republic, Hungary and Poland) or to accession negotiations with the EU.

The smaller parties of the ruling coalition—the Slovak National Party (SNS) and the Slovak Workers' Association (ZRS)—openly promoted cooperation with Russia. Both parties promoted the idea of neutrality, of which the Russian Federation was to become guarantor.[17] The SNS, moreover, advocated Slavic reciprocity. In the second half of the 1990s, it maintained contacts with the Serbian Radical Party and the Liberal Democratic Party of Russia. As early as April 1994, an SNS delegation attended the congress of the Liberal Democratic Party of Russia and the subsequent Congress of Slavic and Orthodox Peoples, during which the All-Slavic Parliament was established. The founding charter of this institution was signed by representatives of the SNS, and the congress also discussed the creation of an 'All-Slavic Armed Forces'.[18] The main coalition party—the Movement for a Democratic Slovakia (HZDS), led by Prime Minister Mečiar—verbally supported Slovakia's membership in the EU and NATO but at the same time initiated practical measures that distanced Slovakia

---

[15] National Council of the Slovak Republic. (1992, June 17). *Stenographic record, 3rd session*.

[16] Mesík, J. (2017). 'Spokojní v provincii: slovenská a česká zahraničná politika po roku 1989', In: Dostál, V. and Mesežnikov, G. (eds) *Maximum možného? 25 rokov samostatnej českej a slovenskej zahraničnej politiky. 25 let samostatné české a slovenské zahraniční politiky.* Praha-Bratislava: AMO – IVO, pp. 36, 36–50.

[17] Marušiak, J. (2010). 'Politický slavizmus v slovenskom zahraničnopolitickom myslení po roku 1989', In Ivantyšynová, T. and Kodajová, D. (eds) *Východná dilema strednej Európy*. Bratislava: SDK SVE – Historický ústav SAV, pp. 214–236.

[18] Wolf, K. (1997, August 15). Od Žirinovského k Le Penovi. *Domino Fórum*, p. 2.

from the West (such as ignoring decisions of the Constitutional Court, thwarting a referendum on the direct election of the Slovak President in 1997, controlling the public media and the secret services, and forcing the intervention of these latter in the political struggle). Therefore, K. Henderson describes HZDS as a 'Europhobic' party.[19] Within the HZDS itself, narratives explaining Slovakia's integration failure as being due to the disinterest or outright hostility of the West prevailed at the official level.[20] Less typical was the view of Mináč that justified the need for a strong Russia as guarantor of Slovakia's security ('Better any Russia than none, better a powerful Russia than none') by proposing a threat from Germany or a Western *Drang nach Osten*.[21]

In terms of public opinion, however, the orientation in favour of European integration was clearly predominant in society, with only 10% of country's population wishing to form an alliance with Russia.[22] The new government of Mikuláš Dzurinda announced measures to accelerate the integration processes but had to face a wave of opposition to the Euro-Atlantic orientation of Slovakia during the Kosovo Crisis in 1999, when the Slovak government allowed NATO air force overflights over the territory of Slovakia. The then-opposition (HZDS and SNS) in Parliament accused the government of 'vassalage' and 'treason', describing the attacks against Yugoslavia as a fight against a 'fraternal Slavic nation'.[23] Despite these conflicts, however, the pro-Western option prevailed in Slovak society, and despite the opposition of the right-wing SNS and

---

[19] Haughton, T. (2001). 'HZDS: The Ideology, Organisation and Support Base of Slovakia's Most Successful Party', *Europe-Asia Studies*, 53(5), pp. 745–769; Henderson, K. (2009). 'Europeanization of Political Parties: Redefining Concepts in a United Europe', *Sociológia*, 41(6), pp. 526–538, p. 531.

[20] Šebej, F., Vašečka, M. and Nič, M. (1998). 'Pohľady predstaviteľov slovenských politických a spoločenských elít na bezpečnosť a vstup SR do NATO', In: Bútora, M. and Šebej, F. (eds) *Slovensko v šedej zóne*. Bratislava: IVO, pp. 219–226.

[21] Mináč, V. (1993). *Odkiaľ a kam, Slováci?* Bratislava: Remedium, p. 21; Duleba, A. (1996). *Slepý pragmatizmus slovenskej východnej politiky: Aktuálna agenda slovensko-ruských vzťahov*. Bratislava: RC SFPA, p. 41.

[22] Bútorová, Z. (1998). 'Vývoj názorov verejnosti na vstup Slovenska do NATO', In: Bútora, M. and Šebej, F. (eds) *Slovensko v šedej zone*. Bratislava: IVO, pp. 175–177, 179–180, 167–184.

[23] National Council of the Slovak Republic. (1999, 14–15 April). *Stenographic record, 12th session*.

the pro-Russian Communist Party of Slovakia (KSS), Slovakia became a member of the EU and NATO in 2004.

Marginalisation of the 'Slavophilic' Agenda After 2000

The first years of Slovakia's EU membership were characterised by a consensus among its decisive political forces on foreign policy issues. This was the period of the governments of Mikuláš Dzurinda (2002–2006)— a coalition of the centre-right parties—and of Robert Fico, the leader of the Smer-Social Democracy (Smer-SD) party (2006–2010). An erosion of this consensus at the level of political elites occurred in 2013–2014, after the so-called Revolution of Dignity triggered by the refusal of Ukrainian President Viktor Yanukovych to sign the Association Agreement with the EU, after which the Russian Federation annexed Crimea and started supporting armed separatists in the Donbas.

Fico, still as leader of the opposition party, first visited Moscow in January 2001, criticising the then-government's policy towards Russia.[24] In later years, he in turn referred to his political role models, the American President Franklin D. Roosevelt and Russia's President Vladimir Putin.[25] In 2005, he criticised the centre-right government of Dzurinda for allegedly ignoring relations with Russia. He also spoke of the need to 'form one's own view' of states such as Russia, Belarus, Cuba or Vietnam.[26] Although he toned down his pro-Russian rhetoric on the eve of the election campaign, he did form a coalition with the former Europhobic parties HZDS and SNS after his 2006 election victory. The new coalition weakened the original Euro-Atlantic dimension of Slovakia's foreign policy, for instance, on the issue of the U.S. missile shield, in which it refused to participate. As prime minister of the Slovak Republic, Fico espoused the idea of Slavic reciprocity in the spirit of Ján Kollár's

---

[24] Lewkowicz, Ł. (2020). *Wpływy rosyjskie w Republice Słowackiej. Prace IEŚ*. Lublin: Instytut Europy Środkowej, p. 65.

[25] Marušiak, J. (2006). 'Fenomén strany Smer: Medzi „pragmatizmom" a sociálnou demokraciou', *Středoevropské politické studie*, 8(1), pp. 19–55.

[26] Marušiak, J. (2010). *Politický slavizmus...*, op. cit.

concepts, i.e. in its cultural dimension—to which, however, some Slovak intellectuals reacted as to the revival of a 'sick and outdated' idea.[27]

On the other hand, despite Fico's pro-Russian statements, we cannot speak of a clear discontinuity in Slovak foreign policy. Slovakia supported Ukraine's aspirations for EU and NATO membership and was also an active supporter of the EU Eastern Partnership programme. On the question of Slovakia's position on the recognition of Kosovo, Slavophilic rhetoric in reaction to NATO military action against Yugoslavia in 1999 was replaced by legalist argumentation in 2007, when Slovakia based its rejectionist position on arguments of international law and of the principle of the inviolability of state borders.[28] This position was adopted by both coalition and opposition parties except for the Hungarian Coalition Party, representing members of the Hungarian minority.

Among the most prominent party actors promoting the principles of Pan-Slavism in the period under review was the SNS, which did gradually abandon its programme of closer cooperation with Russia and rejection of NATO membership. However, it continued to speak of a need to develop 'superior and intensive relations with the Slavic nation states'.[29] The Slavophilic concept was presented in that period primarily as an identity project, not as a political programme. In contrast to the SNS, this agenda was elaborated in more detail by more radical political entities, such as the KSS, which rejected Slovakia's membership in the EU and NATO. During the 2009 presidential elections, its candidate, Milan Sidor—who was also a regional functionary of the Association of Slavic Reciprocity (the successor organisation of the pro-regime Czechoslovak-Soviet Friendship Union operating before 1989)—ran on a Pan-Slavic platform.

Like many other representatives of Slavophilic politics, Sidor presented the cooperation of Slavic peoples, especially in the form of the convergence of Slavic cultures and the cooperation of Slavic states, as a counterbalance to the uncultured tendencies coming to Slovakia 'from across the Atlantic'. Linguistic, cultural and spiritual proximity were to create the preconditions for economic cooperation between Slavic nations. Sidor

---

[27] Kusý, M. (2007, May 11). Chorá a prekonaná idea. *Sme*, 11 May.

[28] National Council of the Slovak Republic. (2007, March 28). *Vyhlásenie NRSR k riešeniu budúceho štatútu srbskej provincie Kosovo.*

[29] Marušiak, J. (2010). *Politický slavizmus...*, op. cit.

combined the 'Slavic' programme with a leftist program, in particular, the promotion of the family and social justice, trade unionism and the legal protection of the interests of the working people.[30] Other, usually marginal, protagonists of 'Slavic' politics were also close to the structures of the pre-1989 communist regime.

In addition to the radical neo-communist left, the radical right-wing nationalist organisation the Slovak Renaissance Movement (*Slovenské hnutie obrody*, SHO) also subscribes to a programme of Slavic reciprocity and, paradoxically, claims the legacy of Andrej Hlinka and Jozef Tiso, President of Hitler's puppet Slovak State (1939–1945), an ally of Nazi Germany whose military forces participated in the war against the USSR. It also opposes the Hungarian and Roma minorities. However, the SHO sees the programme of Slavic reciprocity and 'Slavic Empire' as an alternative to the European or Euro-Atlantic anchoring of Slovakia. The SHO supported the regime of Alexander Lukashenko in Belarus and warned of 'the danger of Freemasonic lodges and Jewish world government'.[31] It was transformed into a political party in 2019 but received only 0.06% of the valid votes in the parliamentary elections the next year.[32]

Similarly, the more successful competitor of the SHO, the association Slovak Community (*Slovenská pospolitnosť*), which since its foundation in 1996 has espoused the ideals of the Slavic civilisational mission and the legacy of the fascist Slovak state, also espoused the ideals of Pan-Slavism. In 2005–2006, it operated under the name National Party-Slovak Community, and, after being banned due to its extremist programme, since 2010 as the People's Party-Our Slovakia (ĽSNS), led by Marián Kotleba. At that time, this party pushed the Slavophilic discourse to the side-lines in favour of an anti-Roma and anti-Western agenda.[33]

---

[30] Marušiak, J. (2010). *Politický slavizmus...*, op. cit. Milan Sidor won 1.11% of the valid votes in the presidential election. See *Elections of the President of the Slovak Republic 2009. First Round*. Retrieved from https://volby.statistics.sk/prez/prez2009/jsp/okres/tab7.jsp.htm

[31] Mikušovič, D. (2004). *Mimoparlamentná krajná pravica na Slovensku*. Bachelor theses. Brno: Masaryk University in Brno, p. 44.

[32] *Elections to the National Council of the Slovak Republic 2020. Valid votes cast for political parties*. Retrieved from https://volby.statistics.sk/nrsr/nrsr2020/en/data02.html

[33] Kluknavská, A. (2013). 'Od Štúra k parazitom: Tematická adaptácia krajnej pravice v parlamentných voľbách na Slovensku', *Politologický časopis – Czech Journal of Political Science*, 20(3), pp. 258–281; Smolík, J. (2010). 'Slovenská neparlamentní krajní pravice: Politické organizace a strategie', *Politologická revue*, XVI(1), pp. 29–52.

Besides the Association of Slavic Reciprocity, the Pan-Slavic Union established in 2009 also subscribed to Pan-Slavic ideas. At the time of its establishment, the cooperation of Slavic nations was understood mainly as a cultural project, not a political one. The idea of a common Slavic state was rejected.[34] On the other hand, the Union advocated the accession of all Slavic states to the EU. However, one of its representatives, Drahoslav Machala, has pointed to the allegedly subordinate position in the EU of the Slavs, who must only 'copy and implement the concepts ... as ready-made recipes put forward by the Germans and the French'. He has also proposed the creation of a grouping based on cultural and historical belonging similar to the British Commonwealth or the Community of Francophone States. In the political sphere, however, he does not talk about the identification of common 'Slavic' interests, nor about the institutional arrangement of their relations. In the cultural sphere, he has spoken of a need to develop cultural exchanges, to create a Permanent Exposition of Slavic Reciprocity with the participation of the individual Slavic nations, or, for example, to create a statue of the Slavic pagan God Perun on Kráľova hoľa Hill.[35] Several collaborators of this organisation were close to the parties of the governmental organisation; Machala, for instance, worked as an advisor to Prime Minister Fico (2006–2010), while the historian Anton Hrnko and the group's chairman Milan Janičina later became deputy chairmen of the SNS, which in 2016–2020 acted as a junior coalition partner of Smer-SD.

In terms of the formation of Slavophilic discourse, the Slovak-Russian Society—whose chairman is Ján Čarnogurský, former chairman of the KDH (1990–2000) and prime minister of the Slovak Republic (1991–1992)—established itself in Slovakia in the post-accession period. Čarnogurský promoted a pan-European agenda rejecting confrontation between the West and Russia. It emphasises the closeness of Slovak and Russian culture and the importance of Russia for European civilisation. In his words, close cooperation with the USA does not serve Slovakia's

[34] Panslovanská únia. (2009). 'Prečo sa hlásime k panslavizmu', In: *Konferencia Panslavizmus, tradícia a perspektívy*. Bratislava: Panslovanská únia, p. 77, pp. 76–79.

[35] Machala, D. (2009). 'Prečo má Slovanstvo budúcnosť, In: *Konferencia Panslavizmus, tradícia a perspektívy*. Bratislava: Panslovanská únia, pp. 65–74.

interests.[36] He has also argued in favour of strengthening bilateral relations with Russia on historical grounds, based on the experience of the generation of the movement inspired by Ľudovít Štúr, the founders of the *Matica slovenská*, and the participants in the anti-fascist Slovak National Uprising in 1944.[37] Even in the post-accession period, he remained opposed to any further expansion of NATO and its military bases to the east: 'Russia is very often perceived by the West as the source of its threat. It is a historic challenge for the European Union to change this perception of the West in Russia'.[38]

In the cultural sphere, the most important writers' organisation in Slovakia is the Slovak Writers' Association, which maintains contacts with the official writers' organisation in Belarus, as well as the *Matica slovenská*. In the period under review, Slavophilic discourse asserted itself primarily as a transnational identity project.[39] Although the ideas of European integration and Euro-Atlantic cooperation on security issues were not openly questioned by its actors, they were perceived with reserve, as a potential source of threat to Slovak sovereignty and the Slavic community. At the same time, however, they did not present political alternatives to Slovakia's Western civilisational orientation. A critical distance from liberalism and an inclination towards traditionalism was also a characteristic feature of Slavophilic discourse.

SLAVICNESS AS AN ALTERNATIVE? THE BEGINNING OF THE CRISIS IN UKRAINE (2013–2014) AND ITS CONSEQUENCES

The immediate impetus for the renewed controversy over Slovakia's foreign policy orientation was the so-called Ukrainian Crisis associated with the Russian intervention in 2014, which resulted in a long-lasting

---

[36] Čarnogurský, J. (2009, July 21). Slovensko ako spojivo medzi Východom a Západom Európy. *Aktuality.sk*. Retrieved from https://www.aktuality.sk/clanok/141216/carnogursky-slovensko-by-malo-zapad-a-vychod-spajat-nie-rozdelovat/

[37] Čarnogurský, J. (2005, March 29). Slovensko kdesi medzi Ruskom a USA. *Pravda*, 29. March.

[38] Čarnogurský, J. (2005). 'Na Európu treba veriť', *OS*, 9(1–2), p. 94.

[39] Paulovicova, N. (2020). 'The Far Right ĽSNS in Slovakia and Its Reconstruction of the Nation', *Rocznik Instytutu Europy Środkowo-Wschodniej*, 18(1), pp. 177–197, https://doi.org/10.36874/RIESW.2020.1.10

conflict between the West and Russia. However, this controversy was foreshadowed by the rise of anti-Western sentiment in the wake of the global financial crisis. In Slovakia, frustration with the social consequences of the post-communist transformation of the 1990s combined with fears of a further deterioration in living conditions. According to the European Bank for Reconstruction and Development (EBRD), more than 70% of Slovak households in 2011 blamed the West for the crisis, followed by Serbia with around 65%. It was in these countries that anti-Western sentiment was strongest among the post-communist states.[40]

The presence of these sentiments contributed to the contradictory reactions of Slovak political elites to the events in Ukraine. While there was a consensus among them regarding support for Ukraine's territorial integrity, a conflict arose as to how to proceed against Russia. While Prime Minister Robert Fico, who was replaced as the head of government by Peter Pellegrini in 2018, and their Smer-SD party verbally criticised the policy of sanctions towards the Russian Federation and refused to label Russia as an enemy, President Andrej Kiska (elected in 2014 with the support of the right-wing opposition parties) supported the sanctions, speaking of Russia's direct involvement in the fighting in Eastern Ukraine on the side of the separatists in the Donetsk and Luhansk regions, and also advocating the establishment of a NATO base in Slovakia. Kiska also accused Russia of conducting a disinformation campaign against the EU. President Kiska's line was continued by the new Slovak President, Zuzana Čaputová, who was elected to office in 2019. Robert Fico referred to the conflict that erupted in Ukraine in 2014 as a geopolitical dispute between Russia and the USA.[41]

Until 2017, only the far-right ĽSNS among relevant political parties clearly supported the pro-Russian stance. In January 2014, its chairman and the then-chairman of the Banská Bystrica Self-Governing Region Marian Kotleba wrote a letter to then-Ukrainian President Viktor Yanukovych in which he urged him 'for the sake of the future of the Slavic peoples, not to give in to groups that are trying to break the territorial

---

[40] European Bank for Reconstruction and Development. (2011). *Transition Report 2011. Crisis and Transition: The People's Perspective.*

[41] Marušiak, J. (2019). 'Slovakia's National Interest and Slovak-Russian Bilateral Relations in the Context of the Ukrainian Crisis (2013–2018)', In: Brhlíková, R. (ed) *Seeking the National Interest: Slovakia after 15 Years of EU and NATO Accession.* Stuttgart: ibidem-Verlag, pp. 155–178.

integrity of his country by street riots and attacks on the government institutions of its representatives'. The letter then went on to describe Slovakia's experience with the EU as one of a loss of sovereignty, dictates from Brussels and economic decline.[42]

The Smer-SD MP Ľuboš Blaha became particularly involved in creating a positive image of Russia, referring to it as a friend of Slovakia and advocating cooperation between the two countries.[43] He blamed the West for the conflict in Eastern Ukraine and the general rise in tensions in international relations, referring to Russia's critics as Russophobes. Not only Blaha but also several pro-Russian websites spread a narrative about the rise of fascism in Ukraine. The annexation of Crimea was openly defended only by marginal politicians, such as the chairman of the Slovak-Russian Society, Ján Čarnogurský—who as an independent candidate in the 2014 presidential elections won only 0.64% of valid votes[44]—or the Nation and Justice (*Národ a spravodlivosť*) Party, led by former SNS politicians Anna Belousovová and Sergei Khelemendik (the latter born in Kyiv).[45] This party also received only marginal support in the European Parliament elections held in the same year (1.38%).[46] The 2016 parliamentary elections were dominated primarily by the refugee crisis, with the issue of relations with Russia taking a back seat.

The politicisation of pro-Russian and Slavophilic discourse can be spoken about after the 2016 parliamentary elections. Although the official course of the Slovak government was oriented towards supporting Ukraine, Slavophilic discourse was mainly developed by the coalition SNS,

---

[42] Aktuality.sk (2014, January 31). Kotleba napísal Janukovyčovi list: Neustúpte! Retrieved from https://www.aktuality.sk/clanok/245111/kotleba-napisal-janukovycovi-list-neustupte/

[43] Blaha zo Smeru pred odchodom do Moskvy: Rusko nie je nepriateľ (2014, June 25). *Plus jeden deň*. Retrieved from https://www1.pluska.sk/spravy/z-domova/blaha-smeru-pred-odchodom-moskvy-rusko-nie-je-nepriatel

[44] Čarnogurský, J. (2014, March 21). Krym patrí Rusku. *Blog.sme.sk*. Retrieved from https://blog.sme.sk/carnogursky/politika/krym-patri-rusku; *Elections of the President of the Slovak Republic 2014. First Round. Results of voting*. Retrieved from https://volby.statistics.sk/prez/prez2014/Prezident-dv/Tabulka7_en.html

[45] Belousovová, A. (2014, March 22). Prečo je dobré mať dobré vzťahy s Ruskom. *Chelemendik.sk*. Retrieved from http://www.chelemendik.sk/_Anna_Belousovova_Preco_je_dobre_mat_dobre_vztahy_s_Ruskom_579680181.html

[46] *Elections to the European Parliament 2014. Results of voting*. Retrieved from https://volby.statistics.sk/ep/ep2014/EP-dv/Tabulka3_en.html

for instance, during visits by its chairman, Andrej Danko (who was also the chairman of the Slovak parliament) to the Russian Federation, where in 2017 he was one of the few EU representatives to be granted the opportunity to give a speech in the State Duma. He justified the need for dialogue with the Russian Federation precisely by its Slavic affiliation ('our culture, history, and perception of our surroundings are intertwined and close'). According to Danko, Slovaks are part of the 'Slavic world' and 'peace is not possible without a strong Russia'.[47]

Danko subsequently visited the Serbian National Assembly, where he delivered a similar Slavophilic speech in which he justified his support for Serbia's EU accession on the grounds of belonging to the 'Slavic world'.[48] Although the SNS did not openly question the foreign policy direction of the Slovak Republic, in practice, it blocked the adoption of basic documents regulating the security policy of the Slovak Republic, such as the Security and Defence Strategy of the Slovak Republic, which referred to the Russian Federation as a security threat. Besides Slavophilic rhetoric, Danko also declared his sympathy for the reforms being implemented in Poland by the PiS and in Hungary by the Fidesz government headed by Prime Minister Viktor Orbán. He himself has declared that he wants to become the Slovak Orbán.[49]

On the eve of the presidential elections in 2019, the so-called National Conference (an allegedly non-partisan forum of 'nationally oriented' intellectuals and politicians) appointed as the presidential candidate of 'all pro-national and pro-Slavic forces' the former President of the Supreme Court of the Slovak Republic nominated during the Mečiar era, Štefan Harabin (1998–2003 and 2009–2014).[50] This ad hoc grouping also formed a shadow cabinet, which included a representative for Slavic reciprocity issues. Part of Harabin's programme was 'deepening the ideas of

---

[47] Danko, A. (2017, November 17). Prejav predsedu NR SR A. Danka v Štátnej Dume RF, *Mepoförum*. Retrieved from http://mepoforum.sk/staty-regiony/europa/staty-eu-plus/vysehradska-4/slovensko/prejav-predsedu-nr-sr-a-danka-v-statnej-dume-rf/

[48] Danko, A. (2018, June 7). Sme Slovania, a preto spoločne zachovajme a rozvíjajme náš slovanský svet. *National Council of the Slovak Republic*. Retrieved from https://www.nrsr.sk/web/Default.aspx?sid=udalosti/udalost&MasterID=54664

[49] Praus, L. (2018, October 24). Danko chce nový program podľa Orbánovho Fideszu, *Sme.sk*, Retrieved from https://domov.sme.sk/c/20945412/danko-chce-byt-ako-orban-zaskocil-tym-aj-vlastnych.html

[50] In 2006–2009 Harabin served as a Minister of Justice, appointed by ĽS-HZDS.

Slavic reciprocity as a cultural and value line'.[51] In the presidential elections, Harabin came in third place at 14.34%, which motivated him to become the electoral leader of the newly formed Fatherland (*Vlasť*) party with a national-populist programme, which, however, did not significantly succeed in the 2020 parliamentary elections, as he received only 2.93% of the vote.[52] Although the party presented a nativist and Eurosceptic programme, it rejected considerations of withdrawal from the EU and NATO. In the election campaign, it described the EU as a source of threat to national identity and sovereignty, especially for small states.[53]

Especially after anti-corruption protests in February–March 2018, which resulted in the resignation of long-time Prime Minister Robert Fico (2006–2010 and 2012–2018), we can also speak of a radicalisation in the politics of the Smer-SD party. The party subsequently strengthened its pro-Russian rhetoric. Its representatives compared the 2018 protests to the Ukrainian 'Maidan' and, in August 2020, to the protests in Belarus against the falsification of the presidential election results: 'In Belarus, I see an attempt to implement the model used in Ukraine, but elements of which we also saw in Slovakia, where the murder of a journalist and his memory were grossly misused politically to attack legitimate government power'.[54] The pro-Russian rhetoric, coupled with expressions of nostalgia for the communist regime, is characteristic of the party's deputy, Ľuboš Blaha, who became deputy chairman in 2020. He describes Russia as a friend of Slovakia: 'Russia is beautiful, Russia is wise, Russia is mature'.[55] He publicly defines himself against anti-communism, right-wing liberalism and Russophobia.[56] Blaha, too, uses Slavic rhetoric to justify his

---

[51] Harabín prijal výzvu stať sa „národným" kandidátom na prezidenta (2018, July 9). *Slovensko-ruská spoločnosť*. Retrieved from http://www.srspol.sk/clanek-harabin-prijal-vyzvu-stat-sa-narodnym-kandidatom-na-prezidenta-16984.html

[52] *Election of the President of the Slovak Republic, First Round 2019*. Retrieved from https://volby.statistics.sk/prez/prez2019/en/data01.html; *Elections to the National Council of the Slovak Republic 2020*, op. cit.

[53] Vlasť. (2019). *Strana Vlasť: Program*.

[54] Trend.sk. Fico: Slovensko by nemalo zasahovať do vnútorných záležitostí Bieloruska (2020, August 19). *Trend.sk*. Retrieved from https://www.trend.sk/spravy/fico-slovensko-nemalo-zasahovat-vnutornych-zalezitosti-bieloruska

[55] Blaha, Ľ. (2019, July 3). V Moskve [Facebook status update]. https://www.facebook.com/LBlaha/videos/2369786069771852/

[56] Blaha, Ľ. (n.d.) Facebook page. https://www.facebook.com/LBlaha

alliance with Russia ('Slavs stick together and will not be upset by the Western secret services'[57]).

However, elements of Slavophilic discourse also appear in environments that do not clearly define themselves as 'national' or 'Slavic' in orientation. This is the case, for example, with the left-wing columnist and peace activist Eduard Chmelár, who served as chairman of the left-wing Socialisti.sk party in 2019–2020. Although he participated in protests against the annexation of Crimea by the Russian Federation in 2014, he gradually began to move closer to the positions of the Russian Federation in his assessments of international developments. He described the West's policy towards Russia as 'chauvinistic'[58] and he is critical of the policy of sanctions against it. He has argued that, thanks to the Putin-Lavrov tandem, 'the Russians have the most capable state leadership since Tsar Peter the Great',[59] and described Russian foreign policy as 'a voice of constructive sobriety and restraint, thanks to which the world is not yet at war'.[60] He has proposed the creation of a grouping of Slavic states within the EU to replace the Visegrad Group, whose potential has supposedly been exhausted. Slavic reciprocity, according to Chmelár, is to 'elevate the sense of...national existence to humanity'.[61] In the 2019 presidential elections, Chmelár received 2.74% of the vote, while in the parliamentary elections the next year, Chmelár's party did not record any significant success, either (only 0.55%).[62]

---

[57] Blaha, Ľ. (2021, April 19). Ak má niekto pocit... [Facebook status update]. https://www.facebook.com/2047997592105476/photos/a.2052950104943558/2931271990444694/

[58] Chmelár, E. (2015, March 13). Fašizmus je vojna. [Facebook status update]. https://www.facebook.com/ChmelarEduard/photos/a.328767897155109/900503179981575

[59] Ruský diplomat Lavrov na Slovensku: Čaká ho kritika od prezidenta?! (2015, April 4). *Čas.sk*. Retrieved from https://www.cas.sk/clanok/312847/rusky-diplomat-lavrov-na-slovensku-caka-ho-kritika-od-prezidenta/

[60] Chmelár, E. (2020, September 23). Porovnajte prejavy týchto dvoch lídrov. [Facebook status update]. https://www.facebook.com/ChmelarEduard/photos/a.328767897155109/3597633013601898/?type=3

[61] Chmelár, E. (2018, November 6). Mier v Európe nie je možný bez mieru medzi slovanskými štátmi. [Facebook status update]. https://www.facebook.com/ChmelarEduard/posts/2126028790762335/

[62] *Election of the President of the Slovak Republic, First Round 2019...*, op. cit.; *Elections to the National Council of the Slovak Republic 2020...*, op. cit.

Pro-Russian sentiments are the result of a range of protest sentiments, whether anti-Western, illiberal or anti-globalist. However, the conflict between the West and Russia has contributed to the revival of the hitherto marginalised Pan-Slavist agenda and its shift from being of a predominantly intellectual character to being part of political debate. Some segments of the pro-Russian scene have begun to instrumentalise these sentiments. If in the past Slavophilic discourse did not necessarily imply an inclination towards Russia, in the post-2014 political sphere one can speak of a merging of Pan-Slavism with the pro-Russian orientation. In this case, appeals to 'Slavicness' may 'soften' the pro-Russian content of some political messages, as it obscures the fact that it is primarily about supporting Russia.

Non-Partisan Actors in Slavophilic Discourse

Slavophilic discourse at the level of political parties has a marginal position. Parties that profile themselves on this agenda generally do not record significant electoral success. On the other hand, the Slavophilic agenda may expand in Slovakia, insofar as polls confirm that Slovakia's identity as part of the West is not a given. This geopolitical and civilisational hesitancy in Slovak society is also confirmed by surveys conducted by the Globsec think tank between 2017 and 2019, when only 21–23% of respondents considered Slovakia to be part of the West, while 9–13% claimed that Slovakia belongs to the East and about half (42–56%) claimed that Slovakia is 'somewhere in between'.[63]

Slavophilic identity concepts are more actively promoted by NGOs. This applies to several organisations active in the field of culture and education, such as the Slovak Writers' Association, where Pan-Slavist ideas appear on, among others, the pages of its magazine *Literary Weekly* (*Literárny týždenník*), but also the *Matica slovenská*, where Slavophilic discourse has been strengthened, especially after the election of Marian Gešper as its chairman in 2017. He defined as partners of the *Matica*,

---

[63] Globsec. (2019). *GLOBSEC Trends 2019 Central & Eastern Europe. 30 Years After the Fall of the Iron Curtain.* Bratislava: Globsec.

in addition to churches and civic associations, also 'national and Slavic-oriented associations'.[64] Given its historical role as a key cultural institution for Slovaks in the nineteenth and twentieth centuries, the *Matica slovenská* enjoys considerable moral authority. Several of its representatives have actively supported national-conservative entities such as the SNS and HZDS, and in later years also Smer-SD. In 2016, its former chairman, Marián Tkáč also received the chairman of the far-right ĽSNS, Marián Kotleba.[65] In later years, however, its political influence waned.

On the other hand, political overlap can be observed in other Slavophilic groupings, such as the Association of Slovak Intelligentsia (ZSI), which since 2019 has been building on the activities of older, similarly focused associations such as the Society of Slovak Intelligentsia '*Korene*' (Roots) and the Permanent Conference of Slovak Intelligentsia Slovakia Plus. It promotes an agenda advocating the 'political neutrality' of Slovakia, 'cooperation with the Eastern states', and the creation of a Community of Slavic Nations and States as an international grouping. Another aim of the organisation is the protection of the state sovereignty of Slovakia and 'the spiritual anchoring of the Slovaks in Christianity and in [...] native culture'.[66] Roman Michelko, a leading representative of the ZSI, was a member of the Vlasť party in 2019–2020, for which he also stood as a candidate in the parliamentary elections. Although he has advocated the decriminalisation of Jozef Tiso, he also collaborates with the portal *Veci verejné* (Public Affairs), which is a follow-up to the radical left-wing and nominally anti-fascist portal *Dav Dva* (Crowd Two).[67] The Slavica association, linked to the Nitrava publishing house through its chairman Miloš Zverina, is also oriented towards promoting 'Slavic reciprocity and the rich cultural heritage of the Slavs'. Zverina, as a candidate

---

[64] Kerný, D. (2018, January 21). Opodstatnenosť Matice a prepojenie národných tém. *Slovenské národné noviny*. Retrieved from https://snn.sk/news/opodstatnenost-matice-a-prepojenie-narodnych-tem/

[65] Golianová, V., and Kazharski, A. (2020). 'The Unsolid', *The RUSI Journal*, 165(4), pp. 10–21, https://doi.org/10.1080/03071847.2020.1796521

[66] Vyšná, M. (2019, November 25). 'Nastupujúca generácia slovenskej inteligencie vyhlásila svoj Generačný program 2020', In: *Združenie slovenskej inteligencie – official website*. Retrieved from https://www.zsi.sk/nastupujuca-generacia-slovenskej-inteligencie-vyhlasila-svoj-generacny-program-2020/

[67] DAV Dva (DAV Two) was supposed to be a continuation of the magazine of Slovak nationally oriented communist intellectuals DAV in the years 1924–1937.

of the ĽSNS for the European Parliament in 2019, advocated for the 'urgent' establishment of the Community of Slavic Nations.[68]

The Pan-Slavist agenda is also present in some paramilitary structures. In addition to the Volunteer Detachment (*Oddiel Dobrovoľník*), which is part of the aforementioned SHO and is named after the Russian military club with which the SHO maintains contacts, another paramilitary organisation, the Slovak Conscripts (*Slovenskí branci*)—which rejects the far-right ideology of the ĽSNS and the legacy of the regime of Jozef Tiso—is better known but does not have a positive attitude towards Slovakia's membership in NATO. The leader of the organisation, Peter Švrček publicly has declared his sympathies towards Russia and the ideas of Slavic cooperation. SHO cooperates with the Russian radical nationalist and Orthodox fundamentalist movement *Narodnyi Sobor* (People's Cathedral/Council) supporting the regime of Vladimir Putin, along with some Serbian and Polish radical right pro-Russian organisations. Švrček received training from the *Stiag* (Flag) and the Russian Cossacks, while the Slovak Conscripts cooperate with Russian ex-Spetsnaz (former Russian special operation forces) instructors.[69] One Slovak Conscripts member, Martin Keprta took part in the war in Ukraine after 2014 on the side of the separatists from Donetsk.[70] Professional soldiers were also involved in the training of the Slovak Conscripts until 2020, after which the cooperation of members of the Slovak Armed Forces with this organisation was banned by the Slovak Ministry of Defence.[71]

The media is an important component of the Slavophilic scene. They are primarily profiled in the online space. In terms of influence on the public, among the most significant are, besides Ľuboš Blaha's Facebook

---

[68] Benčík, J. (2019, May 22). Tak ako, pán Kotleba? Je najvyšší čas vystúpiť z EÚ, alebo kandidovať do Európskeho parlamentu? *DenníkN – blog*. Retrieved from https://dennikn.sk/blog/1474252/tak-ako-pan-kotleba-je-najvyssi-cas-vystupit-z-eu-alebo-kandidovat-do-europskeho-parlamentu/

[69] Mesežnikov, G. and Bránik, R. (2017). *Hatred, Violence and Comprehensive Military Training*. Budapest: Political Capital, pp. 8, 20.

[70] Kern, M. (2015, February 21). Cvičia mučenie, do lesa nosia samopaly, vychovali bojovníka pre Donbas. *Denník N*. Retrieved from https://dennikn.sk/53992/behaju-po-lesoch-samopalmi-vychovali-bojovnika-za-novorusko/

[71] Niňajová, E. (2021, January 13). Slovenskí branci pobehujú ozbrojení po lesoch, šíria nenávisť o Rómoch a LGBTI. *Startitup.sk*. Retrieved from https://www.startitup.sk/slovenski-branci-pobehuju-ozbrojeni-po-lesoch-siria-nenavist-o-romoch-a-lgbti-su-bez-pecnostne-riziko-vravia-odbornici/

profiles, the portal Free Broadcaster (*Slobodný vysielač*), the monthly magazines *Extra Plus* and *Earth & Age* (*Zem a vek*), the online newspapers *Hlavné správy* (*Main News*) and *Hlavný denník* (*Main Daily*), the Internet television *Slovan* and the *Slovenské slovo* (Slovak Word) Internet portal, published by the Pan-Slavic Union, which is committed to a programme of Slavic reciprocity. On the left side of the political spectrum, pro-Russian narratives are also disseminated by the portal Public Affairs (*Veci verejné*), a successor to *Dav Dva*, and the portal *Slovo* (successor to the weekly of the same name). The websites of representatives of political parties (e.g. Eduard Chmelár, Štefan Harabin, the current chairman of Socialisti.sk Artur Bekmatov, and websites close to the ĽSNS and the Republika party) have a significant impact on the public as well, while media oriented exclusively towards Pan-Slavism have a weaker impact. Before the Russian aggression against Ukraine, the Russian portal Sputnik was popular in Slovakia, but it did not have a Slovak editorial office, only a Czech one. However, contacts with Russian media were mediated by, among others, the editor of the *Hlavné správy* portal, Yevgeny Paltsev, who was also an associate of the *Rossiya Segodnya* (Russia Today) agency.[72] Tibor 'Eliot' Rostas, the publisher of the magazine and the Internet portal *Zem & vek*, planned to create a Slavic media holding company and sought the support of the Russian Federation in this regard.[73] The organisations Association of Slavic Reciprocity, *Matica slovenská*, Slavica, the literary historian Viktor Timura, and the publisher Tibor Eliot Rostas formed the core of the Slovak delegation at the 2017 Slavic Congress in Moscow. The congress was conducted in a Russian nationalist spirit; in the words of the chairman of the Russian All-Slavic Union, Oleg Platonov, who organised the congress, the task of the Slavs is 'to liberate the world from the influence of Western civilization', for which it is necessary to create a 'union state of Russia' with Russia at its core and as the guarantor of its success.[74] Pro-Russian and Slavophilic-oriented organised groups as well as informal initiatives and individuals

---

[72] Šnídl, V. (2018, November 14). Propagandu pre Hlavné správy píše Rus, ktorý sa chodí radiť do agentúry Kremľa. *DenníkN*. Retrieved from https://dennikn.sk/128 8348/propagandu-pre-hlavne-spravy-pise-rus-ktory-sa-chodi-radit-do-agentury-kremla-odomknute/

[73] Mesežnikov and Bránik, op. cit., p. 43.

[74] Karpov, M. (2017, May 29). *Gde zh russkiy dux? Vseslavjanskiy syezd reshaet, kak snova sdelat' Rus' velikoj*. Retrieved from https://lenta.ru/articles/2017/05/29/soborno/

form an extensive subculture. NGOs are often linked directly or through their members to political parties and the media, and individual groups support each other.

Slavophilic Discourse in Slovakia

The discourse of the so-called Slavophilic subculture is characterised primarily by support for Russia to varying degrees and, after 2014, by a contrary negative attitude towards another Slavic state, Ukraine, which is why we can speak of pseudo-Pan-Slavism in this case. One of the underlying themes is a negative attitude towards the West, which allegedly does not see Slavs as equals. There are also accusations of anti-Slavic racism: 'As an inferior and obviously inferior race, the Anglo-Saxons are arrogant towards Slavic states not only in politics'.[75] Blaha, for example, regarding the case of the death of Slovak citizen Jozef Chovanec in a police raid in Brussels, spoke of 'racial police brutality', and in the context of the race riots in the USA in 2020 paraphrased the slogan 'Black Lives Matter' into 'Slavic Lives Matter'. According to him, 'Slavic lives do not matter as much as African lives'.[76]

The motif of the victimisation of Russia and Slavs in general is also important. The aim of the West is supposed to be the destruction of Russia, while the Slavic peoples, whom the West is driving against itself, are also dragged into the war against Russia.[77] Russia is portrayed as an object of Russophobia. On the contrary, the West—as represented by the EU and the USA—is portrayed either directly as an enemy or as an actor that limits the sovereignty of Slovakia and the Slavic states.[78] Blaha even equates the West with fascism: 'It will be exactly 80 years since the fascists from the West invaded the Soviet Union and systematically murdered

[75] Harabin, Š. (2020, August 24). Ako k podradným a zjavne menejcenným rasám. [Facebook status update]. https://www.facebook.com/permalink.php?story_fbid=2868043300139163&id=1680731138870391

[76] Blaha, Ľ. (2021, June 29). Otvorený list veľvyslancovi Belgicka vo veci zabitia Jozefa Chovanca. [Facebook status update]. https://www.facebook.com/permalink.php?story_fbid=2990344867870739&id=2047997592105476

[77] Blaha, Ľ. (2022, February 1). Zajtra nad ránom to príde. [Facebook status update]. https://www.facebook.com/photo/?fbid=483285696502050&set=a.394303938733560

[78] Chmelár, E. (2018, November 6). Mier v Európe nie je možný bez mieru medzi slovanskými štátmi. [Facebook status update]. https://www.facebook.com/ChmelarEduard/posts/2126028790762335/

millions of Russians, Belarusians, and Ukrainians. [...] They exterminated a total of 30 million Slavs'. In the context of the anniversary of the Battle of Stalingrad, he said:

> 'Stalingrad is incredibly relevant today. It is a symbol of Western arrogance. [...] This is the same lesson that the West will receive from President Putin if it continues to carve up and further cheer on war. The Russians don't start wars, they end them. [...] Stalingrad is a great symbol of human history. It is a symbol that no matter how hard the West tries to conquer us Slavs, they will never succeed. We will always win.'[79]

In addition to such extreme attributes, there are also associations of the West with 'modern paganism', subversion and Satanism, against which the only hope is the patriotic forces of individual countries and 'the light coming from the East: Christian Russia'.[80] The attributes of fascism are attributed specifically to liberals, the term 'liberal fascism' being specifically adopted by Blaha and Harabin.[81] Regardless of their ideological orientation, the protagonists of Slavophilic discourse are united by their anti-Americanism and their critique of liberalism. The positive image of the communist regime is not only cultivated by Blaha but also by Zverina, for example, who referred to the period when Czechoslovakia was a satellite of the USSR as 'the golden times of the Slavs'.[82]

There are also elements of anti-Semitism in the Slavophilic environment. For example, Rostás published an article 'The Wedge of the Jews among the Slavs', in which he published anti-Semitic statements made by representatives of the Slovak national revival of the nineteenth century, with a commentary in which he indirectly spoke of subversion, the disintegration of society, and an attack on traditions that he associated with

---

[79] Blaha, Ľ. (2021, June 18). *Slováci nemajú dôvod klaňať sa a ospravedlňovať Afričanom*. [Facebook status update]. https://www.facebook.com/2047997592105476/photos/a.2052950104943558/2981587778746448/

[80] Kohút, P. (2018, March 11). *Nedovoľme zdochýnajúcemu Sorosovmu koňovi zničiť Slovensko*. Retrieved from https://www.slovenskeslovo.sk/o-com-je-rec/1394-ned ovolme-zdochynajucemu-sorosovmu-konovi-znicit-slovensko

[81] Kyseľ, T. (2019, October 9). *Prečo je úplný nezmysel, keď vám Blaha či Harabín nadávajú do fašistov*. *Aktuality.sk*. Retrieved from https://www.aktuality.sk/clanok/730 630/preco-je-uplny-nezmysel-ked-vam-blaha-ci-harabin-nadavaju-do-liberalnych-fasistov/

[82] Benčík, J. (2019, May 22). *Tak ako, pán Kotleba?* op. cit.

the influence of Zionism. According to him, 'only Slavic reciprocity and a vision of common strength and prosperity can be the salvation'.[83]

Less concrete are the ideas of the future formulated in the Slavophilic environment. These are based on the protection of the sovereignty of nation-states, but also on the transnational identity of the Slavs. They mostly agree on a line of social conservatism. Thus, in their ideas, the Slovak identity is associated with Christianity and 'traditional family' values. According to the Fatherland Party,

'There are strong efforts to force us to accept perverse, extremely liberal social experiments on people. A dictatorship of only permitted speech and opinion is being created, mass economic illegal migration is being organized, [and] a deviant gender and LGBTI ideology is being imposed on us, which means the disintegration of the normal family.'[84]

The Association of Slovak Intellectuals considers its priority to be 'the protection of human life and its dignity from conception to natural death'.[85] In terms of forging a strategic alliance with Russia, opinions differ. Some, for instance, Viliam Horňáček, claim that 'Russia – whether Tsarist, Soviet, and finally the current democratic Russia – has been and remains the main guarantor of Slavic identity'[86]; others speak openly of the need to integrate Slovakia into the Eurasian Union[87]; others, despite criticism of the 'egoistic, nihilistic West', express doubts about this alternative.[88] Pan-Slavism as a state-building idea, however, is not part of the official agenda of any political party.

---

[83] Potúček, J. (2019, October 30). Hitlerov „Môj boj' vs. Rostasov „Klin Židov medzi Slovanmi'. *Podtatranský kuriér*. Retrieved from https://www.podtatransky-kurier.sk/nazor/hitlerov-moj-boj-vs-rostasov-klin-zidov-medzi-slovanmi

[84] Vlasť. (2019). op. cit.

[85] Vyšná, M. (2019, November 25). Nastupujúca generácia..., op. cit.

[86] Horňáček, V. (2016). 'Slovanstvo a svet súčasnosti', In: Horňáček, V. (ed) *Slovanstvo a svet súčasnosti*. Bratislava: Korene, p. 23, pp. 19–26.

[87] Janco, A. and Janco, T. (2016). 'Postavenie a perspektíva Slovanov v súčasnom svete', In: Horňáček, V. (ed) *Slovanstvo a svet súčasnosti*. Bratislava: Korene, Bratislava, p. 143, pp. 136–143.

[88] Michelko, R. (2016). 'Ľudovít Štúr ako tvorca slovenskej politickej koncepcie', In: Horňáček, V. (ed) *Slovanstvo a svet súčasnosti*. Bratislava: Korene, p. 51, pp. 47–51.

Conclusion

Slavophilic discourse does not stand alone in Slovakia. Currently, it appears most often in the neighbourhood of far-right, traditionalist and nativist discourse, but it is not a necessary part of it. However, it is also present in the agenda of some left-wing circles, and therefore, it does not have clear ideological connotations. Its renaissance is linked to two moments. The first was the global financial crisis after 2008; the second, more important moment playing a significant role in its rise was the crisis in relations between Russia and the West in the context of the political changes in Ukraine after 2014. Slavophilic discourse is almost exclusively oriented towards shaping the perception in Slovak society of Russia—and to a lesser extent Serbia—and is almost completely unrelated to other Slavic states. On the contrary, Ukraine (but also Poland, as a critic of Russia's political influence) are perceived in the optics of the protagonists of Slavophilic discourse in an unambiguously negative way.

Immediately before Slovakia's accession to the EU and somewhat in the first years after EU-accession, there were speculations that the 'Slavic' agenda could become part of Slovakia's European policy, given that the first target countries of Slovakia's development and transformation assistance were states such as Ukraine, Belarus or Serbia. However, in the case of Slovakia, considerations about the possible formation of Euro-Slavism[89] proved to be unrealistic not only in view of the diversification of Slovakia's development assistance policy in later years, but also because Slovak diplomacy did not apply 'Slavic' but mainly 'European' rhetoric in its relations with these states.

The renaissance of the Slavophilic subculture is associated with criticism or outright rejection of the West. As the consciousness of being the part of the West is not deeply rooted in Slovak society, the recent conflict between the West and Russia contributed to the new wave of sympathy towards Russia and, to some extent, to the idea of Slavic brotherhood. However, it manifests itself primarily in the form of identitarianism, less so in the form of practical politics or political programmes. However, it is no longer a topic of purely intellectual debate as it was in 1990s. Although support for the Western orientation in Slovakia is not unequivocal in terms of public attitudes, there are relatively few political parties

---

[89] Marušiak, J. (2010). *Politický slavizmus...*, op. cit.; Troebst, S. (2014). Post-Panslavism?..., op. cit.

that openly question Slovakia's membership in the EU or NATO. The revived pseudo-Pan-Slavism is thus very much part of the protest mood. It appears in the neighbourhood of Slovak illiberalism, but not all Slovak illiberal subjects identify with Slavophilic rhetoric, or else use it only instrumentally, such as Smer-SD or ĽSNS.

An Ethnographic Look on Pan-Slavism

Manifestations of Pan-Slavic Sentiments Among South Slavic Diaspora Communities in the United States of America

Jasmin Hasić and Maja Savić-Bojanić

Introduction

The gradual and continued displacement and resettlement of communities from South Slavic countries in the Balkans to various other countries around the world, predominantly induced by economic instabilities, conflict or other factors, has created generations of people whose identities have developed outside of their own or their parents' countries of origin. They have transformed the original social codes, blended into their host societies, and reformulated and renegotiated some of their conflicting identities and senses of belonging, but they have also often kept and shared some of their 'Pan-Slavic' sentiments and common foundations of belonging. This is especially visible in how the Slavic populations originating in the Balkans, who shared a common past under

---

J. Hasić (✉) · M. Savić-Bojanić
Sarajevo School of Science and Technology, Sarajevo, Bosnia and Herzegovina
e-mail: jasmin.hasic@ssst.edu.ba

M. Savić-Bojanić
e-mail: maja.savic@ssst.edu.ba

© The Author(s), under exclusive license to Springer Nature Switzerland AG 2023
M. Suslov et al. (eds.), *Pan-Slavism and Slavophilia in Contemporary Central and Eastern Europe*,
https://doi.org/10.1007/978-3-031-17875-7_17

communist rule, assign different valuations to how their own identities evolved, to what socialism meant to them and to how it is reflected in their lives.

While the term 'Balkans' nowadays may carry negative and burdened connotations in Europe and elsewhere,[1] the name 'Yugoslavia' is still considered to be something 'attractive' and worthy of self-ascription. Diaspora communities, whose members originate in one of the ex-Yugoslav republics that we now refer to as post-Yugoslav states, frequently underscore the contributions the socialist past had in sustaining and promoting the values of Slavic and Pan-Slavic identities within the national (domestic), regional, and international spheres. Diaspora communities originating in ex-Yugoslav territories carry a number of such 'socialist legacies' within their Slavic and Pan-Slavic identities, and by keeping a specific and largely uncontested memory of socialism alive in their discourses, they also keep Pan-Slavic sentiments alive and sustain them as an important component of their belonging, cultural expression, power, influence and legitimacy.

We will examine in what ways and to what extent so-called Yugoslavism—contextually defined as a distinct and continuous expression of Pan-Slavism among South Slavs in diaspora—exists, what its manifestations are, and how this all fits with the current conceptions of national identity that these diaspora groups have formed and forged outside of their 'homelands'. We will scrutinise the Pan-Slavic identities of said diaspora groups through their conceptualisations and manifestations of identities rooted in the Pan-Slavic notion of 'Yugoslavism' as their own specific discourse. Our aim is to schematise and analyse the performative and practical manifestations of this redefined notion of Yugoslavism among 'Yugoslav' diasporans living in the United States, and to assess the roles it has played in their own notions of belonging, which are also embedded in the cultural and political meanings and discourses of their respective countries of settlement.

We identify two basic manifestations of Yugoslavism, reflexive and objective, and we focus on the following topics: historical and comparative

---

[1] cf. Gallagher, T. (1997). 'To Be or Not to Be Balkan: Romania's Quest for Self-Definition', *Daedalus*, 126(3), pp. 63–83; and Kolsto, P. (2016). 'Western Balkans' as the New Balkans: Regional Names as Tools for Stigmatisation and Exclusion', *Europe-Asia Studies*, 68(7), pp. 1245–1263.

approaches to the development of Yugoslavism; its redefinition and reconceptualisation as a specific form of Pan-Slavism; and its manifestations among different selected South Slavic diaspora communities originating in Yugoslavia (a country which no longer exists as a geopolitical feature of their own individual national identities) and currently living in the United States, through examining the roles of memory, religion and migration experiences in sustaining this common sense of belonging among members of these communities.

THE MAIN ARGUMENTS AND THEORETICAL FRAMEWORK

Traditionally, the term 'Yugoslavism', with a capital 'Y', was used to denote a set of integrative ideologies related to nation- and state-building efforts in the so-called Yugoslav spheres of influence. Yugoslavism is recognised as one of the discourses that helped to frame political action and cultural initiatives for much of the nineteenth and early twentieth centuries.[2] There were several attempts to precisely define and reconceptualise the term in the twentieth century. These have developed into two main variants, integral (or unitarist or centralist) and anti-centralist.[3] These were predominantly ideological and not necessarily ethnic in their nature.[4] Some authors argue that Yugoslavism in the interwar period was not incompatible with or subordinate to Serbian, Croatian or (to a lesser degree) Slovenian national ideas. However, the ways in which the ruling elites adapted ideology over time slowly discredited the Yugoslav national idea and resulted in an increasing delineation and polarisation on the continuum of national ideas present in Yugoslavia.[5] Given that the Yugoslav state never officially recognised the existence of a Yugoslav nation—or of Yugoslavism as a separate national identity—the variances between Yugoslavism and other ideologies, like Serbism, became completely polarised after 1988, as advocates of Serb unification portrayed

---

[2] Robinson, C. (2010). *Yugoslavism in the Early Twentieth Century: The Politics of the Yugoslav Committee*. Routledge, pp. 26–42.

[3] Djokić, D. (2003). *Yugoslavism: Histories of a Failed Idea, 1918–1992*. London: Hurst.

[4] Jović, D. (2003). 'Yugoslavism and Yugoslav Communism: From Tito to Kardelj', In: Djokić, D. (ed) *Yugoslavism: Histories of a Failed Idea, 1918–1992*. London: Hurst.

[5] Troch, P. (2012). 'Between Yugoslavism and Serbianism: Reshaping Collective Identity in Serbian Textbooks Between the World Wars', *History of Education*, 41(2), pp. 175–194.

Yugoslavia as a costly mistake.[6] After Yugoslavia's violent breakup, the ideology lost its position on the spectrum and was reconstructed in debates led by post-Yugoslav social science scholars and philosophers, predominantly as a 'subversive strategy' and an 'alternative view' to dominant nationalist discourses.[7]

In this particular chapter, we re-examine these definitions of 'Yugoslavism' and reconstruct its meaning to fit a Pan-Slavic-induced sense of belonging, constituted through a shared transnational sense of identity. We highlight the existence of new incarnations of 'Yugoslavism' among post-Yugoslav diaspora communities as well as their visions of a common Pan-Slavic memory and cultural space, geographically and emotionally detached from the mutually 'antagonistic' societies ex-Yugoslav territories are most commonly associated with. Our research is centred on investigating individual representations of belonging among diaspora communities of South Slavs. We argue that 'Yugoslavism', specifically denoted with lowercase 'y', emerges as a separate but firmly cohabitated identity in their narrated life stories and discourses, especially with regard to the temporality of events and experiences and the spatiality of communities of belonging both in host countries and on the territories of the former Yugoslavia, as well as in relationships with those who share the same outlooks and sentiments—or with others who (un)willingly reject this type of self-identification.

Our focus revolves around probing three main features: (a) South Slavic diaspora communities in the United States; (b) a sense of belonging to a common regional origin; and (c) the constitutive features of the concept of Yugoslavism as a *performative* transnational social expression of the Pan-Slavic identities of South Slavs in those diaspora communities. We argue that Yugoslavism, as one of the subcategories of Pan-Slavism, can be used as a minimally acceptable supranational identity foundation for South Slavs living in diaspora, and that it is primarily materialised through self-determined notions of something 'to be valued, cultivated,

---

[6] Pavković, A. (1998). 'From Yugoslavism to Serbism: The Serb National Idea 1986–1996', *Nations and Nationalism*, 4(4), pp. 511–528.

[7] Stehlík, P. (2019). Yugoslavism in the 21st Century? On the Afterlife of a Seemingly Retired Idea. In *Fifth International Balkan Studies Conference "Balkan Express"*, 8–9. 11. 2019, Prague.

supported, recognised, and preserved', as well as of a sense of 'groupness' that can allow for collective action once other foundational goals have been identified and agreed upon.[8]

Diaspora communities' hybrid experiences of mixed social, cultural and political attachments are not only manifested through 'where they are from' but also 'where they are at'—a combination of roots and routes.[9] For them, real or imagined events of the past are commonly extrapolated into the present in order to reinforce their sense of a new belonging, and their interactions are a precondition for the narrative construction of the autobiographies through which they identify 'who they are'[10] and how they use the cultural tools in their 'identity-related projects'.[11] As 'imagined communities living far away from a professed place of origin',[12] South Slavic diasporans have developed a distinct, individualised and privatised concept of subjectivity, which relates to their own notion of identity within larger host communities.[13] A feeling of belonging, in this context, is understood as a vital part of identity, and their belonging is accordingly identified with the group notions that an individual attaches to.[14] Their notions of belonging are generally situated in three different spheres: the temporal, related to historical, economic and political developments; the spatial, connected with the ways that different states and societies have experienced historical, political or economic development;

---

[8] Brubaker, R. and Cooper, F. (2000). 'Beyond "Identity"', *Theory and Society*, 29, pp. 1–47.

[9] Kalra, V., Kaur, R. and Hutnyk, J. (2005). *Diaspora and hybridity*. Sage.

[10] Saito, H. (2006). 'Reiterated Commemoration: Hiroshima as National Trauma', *Sociological Theory*, 24(4), pp. 353–376.

[11] Wertsch, James V. (2002). *Voices of Collective Remembering*. New York: Cambridge University Press.

[12] Vertovec, S. (2010). 'Cosmopolitanism', In: Knott, K. and McLoughlin, S. (eds) *Diasporas: Concepts, Intersections, Identities*. London: Zed Books, pp. 63–68.

[13] Wetherell, M. (2008). 'Subjectivity or Psycho-discursive Practices? Investigating Complex Intersectional Identities', *Subjectivity*, 22(1), pp. 73–81.

[14] Colic-Peisker, V. (2010). 'Free Floating in the Cosmopolis? Exploring the Identity-Belonging of Transnational Knowledge Workers', *Journal of Transnational Affairs*, 10(4), pp. 467–488; and Hasić, J. (2018). 'Post-Conflict Cooperation in Multi-ethnic Local Communities of Bosnia and Herzegovina: A Qualitative Comparative Analysis of Diaspora's Role', *Journal of Peacebuilding & Development*, 13(2), pp. 31–46.

and the intersectional, linked to the ways people of the same place and time may be affected differently by a specific politics of belonging.[15]

In both academic literature and policy works, diaspora communities are perceived through two basic categories, as subjects (practice) and objects (analysis),[16] which operate within different lenses of *translocal* and transnational positionalities of belonging towards their hosts and homelands.[17] These '*trans-*' positions allow diaspora communities to sustain their identities within overlapping social fields and to develop relationships with their respective countries of origin or with persons or events there.[18] The cultural and symbolic events and practices that continue to solidify ethnic diaspora identities in their host (adoptive) countries across generations nurture a common sense of belonging and social and emotional attachments,[19] as well as to help to develop further the 'bifocality' of perspectives that relates to diasporans' own identities and their willingness to continue living their lives both 'here' and 'there'.[20]

The South Slavic diaspora, predominantly originating in countries currently situated in the post-Yugoslav space, have been studied with a particular focus on the ethnic belonging, religious ties and political identities that some individuals or groups identify with. The multi-ethnic belonging that persisted in Yugoslavia for quite some time was disrupted by a violent conflict, which not only affected the country's overall existence, bringing mass violence, death and displacement, redrawing the

---

[15] Yuval-Davis, N. (2006). 'Belonging and the Politics of Belonging', *Patterns of Prejudice*, 40(3), pp. 197–214.

[16] Brubaker, R. and Cooper, F. (2000). 'Beyond "identity"', *Theory and Society*, 29, pp. 1–47.

[17] Anthias, F. (2008). 'Thinking Through the Lens of Translocational Positionality: An Intersectionality Frame for Understanding Identity and Belonging', *Translocations, Migration and Change*, 4(1), pp. 5–20.

[18] Levitt, P. and Glick-Schiller, N. (2004). 'Conceptualizing Simultaneity: A Transnational Social Field Perspective in Society', *International Migration Review*, 38(3), pp. 1002–1039.

[19] Waite, L. and Cook, J. (2011). Belonging Among Diasporic African Communities in the UK: Plurilocal Homes and Simultaneity of Place Attachments', *Emotion, Space and Society*, 4(4), pp. 238–248.

[20] Vertovec, S. (2004). 'Migrant Transnationalism and Modes of Transformation1', *International Migration Review*, 38(3), pp. 970–1001.

borders to create new nation-states, but has also contributed to the development of certain types of unity among citizens of the newly formed countries.[21] Comparative studies of diasporan engagement with their (former) homeland spaces suggest that their motivations are incentivised by either a particular identification with the 'image of the homeland' or with a particular ideological basis being promoted at the national or sub-national level.[22] Post-communist political developments within the territories of the former Yugoslavia have, however, left very little political space for uncontested political identities to be cultivated properly, since the highly concentrated ethnonational political environment that has dominated political conversations has skewed perceptions of features of 'common belonging'.

Nonetheless, the 'old generations' of the Yugoslav diaspora, who were physically distant from the violent conflicts taking place in the region and the subsequent post-conflict developments there, have developed some discrete notions of belonging straddled between their individual countries of origin and their new host countries' identities, as opposed to the ones they would have been embedded in otherwise. Their perspectives vary in their ontological and epistemological bases of 'identity' formation from those of people who remained directly attached to or affected by the negative consequences of Yugoslavia's downturn. Their collectively shared memory of Yugoslavia, as a brand and as a lifestyle, sets off a sense of belonging that embodies shared visions of both 'shelter' and 'intimacy', not physically existing but able to be mentally accessed. In this context, 'Yugoslavism' appears as an expression of one's Pan-Slavic identity, which enables access to multiple levels of identification of belonging that are intertwined with a particular history and ways it is remembered.

We label this dichotomy of belonging as 'Yugoslavism', a category of ethnopolitical practice of a distinct, long-distance Pan-Slavic 'groupism' that connects South Slavic diasporans along commonly perceived features of their identity and allows them to cross mental borders between the newly formed nation-states, whose creation they observed only from

---

[21] Hasic, J. (2016). Involvement of Diasporas in Peacebuilding Processes: A Comparative Analysis of Local Elite Perceptions of Bosnian Diaspora's Incorporation in Ownership Frameworks. PhD Dissertation, Université libre de Bruxelles.

[22] Hasić, J. and Telalović, A. (2021). 'Diaspora, Deliberation and Democracy: Examining Externally-Sponsored Initiatives for the Development of Local Fora in Bosnia and Herzegovina', *Innovation: The European Journal of Social Science Research*, pp. 1–16.

a distance, and with which they cannot fully identify in their present discourses and narratives. They self-ascribe as belonging to amalgamated Pan-Slavic, identity-based sentiments, representing a specific notion of memory of a nation-state that no longer exists in reality but which is still alive in the performativity of those individuals and groups that honour its symbolic legacies.

In our attempt to reconceptualise the term 'Yugoslavism' as a Pan-Slavic expression of belonging and identity shared among diasporans who did not directly experience the cultural traumas that caused or followed the breakup of Yugoslavia, we highlight the need to differentiate between various generations of diasporans and their respective visions of the socio-political and historical facts that they might have witnessed. Our conceptualisation of Yugoslavism is contrary to any methodological nationalism[23] that might exist among members of conflict-generated diaspora communities or economic migrants originating in the former Yugoslavia. In our attempt to craft a new definition of Yugoslavism and its application to the older Yugoslav diasporans, our focus is on examining the ability to transcend the affective notions shaped by memories of the Yugoslav wars and the boundaries of the newly formed nation-states. We are set on highlighting a new dynamic of self-identification, where processes of belonging among one or many diaspora communities (originating in a common territory that no longer exists and residing in another) remain open and somewhat inclusive. In this context, ascribing to Yugoslavism via any known process of self-identification does not imply a denial that ethnicity and nation-states among diaspora communities are re-inscribed as irrelevant. The transcendental value of Yugoslavism, as defined in this particular study, mirrors the poststructuralist perspective in social theory, where the bases for defining people's identity are more reflexive and intersectional.[24]

We do not conceptualise Yugoslavism through a 'property of identity being' in an individual's possession, but rather as an expression of an

---

[23] Wimmer, A. and Glick-Schiller, N. (2002). 'Methodological Nationalism and Beyond: Nation-State Building, Migration and the Social Sciences', *Global Networks*, 2(4), pp. 301–334.

[24] Branaman, A. (2010). 'Identity and Social Theory', In: Elliot, A. (ed) *The Routledge Companion to Social Theory*. Abingdon, Oxon: Routledge, pp. 135–155; and Amelina, A. and Faist, T. (2012). 'De-naturalizing the National in Research Methodologies: Key Concepts of Transnational Studies in Migration', *Ethnic and Racial Studies*, 35(10), pp. 1707–1724.

active and socially conscious identity choice that shapes relations among individuals. Our definition serves as an alternative to the 'substantialist ontologies' and is based on shared perceptions of a cultural focus on one or more symbolic elements, shared among community members whose perceived cultural heritage embodies important characteristics that matter to them. Our notion of Yugoslavism is not fully comparable to the 'classic' South Slavic diasporas' individual or community experiences and does not attempt to understand all types of discourses and narratives shared within their own communal 'confines'. In that respect, our definition of Yugoslavism, quite distinctly, opens up space for examining the dynamics of 'supra-identity' construction, which entails particular homeland identification categories that go beyond the private and the national, and reflect the multicultural and multi-ethnic patterns of communal life somewhat characteristic of pre-1990s Yugoslavia.

Research Methodology, Data Collection and Analysis

We draw our data from a multi-sited ethnographic study conducted between March and August 2020. We approached the participants using personal networks and contacts with presidents and regular members of Bosnian diaspora associations in nine cities across the United States and used snowball sampling in order to reach other participants from Serb, North Macedonian and Montenegrin diaspora associations in the United States. Although we are fully aware of the potential sampling bias that may occur in connection with these two methods, their combination is known and often used in ethnographic research, especially because of shifting perspectives among participants.[25] Moreover, considering our focus on identity features, such as memory, belonging, and migration experiences, and their relevance to the aforementioned conceptualisation of Yugoslavism, we posit that personal networks and snowball sampling are crucial to gaining and maintaining trust from participants who may be wary of voicing their stories.

We outlined three main criteria when identifying, contacting and assessing the interviewees: (1) membership in a diaspora association; (2) a date of birth in 1980 or earlier; and (3) migration experience prior to

---

[25] Bryman, A. (2012). *Social Research Methods*. Oxford: Oxford University Press.

Yugoslavia's breakup. The second criterion is deemed important insofar as some personal memory that does not rely purely on parental stories and upbringing is essential when discussing art, holidays and Yugoslav spaces. When it comes to *positionality*, we consider ourselves to be 'partial outsiders' and 'partial insiders'. The 'insider' position mainly relates to our conversations with members of the diaspora community from Bosnia and Herzegovina, with whom we share a common homeland, language and traditions, while the 'outsider' position comes out of the relationships that we established with participants from other diaspora communities, namely from Serbia, North Macedonia and Montenegro.

We have used data gathered from twenty-six interviews conducted in nine cities across the United States with significant diaspora communities and associations from the former Yugoslavia: San Francisco, Cleveland, Saint Louis, Chicago, Milwaukee, Pittsburgh, Des Moines, New York and Detroit. Due to the COVID-19 pandemic, all interviews were conducted online, mostly using the Zoom platform. The interviews lasted anywhere from 30 min up to 2 h and were conducted in the Bosnian/Croatian/Serbian language(s). The interview data presented in this paper is labelled with pseudonyms that we assigned to each participant. Their ethnic affiliation, as well as their age and current city of residence, is a part of their factual data.

We deem it important to emphasise that, although mindful of the role of religion and political orientations in personal bearings towards anything 'Yugoslav', we did not engage in discussions of ethnic preferences in relation to Yugoslav culture, tradition or artistic expression. Instead, we focused on the experiences gained through their membership in diaspora associations and cultural groups, which we have found useful in assessing a specific diaspora community's orientation towards Yugoslavism. It is, hence, through a myriad of personal memories and experiences of the 'old country of Yugoslavia' that we shed light on how Yugoslavism and related ideas are reflected in these modern diasporic communities originating in selected South Slavic countries, formerly members of the Socialist Federal Republic of Yugoslavia, and on how they have influenced local (political) thinking and discourse. As outlined, we will examine their manifestations and what roles they play in sustaining cultural and political meanings and discourses of their respective countries of origin. Through the examination of this data, we have sought to map patterns of symbolic engagement with the aforesaid themes that are shown in it, as well as their change over time.

In the section that follows, these personal memories are used to explore manifestations of Yugoslavism as currently understood and practiced by these four diaspora groups of South Slavs living in the United States. We embraced the participatory approach, which allows us to show how the memory of the past and personal recollections of life during Yugoslavia remain essential in understanding the evolution of modern-day understandings of 'Yugoslavism'.

'WE STILL FIND THINGS THAT UNIFY US!'—NEW FORMS OF 'YUGOSLAVISM' AMONG THE SOUTH SLAVIC DIASPORA COMMUNITIES IN THE UNITED STATES

In an attempt to reconceptualise the term 'Yugoslavism', in whichever form it might appear or resurface among diaspora communities, it is essential to understand that every opinion that emerges inevitably has an ideological background. It is a political statement, willingly or unwillingly expressed through political orientations and intentions. This is how cultural production works: in fact, cultural (re)production is rarely reserved for specific audiences (e.g. music is not absorbed only by youth, nor are books absorbed only by older generations),[26] but instead it serves various power structures that impact the ways in which they produce meaning and impact individual bearings. Examining the meaning and applications of Yugoslavism among South Slavic diaspora communities in the United States incites political meanings, as it relates to 'something of the past' in a former common state, Yugoslavia. Since the end of the 1980s and early 1990s, almost every term relating to Yugoslavia and Yugoslavism could, in fact, be construed as a political statement. Hence, the very fact that the interviewees speak of Yugoslavia and its national holidays, songs, books, places and spaces is, epistemologically, also a political statement. In what follows, we unpack the themes that emerge as primary traits of Yugoslavism among members of the former Yugoslav diaspora in the United States, as theorised in the previous sections. The primary markers of this reconceptualised Yugoslavism, as we will show, are personal commitments to Yugoslav holidays, arts and spaces. They

---

[26] Savić-Bojanić, M. and Jevtić, J. (2015). 'Ethnic Solidarities, Networks, and the Diasporic Imaginary: The Case of "Old" and "New" Bosnian Diaspora in the United States', *New Diversities*, 17(1), p. 71.

ultimately mirror the primary characteristics of what 'former Yugoslavs' consider to still bind them together into a single, South Slavic notion of identity and belonging.

Belma (age 50) is a middle school teacher. She is originally from Bosnia and Herzegovina, and now currently lives in Saint Louis. She says she is still a 'Yugoslav' in many ways:

> 'In my home, we symbolically celebrate religious holidays, and we make sweets. But New Year's Eve is a big celebration, just like it once was back home. We usually go to one of the associations; they bring our singers and we dance until dawn. It is one of those things that still reminds me of life before [the war]'.

Mirjana (age 56), from Serbia and currently living in San Francisco, also speaks of how things were 'back home'. When asked about specific examples, she added:

> 'It means like it was in Yugoslavia, of course. Here in San Francisco many of us are from the former Yugoslavia, and all we care about is meeting for dinner or lunch, speaking a bit in one of the languages, whichever, [laughs] and listening to 'our music'. Our music is music from all over Yugoslavia. It reminds me of my teenage years, back in the seventies in my hometown of Niš'.

The dimension of 'back home' almost instantly translates to 'life in Yugoslavia', while the term 'ours' specifically relates to anything that comes from the space of the former Yugoslavia, regardless of what any specific post-Yugoslav area is called today. Given that the violent breakup of Yugoslavia led to the creation of new states, which established new social and political mythologies based on old forms of identity, like language, ethnic and national origin, religion or confession, it is important to note these transformations of the political context have been well documented in the post-Yugoslav countries[27] but were not readily accessible to all diaspora communities abroad. Namely, the life circumstances that existed during personal experiences both in Yugoslavia and

---

[27] Tomić, C. (2018). 'Literary "Home-Trackers": Narratives of Return in the Era of Post-socialist Transformation Dagmar Gramshammer-Hohl', *Remigration to Post-Socialist Europe: Hopes and Realities of Return*, 3, p. 405.

after Yugoslavia violently broke up still play a role in expressing and self-ascribing belonging among diaspora members to the so-called Yugoslav identity.

What was striking in all the interviews was a clear preference for a Yugoslav identity over an ethnic one, although the latter was not totally disregarded. Such a programmatic insistence on the homogeneity of Yugoslav identity, and the hierarchical educational policy, both created opportunities for multiple sub-national interpretations of Yugoslav unity.[28] Life trajectories have evidently played a role in this, especially for participants born in the 1960s and 1970s, when Yugoslavia was considered a stable country. Equally, the notion of Yugoslavism as a formational Pan-Slavic supra-identity feature among South Slavic diasporans in the United States places more emphasis on transnational connections among communities, rather than inter-ethnic relations in both home and host countries. It does not necessarily serve as an alternative to the political ontologies all interviewees share, but rather it is based on shared perceptions of a cultural focus on more symbolic elements. For example,

'Lately, our 'ethnic' store here in Saint Louis has been selling the 'retro' version of the best candy from the 'Kraš' factory. Kraš candy was very exclusive, expensive stuff when I was young, but the old packaging that is popular today reminds me of Yugoslav stores. I really believe that this is a good way of bringing people back to the old days and reminding them that we had everything'.

These are the words of Lejla (age 47), a sales worker originally from the small town of Goražde in Bosnia and Herzegovina. Today she lives in Saint Louis, a city with a large Bosnian diaspora community. The testimony of Dimče (age 70), originally from North Macedonia and today living in Milwaukee, also reflects similar notions relating to the 'lived' experiences of Yugoslavia through products that remind him of the state's economic power. Their opinions demonstrate that sentiments attached to early life are often reborn via simple objects and memorabilia from a previous era. Such nostalgic attachments to the popular culture industry (cf., Bennett, 2003) are essentially political in their

---

[28] Troch, P. (2010). 'Yugoslavism Between the World Wars: Indecisive Nation Building', *Nationalities Papers*, 38(2), pp. 227–244.

nature, as they imply that notions of Yugoslavism among diasporans are not restricted simply to culture and cultural representations but also to memories of everyday, almost banal things such as cookies or the design of a matchbox or the labels on a bottle of mineral water. To them, these products symbolise well-being and welfare provided by the Yugoslav state, something constitutive of their Pan-Slavic sense of pride.

This identification with everyday objects from the Yugoslav state—symbolically perceived as one of the most advanced state structures that existed during the Cold War—evokes an atmosphere of unity, which is apparent among members of the different ethnic diaspora associations from the former Yugoslavia in the United States. It emerges as a tangible indicator of Yugoslavism, since the notions around which interviewees grew up are reflected in their memorabilia, 'retro' marketing or celebrations. The subjective meanings assigned to objectively shared symbols of products all consumed and deemed as high quality are attached to their Pan-Slavic-induced sense of belonging.

Such identifications with specific products and with Yugoslavia's economic grandeur do not threaten individual ethnic or national identities; quite the opposite, they serve as binders and features of a 'groupism' that connects diasporans in a 'foreign' land through the common features of a once shared national identity. In fact, meaning-making in geographically distant spheres of social engagement not only relies on the existing product or object narratives shared among the group members and between groups, but at the same time also constructs new narratives (of what these meant to them, the status symbols in the country, etc.). This creates a certain sense of 'ontological security',[29] constituted as a feeling of order, a continuity of everyday routines and well-being. The construction of ontological security through the shared memory of material objects and goods are links that the individual uses to connect to the wider communities they perceive and ascribe themselves as belonging to. These identity markers help to change their understanding of belonging as well as the identity links that certain diaspora groups have with their internalised notions of the countries they originate from—and of other countries they have supposed relations with.

Milo, a 71-year-old Montenegrin who has lived in Chicago for over thirty years, also illustrates a similar point:

---

[29] Giddens, A. (1991). *Modernity and Self-Identity: Self and Society in the Late Modern Age*. Stanford University Press.

'I am old enough to be able to say that I am a real Yugoslav. But I am also a Montenegrin as you can tell from my name [laughs].... It was never a problem. We carried multiple ethnic identities but we were always from Yugoslavia, we were Yugoslavs. This is why I don't have a problem with any of the so-called ethnic groups who live here with me side by side. Being a Yugoslav implies that we had a great country, a great leader, that we were all for one and one for all...not this nonsense that they are living now back home'.

In a similar fashion, Amila (age 55) originally from Bosnia and Herzegovina and now living in Des Moines, states:

'I met a lot of people from Serbia, Macedonia, Croatia, but never did we, or so it appeared, think of each other as separate people. We enjoy holidays together and I turn to my neighbour Stefan from Montenegro whenever I need help. It's like a mini-Yugoslavia and we don't have problems with each other. Back home they do now, but here we 'live Yugoslavia''.

Twenty out of the twenty-six participants that we interviewed speak of their life in the United States in a similar fashion. They never question ethnic identity and they actively socialise with 'everybody' they consider their countrymen from Yugoslavia, as long as they are 'good people'. People from the territory of the former Yugoslavia are perceived either as friends, neighbours or simply 'co-nationals'. There is no visible hierarchical structure around geographical or cultural dimensions. Unlike in Yugoslavia, where nations to the 'north' and the 'west' looked down upon those in the 'southern' and 'eastern' parts of Yugoslavia, and where those with historical affiliations to a Western religious denomination, Catholic or Protestant, disdained those who hailed from Orthodox or Muslim backgrounds,[30] a symbolic tug-of-war between Yugoslav Slavs now living in diaspora has never developed.

In fact, the notions of Yugoslavism that these participants shared go beyond their 'ethnic' origins and even galvanised around the former Pan-Slavic slogans of 'brotherhood and unity'. All reported indicators of Yugoslavism appear in expressions of one's common and national identities, which enable the individuals to access multiple levels of identification and belonging, which are intertwined in a particular history and in the

---

[30] Bakic-Hayden, M. and Hayden, R. M. (1992). 'Orientalist Variations on the Theme "Balkans": Symbolic Geography in Recent Yugoslav Cultural Politics', *Slavic Review*, p. 51.

ways it is remembered, despite the geographic distance and time elapsed. Pan-Slavic *yugophilic* discourses contradict the conservative-identitarian quest for roots and legacies, and they are also not in tune with leftist criticisms of the global hegemony of 'the West'. The Yugoslavism among the investigated diaspora groups in the United States is viewed as a part of their intellectual legacy and a memory that merges their own liberal notions and ideas of their common past into a Yugo-revolving Slavophilia.

What is also found in almost all interviews is the sentimentality they attach to the 'Yugoslav era', as outlined by Rijad (age 67), originating from Bosnia and Herzegovina and now living in New York, as well as the criticism most participants share of present times in the post-Yugoslav region.

> 'It was the good times and why not live it and re-live it. Here we remember how it was back then and don't care 'who is who'. If we cared, we would have stayed there and voted for corrupt politicians...we'd steal, hate. Whoever is here likes peace and unity, basically all that we learned from Yugoslavia'.

These descriptors of Yugoslavism can be labelled as 'reflexive' and are more stable in their transfer to younger generations who grew up as first- or second-generation migrants. The reflexive spontaneity of those who narrate 'Yugoslavism' is not a simple form of nostalgic escapism that differentiates those who identified as a Yugoslav or those who still enjoy banal, everyday objects from the past. This type of Yugoslavism erases 'in-betweenness'.[31] Aleksandar (age 58), who moved from Serbia to Pittsburgh, shares a similar sentiment:

> 'Yugoslavia was great. For some, the situation is better today. To me, it doesn't matter. What matters is that the countries of the former Yugoslavia remain at peace with each other and the past. It is not so hard to transfer the concept of 'brotherhood'. It's a small region, interconnected and – I'd dare say – interdependent. Today's countries can all learn from the former 'brotherhood'...and 'unity'...well, very impossible, but not essential'.

---

[31] Waite, L. and Cook, J. (2011). 'Belonging Among Diasporic African Communities in the UK: Plurilocal Homes and Simultaneity of Place Attachments', *Emotion, Space and Society*, 4(4), pp. 238–248.

As outlined, an omnipresent feeling of a 'past that is no more' and a 'present that must be led by the past' supports these individual expressions of Yugoslavism among individual diasporans and diaspora communities in the United States. It is founded on a familiarity with the past, while the future remains uncertain. And indeed, much of the above narrative is guided by individual emotions, motivations and desires to upkeep the Yugoslav notions and transfer them to younger generations. Returning to the 'retro' is a symptom and not an end. Interviewees are pulled to the past because our visions of the future remain unformed.[32] In fact, there is an almost collective action that reflects this:

> 'We must upkeep this spirit of 'brotherhood and unity' for the young. We don't want them to visit their fatherland and get shocked with what goes on there. We must teach our kids that brotherhood with everybody is OK despite what happened in Yugoslavia'.

These words resonate as Irena (age 42), currently living in Detroit, explains her reasons for teaching her children to be friendly with other ethnic groups. She adds,

> 'They [the kids] once came back from a party where somebody played some Ustasha music and they asked me what it was. There was a fight and they left…so see, that's why I am saying this. There is no need to bring these ancient hatreds here and install them into your kids. They have no clue what those songs mean, so they must have heard them from their parents'.

Mehmed (age 50), currently located in Saint Louis, shares a similar sentiment:

> 'Yugoslavism is nostalgia, but it is not long-lived. It will disappear as generations of Yugoslavs disappear'.

If observed from this perspective, which is not unique only to Irena, but is also shared by eleven other interviewees, the question of the durability of manifestations of both 'reflexive' and 'objectified' Yugoslavism is then questioned, inasmuch as newer generations will experience more

---

[32] Guffey, E. (2006). *Retro—The Culture of Revival*. London: Reaktion Books.

difficulties in connecting with the 'old Yugoslav ways', simply because of the lack of lived experience and their present exposure to the opposite notions. What is more, considering that—at least in the case of the four studied diaspora communities in the United States—Yugoslavism is not tied to common history, Yugoslav tradition or the political system, but rather translates into 'retro' in the case of objectified Yugoslavism or into individual perceptions of the common Yugoslav ideas of 'brotherhood and unity'. In the case of reflexive Yugoslavism, the longevity of the very idea of Pan-Slavic Yugoslavism is at stake, but that would be a study in its own right. These self-imaginations of diaspora people reinforce their belonging to a collective 'homeland' community that no longer exists.[33]

What is also noted in a myriad of stories shared by our interviewees is a direction that implies the depoliticisation and historicisation of Yugoslavia. There is little, if any, mention of socialism or those dominant images of Yugoslavia relating to the collective memory of partisanship, camaraderie and the proletariat. For example, Marija's (age 50) statement reflects the passive nature of today's Yugoslavism among diaspora communities:

> 'The 'old days' are gone and we will never again have Yugoslavia. We can only upkeep it in our hearts...and we do that by eating our food and listening to our music, socialising with our Yugoslav neighbours, and celebrating holidays'.

Views like this rest purely on slogans or are reduced to entertainment (e.g. music), food and simple nostalgic memories of the 'good old days'. This short and almost definitional description of Yugoslavism—not connected exclusively with economic, socio-political, identity-bearing and associational manifestations but rather again going back to 'retro'—indicates that intentional nostalgia grows as the old aesthetics of Yugoslavia appear in present-day ordinary consumption and marketing tricks. As noted earlier, such affective attachments to the cultural space representing former Yugoslavia contributes to building trust among diaspora communities, which lack real and present geographic commonalities in their memory recollections. It also translates into momentum for integration with a country's cultural space, and slowly becomes an important part of it. With the decline of political Yugoslavism that may be associated with

---

[33] Sokefeld, M. (2006). 'Mobilizing in Transnational Space: A Social Movement Approach to the Formation of Diaspora', *Global Networks*, 6, pp. 265–284.

socialism, the next generations will be clean of the former ideology, but will still be exposed to its aesthetics and to the sporadic stories inherited from their parents.

Conclusion

Lived experiences of Yugoslavia's violent disintegration and post-conflict developments in the region have all shaped the opinions and perceptions of those Yugoslavs who had previously resettled in various countries abroad. Although distant and unable to directly participate in the day-to-day socio-political processes unfolding in the newly formed states on the former territory of Yugoslavia, Yugoslav diaspora communities have inevitably been affected by the newly formed relationships in the region and the debates on the legacies of Yugoslavia's 'continuities' and 'discontinuities'. Through their perception of 'all things Yugoslav', they are able to broadly exhibit either objectified or reflexive forms of Pan-Slavic belonging, based on the attachments they associate with either 'things' or 'ideas' that were once symbols of their former country.

Such displays and representations of the symbolic implications and dimensions of Yugoslavia's existence—beyond its political, legal or administrative survival, which have developed into socio-spatial discourses enduring among members of post-Yugoslav diaspora communities—we mark as 'Yugoslavism', with a lowercase 'y'. Older generations of diasporans originating from the region practice Yugoslavism with their compatriots as a 'soft' component of their identity base—and in a temporary fashion, until the critical mass of those who share and appreciate these shared values falls below a critical minimum.

Traditionally, the term Yugoslavism was used to denote a set of ideologies related to integrative nation- and state-building efforts in the Yugoslav spheres of influence. However, 'Yugoslavism', in the context of this work, is considered to be the common denominator for a vast number of members belonging to all four investigated Pan-Slavic diaspora communities from south-eastern Europe currently living in the United States. It serves as an important aspect of the definitional process of belonging, and it has the power to cross-reference various social and cultural features that define the communal characteristics existing and coexisting in geographical regions beyond their countries of origin. This Yugoslavism, contextually redefined as a subcategory of Pan-Slavism, revolves around popular geopolitical topics and reflects interviewees' understandings of grassroots ideas, media, opinions and emotions, all attached to their memories of a separate, but firmly cohabitated, identity.

This re-conceptualised Yugoslavism works as a *performative* transnational social expression of the Pan-Slavic identities of the South Slavs living in diaspora communities across the United States and is primarily materialised through self-ascription to a cultivated, supported and mutually recognised 'groupness' that allows for collective action once other foundational goals are identified and agreed upon.

Interethnic Ritual Kinship as Pan-Slavism in Bosnia and Herzegovina

Keith Doubt

Introduction

The exemplification of pan-Slavism in Bosnia and Herzegovina is found in one of its historical kinship practices, namely, the custom of interethnic ritual kinship. Culture is the shared set of normative expectations that structure social relations and common life, and culture is learned through upbringing and witnessing its exemplification in the private and public realms of the community. The Yugoslav ethnographer, Milenko Filipović wrote, 'Ritual kinship of various forms was of great importance among South Slavs in the past, because it widened the circle of relatives beyond the family, the clan, and the tribe.'[1] Filipović noted as well, 'Such brotherhoods (and sisterhoods) are frequently contracted even at present time

---

[1] Filipović, M. (1963). 'Forms and Functions of Ritual Kinship Among South Slavs,' *International Congress of Anthropological and Ethnological Sciences*, 1, p. 77.

K. Doubt (✉)
Wittenberg University, Springfield, OH, USA
e-mail: kdoubt@wittenberg.edu

by two persons belonging to different nations and faiths.'[2] Given the ethnic diversity in Bosnia and Herzegovina, the likelihood of ritual kinship between people from different faiths is greater. Interethnic ritual kinship connects people in socially and ethically important ways and provides stability and solidarity in a polyethnic community.

Two ritual kinships that exemplify pan-Slavism in Bosnia and Herzegovina are *kumstvo* and *pobratimstvo*. *Kumstvo* is what anthropologists call fictive or, better, ritual kinship. Ritual kinship is fictive only in the sense that it is kinship neither by blood nor by marriage. *Kumovi* (the plural for *kum* and *kuma*), in fact, names several types of fictive kin for South Slavs. *Kumovi* may refer to a best man at a wedding, a male or a female witness at a wedding, a godparent at a baptism, a witness at a circumcision, a witness at a child's first communion, a sponsor at a child's first hair cutting, a person who names a family's child, or a woman who nursed a child who was not her own. The ritual kinship gives agnatic kinship a horizontal structure, widens the circle of kin and creates solidarity in a diverse society.

It is important to stress that *kumovi* are not selected from agnatic or affinal kin. Pan-Slavic culture sets clear boundaries on who can be selected. Agnatic and affinal kin are excluded. Friends and neighbours from different ethnic groups, however, are not excluded. Indeed, they are welcomed. In contrast, ritual kin in other cultures may be selected from agnatic or affinal kin. In Latin American communities, for example, ritual kin may be 'chosen exclusively from within one's own family, or perhaps blood kin will be preferred to outsiders.'[3] [My father's best man was his older brother.] From a Pan-Slavic perspective, it is abnormal, even taboo, to ask a blood relative or in-law to be a *kum* or *kuma*. It needs to be stressed that culture provides the mental 'software' that guides decisions and actions with respect to kinship formation.

---

[2] Ibid.

[3] Mintz, S. W. and Wolf, E. R. (1950). 'An Analysis of Ritual Co-Parenthood (Compadrazgo),' *Southwestern Journal of Anthropology*, 6(4), p. 355.

Different Cultures Have Different Sets of Collective Social Programming

A less well-known and much less common ritual kinship is *pobratimstvo* where two friends become blood-brothers or, less commonly, blood-sisters. About this kinship, the Serbian ethnographer Jovan Cvijić writes, 'Love of actual blood relations is not enough, and so we find the institutions of "*pobratimstvo*" and "*posestumstvo*" in which people outside the family take oaths of adoption as brothers and sisters.'[4] The difference between *kumstvo* and *pobratimstvo* is the former serves an important family function (a wedding, a baptism, a circumcision, a first hair-cutting), and the latter is made for its own sake, out of Platonic love. The former has a positive use-value; the latter has no reason other than itself. My colleague Adnan Tufekčić shared this formulation with me while we did research together in Tuzla, Bosnia and Herzegovina.

We can distinguish the habits of the mind, the habits of the fight and the habits of the heart. The habits of the mind are reflected in the laws and political system; they provide a written template for moral action and civic responsibility. The habits of the fight are reflected in the bellicose antagonism and barbaric prejudices ethnic groups may have towards each other.[5] The habits of the heart are reflected in the kinship practices of the community, in this study, in the cultural practice of interethnic kinship.[6]

It needs to be stressed that interethnic ritual kinship reflects pan-ethnicity.[7] The kinship custom reflects neither the habits of the heart of Serbs, the habits of the heart of Croats, nor the habits of the heart of Bosniaks; in Bosnia and Herzegovina, interethnic ritual kinship reflects the habits of the heart of South Slavs. It is what is Pan-Slavic for South Slavs. While these habits of the heart are weaker in comparison with the habits of the mind (as reflected in political systems and state laws) and weaker in comparison with the habits of the fight (as reflected in ethnic antagonism and violence), these habits of the heart at the same time are morally superior. They are where morality itself is located. This Pan-Slavic

---

[4] Cvijić, J. (1930). 'Studies in Jugoslav Psychology (I),' *The Slavonic and East European Review*, 9(26), p. 380.

[5] Veblen, T. (1967). *The Theory of the Leisure Class*. New York: Penquin.

[6] Tönnies, F. (1957). *Community and Society*. Ann Arbor: University of Michigan Press.

[7] Doubt, K., Khamis, H. and Tufekčić, A. (2017). 'Panethnicity and Solidarity in Bosnia-Herzegovina,' *East European Quarterly*, 45(1–2), pp. 57–81.

culture in Bosnia and Herzegovina often answers the question of where we belong, what are we and who are we.

Historical Documentation of Interethnic Kinship

It is worth our while to review the historical documents that bear witness to the cultural heritage of interfaith ritual kinship in Bosnia and Herzegovina. The first historical document comes from the writing of the famous Turkish Balkan travel writer Evliya Çelebi, the second comes the work of the Yugoslav ethnographer, Milenko S. Filipović, the third from the Austrian ethnographer, Kosta Hörmann and the fourth from the cultural studies of Marian Wenzel. These four authors are well-known for their important studies about Bosnia and Herzegovina.

Çelebi on the Bosnian Frontier

Drawing upon an exchange witnessed and recorded in 1660, Evliya Çelebi reports a striking example of sworn brotherhood or *pobratimstvo* on the border of Bosnia. The Great Vizier, Melek Pasha, ordered the execution of a captured Christian soldier. A Muslim warrior, a gazi, pleaded with the Great Vizier to spare the captured soldier's life. The gazi said to the Great Vizier, 'I have a sworn brotherhood with this captive.'[8]

The argument the gazi made was complex. The gazi said, 'If you kill this Christian captive with whom I have a sworn brotherhood, he will go to paradise with my faith, and that will be wretched for me. When I die, the Christian faith of this captive will stay with me, and I will go to hell.' The two had pledged, 'Your faith is mine, and my faith is yours.' It was spiritually imperative for the gazi to intervene and ask the Vizier to stay the execution. In the eyes of Çelebi, the plea revealed the soulfulness of the sworn brotherhood between the opposing warriors from different faiths.[9]

Befuddled, the Great Vizier asked what does this mean? The other gazis explained: When our heroes fall into the hands of the Christians,

---

[8] Bracewell, W. (2016). 'Ritual Brotherhood Across Frontiers in the Eastern Adriatic Hinterland, 16th–18th Centuries,' *History and Anthropology*, 27(3), p. 338.

[9] Ibid., p. 339.

they eat and drink at their table. They swear brotherhood with the Christians. They promise to redeem each other if, on the one hand, a Christian is captured by the Turks or if, on the other hand, a Muslim is captured by the Venetians. They pledge as surety not their honour, but their faith. If a Christian were to die in captivity, he would go to paradise in the Islamic faith and the latter, when he died, would go to hell in the Christian faith. Then, they lick each other's blood. When a blood-brother redeems the other, he restores his faith. The Pan-Slavic custom amazed the Great Vizier. The travel writer, Çelebi, was also amazed at this exchange he witnessed and recorded. The Great Vizier released both men. This particular passage from Çelebi's travelogue, Wendy Bracewell points out, has not been translated into English.[10]

The Great Vizier and Çelebi are befuddled by the enigmatic irony of interethnic kinship. The Muslim gazi proclaims that, while enemies, the Christian captive and he are consubstantial. The rhetorician Kenneth Burke accounts for the irony of the Pan-Slavic custom: 'True irony, humble irony, is based upon a sense of fundamental kinship with the enemy, as one *needs* him, is *indebted* to him, is not merely outside him as an observer but contains him *within*, being consubstantial with him.'[11] The Christian captive and the gazi each offered to their enemy their faith for surety. The Muslim warrior and the Christian warrior each risked apostasy. In doing so, they became consubstantial. Their risk deepened the soulfulness of their lives. The irony of their interethnic kinships was unintelligible from the perspective of the Turkish observers; the Pan-Slavic identity was alien to both the Great Vizier and Çelebi. Although this custom was written neither in the Muslim nor in the Christian prayer books, it was a significant Pan-Slavic custom on the border of Bosnia according to Çelebi.[12] The custom is not found in the habits of the mind; the custom is not written. It is found in the habits of heart.

Bracewell and Bernard Lory point out that the interethnic sworn brotherhood in such stories was idealized during the modern Yugoslav

---

[10] Ibid.
[11] Burke, K. (1989). *On Symbols and Society*. Chicago: University of Chicago Press, pp. 257–258.
[12] Bracewell, W. (2016). 'Ritual Brotherhood Across Frontiers in the Eastern Adriatic Hinterland, 16th–18th Centuries,' *History and Anthropology*, 27(3), p. 339.

era.[13] The origin for the motto of the Yugoslav national identity, Brotherhood and Unity, was said to originate in such historical records. The Yugoslav ideology idealized citizens saying to each other, 'Your faith is mine, and my faith is yours,' hoping to counter the influences of traditional religions and their divisive nationalisms in a polyethnic society. In other words, from within the modern paradigm something more than Catholicism, Islam or Serbian Orthodoxy grounded the socialist solidarity of former Yugoslavia.

Bracewell (2016) contextualizes this account of sworn brotherhood so as to deconstruct the appearance of any moral character in the exchange. She notes that sworn brotherhood is typically contracted between like to like, between two men of the same faith. The solidarity of sworn brotherhood, moreover, she argues, is stronger when homogeneous. Rather than see interethnic ritual kinship as normative (particularly after the recent wars in former Yugoslavia), Bracewell frames the anecdote as an anomaly, which is how the Great Vizier and Çelebi also saw this Pan-Slavic custom. Bracewell advises against idealizing the story as if the story represented an important normative orientation in a shared culture and an authentic basis for solidarity in a polyethnic community. The Pan-Slavic custom instead acquires 'a reputation of losers in politics and ideology' (this citation to editors in this collection, *Examining Pan-Slavism*).

Çelebi's historical account bears witness to the habits of the heart rather than the habits of the mind or the habits of the fight. In Bosnia and Herzegovina, these habits of the heart were historically stronger than in the surrounding countries that chose wars to destroy socialist Yugoslavia to build strong nation-states where one ethnic group (sameness) is privileged vis-à-vis others (difference).

Filipović in a Bosnian Village

Let us consider a second historical example. Milenko S. Filipović visited in 1965 the village called Upper Srebrenik near Tuzla in Bosnia and Herzegovina and recorded his findings.[14] Filipović reported the following

---

[13] Lory, B. (1997). 'Dangers d'ici-bas, promesses d'au-dela. Essai d'anthropologie religieuse des Confins bosniaques au XVIIe sièle,' *Ethnologia Balkanica* 1, pp. 174–177.

[14] Filipović, M. (2017). 'The Mausoleum of Sheikh Sinan-baba and Pobra's Tomb in Srebrenik,' *Spirit of Bosnia* [Online], available at: http://www.spiritofbosnia.org/volume-12-no-4-2017october/sheikh-sinan-of-srebrenik/. [Accessed on June 22, 2021].

folklore which he collected from inhabitants in the village during his visit: Sheikh Sinan-baba came and settled in Srebrenik when multitudes of Ottomans and Muslims were forced to flee Hungry in the early eighteenth century. Upon returning from one of his travels, he passed through several Muslim villages. He, though, was unable to find lodging for the night, as each household declined. He came upon the home of an impoverished Orthodox Christian and asked him if he could stay for the night. His host said he could, but he had nothing for his guest to eat. The Sheikh replied he had supper for both of them. As they dined on barley bread, which the Sheikh had in his pouch, they became friends, in fact, blood-brothers or *pobratim*. Before his death, Sheikh Sinan-baba proclaimed that he was not to receive funeral honours unless such honours were given as well to his blood-brother. He wished none to be placed on his tomb unless Pobra's tomb also received offerings. When Pobra died after Sheikh, he was buried in the Ottoman cemetery as Sheikh ordained. The legend was passed down through generations. People still leave money not only in the mausoleum, but also on Pobra's open tomb nearby, thus preserving the legend.

Filipović notes the theophany in the tale where a divine figure encounters inhospitable people who refuse to give lodging for the night. A poor, hospitable person, however, takes in and houses the divine figure. Filipović said that he heard variations of this folklore about Sheikh Sinan-baba when visiting nearby villages, one being the Sheikh had been a native to Mecca and another being Pobra converted to Islam.

At the end of his report, Filipović said Pobra's grave in Upper Srebrenik is not the only such example of interethnic ritual kinship in the area.[15] He reported hearing about something similar in the village of Čekanići, a village some twenty kilometres on the other side of the provincial town Srebrenik. Filipović included in his report what he heard about Čekanići from his informants while still in Upper Srebrenik. A Muslim was not able to live to see his friend, his blood-brother, *pobratim*, an Orthodox Christian living far away, before his death. While he had sent word to his blood-brother to visit him, he died before his arrival. As the village was waiting to bury the Muslim, his blood-brother arrived after a long journey. The Orthodox Christian died on the spot when he saw his

[15] Ibid.

blood-brother was already dead. The two were then buried together in a *turbe* (a Turkish mausoleum).[16]

Hörmann Among Bosnian Muslims

Let us now turn to a third document regarding interethnic *kumstvo* in Bosnia and Herzegovina. Kosta Hörmann was an Austrian ethnographer in the early nineteenth century, who observed and reported on the interethnic ritual kinship among Bosnian Muslims he befriended. It is worth citing his observations recorded in 1898 at length.

> 'Herzegovinian Mohammedans decide to be godfathers to the children of their close friends in order to make their friendship stronger not just for themselves but for their descendants as well. This is common not only between the two Mohammedans but between the Mohammedan and Christian as well. This custom is solemnly performed in the house of a child's father in this way: If a male child is born to a Mohammedan, his close friend will announce or he will ask whether the child's father and the householders agree that he will be the godfather to a newborn boy. If they agree, they will decide about the day when that ceremony will be performed. This event happens while the child has not had his first haircut as yet, and the ritual must be performed in the morning, while the day is still young. The child's father invites friends and relatives to come to his house, and they come early in the morning, so that the child's mother can welcome the guests in a very festive manner. The child is dressed in the most beautiful clothes. The godfather takes the child and puts him on his lap. One of the relatives brings a glass or porcelain bowl of clean water, and holds it under the child's neck. The godfather takes the scissors and cuts the child's hair, first above his right ear, then in the middle of his head, and lastly above his left ear. The cut hair drops into the water, which is in the bowl.
>
> When the godfather cuts the hair, he throws some coins into the water as well – as much as he can – five or ten coins or even a ducat or more.

---

[16] For further investigation, see "Authentic Syncretism in Čekanići" in Doubt, K. and Tufekčić, A. (2019). *Ethnic and National Identity in Bosnia-Herzegovina*. Lanham: Lexington Books, pp. 9–30.

The gathered people will also throw some coins in. All the collected money will be split among the servants.'[17]

Hörmann notes the strength of the interethnic ritual kinship is its irony, bonding together not like and like but like and unlike.
Hörmann also wrote that 'Haircutting godfatherhood has greatly influenced social and political relations; it often ended hostility among the two families who have become faithful and trusted friends since the start of their godfatherhood relationship.'[18] Similar accounts of *kumstvo's* peacemaking function are found in Christopher Boehm's ethnography *Blood Revenge: The Enactment and Management of Conflict in Montenegro and Other Tribal Societies*.[19] Boehm reported: If a family member murders a member of another family, the offending family offers *kumstvo* to the offended family to quell the passion of revenge. The traditional kinship custom operationalizes the practice of restorative justice which Howard Zehr describes and explains.[20] In order for the offer of *kumstvo* to work as a peace-making offer, the offended family needs to accept the humble and honourable offer of *kumstvo* from the offending family. The prestige of *kumstvo* is the key. Both families need to be involved in the decision-making. When accepted, the offer of *kumstvo* quells the bellicose relationship between the families. Boehm, however, focuses exclusively on intra-ethnic ritual kinship in Montenegro between Orthodox families. He does not mention interethnic *kumstvo*, perhaps because it was not as prevalent in Montenegro as in Bosnia and Herzegovina.

Ritual Kinship in Folklore

Let us consider a different type of example found in the literature rather than ethnography. In her essay, 'A Medieval Mystery Cult in Bosnia and Herzegovina,' Marian Wenzel analyses not only the material culture

---

[17] Hörmann, K. (2019). 'Godfatherhood Among Mohammedans, 1889,' *Spirit of Bosnia* [Online]. Available at http://www.spiritofbosnia.org/volume-14-no-3-2019july/godfatherhood-in-mohammedans/ [Assessed on June 6, 2022].

[18] Ibid.

[19] Boehm, C. (1984). *Blood Revenge: The Enactment and Management of Conflict in Montenegro and Other Tribal Societies*. Lawrence: University of Kansas.

[20] Zehr, H. (2014). *The Little Book of Restorative Justice*. New York: Good Books.

of the Bosnian medieval gravestones called *stećci* but also the non-material culture of folklore in Bosnia and Herzegovina.[21] In the ballad 'Marko Kraljević and the Vila,' Marko Kraljević and Vojvoda Miloš are blood-brothers or pobratimi, who have a treacherous encounter with a supernatural lady called Jelena or "Vila." When Marko and Miloš stop to rest and sleep for the night by the mountain Miroč, Marko asks Miloš to sing for him. Miloš is hesitant.

> 'Ah, my brother, Kraljević Marko,
> Fain would I sing to thee, brother,
> But last night I drank much wine
> With Vila Ravijojala on the mountain,
> And the Vila laid threat upon me,
> If she should hear me sing,
> She will shoot me with arrows,
> Through throat and living heart.'[22]

Marko, however, insists and promises that he, his wonder-horse, Sharatz, and his golden mace will protect Miloš from the Vila. Miloš's song is beautiful. After Marko falls asleep. Miloš continues to sing. The Vila soon hears Miloš singing and joins him in song. Once the Vila discerns that the voice of Miloš is more beautiful than hers, she becomes angry and shoots Miloš in the throat and in the heart with two arrows. When Miloš cries out, he awakens Marko, saying he had known from the start that he ought not to sing and risk offending the Vila. He suffers the consequences of Marko's indiscretion. Marko chases after the Vila and threatens his wonder-horse, Sharatz in the following way:

> 'But if thou overtake not the Vila,
> I shall put out thy two eyes,
> And break all thy four legs,
> And thus I shall eave thee
> To drag thyself from pine to pine,
> Like me, Marko, without my brother.'[23]

---

[21] Wenzel, M. (1961). 'A Mediaeval Mystery Cult in Bosnia and Herzegovina,' *Journal of the Warburg and Courtauld Institutes*, 24(1/2), pp. 89–107.

[22] Koljević, S. (Introduction and Notes) (1984). *Marko the Prince: Serbo-Croat Heroic Songs*. Translated by Anne Pennington. New York: St. Martin's Press, pp. 35–37.

[23] Ibid.

Marko's threat captures the intensity of the sworn brotherhood, *pobratim*. Without Miloš, Marko's life will be like the horse's life if they do not overtake the Vila. Marko, too, will be legless. Marko will drag himself from pine to pine. Without Miloš, Marko's life will become as pitiful as the horse's life will become. Marko and Sharatz, though, overtake the Vila, and Marko forces her to heal the wounds of his *pobratim*. After this, the voice of Miloš becomes even more beautiful, more humble. The transgression of *pobratim*, risking the other's life to satisfy one's selfish desire, led to a higher sense of beauty and being together, of being consubstantial with the other, of being ironically humble, not in a sacred way but in a human way.

In his commentary of this heroic song, Svetozar Koljević wrote, 'It is worth noting that the two greatest heroes of the Serbo-Croat epic tradition are represented in this song as blood-brothers, but Marko—who was historically a Turkish vassal—is seen as the greater hero.'[24] At first glance, the sworn brotherhood is between like to like, making it appear stronger and deeper for this reason. The song, however, inverts the hierarchy of honour between the two Serbian heroes. Miloš, having bravely killed the Sultan, is the more honourable hero; Marko, having fought for the Sultan as the Sultan's vassal, is the less honourable hero, albeit the more popular rogue. Koljević points out that historically Marko and Miloš were enemies making their blood-brotherhood in the song fictionally dramatic. Kenneth Burke's account of true irony again explains the pathos of this song: 'True irony, humble irony, is based upon a sense of fundamental kinship with the enemy, as one *needs* him, is *indebted* to him, is not merely outside him as an observer but contains him *within*, being consubstantial with him.'[25] The Serbian heroes are enemies historically, one being more honourable and the other being less honourable. The folklore ironically inverts their hierarchy. Their difference rather than their sameness makes their sworn brotherhood even more compelling. This Pan-Slavic culture renders the relationship authentic and moral.

---

[24] Ibid., p. 33.
[25] Burke, K. (1989). *On Symbols and Society*. Chicago: University of Chicago Press, pp. 257–258.

Negative Examples of Interethnic Kinship Throughout History

We turn to important albeit negative portrayals of interfaith ritual kinship. The first comes from Vuk Drašković's popular pre-war novel, *Nož* (*Knife*), first published in 1982, the second from Ahmet M. Rahmanović's post-war war novel titled *Black Soul*, published in English in 2010, and finally the canonical literary work in Yugoslav literature, *Gorski Vijenac (Mountain Wreath)*, by Bishop Petar Petrović, known by his pen name Njegoš, published in 1857.

The Betrayal Trope in Vuk Drašković's Novel, Nož

The betrayal trope in the context of interethnic ritual kinship is found in recent war literature. *Nož* (*Knife*) was written by the Bosnian Serb author of several novels, Vuk Drašković, who is a leading politician in Belgrade. Drašković was a close ally of Vojislav Šešelj, who is convicted of crimes against humanity in Bosnia and Herzegovina at the International Criminal Tribunal for the former Yugoslavia. First published in 1982 several years before the war, the novel *Nož* (*Knife*) became a bestseller in Yugoslavia.[26] The novel takes place during World War II and begins with the sadistic killing of a Serbian family by a neighbouring Muslim family. The context of the massacre is pivotal. The Muslim family that murdered the Serbian family were *kumovi* to the Serbian family. When the Muslim kum entered the Serbian home (as the family celebrated Orthodox Christmas), he blasphemed not only the Christian faith but the integrity of the ritual kinship which bonded the Serbian and Muslim families. The violence is depicted in an incendiary manner. Before the gruesome massacre, the Serbian patriarch and Orthodox priest had trusted and honoured his Muslim kum. The violence in the story severs the interethnic interconnecting kinship fabric of *kumstvo*. It, though, is not the violence per se that evokes the novel's constructed gospel of hatred; it is the transgression of the honour of interethnic ritual kinship. The novel was subsequently made into a Serbian movie directed by Miroslav Lekić.[27]

---

[26] Anzulovic, B. (1999). *Heavenly Serbia: From Myth to Genocide*. New York: New York University Press, p. 135.

[27] Lekić, M. (1999). *Nož*. Belgrade: Metrofilm Beograd.

The Betrayal Trope in Ahmet M. Rahmanović's *Black Soul*

The betrayal trope in the context of interethnic ritual kinship is also found in Ahmet M. Rahmanović's popular war novel titled *Black Soul*. The protagonist, Hamza, witnesses from a hilltop, his *kum*, his best man, drive to his weekend home with three others, behead his wife after raping her, and sever his young son with a sharp sword. His *kum* drives away, and Hamza rushes down and holds his headless wife and slaughtered son. Hamza's best man, a Bosnian Serb who was a classmate, is never called by his name, but always by the title, *kum*. The one whom one trusts to protect and support one's family violates this normative trust of *kumstvo* in a grotesque manner. The violent transgression of the moral expectations that culturally structure ritual kin who are from different faiths creates irreconcilable differences.

Black Soul recounts the battles in which Hamza fought to defend Sarajevo during its siege from 1992 to 1995. Hamza is badly wounded during a desperate mountain mission on Mount Igman above Sarajevo. After his recovery, Hamza makes a difficult and lonely migration to Chicago where he settles as a refugee and falls in love. After reuniting with his girlfriend after a long period, the novel ends with Hamza meeting by accident his *kum* in a restaurant in Chicago. Despite Hamza's noble lie thanking his *kum* for sending his wife and son safely to Germany (idealizing the protective role of *kum*), the *kum* protests and declares his murders of Hamza's wife and son. The *kum* attacks Hamza in the restaurant, and Hamza kills him with a knife.[28] In his review of the novel, James Thomas Snyder describes the work as a revenge fantasy.[29]

Mountain Wreath's Rejection of Interfaith Ritual Kinship

Let us now consider a canonical literary work in Yugoslav literature. Bishop Petar Petrović, known by his pen name Njegoš, composed *The Mountain Wreath* in 1857. Marija Mandić writes, 'Considered a masterpiece of South Slavic literature, and required reading in all schools in former Yugoslavia, it was interpreted as a work that promotes ideas

---

[28] Rahmanović, A. (2010). *Black Soul*. Sarajevo: Connectum, pp. 329–338.

[29] Snyder, J. (2010) 'Men of War,' *Dissent*, 20 December, available at: https://www.dissentmagazine.org/online_articles/men-of-war [Accessed June 6, 2022].

of pan-Slavism.'[30] This study questions that interpretation. The literary masterpiece is also a poetic hymn for Serbian nationalism, glorifying hatred of Slavic Muslims and murderous violence against them. Michael Sells interprets the work as a nihilistic poem promoting genocide.[31]

In the poem, set in Montenegro, the Slavic Muslims are confronted with the threat of extinction if they do not convert. The Orthodox say the Slavic Muslims' only choice is between baptism of water or what they call baptism of blood, murder masked with hateful religiosity. The Muslims in Montenegro say there is another choice. They offer a *kum* ceremony, a custom the Montenegrin Orthodox and Muslims share. The Orthodox reject this offer and then slaughter all the men, women and children in the Muslim community. *Mountain Wreath* foreshadows the ethnic violence of the recent war in Bosnia and Herzegovina as well as other pogroms in Balkan history.

The violence is preceded by the rejection of interethnic *kumstvo*. It is helpful to look at the passages in *Mountain Wreath* in which the Muslims offer *kumstvo* to their threatening Orthodox neighbours, not in terms of its dramatic and literary function, but in terms of how it shows things could be otherwise. In *Mountain Wreath,* the Muslims and the Orthodox meet in a council meeting. Hadji Ali Medovitch, an Islamic judge, promises to the Serbian chiefs, 'I will be the first to proceed in front of the kinship sponsors ... just let us be calm [Ja ću prvi poći pred kumama...Tek smirimo].' A few stanzas later, Arslan-Aga Muhadinovitch, a Muslim elder, repeats the offer to the vociferous Serbian chiefs, 'I will gift my son to you, Vuk, if you want that we ask of each other to be *kumovi* [Ja ću ti ga pokloniti, Vuče, tek ako ćeš da se okumimo].' Vuk, however, objects to the peace-making offer, 'It is not *kumstvo* without baptizing [Nema kumstva bez krštena kumstva].' Muhadinovitch objects, 'Hair-cutting *kumstvo* is the same to baptizing [Šišano je isto ka kršćeno].'

---

[30] Mandić, M. (2021) 'The Serbian Proverb *Poturica gori od Turčina* (A Turk is Worse than a Turk): Sigmatizer and Figure of Speech,' in Šístek, F. (ed) *Imagining Bosnian Muslims in Central Europe: Representations, Transfers, and Exchanges.* Berghahn, pp. 170–193, New York, pp. 176–177.

[31] Sells, M. (1996). *The Bridge Betrayed: Religion and Genocide in Bosnia.* Berkley: University of California Press, pp. 41–46.

Vuk then answers, 'A *kum* I will be but never one who assists in a ritual kinship [Kum ću biti, a prikuma nigda!].'[32]

In Njegoš's poem, interethnic ritual kinship is the weapon of the weak.[33] The violence in *Mountain Wreath* is sadistic not because the relations between Slavic Muslims and Orthodox Serbs were distant but because the relations were familiar. The Pan-Slavic cultural of interfaith ritual kinship that Hörmann described tellingly is despised in Njegoš's *Mountain Wreath*. Widely read in Bosnia and Herzegovina and throughout Yugoslavia, the literary work cuts deeply into the Pan-Slavic heritage that held together Bosnia and Herzegovina.

FREQUENCY OF INTERETHNIC RITUAL KINSHIP IN BOSNIA AND HERZEGOVINA

How widely then is the custom of interethnic kinship practiced today in Bosnia and Herzegovina? Has the kinship custom faded with the passing of time and the modern era? Survey questions about ritual kinship were included in an omnibus survey in Bosnia and Herzegovina conducted by Mareco Index Bosnia.[34] Mareco Index Bosnia has experience conducting survey research for universities, embassies and governmental agencies and is a member of Gallup International, following prescribed guidelines regarding ethical inquiry, transparency and protection of human subjects. A clustered, stratified and random sample of 2,500 subjects over the age of eighteen were drawn from the country's population, including the entities Federation of Bosnia and Herzegovina and Republika Srpska as well as Brčko District, a random selection of cantons, and rural and urban populations. The sampling followed the random route technique for selecting households for face-to-face interviews. The technique of nearest birthday was used to select an individual within the household for participation in the survey. The questionnaire in Bosnian/Croatian/Serbian and English,

---

[32] Njegoš, P. (2013). *Gorski Vijenac*, available at: http://institut-genocid.unsa.ba/pdf/GORSKI%20VIJENAC.pdf [Assessed on June 6, 2022]. Translated by the author of this chapter.

[33] Sells, M. (1996). *The Bridge Betrayed: Religion and Genocide in Bosnia*. Berkley: University of California Press, p. 42.

[34] Doubt, K. (2019) *Self-Reported Marriage Practices in Bosnia-Herzegovina, 2017*. Ann Arbor, MI: Inter-University Consortium for Political and Social Research, available at: http://www.openicpsr.org/openicpsr/project/109906 [Accessed June 6, 2022].

Table 1 Interethnic Ritual Kinship by Age
Mareco Index Bosnia, Sarajevo, September 2017 (X^2 [4, $N = 1766$] = 3.96, $p > 0.05$)

	Age					
	18–29	30–39	40–49	50–64	65+	Row Total
Kum or *kuma* from different faith	27.7% (23)	23.2% (69)	21.6% (82)	21.8% (134)	18.9% (74)	21.6% (382)

an SPSS file with the survey's results and a technical report on the survey technique are available online for further study at Open ICPSR was used to select an individual within the household for participation in the survey.

The omnibus survey contained the following categorical question: Is your best man or bride's maid from a different religious tradition than yours [Da li su vaš kum ili kuma različite vjerske tradicije od vaše]? The percentage answering yes was 21.6% ($n = 1766$). This significant minority in the representative sample of the country's population represents a stabilizing centerboard in a polyethnic society. It is helpful to do a crosstabulation first by age (Table 1).

The Pan-Slavic custom of interfaith ritual kinship, the survey shows, is not fading; the variations with each generation are not statistically significant. A recommendation for future research is to repeat the survey to see whether interethnic ritual kinship is being sustained.

It is also informative to do a crosstabulation by ethnicity. The three largest ethnic groups in Bosnia-Herzegovina are named in different ways for various political and historical reasons. One is called Muslim, Bosnian Muslim, and, after the war from 1992 to 1995, Bosniak (spelled Bošnjak in the Bosnian/Croatian/Serbian language, the current way of referring to the language widely used in Yugoslavia and previously called Serbo-Croatian). Another is called Croat, Bosnian Catholic or Bosnian Croat. A third is called Serb, Serbian Orthodox, Bosnian Orthodox or Bosnian Serb. More than ten per cent of the country's inhabitants do not belong to one of these three dominate ethnic groups.[35] Bosnian

---

[35] Dicosola, M. (2016). 'Ethnic Federalism and Political Rights of the Others in Bosnia and Herzegovina.' In Benedizione, L. and Scotti, V., *Proceedings of the Conference Twenty years After Dayton. The Constitutional Transition of Bosnia and Herzegovina*. Rome: Luiss University Press, pp. 97–113.

Table 2 Interethnic Ritual Kinship by Ethnicity
Mareco Index Bosnia, Sarajevo, September 2017 (X^2 [4, $N = 1766$] = 3.96, $p > 0.05$)

	Bosniak	Croat	Serb	Row Total
Kum or kuma from different faith	27.8% (235)	26.5% (76)	11.2% (71)	21.6% (382)

Jews and Bosnian Roma are small, notable minority groups. No longer is Yugoslav used as an ethnic or national identity as it was just several decades ago.[36] The study follows current usage (which is problematic in that reifies ethnic identities) and employs the terms Bosniak, Croat and Serb.

The Pan-Slavic custom of interethnic ritual kinship is practiced in each of the major ethnic groups in Bosnia and Herzegovina, notably, more so by Bosniaks and Croats than by Serbs (Table 2).

The Pan-Slavic custom is shared throughout the polyethnic society although Serbs at a statistically significant lesser frequency.

THE IMPACT OF WAR ON INTERETHNIC RITUAL KINSHIP

What happened to interethnic ritual kinships during the recent war? Hariz Halilovich points out, 'The ethnic conflict in Bosnia destroyed many such relationships, which in many cases crossed ethnic lines.'[37] While the destruction of this interfaith kinship structure seems to have been a fatal wound to Bosnia and Herzegovina as a polyethnic society, relations to a *kum* or *kuma* from another ethnic group, as the survey indicates, persist to this day. For many, the thought that it was one's *kum* or *kuma* killing members of one's family destroyed the ritual kinship. Being harmed, being killed, by one's sworn kin was unthinkable.

A woman in Sarajevo lost her teenage daughter during the siege of the city that lasted four years. Her daughter was killed by a Serbian sniper

---

[36] Sekulić, D., Massey, G. and Hodson, R. (1994). 'Who Were the Yugoslavs? Failed Sources of a Common Identity in the Former Yugoslavia,' *American Sociological Review*, 53(1), pp. 83–97.

[37] Halilovich, H. (2013). *Places of Pain: Forced Displacement, Popular Memory, and Trans-Local Identities in Bosnian War-Torn Communities*. New York: Berghahn, p. 78.

in the mountains. The woman's *kuma* was Serbian, and they had been close high-school friends in Sarajevo. She, in turn, was her friend's *kuma*. Her *kuma* left without saying good-by as soon as the war started, and her *kuma's* brother became a military officer in the Serbian army that shelled Sarajevo and killed many civilians including her daughter. The woman could not accept that her *kuma* never called to ask about her daughter after her death or that her *kuma's* brother was a military officer in the army that had murdered her daughter and might have been the commander of the soldier who shot her daughter.

While there are stories of betrayal during the war, there are also stories of loyalty and keeping the faith of this Pan-Slavic custom. A woman in Sarajevo shared the story of her father and his *kum*, who was the best man at her parents' wedding. Her family lived in Prijedor in northwest Bosnia-Herzegovina. At the start of the war, nationalist Serbs established the death camp called Omarska for Bosniak and Croat men and women in the town. Her father was taken and held in Omarska but survived. While he was in the death camp, his wife died of a heart attack leaving their young children alone and helpless during the violence occurring in the town of Prijedor. The father's *kum*, who was an Orthodox Serb, arranged for and paid for the funeral of her mother, while her father was in Omarska. After the war was over, the father returned to Prijedor and met with his *kum* in a coffee shop. The two sat together in silence for two hours. They then departed without saying a word. Their silence bore witness to the honour of *kumstvo*; their departure to its end.

Young Bosniak couples who survived Sarajevo's siege will still ask a Serbian friend to be *kum* at their wedding. When one Bosniak couple asked a Serbian friend, the friend worried he would have to pay for their wedding, which is the custom in Serbia. In Bosnia and Herzegovina, the role of *kum* is more of a figurehead. The Bosniak couple asked their Serbian friend because the Pan-Slavic custom deepens the character of their marriage and their family's connection to others in their polyethnic society. Despite resistance from traditional parents, the young couple wanted to preserve this 'soft' Pan-Slavic custom in their everyday lives.

The reason the violence during the war in Bosnia and Herzegovina was so sadistic and cruel was not because interethnic relations were distant and hostile but because interethnic relations were often intimate and close. In *Waiting for Elijah: Time and Encounter in a Bosnian Landscape*, Safet HadžiMuhamedović criticizes Eugene Hammel's classic work *Alternative Social Structures and Ritual Relations in the Balkans* for devoting only one paragraph to interethnic *kumstvo*.[38] Hammel argues that ritual kinship in Serbia and Montenegro *kumstvo* is longer lasting when *kumstvo* is between like and like, ethnically homogeneous. Carried out in Bosnia and Herzegovina after the war that ended in 1995, HadžiMuhamedović's study argues in contrast that, when *kumstvo* is between like and unlike, ethnically heterogeneous, *kumstvo* is stronger. One of HadžiMuhamedović's informants reports: 'It was never really Muslim with Muslim or Serb with Serb, but exclusively Serb-Muslim.'[39] Interethnic *kumstvo* offers a *formula of rapport* and 'is manifested as a reciprocal bonding act.'[40] Interethnic ritual kinship reflects what is special and compelling about Pan-Slavic culture, providing a window into the particularity of the Slav heritage in Bosnia and Herzegovina.

Conclusion (and a Note on Interethnic Ritual Kinship in Ukraine)

By way of conclusion, I point out (without providing further elaboration given the particular focus of this study) that interethnic kinship is common between Orthodox Ukrainians and Orthodox Russians. The interethnic kinship is being deeply wounded if not destroyed during the current violent war in Ukraine. During a television interview, a Ukrainian woman in Kiev whose home was destroyed by Russian shelling pleaded for her disbelieving *kuma* from Moscow to come now and see the home her *kuma* had visited so often. The woman's use of the word, *kuma*, was frequent and emphatic.

To give a political example, Viktor Medvedchuk, a Ukrainian politician close to Russian President Vladimir Putin, was recently seized and charged with treason, accused of selling military secrets to Russia and looting natural resources. In *Al Jazeera*, Mansur Mirovalev reported that Putin baptized Medvedchuk's youngest daughter in a Saint Petersburg cathedral in 2004.[41] Putin is *kum* to Medvedchuk's family. Mirovalev

---

[38] HadžiMuhamedović, S. (2018). *Waiting for Elijah: Time and Encounter in a Bosnian Landscape*. New York: Berghahn, p. 133.

[39] Ibid., p. 131.

[40] Ibid.

[41] Mirovalev, M. (2022). 'Who Is Viktor Medvedchuk, Putin's Main Man in Ukraine?' *Al Jazeera*, 13 April, available at: https://www.aljazeera.com/news/2022/4/13/who-is-viktor-medvedchuk-putins-main-man-in-ukraine [Assessed June 6, 2022].

reported that, after Medvedchuk's arrest, Putin accused Kyiv of 'purging the political field of all the forces that stand for a peaceful resolution.' This study helps frame the sardonic irony of Putin's comment. The study of interethnic ritual kinship in Ukraine and the war's impact on the kinship custom would be another opportunity to understand pan-Slavism and its fragility.

Acknowledgements I thank Professors Adnan Tufekčić, Nermina Mujagić, Rusmir Mahmutćehajić, and Aida Hadžiavdić-Begović for their insightful discussions that were invaluable to the development of this study.

Afterword

Marlene Laruelle

The existence of contemporary Pan-Slavism has not spurred many serious scholarly inquiries, and yet still we find it residually in many political discourses, as well as in external analyses, e.g., Aren't Russia and Serbia supporting each other because of their Slavic-Orthodox ties? Doesn't Vladimir Putin justify his invasion of Ukraine by the need to recreate a pan-Eastern Slavic nation? This volume has tried to fill this gap by giving us the first and most detailed exploration ever of what remains of Pan-Slavism today.

But this volume has offered much more than just that. It proposes to rediscover that ideologies are not always 'thick' or 'thin', to use Freeden's typology, but rather may be just a coalescence of metaphors, historical myths, and imaginaries—some vague geopolitical ideas that can be activated as the occasion calls for. This fruitful conceptualisation of Pan-Slavism allows for the capture of many dormant features of ideologies, and I would welcome seeing that conceptual framework applied to other regions of the world: the elusive place of Pan-Americanism in US political life would fit well as a comparandum. If we indeed live in a post-modern

M. Laruelle (✉)
George Washington University, Washington, DC, USA
e-mail: laruelle@email.gwu.edu

© The Editor(s) (if applicable) and The Author(s), under exclusive license to Springer Nature Switzerland AG 2023
M. Suslov et al. (eds.), *Pan-Slavism and Slavophilia in Contemporary Central and Eastern Europe*,
https://doi.org/10.1007/978-3-031-17875-7

world, then eclecticism, allusions, and loose collections of ideas are the norm of our *Weltanschauung*.

The second element that this volume has brought us is a long-awaited contradistinction between pan-nationalism (a supranational unity for kin-related nations) and macro-nationalism (a nation projecting itself beyond its current borders), as well as their sometimes-overlapping narratives. I would connect that discussion to the question of civilisational identity, which—at least in the Russian case—has become a central discursive point brought forward to explain the country's refusal of Western normative power, as well as the existence of 'auratic bodies' outside its official borders. Indeed, Russia's civilisational language repeats many of the features the volume's editors have noticed in Pan-Slavism: that it is an amorphous discourse that can be promoted by different groups and received by different audiences, allowing for a feeling of sharedness even as the contents of the 'civilisation' can be divergent.

So how can such an elusive concept be politically useful today? It confirms, if any confirmation is needed, that governmentality—i.e., the way people accept to be governed—covers much more than the technocratic choices made by ruling elites (whether elected or not); rather it is about sharing a collective imaginary and performing it in both domestic and international politics. When, for instance, Gazprom Neft funds the restoration of the majestic interior of Belgrade's St. Sava Orthodox Cathedral, and Serbia's president, Aleksandar Vučić declares that it will become the new Hagia Sophia of the Orthodox world now that the original one in Istanbul has been (re)converted to a mosque, they are performing and projecting a Slavic geopolitical imaginary.

Concepts such as Slavic identity or Slavic unity are largely empty signifiers that can be filled with different contents. In the case of Pan-Slavist reminiscences, anti-Westernism has been a key, permanent feature, inviting the securitisation of this supposed Slavic identity and unity against the cultural and/or politically normative pressures coming from 'the West'. Pan-Slavism thus belongs to the broad repertoire of anti-colonial discourses coming from the 'periphery' of Europe as a way of expressing dissatisfaction and anxiety at a power hierarchy that favours Western Europe against Central and Eastern Europe.

In today's political terms, Pan-Slavism is thus intrinsically articulated within a right-wing populism that expresses itself both in domestic policies (as calls for majoritarian solutions and cultural homogeneity) and on the international scene (by being pro-Russian). It can be found both in dominant narratives by state leaders—with Serbia as the flagship here—and in fringe discourses emanating from certain radical rightist groups. Indeed, Pan-Slavist tones have been present in almost all radical right subcultures in countries with a Slavic background, as they permit an emphasis on the existence of a primordial cultural kin/ethnos/race to be regenerated and protected. The importance of demographic anxieties all over Central and Eastern Europe—explainable by large emigration flows—offers a fertile background for primordialist visions of the nation.

Pan-Slavism has never been an easy project to sell: Imperial Russia and Rzeszpospolita Poland competed against each other for centuries, and Russia's size as well as its internal ethno-diversity has always challenged the credibility of any future Slavic Union. In more contemporary settings, Slavic pan-nationalism has indisputably failed: the Yugoslav Wars have largely destroyed the idea of any Slavic unity, and even today the difficulties some of the Western Balkan countries with Slavic backgrounds (Serbia, Montenegro, North Macedonia) have in working together is a testament to the lack of any Slavic political unity.

Last but not least, Russia's invasion of Ukraine in February 2022 has put a final full stop on the Pan-Slavist ideal, not only directly because of the fighting between the two so-called brother nations of the Russians and the Ukrainians but also because Central European countries with Slavic roots (Poland first, then the Czech Republic and Slovakia to a lesser extent) have led the geopolitical battle against Moscow and posit themselves as an avant-garde of the Atlanticist worldview. This is not new, as already in the nineteenth-century competition between Russia and Poland was the Achilles heel of any theory of Slavic unity. As such, Pan-Slavism seems to have failed in its fight against the empires: the borders between the Austro-Hungarian, the Ottoman, the Russian, and the Prussian empires have held out better over the centuries in framing cultural and political modes of citizenship and collective belonging than the romanticised projection of a political community based on a shared Slavic past.

This failure probably explains why Pan-Slavism is so intimately interrelated with Pan-Orthodoxy for those countries who share both features: excluding the Catholic and Protestant Slavic nations from the expected Slavic unity, due to their 'romano-germanisation' (the nineteenth-century explanation) or to their domination by a decadent West (in today's formulation), is a way of expressing disappointment in their lack of (cultural or political) solidarity and of refocusing on Orthodox Slavism. This may entail adding Greece to this geopolitical imaginary, but this is easier to digest than solving the issue of non-Orthodox Slavs. We see it also in the Kremlin's ideological repertoire today, where references to Russia as an Orthodox civilisation have been much more developed than those to Slavic identity.

In many respects, Russia is an exception among Slavic countries because it is the only case where a Slavic nation was at the centre of an imperial construction and not in a peripheral situation. Moreover, Slavic identity is too restricting for a post-imperial nationhood: with its 20% ethnic minority population and the growing place given to Islam as its second religion after Orthodoxy, Russia cannot be satisfied with a one-sided identity. This makes any case of Pan-Slavic allusion even more instrumentalist, especially as the Putin regime has become master at playing with ideational constructs, including the Eurasianist one, in order to advance multifaceted identities adaptable to each audience and context. In this pro-diversity framework, Slavic identity has always played a very minor role compared to Orthodox identity.

The notion of the Russian World has long been used for expressing the 'auratic bodies' of those who were not Russian citizens but shared something (the Soviet past or the Russian language) with Russia, yet the Slavic undertone of the Russian World has never been dominant compared to the Pan-Orthodox one. Even so, it has been revived in some ways—and in the most bellicose manner—with Putin's Eastern Slavic imperialism that claims Ukrainians are just Russians ignorant of themselves due to Western domination. Even if, in this case, one cannot really speak of Pan-Slavism but rather of classic imperialism—as the goal is more about the absorption of Ukrainians' 'peripheral' identity into the Russian 'core'—Moscow has probably forever tainted Pan-Slavism with an Eastern Slavic imperialist connotation that will not be able to be erased.

Thanks to Mikhail, Marek, Vladimir, and their co-authors, we now have a seminal work on Pan-Slavism that will constitute a milestone in our studies of both Eastern Europe and the field of intellectual history.

Appendix

See Figs. 1, 2, 3, 4, 5, 6, 7, 8, 9, 10, 11, 12, and 13.

Fig. 1 All-Slavic Congress in Prague 1848—Ceremonial Mass (Photo: Archive of authors)

© The Editor(s) (if applicable) and The Author(s), under exclusive license to Springer Nature Switzerland AG 2023
M. Suslov et al. (eds.), *Pan-Slavism and Slavophilia in Contemporary Central and Eastern Europe*,
https://doi.org/10.1007/978-3-031-17875-7

Fig. 2 All-Slavic Congress in Prague 1997—information brochure about the progress of the convention (Photo: Miroslav Mareš)

APPENDIX 405

Fig. 3 All-Slavic Congress in Moscow 2015—promotional graphics (Photo: Archive of authors)

Fig. 4 Sticker of football fans of the Sparta Prague football club with the depiction of the Pan-Slavic symbol "kolovrat" (spinning wheel) and pro-Serbian inscriptions (Photo: Miroslav Mareš)

Fig. 5 The 'Night Wolves' motorcycle gang on one of their 'Freedom Journeys' on the occasion of the end of the Second World War, Brno, Czech Republic 2021 (Photo: Marek Čejka)

Fig. 6 Various pro-Russian and pan-Slavic symbols are often found at the events of the 'Night Wolves' motorcycle gang, Brno, Czech Republic 2021 (Photo: Marek Čejka)

Fig. 7 Various pro-Russian and pan-Slavic symbols are often found at the events of the 'Night Wolves' motorcycle gang, Brno, Czech Republic 2021 (Photo: Marek Čejka)

Fig. 8 The ribbon of St. George is a frequent symbol of pro-Russian and pan-Slavic attitudes. The photo shows one of the members of the 'Night Wolves' biker gang (Photo: Marek Čejka)

APPENDIX 411

Fig. 9 Pan-Slavic inscription 'Brother for brother' (written in Russian alphabet) stuck on a Slovak car (Photo: Marek Čejka)

Fig. 10 Ultra-nationalist demonstration in Brno (Czech Republic, 2015) at which a number of pro-Russian and Pan-Slavic symbols appeared (Photo: Marek Čejka)

Fig. 11 From Pan-Slavism to Pan-Orthodoxy? T-shirt on a stand in Belgrade, 2021 (Photo: Marek Čejka)

414 APPENDIX

Fig. 12 Slavic symbols on the flags of the paramilitary organization 'Slovak Conscripts' (Photo: Miroslav Mareš)

APPENDIX 415

Fig. 13 Slavic symbols on the flags of the paramilitary organization 'Slovak Conscripts' (Photo: Márty Surma)

Index of Persons

A

Alexander the Great, 226, 227
Amfilohije (Metropolitan Bishop), 285, 288, 289, 292, 294, 296, 299–301

B

Battenberg, Prince Alexander, 268
Bekier, Bartosz, 170, 171
Beneš, Edvard, 54, 57
Bielawski, Paweł, 179
Blaha, Ľuboš, 343, 345, 346, 349, 351, 352
Boehm, Christopher, 387
Borisov, Boyko, 272, 277, 279
Borovský, Karel Havlíček, 49, 51, 314
Bracewell, Wendy, 382–384
Bulatović, Momir, 285, 288
Burke, Kenneth, 383, 389

C

Čarnogurský, Ján, 334, 340, 341, 343
Çelebi, Evliya, 382–384
Chernozemski, Vlado, 218
Chernyaev, Mikael, 65, 66
Chmelár, Eduard, 346, 350, 351
Chornovil, Viacheslav, 241
Chupovski, Dimitrija, 214, 216, 217
Cieśluk, Adam, 177
Cieszkowski, August, 48
Cvetković, Mirko, 144, 145
Ćwik, Grzegorz, 177, 179
Cyril and Methodius, Saints, 85, 219, 231, 236, 267, 333
Czartoryski, Adam Jerzy, 171

D

Dabčević-Kučar, Savka, 194
Danilevsky, Nikolai, 37, 65, 83
Danko, Andrej, 344
Đinđić, Zoran, 138, 139
Dmowski, Roman, 54, 55, 159, 160
Dobrovský, Josef, 47, 49
Dostoevsky, Fedor, 89, 94, 99

418   INDEX OF PERSONS

Drašković, Janko, 190
Drašković, Vuk, 390
Dugin, Aleksandr, 14, 87, 88, 98, 170
Đukanović, Milo, 285, 287–291, 305, 306
Dzermant, Aliaksei, 106, 114
Dzurinda, Mikuláš, 336, 337

F
Feldon, Antoni, 165–167
Fico, Robert, 337, 338, 340, 342, 345
Filipović, Milenko S., 379, 382, 384, 385
Fudali, Robert, 177

G
Gaj, Ljudevit, 61–64, 66, 67, 72, 190, 191
Garašanin, Ilija, 64
Giedroyć, Jerzy, 173
Gromada Białożar, 179
Gruevski, Nikola, 226, 227

H
HadžiMuhamedović, Safet, 396, 397
Halilovich, Hariz, 395
Hammel, Eugene, 396, 397
Harabin, Štefan, 344, 345, 350–352
Herder, Johann Gottfried von, 49, 60, 61, 64, 235
Hlinka, Andrej, 339
Hörmann, Kosta, 382, 386, 387, 393

I
Ignatiev, Nikolai, 65
Irinej (Patriarch of the Serbian Orthodox Church), 284
Ivanov, Gjorge, 226

J
Jungmann, Josef, 47, 49

K
Karadžić, Vuk, 61, 63
Karamarko, Tomislav, 195, 203
Kastsyan, Siarhei, 111, 112
Kayalovich, Mikhail, 107, 108
Khomiakov, Alexis/Aleksei, 36, 84, 130, 236
Khuen-Herdervary, Karoly, 68
Kirill (Patriarch of the Russian Orthodox Church), 85, 94, 118, 284, 287, 303
Kirill, Russian Patriarch of Moscow and All Russia, 278
Kiska, Andrej, 342
Knežević, Milan, 296, 297
Koljević, Svetozar, 388, 389
Kollár, Ján, 47, 48, 190, 314, 315, 331, 337
Konuzyn, Aleksandar, 147
Koštunica, Vojislav, 139–141, 143, 152
Kotleba, Marian, 339, 342, 343, 348
Kramář, Karel, 54, 55, 314–317, 324
Kravchuk, Leonid, 241
Križanić, Juraj, 189
Kuchma, Leonid, 231–234
Kusturica, Emir, 87

L
Lelewel, Joachim, 48, 237
Lepper, Andrzej, 167–170
Lubomirski, Jerzy, 48, 50, 52
Lukashenka, Aliaksandr, 101–103, 106, 108–116, 119, 121, 122
Lukashenko, Alexander, 102, 113, 119, 120, 137, 169, 321, 339

INDEX OF PERSONS

M
Mandić, Andrija, 292, 296, 297
Masaryk, Tomáš, 55, 56, 69, 191, 314–316
Matić, Predrag, 196
Mečiar, Vladimír, 329, 334, 335, 344
Merunka, Vojtěch, 324
Mider, Daniel, 166
Mikhalkov, Nikita, 94, 99
Milačić, Marko, 298
Milošević, Slobodan, 134–136, 138, 140, 142, 146, 149, 152, 195, 285, 292
Mináč, Vladimír, 333, 336
Misirkov, Krste Petkov, 214–217

N
Nikolić, Tomislav, 147, 149, 151
Ninova, Kornelia, 276, 277

O
Orvini, Mavro, 189

P
Paisius of Hilendar, 266, 267
Palacký, František, 50–52, 314
Paterek, Patryk, 179
Patriarch Cyril, 232
Petrović-Njegoš, Petar II, 390, 391
Philip of Macedon, 227
Piasecki, Bolesław, 56, 174
Piłsudski, Józef, 172, 174
Piskorski, Mateusz, 167–170, 177
Pludek, Alexej, 320, 324
Pribojević, Vinko, 189
Prokhanov, Alexander, 111
Putin, Vladimir, viii, 1, 4, 9–11, 39, 77, 97, 113, 137, 141, 143, 145, 147, 150, 151, 180, 232, 234, 247, 251, 252, 297, 303, 309, 323, 337, 349, 352, 397–399, 402

R
Radev, Rumen, 277
Radić, Stjepan, 71, 191, 192
Rahmanović, Ahmet M., 390, 391
Rasputin, Valentin, 82, 86, 89, 99
Ridiger, Aleksii II, 116

S
Šafařík, Pavel Josef, 191
Sells, Michael, 392, 393
Semashko, Iosif, 119
Šešelj, Vojislav, 390
Šimečka, Milan, 334
Stachniuk, Jan, 174, 177
Stambolov, Stefan, 268
Stanishev, Sergey, 276
Staszic, Stanisław, 48
Stoilov, Vassil, 268
Strossmayer, Josip Juraj, 191
Štúr, Ľudovít, 47, 49, 51, 331, 341, 353
Supilo, Fran(j)o, 68, 70, 191
Szczepański, Tomasz, 158, 160, 162, 163, 173–177, 179

T
Tadić, Boris, 144–146
Tatarka, Dominik, 333
Tejkowski, Bolesław, 90, 159, 162–165
Tiso, Jozef, 339, 348, 349
Tito, Josip Broz, 29, 72, 73, 133, 192, 193
Tomašević, Tomislav, 196
Trashchanok, Yakau, 111
Tripalo, Miko, 194
Trumbić, Ante, 68, 70, 191

Tudman, Franjo, 202, 203
Tupeko, Veniamin, 121

V
Veblen, Thorstein, 381
Vučić, Aleksandar, 2, 79, 92, 137, 149–152, 297, 400

W
Wacyk, Antoni, 166, 177
Wenzel, Marian, 382, 387, 388

Wylotek, Andrzej, 165

Y
Yanukovych, Viktor, 232, 234, 337, 342
Yeltsin, Boris, 137, 143

Z
Zap, Karel Vladislav, 50
Zeman, Miloš, 323
Zyuganov, Gennady, 112, 164

Index of Subjects

A

Agency for the Bulgarians Living Abroad, 270
Aggression of the West, 80, 136
Ambient Slavophilism, 255
Annexation of Crimea, 95, 120, 150, 232, 295, 343, 346
Anti-communism, 345
Anti-fascist, 318, 341, 348
Anti-Western, 9, 10, 13, 14, 30, 36, 88, 111, 140, 151, 152, 232, 239, 248, 285, 295, 297, 306, 307, 327, 339, 342, 347
Anti-Westernism, 2, 29, 80, 96, 136, 142, 150, 153, 400
Aryans, vii, ix, 44, 105, 178, 180, 247, 248, 318
Auratic geopolitics, 21
Austromarxism, 316
Austro-Slavism, vii, 7, 49, 54
Authoritarian, 4, 9, 12, 189, 234, 235, 250, 314, 315, 317, 323, 335
Autocephaly, 121, 266, 300, 303–305, 307, 308

B

Balkans, v, 14, 24, 28, 31, 36, 59, 65, 68, 78, 96–98, 130, 137, 143, 150, 152, 186, 197, 202, 205, 216, 217, 225, 267, 284, 285, 293, 298, 300, 303, 306, 310, 359, 360
Baltics, 106, 114, 172–174, 210
Belarusianisation, 105
Belarusian Orthodox Church (BOC), 103, 107, 109, 116, 118–122
Belarusian Revolution, 115, 121, 122
Belonging, 3, 5, 78, 86, 109, 111, 198, 201, 207–209, 211, 213, 222–224, 226, 227, 241, 242, 250, 253, 257, 271, 279, 302, 330–332, 334, 340, 344, 359–367, 370–374, 376, 377, 380, 401
Betrayal trope, 390, 391

Bosnia and Herzegovina, 8, 36, 65, 66, 224, 365, 368, 370, 371, 373, 374, 379–382, 384, 386–388, 392–397
Brotherhood, 22, 54, 88, 92, 97, 99, 109, 125, 129, 131, 135, 136, 140, 145, 148, 160, 185, 234, 240, 244–246, 249, 252, 256, 284, 285, 374, 379, 382–384, 389
Brotherhood and unity, 114, 133, 134, 189, 205, 208, 219, 305, 373, 375, 376, 384
"Brotherly peoples", 244
BSSR, 105, 106
Bulgarian Orthodox Patriarchy, Synod, 278
Bulgarian Socialist Party, 276

C
Charitable Slav Society, 214, 215
Civilization, 9, 37–39, 71, 87, 89, 135, 136, 233, 247, 257, 333, 347, 350
Cold War, 13, 91, 125, 132, 173, 223, 372
Communism, 163, 176, 195, 196, 203, 207, 221, 240, 319, 334
Communist Party of Bohemia and Moravia, 319, 323, 326
Communist rule, 265, 360
Conservatism, 16, 29, 45, 80, 83, 94, 100, 353
Constitutional Court, 262, 273, 274, 276, 336
Continentalist discourse, 14
Cossackdom, 236
Cossacks, 349
Crna Duša (Black Soul), 390, 391
Croatian National Party, 68
Croatian War of Independence, 195

Czech-Moravian Slavic Union, 321, 324
Czechoslovakia, 56, 58, 134, 164, 172, 173, 316, 317, 319, 320, 326, 352

D
Democratic Front (DF), 290, 293, 295–297, 301, 302, 307, 308
Democratic Party of Socialists (DPS), 287, 289–292, 296, 299, 300, 302, 305, 308

E
East Slavonic imaginary, 241, 253, 255, 257
East, the, 12, 13, 55, 89, 97, 98, 108, 114, 134, 145, 147, 159, 179, 201, 202, 233, 243, 252, 255, 303, 330, 333–335, 347, 352
Educational policy, 371
EU membership, 125, 141, 152, 208, 223–226, 265, 323, 337, 338
Eurasian Economic Union (EAEU), 97
Eurasianism, vii, 5, 7, 14, 15, 29, 97, 98, 103, 113, 114, 120
Euro-Atlantic integration, 197, 245, 299
Euro-Atlantic membership/Euro-Atlanticism, 271, 280
Europe, 2–4, 12, 20, 28, 35–38, 48, 50, 51, 55, 56, 66, 70, 71, 78, 91, 96, 98, 104, 105, 114–116, 125, 134, 135, 139, 140, 143, 144, 152, 164, 165, 171, 172, 176, 179, 180, 186, 197, 201, 202, 205, 207, 211, 213, 217, 223, 224, 229, 235, 255, 256, 262–265, 271, 275, 277, 281,

285, 315, 320, 330, 332, 360, 370, 377, 400–402
Europeanization, 139, 140, 198, 336
European Union (EU), viii, 12, 13, 15, 18, 25, 88, 90, 91, 99, 114, 125, 138–141, 144, 145, 147–149, 151, 152, 161, 166, 169, 171, 173, 188, 197, 198, 205, 207, 208, 211, 222–225, 227, 229, 233, 234, 262, 263, 266, 271, 289, 295, 298, 306, 311, 329, 334, 335, 337, 338, 340–346, 351, 354, 355
Exceptionalism, 134, 136, 153
Extremism, 310, 320–322

F
Falanga, 56, 170, 171
Fascism, 80, 90, 96, 99, 144, 164, 167, 170, 179, 343, 351, 352
Freedom and Direct Democracy, 324
Friendship, v, 125, 129, 131, 141, 142, 144, 146, 151, 158, 159, 307, 386

G
Galicia, 41, 238, 239
Gender, 262, 264, 272, 273, 275, 278, 280, 281, 353
Genesis of Croatian political identity, 190
Geopolitical discourses, 16, 126, 127, 134, 152, 263, 264, 280, 281
Geopolitical identity, 262, 264, 265, 278
Geopolitical populism, 19, 86–88
Gorski Vijenac (Mountain Wreath), 390
Great Patriotic War, 92, 161
Grossraum, 14, 21, 22

H
HDZ (Croatian Democratic Union), 195, 198, 202, 204
Holy Rus', 110, 117
Human rights, 261, 262, 265, 275, 279, 280
Hybrid interference, 312, 326
Hybrid threats, 309, 311–313, 322

I
Identitarian conservativism, 45, 80
Identity, vi, viii, 2, 4, 5, 7, 14–17, 19, 20, 27, 29–31, 36, 38, 60, 63, 66, 78, 79, 84, 85, 87, 88, 90–92, 100, 107, 118, 119, 124, 126, 132, 134, 135, 139–141, 145, 148, 152, 168, 185, 186, 189–194, 198, 200, 202, 203, 205, 207–214, 216–229, 237, 238, 241–243, 248, 255, 256, 263–265, 271, 272, 275, 276, 281, 285–287, 290, 291, 299, 304–308, 313–319, 321, 327, 338, 341, 345, 347, 353, 359–367, 370–373, 377, 378, 383, 384, 395, 400, 402
Identity complexes, 242
Identity politics, viii, 28, 78, 199
Ideology, vii, 1, 3, 4, 7, 9, 12, 13, 15, 16, 19, 20, 29, 35, 38, 39, 45, 47, 53, 58, 59, 64, 66, 72, 77–80, 82, 85, 88, 97, 100, 102, 103, 108, 110, 112, 113, 119, 120, 125, 128, 129, 133–135, 166, 193, 195, 196, 200, 212, 218, 219, 221, 229, 239, 240, 248, 256, 257, 265, 267, 269, 277, 280, 286, 293, 300, 302, 306, 308, 320, 330, 333, 349, 353, 361, 362, 377, 384, 399
Illiberalism, 325, 355
Illyrianism, 50, 62, 64, 190, 191

Illyrian movement, 62, 66, 190, 217
Imagined communities, 19, 189, 240, 253, 363
Institute of Slavic Strategic Studies, 323
Interethnic ritual kinship, 15, 31, 379, 381, 384–387, 390, 391, 393–395, 397, 398
Intermarium (*Międzymorze* in Polish), 115, 157, 171, 172, 174–177, 180
Istanbul Convention (Council of Europe Convention in Preventing and Combating Violence against Women and Domestic Violence), 261–266, 268, 271, 272, 275–279
Izborsky Club, 88, 96

J
Jugoslovenski Pokret, 68

K
Katechon, 96
Kievan Rus', 116, 120
Kinship, 82, 86, 88, 97, 113, 124, 128–130, 140, 153, 269, 271, 379–383, 387, 389, 390, 392–395, 397, 398
Kosovo, 24, 63, 94, 96, 135–138, 140–144, 146, 147, 150, 152, 211, 225, 287–289, 291–293, 296, 298, 307, 327, 336, 338

L
"Larger Eurasia" concept, 97
Law on Religious Freedom, 301, 308
Liberation from fascism, 133
"Little Russians", 83, 108, 235–238

M
Macedonian Scientific and Literary Society, 214, 215
Macro-nationalism, vi, 2, 4, 5, 21, 41, 268, 400
Martyrdom, 95
Matica slovenská, 341, 347, 348, 350
Messianic narrative, 96
Messianism, 14, 44, 45, 80, 89
Metropolitanate of Montenegro and the Littoral (Metropolitanate, MML), 283
Mitteleuropa, 172, 197
Montenegrin Orthodox Church (MOC), 284, 288, 300–305, 307
Montenegrins, 66, 284, 285, 287, 299, 301, 307, 308
Montenegro, 3, 7, 8, 30, 63, 65, 70, 224, 283–285, 287–291, 293–308, 368, 387, 392, 397, 401
Moscow, 3, 4, 9, 12, 37, 41–44, 52, 53, 57, 58, 65, 83, 84, 87, 89–92, 95, 98–100, 103, 113, 114, 117, 119–122, 133, 136, 142, 144–146, 149, 160, 162, 167, 168, 171, 180, 234, 240, 248–250, 292, 294–296, 298, 303, 318, 326, 327, 337, 350, 397, 401, 402
Movement for Democratic Slovakia (HZDS), 335–337, 344, 348
Multi-dimensional, 17
Multiple civilizations concept, 78

N
Nacertanje, 64
Nagodba, 68
National awakening, vi, 4, 35, 77
National Fascist Community (NOF), 317

INDEX OF SUBJECTS 425

Nationalism, vi, vii, ix, 3, 4, 7, 8, 16, 18, 20, 38, 44, 64, 69, 71, 80, 83, 100, 105, 106, 119, 159, 162, 163, 166, 172, 187, 190, 195, 205, 218, 220, 228, 229, 233, 235, 236, 238, 239, 256, 268, 270, 284, 287, 291, 304, 306, 315, 320, 366, 384, 392
National Socialist Black Metal (NSBM), 167, 177
National Social Union (USN), 165–167
National sovereignty, 262, 264, 277, 280
NATO, 8, 18, 23, 24, 88, 90, 91, 95, 96, 98, 135–141, 146, 148, 161, 165, 166, 169, 171, 188, 197, 198, 202, 208, 222, 225, 227, 229, 289, 293–299, 306, 311, 321, 322, 327, 329, 334–338, 341, 342, 345, 349, 355
Nazi, 10, 56, 57, 175, 177, 180, 232
Neo-Slavism, vii, 15, 44, 53, 54
Niklot, 167, 168, 174, 175
Nordic civilization, 100
Nož (Knife), 390

O

Orthodox (Christianity; civilization), viii, 4, 14, 21, 22, 27, 62, 85, 111, 114, 115, 130, 156, 207, 222, 225, 239, 255, 262, 263, 265, 269, 284, 287, 303, 306, 325, 385, 402
Ottoman Empire, vi, 8, 36, 37, 60, 62, 64, 66, 71, 98, 129, 132, 211, 214–216, 266

P

Pan-nationalism, vi, vii, 2–8, 15, 17–22, 78, 89, 213, 280, 310, 400, 401
Pan-Slavic Committee, 57
Pan-Slavic solidarity, 9, 13, 15, 36, 133, 135
Pan-Slavism, v–ix, 1–4, 6, 9, 13–16, 19, 22–25, 27–30, 35–39, 45, 47, 48, 51, 53, 57, 59–61, 64, 66, 68, 69, 71, 77, 78, 80–82, 87, 89, 92, 97, 98, 100, 102, 105, 109–111, 119, 121–124, 127, 129, 132–134, 137, 156–159, 161, 162, 166–168, 174, 179, 180, 185–188, 190–193, 199, 203, 205, 213–216, 227, 228, 239, 240, 247, 253, 255, 263, 267–269, 309, 310, 313–316, 318, 319, 326, 327, 330–332, 338, 339, 347, 350, 351, 355, 360–362, 377, 379, 380, 392, 398–402
Party of European Socialists, 276
Party of Regions, 233, 246
People's Party Our Slovakia (ĽSNS), 339, 341, 342, 348–350, 355
Performative transnational social expression, 362, 378
Poland, 3, 28, 29, 40, 43, 48, 49, 51, 53–58, 104, 155–159, 161–176, 178–181, 335, 344, 354, 401
Polish-Lithuanian Commonwealth, 172, 235
Polish National Community-Polish National Party (PWN-PSN), 164, 165
Political Orthodoxy, 288, 308
Polyethnicity, 380, 384, 394–396
Populism, 2, 16, 18, 19, 29, 40, 80, 86, 87, 264, 265, 271, 279, 280, 298, 400

Post-Yugoslav diaspora, 362, 377
Prague Uprising, 51
Putinism, 9, 10, 79, 80

R

Regime ideology, 9, 77, 79, 80, 83, 87, 92, 100
Rodzima Wiara, 174, 177
RUN-vira ("Native Ukrainian Faith"), 247
Ruś (Kyivan Rus), 240
Russia, vi–ix, 1–15, 19, 22, 28–30, 35–45, 49, 51, 53, 55–57, 60, 66–68, 77–82, 84–87, 91, 94–100, 103–105, 108, 110, 112–122, 124, 125, 129–133, 135–138, 140, 142–153, 156–162, 164, 166, 168, 170–172, 180, 186, 191, 211, 213, 215–217, 222, 225, 227, 228, 233–235, 237, 242, 244–246, 248, 249, 251, 252, 255, 257, 267–269, 279, 283, 288, 289, 291, 293–296, 298, 300, 302–304, 306, 307, 310, 312, 315, 317, 321, 323, 326, 327, 330, 331, 334–338, 340–347, 349–354, 397, 399–402
Russian Federation, 4, 96, 117, 164, 168, 198, 330, 332, 335, 337, 342, 344, 346, 350
Russian Orthodox Church (ROC), 40, 51, 116–118, 121, 122, 130, 232, 235, 239, 284, 285, 287, 288, 291, 293, 297, 300, 302–305, 307, 308
Russian-Serbian brotherhood, 92, 97
Russian-Ukrainian "brotherhood", 242
"Russkii mir" (Russian World), 113, 250, 255
Russo-Georgian War, 95
Russophilia, 125, 250, 267, 268, 276, 280, 293, 299, 303, 306, 307, 315, 333
Russo-Ukrainian conflict, 244

S

Saviour, 98, 110, 112, 113
Securitization, 38
Security, 16, 22, 113, 115, 118, 198, 205, 272, 306, 311, 312, 322, 330, 335, 336, 341, 344, 372
Self-Defense (*Samoobrona* in Polish), 169
Serbia, 1–3, 7, 8, 11–13, 28, 29, 59, 63–68, 70, 71, 79, 82, 84, 88, 91, 92, 95, 96, 98, 110, 124–132, 134–153, 166, 186, 191, 195, 200, 206, 211, 217, 228, 268, 283, 285, 287–291, 295, 296, 298, 300, 301, 304, 306, 327, 332, 342, 344, 354, 368, 370, 374, 396, 397, 399–401
Serbian Orthodox Church (SOC), 132, 141, 283–288, 290–293, 299–308
Serbs, v, 8, 41, 43, 56, 61, 62, 65, 66, 68–70, 84, 92, 95–98, 109, 131, 135, 138, 150, 161, 186, 191, 192, 194, 195, 199–201, 205, 206, 217, 284, 285, 287, 292, 299, 301, 304, 307, 308, 381, 393, 395, 396
Skopje 2014, 226
Slavdom, 40, 42, 43, 295, 303, 306
Slavia Orthodoxa, 240, 253, 255
Slavic brotherhood, 28, 88, 93, 101, 108–110, 114, 120, 148, 190, 267, 354
Slavic civilization, 7, 36, 37
Slavic closeness, 125

INDEX OF SUBJECTS 427

Slavic Committee, 52, 58, 110, 111, 165, 267, 270, 321
Slavic Committee of the Czech Republic, 321, 323, 326
Slavic Congress, 49, 52, 54, 57, 113, 164, 314, 315, 318, 320, 321, 350
Slavic fantasy, 85
Slavic mutuality, 313, 326
Slavic-Orthodox civilization, 14
'Slavic Talks', 269
Slavic Union, 3, 4, 13, 20, 28, 40–42, 56, 81, 83, 191–193, 198, 203, 208, 320, 324, 325, 401
Slavic world, v, vii, ix, 13, 29, 40, 43, 44, 82, 85, 90–92, 94–96, 103, 104, 106, 108–110, 113, 135, 167, 209, 237, 264, 266, 269, 271, 332, 344
Slavo-Eurasian union, 98
Slavophiles, 16, 36, 37, 84, 89, 110, 122, 236–238, 248, 256, 324
Slavophilia, viii, 8, 14–17, 25, 27, 30, 77–80, 82, 88, 93, 96, 98, 100, 102, 103, 110, 112–114, 116, 121, 122, 207, 209, 210, 213, 250, 255, 257, 263–270, 275, 277, 279, 280, 307–310, 313–315, 318–321, 324, 325, 327, 330, 334, 374
Slavophilism, ideology of, 35
Slavs, the, 12, 19, 36–38, 41–44, 48, 49, 53, 60, 64, 78–81, 83, 84, 87–91, 93, 97, 99, 156, 158, 172, 238, 266, 340, 348, 350, 352, 353
Slovak National Party (SNS), 335–338, 340, 343, 344, 348
Smer-SD (Direction–Social Democracy), 337, 340, 342, 343, 345, 348, 355
Social ambivalence, 241, 256

South Slavism, 185–189, 193, 197, 199–203, 205
Special relationship, 127, 129, 138, 152, 153
Stereotypes, 131, 264
Sufferings of the Slavs, 90
"*Szturm*", 175, 179

T
Third gender, 275, 276, 278
"Third way", 81, 93, 134
Traditional/family values, 30, 225, 281, 353
Translocal positionality, 364
Transnational positionality, 364

U
Ukraine, 1, 3, 5, 9–14, 29, 30, 39, 66, 81, 84, 102, 108, 113, 115–117, 119, 121, 149–151, 164, 169, 171, 172, 179, 180, 231–235, 237–242, 244, 245, 247–253, 255–257, 298, 303, 304, 311, 323, 326, 329–331, 338, 342, 343, 345, 350, 351, 354, 398, 399, 401
Ukrainian Orthodox Church (of the Kyiv Patriarchate vs. Moscow Patriarchate), 248, 288
Uniate (Greek Catholic) Church, 107, 237
United Kingdom of Serbs, Croats, and Slovenes, 71

V
VMRO-DPMNE (VMRO-Democratic Party for Macedonian National Unity), 225–227
Vrbětice case, 310, 312, 325, 327

W

War in Donbas, 13
War in Ukraine (2014–), 13, 349
War in Ukraine (2022–), 11, 79, 83, 397
Westernization, 36
Western world, 6, 108, 109
World War II, 56, 57, 72, 90, 92, 168, 173, 174, 180, 192, 219, 270, 318, 326, 390

Y

Young Czechs, 54
Yugoslav diaspora, 365, 369, 377
Yugoslavia, 8, 50, 56, 70–73, 91, 128, 134, 164, 169, 173, 186, 189, 192–195, 197, 200, 202, 203, 205, 206, 210, 212, 213, 217–220, 223, 227–229, 285, 287, 288, 319, 322, 334, 336, 338, 360–362, 364–377, 384, 390, 391, 393, 394
Yugoslavism, 29, 31, 133, 186, 188, 189, 192, 193, 196, 199, 200, 202, 203, 213, 217–221, 226–229, 360–362, 365–369, 371–377

Z

Zadruga, 174, 177, 178

Printed in the USA
CPSIA information can be obtained
at www.ICGtesting.com
LVHW011957160324
774517LV00004B/443